For Nancy,
Becky, Eva, Jennifer, and Sandra

Contents

========= **PART III   The Policy Process** =====================================

THREE

The Public   50

FOUR

Interest Groups   74

FIVE

Congress   93

SIX

The Bureaucracy   114

Preface

The primary purpose of this book is to provide an introduction to contemporary American foreign policy issues and the policy-making process. However, it also provides an overview of major trends in world politics, and it discusses many policy problems in a global context. It furthermore includes analytic models of world politics that emphasize the importance of factors other than policy-process variables in foreign policy making. The emphasis, however, remains on the effects of process on policy.

This third edition incorporates recent information and literature concerning American foreign policy, including in particular material on economic policy issues, such as trade, foreign direct investment, and monetary affairs. It also reflects the dramatic changes in the USSR and elsewhere in Eastern Europe in recent years, as well as changes in the U.S. administration.

The specific content of the book naturally reflects my own methodological, theoretical, and pedagogical convictions. I believe, for instance, that good foreign policy analysis combines the objectives and the methods of both the scientific and the humanistic approaches to political analysis. I have therefore drawn upon existing case studies, quantitative studies, systematically collected data sets, and more impressionistic surveys as appropriate. Although I have emphasized empirical analysis, I have given some attention to normative analysis as well. The resulting discussion is therefore methodologically eclectic.

The analysis is also eclectic in its theoretical approach; it describes, evaluates, and applies ten conceptual models. I have tried to be fair in the treatment of each analytic model; but because I have necessarily summarized and evaluated each one only briefly, you may find some models slighted. Any such problem can be easily remedied by more specialized additional readings that emphasize one or more of the models.

Finally, I believe that an introductory discussion should be rich in concepts and facts but nevertheless written in a style that is appropriate to the audience. I have therefore not hesitated to include any conceptual and factual material that seems appropriate for a serious and rigorous introduction of American foreign policy. At the same time, however, I have tried to present the material in clear, straightforward prose.

ACKNOWLEDGMENTS

I am indebted to the late George Lipsky, who reinforced my early interest in world politics. Karl Deutsch inspired and encouraged me during graduate school and after. Terry Nardin guided me and yet gave me independence while I wrote a dissertation. Others who have contributed indirectly to this book include Harold Lasswell, Lester Milbrath, Zvi Namenwirth, Karl O'Lessker, Charles Planck, Donald Puchala, Dennis Quinn, Warren Roberts, Warren Shearer, Jerome Slater, Gaddis Smith, Glen Snyder, and Philip Wilder.

Jennifer Brewer provided excellent research assistance for this third edition. My family, individually and collectively, continued to inspire and motivate me as I undertook this revision. I am, as always, indebted to them. I am particularly grateful to my wife, Nancy Starke Brewer, who continues to inspire, cajole, tolerate, and support.

Three reviewers for this edition provided numerous helpful suggestions (Richard Thomas Cupitt, University of Georgia; Gary Prevost, St. John's University; and Henry A. Shockley, Boston University), as did the editorial and production people at Prentice Hall. In particular, Karen Horton, Linda Pawelchak, and Dolores Mars were consistently helpful throughout the editorial and production stages.

ONE

American Interests and Power in a Changing World

"The Cold War is now behind us. Everyone must change."—Soviet President Mikhail Gorbachev in a speech at Stanford University, June 4, 1990.

Summit meetings between U.S. and Soviet leaders provide dramatic glimpses into the interplay of interests and power that are central to American foreign policy making. They also often mark important turning points and trends in global political and economic contexts that influence American foreign policy. In recent years, there have been numerous significant changes reflected in these summit meetings: political and economic revolutions in the Soviet Union and other East European countries; decreasing hostility between those countries and the countries of Western Europe and North America; and increasing economic interactions between East and West. The liberalization of the Soviet political and economic systems, represented by *glasnost* and *perestroika,* are but some of the dramatic changes in the global environment of American foreign policy. There have also been significant changes in the developing countries of the "Third World": the establishment of democratic political processes in Argentina, Brazil, and elsewhere; the emergence of internationally competitive industries in Southeast Asia; and severe difficulties in repaying external debts by scores of countries. Most dramatic, though, was the emergence of Iraq as a significant military power and its defeat in the Persian Gulf War of 1991.

The stake of individual Americans and their local communities in such developments in the world can be illustrated by an examination of a single American city. Although you may not normally think of the people of Columbus, Ohio, as being involved in world politics and economics, they do in fact have substantial interests at stake. Their interests are evident in numerous statistics.[1]

1

In a single year, more than $130 million in machinery, scientific equipment, chemicals, and other manufactured goods were exported from Columbus. During the same year, there were also $88 million in direct imports into Columbus—not including goods first imported into other American cities and then transshipped to Columbus. Most of this trade was with Western European countries, but there was also trade with Japan, Israel, Canada, Mexico, and South Africa.

A dozen Columbus firms own nearly 200 factories and other facilities abroad. Thirty-four companies have daily contacts with foreign firms. Representatives of Columbus businesses make nearly 1,200 foreign trips each year to countries on all continents. The banks in Columbus maintain business contacts with 500 foreign banks. One of the insurance companies has 400 employees stationed in West Germany and Puerto Rico. A large nonprofit research organization with headquarters in Columbus has research centers in Switzerland and West Germany.

The agricultural industry in the county surrounding Columbus is heavily dependent on exports for its profits. Nearly two-thirds of its wheat crop is exported. Its annual export sales of wheat, corn, soybeans, and oats total more than $50 million. Consumers in the area purchase food imported from numerous countries—bananas from Panama, cocoa from Ghana, wine from Italy, and another seventy food items imported from other countries.

The people of Columbus have also had direct contact with foreign countries. About 18,000 of them were born abroad. Another 48,000 have one or more foreign-born parents. Altogether, about 6 percent of the local population have such a tie to a foreign country. In one year, these and other Columbus residents purchased 29,000 airline tickets to foreign countries—purchases that provided 60 percent of local travel agents' sales.

Finally, wars have left their mark on Columbus. There are more than 60,000 veterans of World War II and 30,000 veterans of the Vietnam War in Columbus. Altogether, five wars in this century have killed more than 3,000 Columbus citizens. In a nuclear war, the entire population might be killed.

These figures about Columbus, however, are only a mere suggestion of the importance of world politics and foreign policy to the entire United States. To obtain a more comprehensive and refined understanding of American interests—and American power—in world politics, we will consider the following questions: What are the significant characteristics and trends in the world political system? What is the distribution of military capabilities in the world political system? What economic, technological, and environmental developments are impinging on world politics? How do these conditions affect American interests and power?

THE WORLD POLITICAL SYSTEM

Actors

The world political system includes approximately 165 national governments. The United States maintains formal diplomatic relations with nearly all of them and has embassies in all but a few of their capitals. More than formal diplomatic relations are involved in American relations with these national governments, however. The American government interacts with most of these national governments across a broad spectrum of economic, military, technological, and cultural domains. Since the interests and circumstances of each country are distinctive, there is considerable diversity and complexity in American relations with them. (The statistical data in the appendix to this chapter provide additional information about each country.)

National governments, however, do not always act as single, monolithic actors. Sometimes, they act instead as several partially autonomous government bureaucracies. This is so because the foreign affairs, defense, intelligence, economic, and technological ministries of governments maintain relations with their counterparts in other governments, and those relations are often carried on rather independently of any effective centralized governmental controls. Since each national government has as many as ten or even more such bureaucracies commonly involved in foreign relations, there are many hundreds of national governmental bureaucratic actors in the world political system.

Although national governments remain the principal actors on most issues, they must often contend not only with one another but with numerous intergovernmental and nongovernmental actors as well. There are more than a hundred intergovernmental international organizations.[2] The most prominent, of course, is the United Nations, which provides general diplomatic functions, supervises specific peacekeeping operations, and oversees numerous other programs. In its General Assembly, members have negotiated agreements on arms control and provided guidance for peaceful settlements of disputes. The UN Security Council has authorized numerous peacekeeping forces: in southern Lebanon to try to maintain peace between the various warring groups; in the Sinai peninsula to separate Israeli and Egyptian troops; in Cyprus to reduce violence between Greek and Turkish ethnic groups; and in Zaire (formerly the Congo) to try to restore order in a civil war. The UN Relief and Works Agency provides subsistence support for more than a million displaced Palestinians, many of them in refugee camps scattered over the Middle East. The UN Economic and Social Council monitors the activities of more than a dozen affiliated specialized agencies and other programs in the United Nations system—for instance, the Food and Agriculture Organization, which conducts agricultural research and education programs. The UN also invoked economic sanctions against Iraq in an effort to isolate Iraq after its invasion of Kuwait. It subsequently passed a resolution authorizing the use of force in January 1991 when Iraq refused to leave Kuwait.

The World Bank Group, the International Monetary Fund, and the General Agreement on Tariffs and Trade (GATT) are especially important among economic organizations. GATT provides the framework within which worldwide negotiations on trade policy are periodically undertaken and within which trade disputes between countries are often resolved. The International Monetary Fund is principally concerned with countries' balance of payments, which it often helps to finance when countries' imports exceed their exports. As a condition of providing countries with loans, it often requires governments to adopt austerity measures in their economic policies. The World Bank Group is actually several closely related agencies, each with a slightly different emphasis, although their common purpose is to facilitate the flow of capital to developing (Third World) countries and hence contribute to their long-term growth. The activities of the World Bank thus include lending for development projects, providing economic adjustment assistance, issuing guarantees to foreign corporate investors against certain types of noncommercial risks, and undertaking projects in cooperation with private investors.

There are dozens of other intergovernmental organizations with more restricted memberships and functions. The Organization of Petroleum Exporting Countries (OPEC), for instance, consists of thirteen countries whose representatives meet periodically to try to coordinate oil export prices. Several of the most conspicuous intergovernmental organizations in American foreign policy are the regional military alliances, such as the North Atlantic Treaty Organization (NATO). There are also a large number of regional organizations that channel economic development funds or promote economic cooperation.

A multitude of nongovernmental organizations are also actively involved in world politics.[3] This diverse group of actors includes such religious organizations as the Roman Catholic Church and the World Council of Churches. It also includes giant multinational corporations engaged in global industrial and commercial activities. Other nongovernmental organizations represent the interests of particular economic sectors or groups of workers; the International Air Transport Association and the International Airline Pilots Association, for instance, have been active in seeking action against terrorist skyjacking. The terrorist organizations themselves are, of course, also nongovernmental actors in world politics. Such other nongovernmental organizations as Amnesty International and the International Red Cross devote their resources to humanitarian purposes. Altogether, there are several thousand nongovernmental organizations engaged in a variety of activities in world politics.

The world political system, therefore, is a diverse array of literally thousands of governmental, intergovernmental, and nongovernmental organizations. Such a complex image of world politics has several important implications for American foreign policy. One is that American policy makers must take into consideration a large number of other actors in world politics, and all of them exercise power. Individually, the power of the other actors is often marginal and limited to a narrow issue; in particular policy areas, however, such individual organizations can have an important impact. Furthermore, their number and significance have been increasing, especially in economic policy areas. For example, as much American economic development assistance is now provided to other countries indirectly through multilateral international organizations as through bilateral programs administered directly by the United States. Private corporations, moreover, transfer more capital to foreign countries than the American government does through the official bilateral and multilateral economic-assistance programs combined.[4]

Interactions

The number and diversity of the actors in world politics are also significant for American foreign policy because they mean that the system generates an immense number of diverse interactions among the actors. During the course of a year, more than a million cabled messages flow in and out of the U.S. State Department, and as many as one hundred thousand of these messages are sufficiently important or sensitive to require special handling through the department's Operations Center. To these, we can add the interactions that occur in face-to-face meetings and in other forms. For example, sixty-some diplomatic couriers travel more than sixteen million miles per year to deliver correspondence and documents. State Department representatives attend approximately a thousand international conferences each year.[5] We can further add the interactions involving the White House, the Defense Department, the CIA, and other U.S. government organizations. The American government is involved in millions of interactions in world politics during a year, and thousands in a single day.

As a result, American policy makers are confronted by an overwhelming and bewildering flow of information—much of it posing problems affecting American interests. One way to gain an appreciation of the diversity of problem areas involved in American foreign policy is to note the large number of entries concerning foreign relations in the *U.S. Code,* which is a compilation of currently effective federal laws. In Table 1–1, the titles listed in the *U.S. Code* that contain portions concerning foreign relations are indicated.

MILITARY CAPABILITIES

The Problem of War

The statistics on the wages of war provide compelling and tragic evidence of war's importance as a foreign policy problem. Table 1–2 lists the battle-connected deaths among military personnel in wars involving the United States since the early

TABLE 1–1 *U.S. Code* Titles containing Material Pertaining to Foreign Relations

TITLE	TOPIC
7	Agriculture
8	Aliens and nationality
10	Armed forces
12	Banks
15	Commerce and trade
16	Conservation
18	Crimes
19	Customs duties
20	Education
21	Food and drugs
22	Foreign relations and intercourse
26	Internal Revenue Code
32	National Guard
33	Navigation
37	Pay and allowances of uniformed services
38	Veterans' benefits
46	Shipping
48	Territories
49	Transportation
50	War and national defense

TABLE 1–2   Military Battle Deaths in American Wars (1816–1991)

	MILITARY BATTLE DEATHS*	
WARS	U.S.	OTHER COUNTRIES
Persian Gulf	139	na‡
Indochina†	46,000	1,000,000
Korean	54,000	2,000,000
World War II	408,300	15,000,000
World War I	126,000	9,000,000
Second Philippine	4,500	na‡
Spanish-American	5,000	5,000
Mexican-American	11,000	6,000

*Battle-connected deaths among military personnel only.
†Figures are for 1960–1975.
‡Not available.

Sources: J. David Singer and Melvin Small, *The Wages of War, 1816–1965* (New York: Wiley, 1972), pp. 60–75, tables 4–2 and 4–4. Indochina war figures are from Congressional Quarterly, *Congress and the Nation* IV, 1973–76 (Washington, DC: Congressional Quarterly, 1977), pp. 908–10. Persian Gulf figure is from the U.S. Department of Defense.

nineteenth century. They number over 600,000 for the United States alone and total 27 million for the militaries of all countries involved.

Even those figures, however, do not represent the total destructiveness and cost of war. Civilian deaths in World War II are estimated to have been between 20 and 35 million.[6] Civilian deaths in South Vietnam from 1965 to 1975 are estimated to have been half a million, with another million wounded. There were 300,000 wounded American military personnel in the Vietnam War and several million wounded South Vietnamese, Vietcong, and North Vietnamese military personnel.[7]

The economic costs of war also indicate the magnitude of the American interests involved. The war with Iraq cost hundreds of millions of dollars per day. The direct cost of the Vietnam War to the United States alone has been estimated to be $195 billion, if veterans' benefits and the interest on government borrowing are included; to that, we should add more than $30 billion in economic and military assistance provided by the United States to the government of South Vietnam. The American cost of World War II was more than $600 billion (mostly in uninflated pre-1950 dollars).[8] Finally, the inflationary pressures created by war impose many indirect economic and social costs. Thus, a major contributing factor to the relatively high inflation rates in the United States in the late 1970s was the earlier U.S. involvement in the war in Southeast Asia—and the failure of the government to raise taxes or reduce other expenditures at that time.

As the Persian Gulf War demonstrated, developments in weapons technology have increased the destructiveness of military forces. The improved accuracies of "precision guided" munitions, for instance, have substantially increased the percentage of hits by bombs and tactical missiles, so that the destructive potential of a given number of such weapons is now much greater than it was in the past.

Other statistics about the incidence of war and its human consequences suggest the magnitude of the problem of war in contemporary world politics. An organization that monitors international conflict found forty wars in progress in 1988.[9] They involved nearly five million combat troops and forty-five countries. They were estimated to have caused one to five million deaths and another three to fifteen million wounded.

The proliferation of nuclear weapons to additional countries increases the potential destructiveness of such wars. One relatively "small" nuclear weapon, similar to the one dropped on Hiroshima, can destroy a medium-sized city and inflict casualties of a hundred thousand or more. A large nuclear bomb or warhead can destroy much of a major city and inflict casualties of more than a million. Since nuclear bombs can be delivered by common aircraft, or even by simple ground vehicles, the mere acquisition of a few nuclear bombs gives a country at least a primitive nuclear force, even without the technologically advanced delivery capabilities of long-range missiles.

By 1991, eight countries had tested nuclear devices or were widely presumed to possess them. They included the United States and the Soviet Union, with more than ten thousand nuclear bombs or warheads each, and the United Kingdom, France, and China, with a few hundred each. India exploded a nuclear device in 1974 (but claims not to have produced any weapons subsequently). Although Israel has asserted that it would not be the first to introduce nuclear weapons into the Middle East, it was widely believed to have produced a dozen or more by the late 1970s. South Africa was reported to be preparing for a nuclear test explosion in 1977 when the United States, the Soviet Union, and France dissuaded it from proceeding. In addition, Pakistan and Iraq have had advanced nuclear research programs that could give them nuclear weapons' capabilities. Iraq's nuclear weapons program, however, was substantially destroyed in the early days of the 1991 war.

Military Forces as a Source of Power

The possession of such highly destructive military weapons conveys potential power in the limited sense of the ability to do damage. The actual use of military forces may enable a country to deny its adversaries the opportunity to achieve their objectives or at least to impose great costs on them.

But military forces do not necessarily otherwise convey power. Paradoxically, the increased destructiveness of military forces can make them less effective as a source of power because their threatened use is less credible. This paradox is most obvious in the case of nuclear weapons: A threat to use them, except in the most dire circumstances, is not likely to be credible because their use might invite nuclear retaliation. Furthermore, there are other sources of power in world politics besides military capabilities; economic, technological, and scientific development are all obvious sources of power. Yet a country's ability to punish other countries, to deny them their objectives, or to defend itself against attack establishes its basic political position in the world. The absolute and relative military-force levels of countries are among the most important indicators of their potential power in world politics.

Military personnel and expenditure figures reveal that a small number of countries have dominant military superiority.[10] American and Soviet annual military expenditures of over $400 billion each are greater than all other countries' expenditures combined. Moreover, the United States and the Soviet Union plus West Germany, China, France, and the United Kingdom account for about three-fourths of the world's annual military expenditures. If we use personnel statistics, we also find a considerable concentration, although the precise rankings are slightly different. The Soviet Union, China, the United States, and India, with over two million troops each, account for about one-half of the world's uniformed military personnel.

However, the distribution of military capabilities is constantly changing. Whereas the military forces of the industrialized countries have remained relatively stable, the military forces of the less developed countries have increased substantially. Moreover, a few countries are achieving regional military superiority. Although their military capabilities are still far below those of the United States and the Soviet Union, their increasing military forces are altering regional balances of power. Iraq, for instance, had a million troops by early 1991.

Not only have the numbers of troops increased in the less developed countries; so has their stock of military equipment. And much of it has been transferred from the industrialized countries. By the early 1990s, the industrialized countries were annually transferring more than $20 billion in military supplies to less developed countries.[11]

Thus, although a few countries continue to have predominant military superiority, the extent of their predominance is declining. This means that the world is becoming more polycentric, or multipolar, in terms of military capabilities. It is no longer such a bipolar system dominated by the Soviet and American military capabilities, as it was a few decades ago. This diffusion of military capabilities and the emergence of regionally dominant military powers are reinforced by similar trends in the world economy.

ECONOMICS

The Distribution of Wealth

Economic wealth, no matter how it is measured, is very unevenly distributed among the world's 165 countries. The United States alone accounts for about one-fourth of the world's annual gross production of goods and services. The twelve countries of the European Community account for one-fifth; the Soviet Union accounts for one-seventh; Japan accounts for about one-tenth. None of the remaining 150+ countries individually accounts for more than 5 percent of world economic activity; collectively, they account for only one-third.[12]

However, unusually fast growth rates in a few countries have made these countries dominant, not only regionally but globally, as major economic centers. In particular, Japan, West Germany, the Middle Eastern oil-producing countries, and the newly industrializing countries (NICs) of Southeast Asia have all enjoyed greater increases in their gross national products than the rest of the world. Their exports and their holdings of foreign currencies have also been increasing relatively rapidly. Meanwhile, American gross national product and exports were declining as shares of the world totals. Between 1960 and 1990 the American share of world gross product declined from 34 percent to about 20 percent, and its share of world exports declined from 17 percent to about 10 percent.[13]

The emergence of economic multipolarity and the declining American position in the world economy pose new foreign policy problems for the United States. American trade relations with Japan and some NICs became highly conflictual as their exports became increasingly competitive with American products. We will explore the implications of these and other developments more fully in later chapters; here we need only note that these economic problems rank with the problem of war as central items on the foreign policy agenda.

Another important change in the world economy during recent decades has been an increase in international interdependence.

Interdependence

There has always been a degree of interdependence in world politics, inasmuch as countries' interests and actions depended on one another. Indeed, since the advent of nuclear weapons and long-range missiles, every country's very existence has depended on the restraint of other countries' leaders in their use of those weapons. Countries have also been economically interdependent, particularly in matters of trade.

But the degree, the forms, and the significance of interdependence all change periodically.[14] During the past few decades, there have been several such changes. In 1960, for example, world exports were 9 percent of gross world product; by 1985, they had increased to approximately 15 percent. Countries vary considerably, however, in the share of their gross national product that comes from exports. More than one-half of some countries' GNP is based on exports. Only about 12 percent of American GNP is directly based on export sales—but that is up from 4 percent in 1960.[15]

There was also an increase in economic interdependence in the form of investments. This was especially true for the United States. Between 1960 and 1985, the value of direct American investments in foreign countries increased roughly by a factor of five. In recent years, the ten largest American banks have collectively earned more than half their profits from overseas activities. There has also been an increase in the flow of foreign capital into the United States. Between 1960 and 1985, total direct foreign investments in the United States more than quadrupled.[16]

In the late 1980s, there was a substantial surge in foreign investment in the United States, particularly by Japanese firms. These Japanese investments included automobile assembly facilities in California, Illinois, Indiana, Ohio, Kentucky, and Tennessee, in addition to Michigan, and also scores of automobile supplier firms. These projects and Japanese investments in real estate—hotels in Honolulu, office buildings in Los Angeles, Washington, DC, and New York City (including majority ownership of Rockefeller Center)—became symbols of the changing relationship between the American economy and the rest of the world economy.

Furthermore, these investments and investments by firms from other countries were posing new issues for American foreign policy makers at the national level as well as government officials at the state and local levels during the 1990s.

Energy interdependence from trade and foreign direct investment has also increased for the United States and other countries. About one-fifth of total United States energy is from foreign sources, as is nearly half of the oil it consumes. Japan and the continental countries of Western Europe are even more dependent on foreign oil and other energy sources. In fact, all of Japan's oil is from foreign sources. There is also international interdependence in other natural resources. The United States imports over half of its annual consumption of several metals used in making steel and in other manufacturing processes. Among them are chromium, cobalt, manganese, nickel, tin, tungsten, zinc, and bauxite (the principal component of aluminum). Japan and the European Community countries import 100 percent of their bauxite, nickel, and tungsten and over 90 percent of several other metals as well.[17]

These forms of interdependence affect American interests in several ways. American economic interests, particularly incomes and prices, are sensitive to the economic and political conditions in other countries. Wars and other forms of political instability, for instance, can interrupt the supply of imported raw materials used in manufacturing processes in the United States. Economic recession in other countries reduces American exports and, therefore, American employment and American profits. Oil price increases create inflationary pressures on American transportation, plastic products, and food—all of which directly depend on petroleum products in their manufacturing processes.

Interdependence also affects American power in world politics.[18] When a country imports a substantial proportion of its consumption of any economically important commodity, its dependence on those imports can be used as a source of power by the country that provides the commodities.

The full impact of interdependence on national power, however, is more complex than that. In the first place, vulnerability to threatened or actual interruptions in imports varies according to the degree to which internal reserves, stockpiles, or substitutes can alleviate shortages. For instance, the United States has domestic oil sources still available; it has a several months' stockpile of oil; and it has internal supplies of coal, natural gas, and nuclear fuels that can be used as partial substitutes for oil to generate electricity. Yet, U.S. sensitivity to oil prices was dramatically demonstrated by the Persian Gulf crisis.

The political consequences of interdependence are also complicated by the fact that interdependence varies among economic sectors. The United States is dependent on foreign oil and several metals, but it is not very dependent on foreign aircraft manufacturers or communications equipment. In fact, many countries are highly dependent on American sources in these sectors. As the term *interdependence* suggests, therefore, there is mutual dependence among many pairs of nations. Although the United States depends on Saudi Arabian oil, Saudi Arabia depends on

American technology and military supplies. The interdependencies are often asymmetrical, however. For any pair of countries, they do not necessarily balance, so that one country may have an advantage over the other.

International economic interdependencies also create pressures to expand the functions and the authority of international organizations. Individual countries are less able to influence their own economic conditions through their own separate policies, for economic conditions in each country are highly dependent on the economic conditions and policies of other countries. Therefore, the need for international cooperation increases.

Transnational economic interdependence also has important implications for internal political processes. Individual and group economic interests within the United States, for instance, are significantly affected by the economic conditions and policies of other countries and, therefore, by American foreign economic policies. The availability, quality, and price of many common American consumer goods are partially determined by American foreign trade policies and other elements of American foreign economic policies. Employment and income are also widely affected by international economic relations.

As the internal impact of foreign policy increases through transnational economic interdependence, domestic political pressures on foreign policy makers also increase. However, since the economic consequences of any given policy alternative are obviously distributed unevenly among domestic groups, domestic conflict becomes more likely. Foreign economic policy making, therefore, tends to be marked by considerable pluralism: Multiple-interest groups struggle to have their policy preferences prevail so that their economic interests will be advanced.

There is another way in which economic activities affect world politics: by depleting the global reserves of natural resources and by polluting the natural environment. The publication of a book titled *The Limits to Growth*[19] and periodic environmental disasters have focused attention on additional problems that affect American foreign policy. Simply stated, the central problem is that increases in world population and industrial production are imposing burdens on the natural environment, the supply of raw materials, and food-production capacities. Global warming, for instance, has become an important foreign policy issue.

The general nature of the problem and the relationships among several key trends are depicted in Figure 1–1. The basic forecast is that in the twenty-first century, per capita industrial production will peak and then decline precipitously as a result of the severe scarcity of natural resources, such as fuels and metals. According to this scenario, although the pollution created by industrial processes would continue to increase for a while, it would then decline because of the decline in industrial production. Population would continue to increase until after food production peaked, and then it would decline. In short, this simplified model indicates the possibility of economic collapse and starvation on a massive scale.

One should be careful, however, not to take such forecasts as certain or precise. Like all forecasts of the future, they are based on assumptions that may turn out to be wrong; further, these particular forecasts ignore the effects of price changes. The

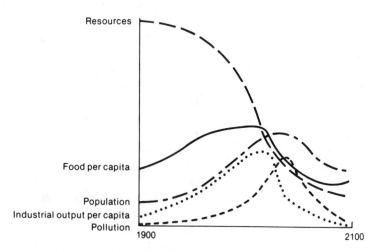

FIGURE 1–1   "The Limits to Growth": World Model. This is the "standard run,"
which assumes a continuation of past relationships among
physical, economic, and social variables.

*Source: The Limits to Growth: A Report for the Club of Rome's Project on the Predicament
of Mankind,* by Donella H. Meadows, Dennis L. Meadows, Jørgen Randers, and William W.
Behrens III. A Potomac Associates book published by Universe Books, New York, 1972.
Graphics by Potomac Associates.

rates of increase in energy consumption and population, for example, have already
slowed since the projections were made. Furthermore, the model ignores important
regional variations.[20] Starvation could be widespread in some regions (as it already
has been) but virtually nonexistent in others.

Although the precise impact of scarce resources on an individual country's
political position depends on many complex factors, a few simple statistics are
suggestive. Two-thirds of the world's proven oil reserves are in the Middle East and
North Africa. Saudi Arabia alone has over one hundred billion barrels, one-fifth of
the world total. Kuwait, Iran, Iraq, Libya, and Abu Dhabi also have major portions,
with over twenty billion barrels each. Outside the Middle East, the other major
reserves are located in only a few countries, including the Soviet Union and the
United States.[21] The world's reserves of several important metals are also highly
concentrated in a few countries. Nearly two-thirds of the world's bauxite reserves are
located in four countries: Guinea, Jamaica, Australia, and Surinam. Four-fifths of the
world's copper reserves are in Chile, Peru, Zambia, and Zaire.[22]

Economic interdependence has made the traditional distinction between foreign affairs and domestic affairs often ambiguous. Economic policy cannot be
thought of as only domestic policy. Because economic issues involve both international and domestic aspects, they are now sometimes referred to as "intermestic"
affairs.

THE NATURE OF POWER

Political power is a central concept in American foreign policy analysis. But there are several types of power, and it is often a subtle and complex phenomenon.[23] Four distinct notions of power can be identified.

Power can be defined as *control over pertinent resources*. Military forces, population, and GNP are resources commonly used to indicate national power in international political relations. Or, similarly, the number of staff personnel, membership, and funds spent by interest-group organizations are frequently used to indicate their power within the policy process. Such a notion of power is so common partly because the indicators are familiar and intuitively appealing ones but also partly because data are readily available so that pertinent actors' power can be measured quantitatively.

There are several limitations to this notion of power, however. One is that there are many different types of power resources, and their significance varies across issues, time, and other situational characteristics. Thus, one must be careful to relate a particular power-resource indicator to a particular situation of interest. A second limitation of this concept of power is that mere control over such resources does not necessarily lead to their effective use. Indeed, there is usually some kind of conversion process through which such resources are brought to bear on specific situations in order for them to have some kind of effect. Since such resources may or may not be actually applicable, their possession is often referred to as indicating only "potential power" rather than "actual power."

Thus, power can be defined as a *relationship* in which one country influences another country's actions by the threatened or actual use of force. For this type of power, the possession of military capabilities is clearly an important asset in world politics. There are many other variables, such as diplomatic and administrative skills, that determine the extent to which military capabilities can be used as a source of power; but military capabilities do provide one rough indicator of a country's potential power in this sense. National economic resources can also be used as a source of power in influence relationships. By promising or actually rendering economic assistance in any of several ways, or by withdrawing or threatening to withdraw such assistance, a country may be able to affect another country's actions.

The aggregate American military and economic resources that can be used in such influence relationships are substantial—even predominant in relation to nearly all countries in the world. But they are declining in relative terms even as they increase or remain constant in absolute terms. The increasing military capabilities and economic resources of a few other countries are enhancing their individual political positions in world politics; they are also contributing to a more multipolar world political system. The United States is increasingly constrained in world politics by these changing distributions in military capabilities and economic resources.

The United States is also constrained by the degree to which it is dependent on foreign sources of economic goods and services. However, since most international economic relationships involve mutual dependency, American power is also enhanced to the extent that other countries are dependent on American supplies (and purchases) of goods and services. And that dependency remains substantial.

Another type of power occurs when someone makes a *decision that affects the allocation of values* among a group of people. For instance, when a large corporation decides to build a new manufacturing plant in one country rather than another, it affects the distribution of income, employment, and other economic and social conditions; in that sense, it is allocating values and exercising power. A large number of diverse intergovernmental, nongovernmental, and governmental organizations exercise this type of power in world politics. International capital-investment decisions (to build new manufacturing plants, for example) are made by the World Bank and several other international organizations, by hundreds of large private corporations, and by the foreign aid and other bureaucracies of national governments.

Yet another type of power refers to the *ability to achieve objectives.* Thus, to the extent that a country can achieve security and prosperity, for instance, it is powerful. Several economic, environmental, and technological trends are imposing constraints on all countries' power in this sense. As international economic interdependence continues to increase, a national government's ability to achieve many of its economic policies through unilateral actions declines (although its citizens' standards of living may nevertheless increase directly or indirectly as a result of the increase in international commerce). As environmental pollution spreads from its source in one country to do damage to the air, water, industry, and health of the citizens of other countries, national governments find that they cannot be responsive to their constituents' desires for improved environmental quality without the cooperation of other governments. As improvements in the technology of warfare occur—and, therefore, as war becomes more destructive—governments are less able to provide for national security, except by increasing their own expenditures on military technology for defense. Thus, achievement of national security objectives becomes more expensive and/or less successful.

In sum, power can be defined as controlling resources, exercising influence in a relationship, making a decision that affects people's lives, or achieving objectives. Depending on the context, one or more of these may be pertinent in American foreign policy making. In any case, however, there are always costs associated with power, and there are always constraints. Much of the complexity and uncertainty—and much of the drama as well—in foreign policy stem from the multiplicity of types of power, and the costs and constraints that policy makers face, as they try to impose their preferences on others.

As the analytic models discussed in Chapter 2 make clear, questions of power are important domestically in the interactions among participants in the policy process as well as externally in U.S. relations with other countries.

Data on selected indicators of countries' military and economic resources and evidence of the extent of achievement of physical quality-of-life goals are presented in the appendix to this chapter.

Appendix to Chapter 1

The purpose of the table in this appendix is to provide data on selected indicators of countries' political, economic, military, and social features. Although they change from year to year for each country, their relative magnitudes across countries do not usually change much over a period of a few years. The table is thus useful for approximate cross-national comparisons. The United States has been placed in the first row to facilitate comparisons between it and other countries. The relatively large values for the United States on all of the indicators are not likely to be surprising. On the other hand, some information for other individual countries may change your basic perceptions of the world in important ways—for instance, the relatively large economic size of Brazil (as indicated by its GNP), or the high literacy rate in Argentina, or the large population of Bangladesh. The reader is invited to use the table as needed to look up particular information about specific countries, or to browse through it for more impressionistic and serendipitous scanning of the global environment of U.S. foreign policy.

NATIONAL STATISTICS*

	MILITARY CAPABILITIES		HUMAN AND ECONOMIC RESOURCES		LIVING CONDITIONS		
	PERSONNEL** (THOU.)	EXPENDITURE† (U.S. $ MIL.)	POPULATION†† (MIL.)	GNP‡ (U.S. $ MIL.)	LIFE## EXPECTANCY (YRS.)	PER§ CAPITA GNP (U.S. $)	LITERACY§§ RATE (%)
United States	2,279	296,200	243.8	4,527,000	73	18,570	99
Afghanistan	55	na	14.2	3,083	41	217	12
Albania	42	151	3.1	2,940	69	953	75
Algeria	170	1,930	23.5	65,200	55	2,779	46
Angola	74	na	8.0	na	41	na	20
Argentina	118	1,100	31.1	76,850	69	2,467	94
Australia	70	4,986	16.1	197,900	73	12,320	99
Austria	39	1,447	7.6	116,800	72	15,440	99
Bahrain	4	160	0.5	3,865	66	8,328	40
Bangladesh	100	321	107.1	17,480	46	163	25
Barbados	1	na	0.3	1,349	70	5,277	97
Belgium	109	4,163	9.9	137,600	72	13,940	99
Benin	4	na	4.3	1,646	46	379	20
Bolivia	30	127	6.3	4,160	49	659	63
Botswana	4	24	1.1	1,094	48	952	30
Brazil	541	2,200	147.1	291,300	62	1,980	75
Bulgaria	191	6,656	9.0	64,780	72	7,229	95

*Data based on monetary values are only approximately comparable across countries since they do not precisely reflect comparable purchasing power and since they are based on currency conversions using fluctuating exchange rates.

Sources: **,†U.S. Arms Control and Disarmament Agency, World Military Expenditures and Arms Transfers, 1988 (Washington, DC: June 1989). Data are for 1987—latest available.
††,‡,##,§,§§Europa Yearbook, 1984 (London: Europa Publications, 1984). Population data are for 1980, GNP data for 1983, life expectancy for 1975–1980, literacy for 1982.

NATIONAL STATISTICS* (continued)

	MILITARY CAPABILITIES		HUMAN AND ECONOMIC RESOURCES		LIVING CONDITIONS		
	PERSONNEL** (THOU.)	EXPENDITURE† (U.S. $ MIL.)	POPULATION†† (MIL.)	GNP‡ (U.S. $ MIL.)	LIFE## EXPECTANCY (YRS.)	PER$ CAPITA GNP (U.S. $)	LITERACY§§ RATE (%)
Burkina Faso	9	51	8.3	1,638	na	198	na
Burma	210	281	38.8	9,357	53	241	78
Burundi	10	37	5.0	1,192	41	238	25
Cambodia	40	na	6.5	na	na	na	na
Cameroon	15	246	10.3	12,080	46	1,256	34
Canada	86	8,835	25.9	402,100	74	15,550	99
Cape Verde	4	na	0.3	175	60	507	37
Central African Republic	5	na	2.7	1,056	42	396	16
Chad	30	34	4.6	968	40	208	15
Chile	127	683	12.4	17,110	66	1,375	90
China, People's Republic	3,530	20,660	1,074.0	470,700	67	438	70
China, Taiwan	365	4,701	19.8	101,300	68	5,126	89
Colombia	86	371	30.7	33,870	62	1,105	82
Congo	14	105	2.1	2,298	46	1,104	80
Costa Rica	8	26	2.8	4,288	70	1,525	90
Cuba	297	na	10.3	26,420	73	2,576	96
Cyprus	13	35	0.7	3,733	72	5,460	89
Czechoslovakia	215	10,320	15.6	151,300	70	9,709	99
Denmark	28	2,141	5.1	97,810	74	19,100	99
Dominican Republic	21	64	7.0	4,631	60	665	68
Ecuador	44	250	10.0	9,715	60	976	84
Egypt	450	6,527	51.9	71,170	55	1,370	40
El Salvador	49	178	5.3	4,546	62	864	58
Equatorial Guinea	2	na	0.3	109	46	319	20

NATIONAL STATISTICS* (continued)

	MILITARY CAPABILITIES		HUMAN AND ECONOMIC RESOURCES		LIVING CONDITIONS		
	PERSONNEL** (THOU.)	EXPENDITURE† (U.S. $ MIL.)	POPULATION†† (MIL.)	GNP‡ (U.S. $ MIL.)	LIFE‡‡ EXPECTANCY (YRS.)	PER§ CAPITA GNP (U.S. $)	LITERACY§§ RATE (%)
Ethiopia	300	442	46.7	5,217	39	112	8
Fiji	3	na	0.7	1,069	71	1,475	75
Finland	37	na	4.9	85,130	73	17,250	99
France	559	34,830	55.6	868,300	74	15,620	99
Gabon	9	na	1.0	3,058	44	2,930	40
Gambia	1	na	0.8	136	41	179	12
Germany, Dem. Rep.	241	14,440	16.6	196,900	72	11,860	99
Germany, Fed. Rep.	495	34,130	61.0	1,126,000	72	18,450	99
Ghana	11	45	13.9	4,936	48	354	30
Greece	203	2,902	10.0	46,710	73	4,677	95
Guatemala	43	104	8.6	6,768	58	785	47
Guinea	24	na	6.7	1,662	44	247	15
Guinea-Bissau	11	4	0.9	122	41	131	9
Guyana	5	na	0.8	247	69	323	85
Haiti	8	40	6.2	2,231	51	361	23
Honduras	22	133	4.8	3,624	57	752	47
Hungary	116	4,525	10.6	87,640	70	8,260	98
Iceland	0	0	0.2	5,165	76	21,110	100
India	1,502	9,632	800.3	246,000	49	307	36
Indonesia	281	1,367	180.4	65,780	48	365	64
Iran	350	na	50.3	257,800	54	5,129	48
Iraq	900	na	17.0	56,520	55	3,331	30
Ireland	14	na	3.5	25,750	72	7,285	99
Israel	180	5,536	4.2	33,440	72	7,921	88

NATIONAL STATISTICS* (continued)

	MILITARY CAPABILITIES		HUMAN AND ECONOMIC RESOURCES		LIVING CONDITIONS		
	PERSONNEL** (THOU.)	EXPENDITURE† (U.S. $ MIL.)	POPULATION†† (MIL.)	GNP‡ (U.S. $ MIL.)	LIFE## EXPECTANCY (YRS.)	PER§ CAPITA GNP (U.S. $)	LITERACY§§ RATE (%)
Italy	531	18,350	57.4	746,400	73	13,010	98
Ivory Coast	8	178	10.8	9,440	46	877	22
Jamaica	3	26	2.4	2,310	70	950	82
Japan	244	24,320	122.0	2,369,000	76	19,410	99
Jordan	100	646	2.7	4,646	60	1,690	58
Kenya	21	182	22.4	7,618	54	340	40
Korea, Dem. People's Rep.	838	5,800	21.4	25,900	63	1,208	85
Korea, Rep.	604	5,626	42.2	118,000	63	2,796	92
Kuwait	20	1,330	1.9	25,720	69	13,800	80
Laos	50	na	3.8	na	44	na	28
Lebanon	37	na	3.3	na	65	na	75
Lesotho	2	na	1.6	517	50	319	55
Liberia	6	40E	2.4	1,063	53	446	24
Libya	91	3,063	3.8	27,560	55	7,188	40
Luxembourg	1	73	0.4	8,682	72	23,710	100
Madagascar	26	44E	10.7	1,825	46	170	53
Malawi	7	18	7.4	1,246	46	168	25
Malaysia	106	937	16.1	28,970	63	1,803	na
Mali	8	47	8.4	1,925	42	228	na
Malta	1	26	0.4	1,679	71	4,575	na
Mauritania	16	37	1.9	869	42	466	17
Mauritius	1	3	1.1	1,724	64	1,597	61
Mexico	141	726	81.9	139,200	64	1,701	76
Mongolia	32	na	2.0	na	63	na	95

NATIONAL STATISTICS* (continued)

	MILITARY CAPABILITIES		HUMAN AND ECONOMIC RESOURCES		LIVING CONDITIONS		
	PERSONNEL** (THOU.)	EXPENDITURE[†] (U.S. $ MIL.)	POPULATION[††] (MIL.)	GNP[‡] (U.S. $ MIL.)	LIFE[##] EXPECTANCY (YRS.)	PER[§] CAPITA GNP (U.S. $)	LITERACY[§§] RATE (%)
Morocco	200	1,114	24.4	15,640	55	642	24
Mozambique	65	103	14.5	1,237	46	85	14
Nepal	30	33	17.8	2,775	43	156	20
Netherlands	106	6,543	14.6	213,700	75	14,590	99
New Zealand	13	755	3.3	33,910	73	10,230	99
Nicaragua	80	na	3.3	33,170	na	9,994	na
Niger	5	na	7.0	2,370	55	339	87
Nigeria	138	180	108.6	23,270	42	214	5
Norway	38	2,775	4.2	80,790	75	19,330	99
Oman	27	1,516	1.2	6,510	48	5,306	5
Pakistan	573	2,226	104.6	34,210	47	327	na
Panama	12	105	2.3	5,160	51	2,268	23
Papua New Guinea	3	na	3.6	2,759	70	774	85
Paraguay	16	47	4.3	4,566	50	1,074	32
Peru	127	2,198	20.7	44,580	64	2,150	82
Philippines	161	458	61.5	34,620	57	563	72
Poland	441	17,950	37.7	259,500	61	6,879	88
Portugal	103	1,131	10.3	34,870	71	3,380	98
Qatar	11	na	0.3	4,206	57	13,320	70
Romania	248	7,609	22.9	146,000	70	6,365	98
Rwanda	5	42	6.8	2,087	50	306	25
Sao Tome and Principe	1	na	0.1	na	na	na	na
Saudi Arabia	80	10,490	14.8	82,270	53	5,563	75
Senegal	18	97	7.1	4,397	42	622	10

NATIONAL STATISTICS* (continued)

	MILITARY CAPABILITIES		HUMAN AND ECONOMIC RESOURCES		LIVING CONDITIONS		
	PERSONNEL** (THOU.)	EXPENDITURE[†] (U.S. $ MIL.)	POPULATION[††] (MIL.)	GNP[‡] (U.S. $ MIL.)	LIFE[##] EXPECTANCY (YRS.)	PER[§] CAPITA GNP (U.S. $)	LITERACY[§§] RATE (%)
Sierre Leone	6	na	3.9	935	50	242	15
Singapore	55	na	2.6	20,550	71	7,854	76
Somalia	50	na	7.7	1,540	43	199	5
South Africa (incl. Namibia)	102	3,400	34.3	77,130	60	2,248	35
Spain	314	6,906	39.0	284,000	73	7,282	93
Sri Lanka	30	204	16.4	6,534	65	398	81
Sudan	59	231	23.5	8,691	47	369	20
Suriname	3	na	0.4	1,086	67	2,794	na
Swaziland	3	8	0.7	591	46	827	65
Sweden	66	4,434	8.4	155,000	75	18,490	99
Switzerland	20	3,726	6.6	179,400	75	27,300	99
Syria	400	3,364	11.1	28,230	64	2,532	50
Tanzania	40	na	23.5	2,831	15	120	60
Thailand	275	1,657	53.6	45,070	60	840	84
Togo	8	40	3.2	1,204	46	373	10
Trinidad and Tobago	2	na	1.2	4,160	69	347	92
Tunisia	38	289	7.6	9,184	58	1,215	62
Turkey	879	2,890	53.0	65,460	61	1,235	70
Uganda	15	na	15.9	3,762	53	236	25
USSR	4,400	303,000	284.0	2,460,000	70	8,662	99
United Arab Emirates	44	na	1.8	23,290	62	12,610	53
United Kingdom	328	31,580	56.8	667,000	72	11,730	99
Uruguay	28	na	3.0	7,222	70	2,437	94
Venezuela	69	1,379	18.3	38,370	66	2,098	86

NATIONAL STATISTICS* (continued)

	MILITARY CAPABILITIES		HUMAN AND ECONOMIC RESOURCES		LIVING CONDITIONS		
	PERSONNEL** (THOU.)	EXPENDITURE† (U.S. $ MIL.)	POPULATION†† (MIL.)	GNP‡ (U.S. $ MIL.)	LIFE## EXPECTANCY (YRS.)	PER$ CAPITA GNP (U.S. $)	LITERACY§§ RATE (%)
Vietnam	1,300	na	63.6	12,700	53	200	78
Yemen, (Aden)	40	na	2.4	941	41	400	12
Yemen (Sanaa)	28	324	6.5	4,518	44	692	25
Yugoslavia	234	1,317	23.4	60,450	69	2,580	85
Zaire	53	na	32.3	5,349	46	165	40
Zambia	17	na	7.3	1,660	48	228	50
Zimbabwe	45	283	9.4	5,714	54	610	45

Analytic Models

Foreign policy analysis can be undertaken for any of several reasons. Sometimes its purpose is to analyze facts so that one can reach conclusions about what has occurred or why it has occurred—in other words, to describe or explain policy; since description and explanation are based on factual observations, they are forms of empirical analysis. Sometimes the purpose of analysis is to predict future policy; although such forecasts are inherently speculative, they also typically depend partly on empirical analysis of the past and present. Normative analysis, which inevitably involves values as well as facts, is also common; values are involved when policy is evaluated or prescribed.

Thus, one may want to know the following about U.S. trade with Japan: What restrictions—if any—does the United States impose on imports from Japan? (description). Why has the United States pressured the Japanese government into limiting its exports of automobiles to the United States in some years? (explanation). Will the establishment of Japanese-owned automobile plants in the United States decrease or increase imports of automotive parts from Japan? (prediction). Is the general policy of allowing foreign firms to invest in the United States without restrictions desirable, and are the exceptions to this generally open policy advisable? (evaluation). What should the U.S. government do, if anything, about state and local government subsidies to attract Japanese (and other countries') firms to establish facilities in their areas? (prescription).

Another series of questions may concern American policies in arms control negotiations with the Soviet Union. In that case, we could try to answer several questions: What are the American policies in those negotiations? (description). Why did the United States adopt these policies? (explanation). Is the United States likely to reach additional arms control agreements with the Soviet Union in the near future? (prediction). Are the existing treaties beneficial? (evaluation). What other agreements should the United States try to reach? (prescription).

Instead of questions about a particular issue, we may want to ask more general questions: In how many wars has the United States been involved? Why has the United States fought in some wars but not others? Is the United States likely to become involved in more wars or fewer wars in the future? Has the United States been too willing or too reluctant to become involved in wars? What policies should the United States adopt to reduce the incidence of war?

These illustrative questions readily indicate that foreign policy analysis includes a diverse variety of analytic tasks. It involves values as well as facts, the future and the past as well as the present, and general categories of cases as well as particular individual issues. Foreign policy analysis is further complicated by the number and complexity of the facts and values that are pertinent to the questions that we try to answer.

Fortunately, there are a large number of analytic models that can help us deal with the complexities by structuring our analyses. *Analytic models* are generalizations that can help us pose and answer questions about American foreign policy. Since their nature and utility will become clear as we consider the particular models available to us, we can simply note here that they include concepts and empirical assumptions that are helpful as we describe, explain, and predict American foreign policy; and they also include concepts and normative guidelines that are helpful as we evaluate and prescribe policy.

Although some of the concepts in these models may be unfamiliar and even seem esoteric, many of the basic ideas are nevertheless probably quite familiar. In fact, many observers already have the basic ideas in their heads and use them to analyze American foreign policy (and so do policy makers). However, we need to develop those rudimentary ideas into more comprehensive, more refined, and more explicit models so that they can be more useful.

COMPREHENSIVE RATIONAL DECISION MAKING[1]

Everyone agrees that American foreign policy should be rational, that it should be formulated and implemented rationally. Many people, however, believe that policy is not typically made through a rational policy process. But what do such statements mean? To make the notion of rationality analytically useful, we will develop it into a complex set of assumptions about foreign policy making—now commonly referred to as the rational or "strategic" decision-making model.

According to this model, for a decision to be made rationally, five sets of criteria must be met. The first set concerns a decision maker's goals: They must be clearly specified. Three commonly stated foreign policy goals, for instance, are the promotion of the national interest, or the protection of national security, or the maximization of national welfare. But the meanings of these terms are normally vague. On the other hand, examples of more clearly specified goals are the avoidance of nuclear war or the achievement of an open international trade system.

A second set of criteria for rational decision making pertains to the decision maker's perception of the environment, or "definition of the situation," as it is often called. In particular, the decision maker needs accurate and comprehensive information about the nature of the threats and opportunities that arise in the international environment.

Third, rational decision making entails consideration of all major alternatives, or "options," as they are often called in the government. And those alternatives must be clearly specified.

The fourth set of criteria for rational decision making is the most elaborate and also the most demanding. These criteria require that the evaluation of alternatives includes estimation of the possible advantageous and disadvantageous outcomes (costs and benefits) that might result from each of the alternatives. Such costs and benefits might include not only specific, measurable economic costs and benefits but also all other kinds, such as general political costs and benefits. Moreover, in its most extreme form, the rational decision-making model assumes that estimates are made of the approximate probability that each such possible cost and benefit will actually occur. These probabilities can be combined with the estimates of the costs and benefits to yield "expected" costs and benefits. Then, taking into account all expected costs and benefits, the "net expected benefit" of each alternative is determined as the excess of expected benefits over expected costs.

Finally, the rational choice is made—namely, the selection of the alternative with the maximum expected net benefit.

Although this is the essence of the rational decision-making model, as that term is now commonly used, we can add two additional complementary components— planning and learning—which are also consistent with common notions of rational decision making. Rational decision making entails active planning ahead in order to cope effectively with anticipated situations rather than passively waiting for situations to develop and then reacting to them.[2] But rational decision making involves not only forecasting and planning for the future; it also involves learning from the past. It specifically involves the feedback of information about the effects of past decisions so that present and future decisions can be adjusted to minimize the unfavorable outcomes and maximize the favorable outcomes.[3]

Figure 2–1 summarizes this model of foreign policy making in diagram form.

The accuracy of this model as a set of empirical assumptions about American foreign policy is arguable. Indeed, many of the assumptions lack plausibility simply on common intuitive and impressionistic grounds. There is so much complexity and uncertainty in foreign policy making that it would be quite difficult, and perhaps even impossible, for policy to be based on such comprehensive calculations, even by the most capable and dedicated decision makers.

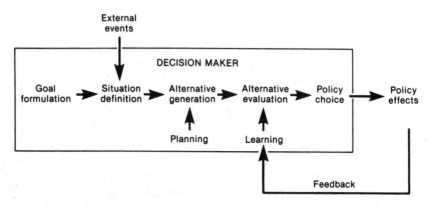

FIGURE 2–1 Comprehensive rational decision-making model

We also know from ordinary observations that such a model is implicitly based on dubious assumptions about human behavior. For of course human beings do not always process information in such a thorough and reliable manner.

Furthermore, we know that foreign policy decisions are not made by a single person or a unified collectivity of people, and we know that not all the people making decisions want the same policy. They have different personal stakes in decisions, prefer different goals, and even have different conceptions of the national interest. In other words, politics plays a part in foreign policy making.

The rational decision-making model, therefore, suffers from three flaws as an empirical model for American foreign policy analysis. It ignores the complexity of foreign affairs; it ignores the human dimension of policy making; and it ignores the political conflicts in policy making. As a consequence, we have to turn to other models of policy making to take these factors into account.

Yet we should be careful not to dismiss the rational decision-making model as useless simply because it suffers from these shortcomings. For we do find that such rational decision-making calculations are present to some extent in foreign policy . making. Furthermore, even though policy making deviates from the rational model assumptions in several respects, the rational model provides a useful starting point for many empirical analyses.

What about its value as a source of normative criteria and guidelines to help us evaluate and prescribe foreign policy? If we consider both what the model includes and what it excludes, we find that it even has limitations for normative analysis. In terms of what is included, the model is so demanding in its requirements for comprehensive calculations that it could be counterproductive. While such comprehensive calculations are proceeding, time is passing, the situation confronting decision makers may be changing, and hence problems may become more severe. Delays, in other words, can be costly.

In terms of what is excluded, the model does not help us answer a central normative question about the policy process: Who should make decisions? Furthermore, although the rational decision-making model indicates how rational decisions can be reached, it does not offer any guidance on the specific substance of rational decisions. In other words, it does not tell us which particular interests or goals ought to be pursued. Interests are usually not self-evident; they must be defined. Goals are not merely derived from definitions of interests; they depend on particular situations. So we will have to turn to other models for additional guidance in our evaluations and prescriptions.

In spite of these limitations, the rational model provides a useful set of criteria and general guidelines if we do not employ them literally or exclusively. It is obviously better to have clearly defined goals than vague ones. It is better to consider several alternatives instead of only one. It is better to consider both costs and benefits rather than only one or the other. It is better to take into account the likelihood of possible outcomes, even if only intuitively and approximately, rather than ignore them altogether. And it is better to plan for the future and learn from the past than to neglect them completely.

INCREMENTAL DECISION MAKING[4]

Another model of policy making also focuses on the information-processing aspects of decision making. But it takes into account the burdens placed on decision makers by complexity and uncertainty, and it also takes into account the inherently limited information-processing capabilities of individual and organizational decision makers. In other words, this model of policy making recognizes that the information-processing requirements of the comprehensive model are unrealistic and even counterproductive. Policy makers must adapt to the realities of making decisions in an almost infinitely complex world with only finite information-processing resources.

Because of the analytic difficulties involved in establishing precise goals for the future, the incremental model assumes that policy makers have only rather general and even vague goals. Hence, they focus their attention on moving away from present problems.

Decision makers further cope with complexity and uncertainty by limiting the number of alternatives and the possible consequences of each one that they consider. In particular, they tend to limit serious consideration to those alternatives that are only marginally different from existing policy. Such an approach reduces complexity by limiting the number of alternatives and consequences that are considered. It reduces uncertainty by limiting policy changes to only incrementally different alternatives. If an alternative is only marginally different from present policy, the consequences are also likely to be only marginally different.

Nor, according to the incremental decision-making model, is there much emphasis on planning ahead. Since there are so many possible future contingencies for which policy makers might plan, it is preferable to deal with the problems on an ad hoc basis as they arise.

Finally, according to the incremental model, learning processes are limited. They are narrowly focused on a few short-term consequences of present policy. Thus, policy may be changed on the basis of experience, but it is only through limited feedback focused on short-term effects. Policy making is essentially a trial-and-error process, in which policy alternatives are tried and then adjusted incrementally as deemed appropriate on the basis of short-run experience. Such an approach to decision making has been referred to as *muddling through*. It is diagrammed in Figure 2–2.

As an empirical model, this set of assumptions is more nearly accurate than the comprehensive rational decision-making model in some respects. But it also suffers from a neglect of the human and political dimensions of policy making.

Its value as a normative model, however, is more controversial. On the one hand, it helps to identify a problem in policy making that ought to receive our attention: How should policy makers cope with complexity and uncertainty? On the other hand, critics have argued that it encourages a defeatist, escapist, and amateurish approach to policy making; "muddling through" on the basis of minimal analysis of immediate problems is considered a virtue. Policy making that emphasizes the short term, after all, can lead to policies that are disastrous in the long term.

In addition, this model of policy making has been criticized on normative grounds as being inherently conservative in the sense of favoring the status quo. If only incremental changes in policy receive serious attention, then the problems are not likely to be substantially solved but only marginally ameliorated. It may be true, as advocates of incrementalism argue, that a large number of small changes add up to a large change over time. But that means problems will be solved only over the long term, a prospect that may be intolerable. Thus, whether we find incrementalism to be a desirable or undesirable approach to policy making depends very much on how desirable or undesirable we find the status quo.

HUMAN BEHAVIOR[5]

Another model of policy making focuses on the fact that decision makers are human beings. Its concepts and assumptions are therefore quite naturally derived from psychology's emphasis on personality, perceptions, and the social context of behavior. The psychological model of policy making emphasizes the extent to which the goals of policy makers are dependent on the individual policy makers' own personalities and backgrounds. Some policy makers place considerable, even exclusive, emphasis on power and status as foreign policy goals; others place some emphasis on such goals as reducing poverty, poor health, and injustice. Although such differences

FIGURE 2–2 Incremental decision-making model

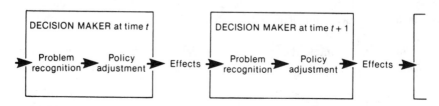

may be partly the result of different conclusions based on careful, thoughtful analysis, they are also partly the result of different personal experiences and backgrounds.

Indeed, they may even be a reflection of deep, unconscious personal needs. A considerable amount of psychological analysis, for instance, has focused on the nature, origins, and consequences of a particular personality trait: authoritarianism. Its characteristics include a tendency to be aggressive, domineering, and generally controlling in human relations. These tendencies, which are commonly defensive reactions to ego-damaging experiences during childhood or youth, lead to a relatively strong emphasis on power and status in politics. In some cases, authoritarian personality tendencies can also lead to paranoia—the exaggeration of threats in the environment—a tendency that can clearly affect policy makers' perceptions of the situations they confront.

More generally, we know from psychology that people often misperceive their environment. Even in the best of circumstances and with a concerted and open-minded effort, it is difficult for policy makers to obtain accurate perceptions of the situations they confront. But given such common human tendencies as wishful thinking, stereotypic thinking, and dogmatic thinking, it is not surprising that policy makers' images of reality are often distorted.

Individual policy makers' personality traits can also affect the generation, evaluation, and choice of policy alternatives. For instance, some policy makers are prone to conform to a consensus supporting a particular policy alternative. Thus, the generation of other policy alternatives may be stifled, and the evaluation of the favored alternative may be biased or even prematurely discontinued. Since government policy discussion typically occurs in the context of a group meeting, such tendencies as conformism or other elements of small-group behavior may be pervasive in the policy process.

Personality traits and group behavior tendencies are also important factors in the selection of alternatives. Some policy makers prefer high-risk alternatives; others prefer low-risk alternatives. Some policy makers prefer to plan for the future; others prefer to muddle through. Some are open-minded enough to change policies when they receive information indicating failure; others are so closed-minded they continue to support policies that are clearly failures.

A study of a series of American foreign policy cases suggests that a whole syndrome of dysfunctional decision-making tendencies, "group think," arises from the cohesiveness of small groups in the government.[6] These tendencies include illusions of invulnerability as well as stereotypic, conformist, and dogmatic thinking.

Psychological foreign policy analysis, then, emphasizes the role of human behavior in policy making, particularly the role of dysfunctional and even irrational behavior; and it emphasizes the variations among individuals and groups. Its basic components are indicated in Figure 2–3.

How much and in what ways does the human behavior model help our empirical analyses of foreign policy? In the first place, it provides a corrective to the unrealistic assumptions about human behavior that are implicit in the comprehensive rational decision-making model. It also alerts us to the potential impact of individual perceptions, preferences, and experiences on policy making.

But as an empirical model, it also suffers from several flaws. Although its

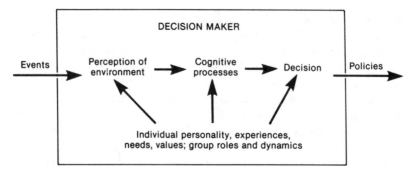

FIGURE 2–3 Human behavior model

assumptions have some appeal on the basis of our common observations of human behavior, it may lead us to exaggerate the impact of individual behavior in policy making. In particular, it may lead us to see policy as simply the direct result of the preferences of individual decision makers. Also, to the extent that its assumptions are based on psychoanalytic notions about the roles of traumatic emotional experiences and subconscious emotional needs, psychological foreign policy analysis unfortunately rests on ambiguous evidence. Such psychoanalytically derived foreign policy analyses are inevitably rather speculative. They are difficult either to document or to disprove, since they are not based on hard evidence. Furthermore, taken to an extreme, the psychological approach depoliticizes policy making—it explains away conflicts, for instance, as the result of misperceptions and explains away interests and policy preferences as merely reflections of deep-seated personal emotional needs.

What about its normative value? The normative guidelines that emerge from the psychological approach tend to be either banal or unrealistic. The implication that policy makers should be emotionally stable people with healthy psyches is obvious, and the suggestion that they should be subjected to psychoanalytic evaluation to determine their fitness to hold such responsible positions seems unrealistic—at least as far as any publicly visible high-level officials are concerned. Yet it is nevertheless true that policy makers and publics alike should be on the alert for signs of dysfunctional and potentially disastrous human behavior in the policy process.

In any case, psychological analysis of policy making does provide us with occasional insights into foreign policy. They are insights that may be subtle and even based on tenuous evidence, but they are significant. And we can gain insights only after we are sensitized to the subtleties and even perversities of human behavior by exposure to the concepts and assumptions of psychology and psychoanalysis.

Finally, we do not have to accept the basic tenets of psychoanalysis; we do not have to assume that human behavior tends to be pathological; and we do not have to probe the experiential and subconscious origins of human behavior. We can simply recognize that the thought processes of policy makers have an impact on policy making. In other words, we can analyze policy makers' cognitive processes without imputing pathological behavior or unconscious motives. We can merely assume that policy makers necessarily deal with enormously complex problems and that their cognitive processes as they do so are important and often imperfect.[7]

ORGANIZATIONAL BEHAVIOR[8]

Our fourth model is based on the recognition that policy making occurs in an organizational context and that certain tendencies in organizational behavior have important foreign policy consequences.

One characteristic of government foreign policy organizations is that their core personnel belong to professional career groups with distinctive belief systems that are fostered through organizational recruitment, training, and promotion processes. Such factors account for the often narrow perspectives of government bureaucrats. In the case of American foreign policy making, the most conspicuous of these career groups are the military and the foreign service.

Another tendency of organizations is that they protect and promote their own interests, which often include organizational survival, expansion, and the exercise of influence in policy making. In addition to such obvious interests, however, there is also considerable concern about protecting organizational missions, that is, the presumed central purposes of the organization. In fact, organizations sometimes resist expansion into new domains because they do not view them as part of the organizational mission.

The governmental organizations involved in foreign policy are large, but they are not monolithic. They consist of many suborganizations, each of which has a distinctive function within the larger organization. Specialization by function (or division of labor) is one of the earmarks of organizations. Governmental organizations are not only functionally decentralized; they are also geographically decentralized. They have large numbers of employees situated in different cities and countries. As a result, problems tend to be "factored," that is, divided into parts; and power tends to be "fractionated," that is, decentralized.

Organizations are also hierarchical. They are arranged so that everyone is in a relationship of superior or inferior authority to someone else. Although such an arrangement facilitates the efficiency and control of the organization, it also tends to foster conformist thinking and behavior.

Another way organizations facilitate efficiency is by adopting standard operating procedures (SOPs), which are narrowly prescribed routines. But because organizations follow routines, they are difficult to change; they have strong tendencies toward inertia. They resist being moved to undertake new responsibilities, and they resist measures to stop them once they are started.

Organizational personnel also like stability because stability enables them to maximize the use of standard operating procedures; it enables them to function smoothly and efficiently.

Finally, they frequently like secrecy because secrecy maximizes power and minimizes embarrassment.

Such tendencies affect foreign policy making in numerous ways, but principally through organizations' informational and operational capabilities. Information processing is an important part of policy making, since it is inevitably involved in defining situations, estimating consequences of alternatives, planning for the future, and learning from experience. Most of the information that goes into these policy-making activities is channeled through governmental organizations, such as the CIA.

But organizations frequently distort the content of information and/or restrict its distribution. Sometimes they do so inadvertently, sometimes intentionally. But the combination of their self-interest, specialized, decentralized, conformist, routinized, and secretive tendencies clearly constrains the wide distribution of undistorted information.

The operational capabilities of organizations become particularly important in the implementation of policy decisions. High-level government officials, whether in Congress or the executive branch, can rarely implement their individual or collective policy decisions without organizational assistance. Such dependence on organizations' operational capabilities is obvious and dramatic in wars, for instance. But it is also substantial in more routine, less obvious cases, such as negotiation of tariff reductions or implementation of economic-assistance agreements or arms transfer agreements.

The interests, routines, and inertia of the implementing organization can fundamentally affect policy. Indeed, sometimes policy decisions are not implemented at all; other times policies are implemented even though they have not been decided by responsible officials. Since there are often several organizations that are implementing policy, there are often several policies, which may even be contradictory. At a given time, on a given issue, there may be not one American policy but rather several organizational policies: a Defense Department policy, a State Department policy, a Treasury Department policy, an Energy Department policy. Such a multiplicity of organizational policies is evident in Figure 2–4.

FIGURE 2–4 Organizational behavior model

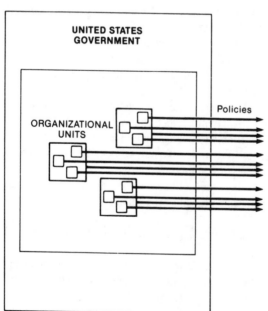

The organizational behavior model alerts us to the conceptually and empirically significant difference between policy as decided by high officials and policy as implemented by organizations. It also helps us to recognize the importance of organizational processing of information. And it underscores the conservative, status quo–maintaining tendencies that result from narrow professional belief systems, standard operating procedures, and inertia.

In a normative vein, the organizational behavior model suggests that the way to improve policy is to improve the organizations that formulate and implement it. For instance, personnel policies should be adopted that will combat the development and maintenance of closed career groups. High-level organizational positions should be occupied by noncareer personnel who are responsive to current policy decisions. Centralized organizational units and procedures should be established to control and coordinate policy. Several separate organizations involved in the same policy area should be integrated into one organization.

There are numerous additional organizational reform possibilities, but they generally suffer from two limitations. One is that they all involve trade-offs, so that any given organizational reform strategy may achieve one objective, but it necessarily sacrifices another. For example, centralization of policy making may facilitate control and coordination. But it also encourages conformism and perhaps an undesirable concentration of power.

Another problem with the organizational behavior model as a source of normative guidelines is that it encourages us to focus our attention on the policy-making process rather than substantive policy issues. Although improving the policy-making process may improve the policies that result from it, tinkering with the organizational machinery may have only a marginally beneficial effect on the substance of policy. In any case, focusing our attention exclusively on the organizational process diverts our attention from the more fundamental issues of policy content (such as how to improve relations with Cuba, or whether initiation of the war with Iraq was desirable).

Since the organizational behavior model ignores the national political context in which governmental organizations exist, we turn to several models that focus specifically on political factors. One of them is the democratic model of policy making.

DEMOCRATIC POLITICS[9]

The central empirical assumption of the democratic model is that policies reflect public preferences. Although public preferences may not directly determine policy, they are assumed to do so indirectly through electoral processes and representative institutions.

These general assumptions depend, in turn, on several more specific assumptions concerning citizens' voting behavior and elected officials' policy-making behavior. For the assumptions of the democratic model to hold, large numbers of citizens must vote, and they must base their votes on a comparison of the candidates' positions on the issues with their own policy preferences. Furthermore, officials must know the public's preferences on a more or less continuous basis between elections and adopt those preferences as their policies. Finally, members of Congress must have equal influence on policy through institutional procedures that provide equal representation.

These assumptions, however, are not consistent with a variety of widely known facts. Large portions of the potential electorate do not vote—nearly one-half in presidential elections and typically over one-half in congressional elections in recent years. Among those who do vote, substantial proportions do not base their votes on specific policy issues. For these and other reasons, election outcomes do not constitute clear indications of the public's policy preferences. Nor do officials always have accurate perceptions of public preferences on issues between elections. Even when they do know what a majority of the public wants, they do not necessarily adopt those preferred policies.

Moreover, the institutional arrangements do not assure that policies will be responsive to public opinion. Although the principle of one person–one vote may be operative in elections and congressional voting procedures, there are many other determinants of individual citizens' and individual members of Congress's actual impact on policy. Even within the executive branch, governmental organizations are only partially responsive to the specific current policy preferences and decisions of the president and other politically responsible officials.

Yet, in spite of such obstacles to the translation of public preferences into policies, we cannot ignore the roles of public attitudes, the electoral process, or the Congress and the presidency as representative institutions. To some extent, policy makers' goals are affected by public opinion. Although policy makers' perceptions of their external environment and the problems it poses may not closely correspond to public perceptions, neither can policy makers entirely ignore what seems important to the public. Furthermore, the generation, evaluation, and choice of alternatives may be affected by policy makers' assumptions about anticipated public reactions. If a given policy alternative is likely to prompt a strong negative public reaction, it is less likely to receive serious consideration or final selection (Figure 2–5).

What about the democratic model as an ideal to be sought? Surely there are no grounds on which it can be criticized in this respect, we might suppose. There is, however, one set of concerns that is often raised: If the public is not now, and is not likely to become, very knowledgeable about foreign affairs, should it have much impact on policy? Although we will not attempt to resolve this difficult question here, in Chapter 3 we will consider an abundance of data on the public's knowledge of foreign affairs that can help us deal with the question in a more informed way.

In any case, this normative issue and the large number of empirical reservations about the democratic model have led to the formulation of a modified democratic model, which is commonly called the pluralist model.

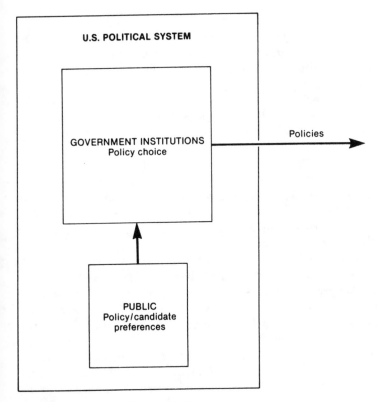

FIGURE 2–5 Democratic politics model

Source: From *The Domestic Context of American Foreign Policy* by Barry B. Hughes. Copyright © 1978 by W. H. Freeman and Company. Reprinted with permission.

PLURALISTIC AND BUREAUCRATIC POLITICS[10]

A central assumption of the pluralist model is that the public has less actual influence on foreign policy making than it could potentially have. Although the public could exercise more direct and substantial influence through elections and political pressure on office holders, most of the public is not sufficiently interested, informed, or active enough to do so.

Instead, the public's influence occurs mostly through organized interest groups (often called pressure groups or lobbies), which represent the interests of segments of the public. In the pluralist model, the public is conceived as a heterogeneous and varied society composed of different groups with different interests. Because those interests are so diverse, however, policy conflicts among the groups are inevitable. Policy making is, therefore, a highly politicized conflict-resolution process.

Only a small fraction of the population participates directly in that conflict-resolution process. The participants include members of Congress, the president and his advisers, bureaucrats, interest-group representatives, academic experts, and members of the press. Ordinary citizens are bystanders, only casually attentive to the policy-making conflicts.

Furthermore, the policy process is decentralized in the sense that there are several different influential individuals, groups, and organizations concerned with any given issue. In other words, there are multiple power centers in the policy process.

Certain structural characteristics of the governmental system create this multiplicity of power centers. The separation of the legislative and executive institutions, the division of the legislative institution into two houses, and the various well-known provisions for "checks and balances" all have a decentralizing effect. As a result, a large number of governmental individuals and organizations have a virtual veto over policy alternatives they do not like.

Some individuals and groups outside the government are also influential—often because they are wealthy, and they know how to use that wealth to exercise influence. Still other people, either inside or outside the government, are especially influential because they are unusually knowledgeable in a particular policy area or because they are unusually active and skillful in promoting particular policy alternatives. Further, such government organizations as the Defense Department, the Treasury Department, and the CIA are influential because of their informational and operational capabilities. Thus, the sources of influence—official position, wealth, expertise, political skills, information, and operational capabilities—are distributed widely among individuals, groups, and organizations inside and outside the government.

Since there are so many people who can influence policy, and since they disagree about what policy should be, they must bargain and compromise with each other to avoid stalemates. Such bargaining and compromising sometimes occur through a simple procedure. When Congress and the president disagree about how much money should be appropriated for a particular program, for example, they often resolve their differences by agreeing to a compromise funding level that is in between what each wants. Often, however, the bargaining and the compromise outcomes are much more complicated and confusing because they involve numerous participants and more than one issue. Because there are many issues being considered at any one time, it is possible to arrange compromises that cut across issues. If the president and a group of senators are at odds on two issues, they may arrange a compromise whereby each gets most of what it wants on one issue but only a small part of what it wants on the other issue.

Because it must be based on the compromise outcomes of a bargaining process, policy changes incrementally. Although several participants may agree that they want major changes in policy, they disagree about what changes would be best. Some may want a substantial increase in the funding for a particular project, others a substantial decrease. Since they are likely to compromise on a small increase or small decrease, policy changes only incrementally.

The traditional version of the pluralist model focuses on Congress, the president, and interest-group organizations. An extension of the pluralist model focuses on the executive-branch bureaucracy, and it has been labeled the bureaucratic politics model.[11] It is based on many of the concepts and assumptions of the pluralist model (as well as the organizational behavior model). But it further assumes that the governmental bureaucracy has an especially important impact on policy. Therefore, it applies particularly to the intra-executive–branch political games played by the president, other high-level administration officials, and bureaucrats.

The bureaucratic politics model focuses on the political tactics used by the executive-branch policy makers as they promote individual and organizational interests and policy preferences. They form factions to promote or oppose particular policy alternatives. They "leak" sensitive information to the press to embarrass their opponents. They withhold information from other organizational units to prevent them from exercising influence. They circulate rumors to discredit one another.

This conception of policy making in the bureaucratic and pluralistic politics model suggests that the notion of a national interest from which specific policy goals are derived is largely irrelevant to foreign policy making. There are group interests, there are bureaucratic interests, there are institutional interests, and there are individual interests—all of which are important determinants of foreign policy goals. But there are rarely widely accepted conceptions of a national interest. Policy problems are not easily defined by policy makers as situations that represent threats to the national interest. Indeed, much of the struggle of policy making is precisely over which situations are problematic and which are not. And that, of course, is because participants in the policy process have different self-interests or different conceptions of the national interest.

Policy alternatives are generated and evaluated not by dispassionate information processors but rather by individuals, groups, and organizations with interests that will be affected by those alternatives if they become policy. Hence, some participants push some alternatives onto the policy-making agenda and advocate them on the basis of selective evaluations that emphasize their benefits and neglect their costs. Other participants try to prevent those alternatives from getting much attention or evaluate them selectively to emphasize their costs and deemphasize their benefits.

The pluralist model, then, provides us with a much more complex image of foreign policy making, as shown in Figure 2–6. This model includes a minor role for the public; but it focuses on a continuing struggle among influential individuals, groups, and organizations, who persuade and bargain with one another as they promote policies based on their particular interests or preferences. Policy results almost willy-nilly from the chaos.

Although this image may conform with many of our casual observations of American foreign policy making, it has been criticized on several empirical grounds. In particular, its assumptions about the level and sources of public apathy and ignorance about foreign affairs, about the sources and distribution of influence, and about the degree of conflict have all been questioned—as we shall note in our discussion of the ruling elite model.

The normative implications of the pluralist model are also subject to con-

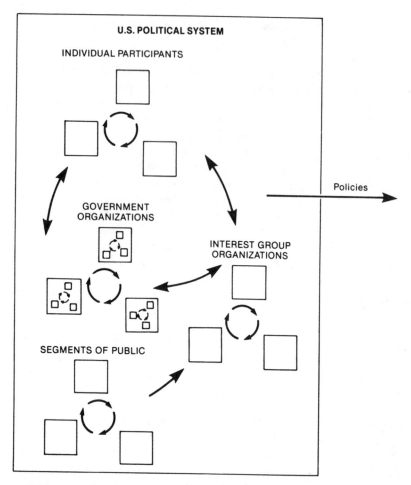

FIGURE 2–6   Pluralistic and bureaucratic politics model

Source: From *The Domestic Context of American Foreign Policy* by Barry B. Hughes. Copyright © 1978 by W. H. Freeman and Company. Reprinted with permission.

troversy. Defenders of the pluralist model argue that it represents a semidemocratic system in which the public may have only marginal and indirect influence, but this limited influence is better than none. And in any case, it is the most that can reasonably be expected. They further argue that it is desirable to have only limited public influence, since the public is not very well informed. Besides, the compromises reached by the more directly influential individuals and organizations serve the public interest reasonably well. In short, it is a practicable and acceptable compromise between the classical democratic ideal and the realities of politics and human behavior.

On the other hand, critics argue that it is a system in which the democratic ideal of maximum individual participation in the decisions that affect people's lives is severely and unnecessarily compromised. They also argue that such a system does not yield policies that are in the common interests of the whole country. Instead, it leads to policies that are in the interests of particular segments of society: special interests.

The pluralist model has also been criticized for fostering ineffective policies because those policies are based on responses to short-term internal political pressures rather than on calculations about long-term interests in the external political context. Furthermore, it is an ineffective way to make policy, because the bargaining-compromising process often produces long delays.

Finally, such a model of policy making has been criticized on the additional normative ground that it is too conservative, even reactionary. Incremental policies, by definition, do not change the status quo much. If the status quo is objectionable, the merely marginal changes in policies that result from a pluralistic process are also objectionable.

These empirical and normative objections to the pluralist model have led to the formulation of yet another model of American foreign policy making: the ruling elite model.

RULING ELITISM[12]

The ruling elite model assumes that the policy process is undemocratic and that the policies that result from it are imperialistic. In this model, power is assumed to be concentrated in a relatively small and cohesive group of political elites who have common interests and policy preferences. Internally, they manipulate the public and ignore its preferences; externally, they pursue policies that are self-aggrandizing and detrimental to world peace, prosperity, and justice (Figure 2–7).

Although the several versions of the ruling elite model all have these central tenets in common, they also differ in important respects, including the assumed composition of the ruling elites. One version assumes there is a "ruling class" of socioeconomic elites comprised of a small number of prominent wealthy families, such as the Rockefellers, Harrimans, Du Ponts, Fords, Morgans, and Mellons. In this version, government officials are little more than their pawns. In a second version, the ruling elites include the military establishment, who, along with defense industries, make up the "military-industrial complex." In a third version, the dominant group is much more disparate, including not only the military and the owners and managers of big corporations but also government officials and members of Congress, labor unions, and universities. Thus, the first version emphasizes the capitalistic origins of American foreign policy; the second emphasizes the militaristic sources; the third includes both.

Another important difference among the ruling elite model versions concerns their opinions about conspiracy. Some versions assume that the elites directly and secretly communicate and cooperate with one another to develop a coordinated policy—in short, that they conspire. Indeed, such conspiracy-oriented versions sometimes name such specific organizations as the Council on Foreign Relations or the Trilateral Commission as the presumed locales of the conspiracies. (We should

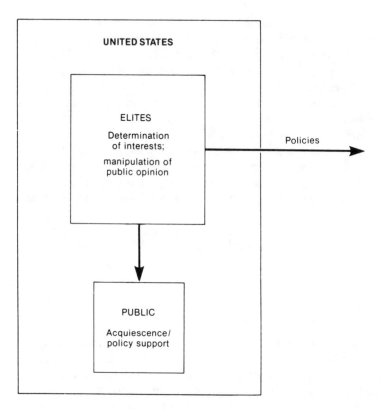

FIGURE 2–7   Ruling elite model

Source: From *The Domestic Context of American Foreign Policy* by Barry B. Hughes. Copyright © 1978 by W. H. Freeman and Company. Reprinted with permission.

note that some conspiracy theories assume that there is a conservative-capitalist-militarist conspiracy. Others contend that there is a liberal-intellectual conspiracy. Although some of the same organizations are named in both, liberal conspiracies are generally presumed to take place at the Ford Foundation, the Brookings Institution, or Harvard University.)

More subtle and complex versions of the ruling elite model assume there is no such conspiracy but rather a convergence of interests that lead disparate individuals, groups, and organizations to prefer similar policies. Thus, all of the following may separately support high defense expenditures because they have a convergence of interests, even though they have some conflicting interests as well: professional military personnel; civilian bureaucrats in the Pentagon; the stockholders, managers, and factory workers in the aerospace industry; small-business owners near military installations or aerospace factories; and the members of Congress from those areas.

Many familiar facts and anecdotes lend at least superficial credence to the ruling elite model. The United States has spent over $2 trillion on the military since the end of World War II, much more than any other country; it has supported repressive anti-Communist factions in numerous countries; and it has tried to overthrow or assassinate Communist leaders in other countries. Active and retired military personnel are pervasive and influential throughout the policy process—in Congress, in executive agencies, in defense industries, and in a variety of other nongovernmental organizations.

But there is also abundant evidence to give us pause before we accept these general assumptions without qualification or skepticism. Such "ruling class" family members as John and Ted Kennedy, Averell Harriman and Nelson Rockefeller have been widely regarded as leaders of the "liberal" factions within the Democratic and Republican parties. It was a retired army general, President Eisenhower, who imposed reductions in military expenditures. Thus, when we begin to examine specific facts, we find that the evidence on the empirical accuracy of the ruling elite model assumptions is mixed.

Yet in a general way, it surely provides some important qualifications and supplements to the other models of policy making. It reminds us that the foreign policy goals pursued by policy makers are to some extent derived from ideologies, such as capitalism. Furthermore, it reminds us that their perceptions of reality are also at least partially determined by their ideological perspectives. Some policy alternatives rarely receive serious consideration because they are outside the ideological mainstream. Indeed, many of the conflicts over policy that are so central to the pluralist and bureaucratic politics model are trivial in contrast to the large number of vastly different alternatives that might be considered. Policy conflicts are often only small differences over tactics, not significant differences in definitions of reality or grand foreign policy goals or radically different policy alternatives.

Thus, although the ruling elite model may contain some oversimplification compared with the complexity of the pluralist and bureaucratic politics model, it is also more encompassing than those more narrowly based models. Furthermore, although the ruling elite model may be overly cynical, it may also be more realistic than the naive assumptions of the democratic model.

As a source of normative guidelines, it encourages us to take a critical look at the policy process and the policies it yields. In fact, it suggests that fundamental changes are needed. The minor reforms that might be achieved by tinkering with the machinery of government or adopting incrementally different policies are not sufficient. Only basic structural changes in the policy process to provide "participatory democracy" and revolutionary changes in the socioeconomic system will yield policies that will promote peace, prosperity, and justice.

Yet such sweeping evaluations and prescriptions ignore many difficult issues—including, for instance, the nature of the world in which American foreign policy is conducted. American policy makers may be part of a capitalistic society with a sizable military establishment, making them prone to define situations as threats in ideological and military terms. But many of the threats that they perceive are not entirely figments of their imaginations.

INTERNATIONAL POLITICS[13]

The international politics model assumes that American foreign policy is a response to the problems posed by an international political system of 165 nation-states. Since each of the governments of these nation-states is trying to maximize its own security and status, the international political system is marked by conflict and competition. It is also marked by distrust and suspicion arising from ideological and cultural differences. Because the system lacks an effective centralized authority to restrain the conflict and competition, there are strong tendencies toward violence. It is a dangerous, even anarchic, world (Figure 2–8).

All countries, including the United States, pursue policies designed to protect and promote their national interests, particularly security, in the midst of anarchy. They do so by developing national power capabilities, which include wealth, population, natural resources, and military forces. In addition to developing their own national power capabilities, they enter into alliances with one another to supplement those capabilities and to try to match or exceed the power capabilities of their adversaries. Thus, they try to maintain a balance of power; or, more precisely, they try to achieve an imbalance in which they enjoy the advantage.

This model relegates internal policy-making processes to a negligible role. Indeed, it views the public, interest groups, and governmental institutions mostly as hindrances to effective diplomacy. One central normative guideline of this model is to conduct diplomacy in such a way as to promote the long-term national interest by creating a stable peaceful world based on a balance of power. Such a strategy requires subtle diplomatic maneuvering externally and sustained development of national

FIGURE 2–8 International politics model

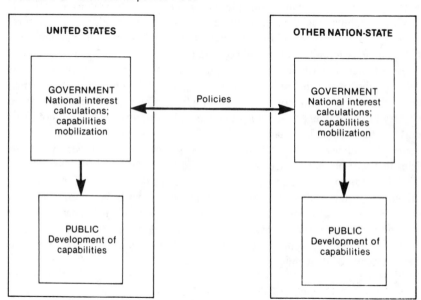

power capabilities internally. The required effort, subtlety, national perspective, and long-term focus are not likely to be widely understood or supported, however, unless diplomacy is based on a degree of secrecy in negotiations and exhortation in domestic politics.

Empirically, such a model helps us recognize that foreign policy goals and problems have their origins at least partly in the basic nature of the international system and that specific goals and problems are embedded in a larger international political context. Although the individual problems and goals arising out of particular circumstances vary considerably and depend on the specific perceptions and values of policy makers, there is a tendency for them to share an underlying basic concern with security and status. In other words, there is substantial continuity in the issues and goals of American foreign policy.

The international politics model also helps us recognize that the actual consequences of policy depend very much on American power capabilities and the nature of the international system.

As a source of normative guidelines, however, the model may be somewhat shortsighted. Its policy prescriptions tend to perpetuate a system that may be quite destructive in the long run. Policies that promote fundamental changes in the system may be more beneficial in the long run than policies that promote stability in the short run.

Furthermore, such an approach to policy making might be criticized for being too conservative and hence perpetuating an unjust status quo. It may also be criticized for being too parochial, since its central policy prescriptions are to promote narrow national interests through national and alliance power capabilities. Again, however, our reactions to the normative implications of the international politics model depend very much on our own values.

The international politics model has also been criticized for being too narrow empirically. It ignores many significant aspects of contemporary world politics. Indeed, it almost entirely neglects a variety of important developments in world politics in the past several decades. It exaggerates the independence, autonomy, and sovereignty of nation-states. It underestimates the significance of international organizations and nongovernmental organizations in world politics. It underestimates the importance of economic goals independent of their relationship to national security and status. It ignores the cooperative aspects of world politics (except for alliances). Finally, it relies on a narrow notion of power, with undue emphasis on military forces as a power capability.

These concerns about the empirical limitations of the traditional international politics model have led to the formulation of yet another model: the transnational politics model.

TRANSNATIONAL POLITICS[14]

The transnational politics model emphasizes the actors and interactions that cut across national boundaries, rather than the national government actors and their interactions that the traditional international politics model emphasizes.

Such an emphasis is the result of a variety of technological, industrial, and commercial developments, which have led to a change in the degree and nature of interdependence among societies. These changes are especially evident and politically significant in economic activities in general; and they include many specific forms of interdependence in energy, raw materials, and agricultural products. Although the security of societies has involved interdependence for a long time (particularly since the advent of nuclear weapons on long-range missiles) and although international trade and other forms of international economic relations have all yielded interdependence in the past, recent trends have made interdependencies more salient and more politically significant. The development of large multinational corporations and other kinds of nongovernmental transnational organizations has added an important new set of actors to world politics.

The significance of interdependence and nongovernmental actors for foreign policy analysis lies primarily in their impact on interests and power. In the first place, they create new transnational interest groups—groups whose specific interests transcend national boundaries. For instance, the interests of large multinational energy corporations are not simply subinterests within the context of the national interests of any one country; rather, they are interests that partly parallel and partly diverge from the interests of several countries. At least in the short run, their interests are specifically in high levels of energy production and consumption, high energy prices, and low production costs. In other words, some significant actors in world politics do not define their interests in relationship to any one country's national interests; they define them in terms of their relationship to some transnational economic activity.

Interdependence and nongovernmental transnational actors also alter the patterns of power in world politics. A given nation's power depends not only on such traditional capabilities as military forces but also on the nature and degree of its interdependence with other nations. When interdependence is asymmetrical—when one country is more dependent on the other—its power position is relatively weak. Since there are many different areas of interdependence, the calculation and exercise of power become more complex, subtle, and uncertain than is the case with traditional notions of power based on national capabilities. Furthermore, transnational actors, especially multinational corporations, sometimes exercise power independently of, and even in opposition to, national governments. In fact, transnational organizations sometimes constrain the ability of governmental policy makers to achieve their goals, or at least increase the political costs of achieving them. However, they also sometimes act in cooperation with national governments in pursuit of common goals. The political environment of foreign policy making thus becomes more complex and confusing (Figure 2–9).

The transnational politics model, therefore, emphasizes recent changes in the actors, the problems, and the sources of power involved in foreign policy making. In doing so, it facilitates our analysis of policy concerning the resources issues (economics, energy, raw materials, and food), which have joined the traditional security issues as central items on the foreign policy agenda. It also puts foreign policy making into a larger context, which includes the economic system.

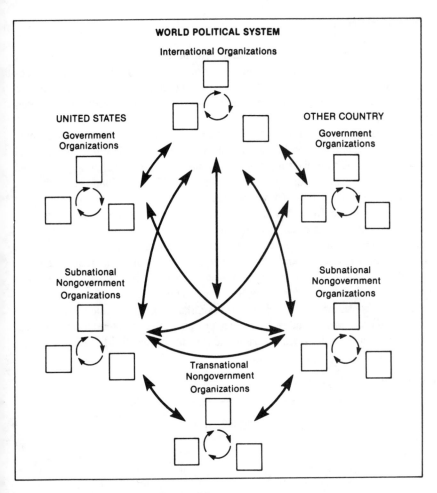

FIGURE 2–9   Transnational politics model

We must be careful not to exaggerate the significance of the elements of the transnational politics model in our foreign policy analyses. But it does expand the potential range of our analytic concerns, and it does provide a basis for insights into a variety of topics.

Its normative value, however, is more limited. It does not offer any specific normative guidelines—only the general admonitions that policy makers should take nongovernmental actors seriously as potential facilitators or constrainers of their power and that they should recognize that power depends on numerous and complex forms of interdependence as well as the more familiar national capabilities.

For more encompassing empirical and normative concerns, we need to turn to a final model: the world systems model.

WORLD SYSTEMS[15]

The final model is the most encompassing in its analytic range. It is the most encompassing because it places foreign policy making not only in a global perspective but also in the context of social, physical, biological, scientific, and economic processes. It thus reflects a dictum of general systems theory that everything is related to everything else (Figure 2–10).

The systems approach is, therefore, an interdisciplinary approach. It encourages us to consider how nonpolitical conditions and trends may impinge on American foreign policy. It reminds us, for instance, that major changes in economics or human values or the climate or medicine or technology can all have profound consequences for American foreign policy. They may create new problems for the foreign policy agenda; they may make different policy alternatives more feasible; or they may make traditional goals more difficult to attain. In short, they set many of the parameters within which policy makers operate, at least in the short term.

The world systems model not only encourages us to think in broad spatial and interdisciplinary terms, it also encourages us to think in broad temporal terms. It is a future-oriented approach to foreign policy analysis that is especially concerned with the long-term consequences of policies. It is similarly focused on the anticipation of future global problems so that measures can be taken to avert potential catastrophes. In particular, much of the work from a world systems perspective has focused on the

FIGURE 2–10   World systems model

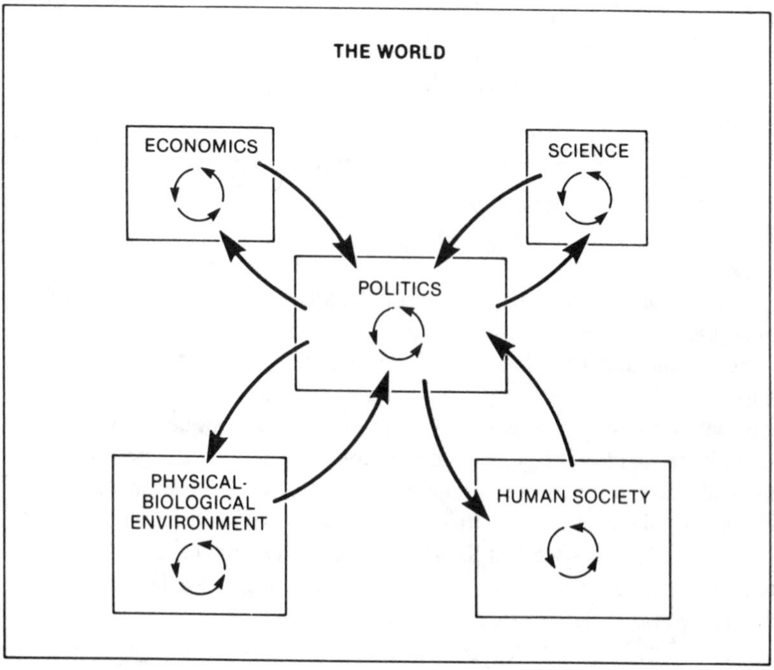

problems posed by increasingly scarce resources. Thus, economic development, population, food, energy, and pollution problems have received great emphasis.

Although many world systems analyses have tried to forecast future conditions, there are also strong normative implications of many of the descriptions and projections of regional and global conditions depicted in world systems analyses. Put simply, a central normative implication is that the makers and students of American foreign policy should take into account the long-term global consequences of policies in their evaluations.

Although the world systems approach tends to be rather general both empirically and normatively, it is nevertheless useful in helping us to keep foreign policy analysis in a broad spatial, temporal, and value context. It thus reminds us of the magnitude of the stakes and responsibility involved in making and analyzing American foreign policy.

CONCLUSION

Clearly, no one of these ten models by itself is an adequate basis for empirical and normative analyses of American foreign policy. Each one can help us somewhat by drawing our attention to certain facts or values; but each one also has limitations. Each one provides us with only a partial picture of reality for our empirical analyses; each one suggests some criteria that are relevant to our normative analyses but neglects others.

The models are substantially complementary, however, rather than entirely competitive. Although some of their empirical assumptions and normative guidelines are contradictory, many concern different points. Furthermore, many of their seeming contradictions merely reflect different emphases rather than fundamentally opposed analyses. For instance, whereas the democratic model emphasizes the influence of the public in policy making, the bureaucratic politics model emphasizes the influence of executive agencies; those models' assumptions about the public and the executive agencies, however, are otherwise generally compatible with one another. This mixture of complementary and competitive relationships among the models is evident in their empirical assumptions and normative guidelines about the actors in policy making, the policy problems they face, their policy-making behavior, and the policies they adopt. Their emphases are briefly summarized in Table 2–1.

To an extent, the models do contain different emphases and even some contradictory assumptions and guidelines. But we can further reduce their conflicting analyses by noting that the relative analytic utility of each model depends on variations in the characteristics of issues and situations.[16] For instance, active involvement in policy making during military crises is likely to be limited to a small number of high-level executive-branch policy makers who urge maintaining national security and the status quo. Thus, assumptions of the ruling elite, bureaucratic politics, and international politics models are likely to be especially pertinent. Revisions of foreign trade legislation, however, involve conflicts among large numbers of governmental and nongovernmental groups with diverse interests. Thus,

TABLE 2–1 Summary of Models' Analytic Emphases

MODELS	PARTICIPANTS	ANALYTIC EMPHASIS		
		POLICY PROBLEMS	POLICY-MAKING BEHAVIOR	POLICIES
Rational Decision Making	—*	—	value maximizing calculations	strategies
Incremental	—	inadequacies of current policy	constrained calculations	marginal changes
Human Behavior	individuals and small groups	Individual perceptions and preferences	individual variations	—
Organizational Behavior	executive agencies	organizational interests	organizational routines	organizational operations
Democratic Politics	public, Congress, president	public interests	representative processes	public preferences
Pluralistic Politics (Bureaucratic Politics)	multiple-interest groups (executive agencies)	group interests (bureaucratic interests)	group bargaining (bureaucratic game playing)	compromise outcomes
Ruling Elitism	dominant interest group	threats to status quo	self-interested calculations	capitalistic, militaristic tendencies
International Politics	national governments	threats to national security status	interest and power calculations	strategies
Transnational Politics	intergovernmental and nongovernmental organizations	transnational economic interdependencies	—	—
World Systems	—	"nonpolitical" global trends	—	—

*No particular emphasis

the transnational politics and pluralistic politics models are likely to be the most pertinent to an understanding of policy making on such issues. Finally, policy making on technical, long-term environmental problems is more likely to be dominated by a few highly specialized governmental organizational units. The world systems model and the organizational behavior models would probably be the most useful in analyses of these problems.

Much of the challenge in applying the models to specific analytic problems is to determine which particular elements of various models are the most pertinent to the analytic task at hand. Which assumptions of which models seem the most plausible? What normative prescriptions are the most compelling? What predictive implications are the most realistic? The analytic utility of the models is ultimately dependent on the analyst's ability to apply them thoughtfully to the diverse array of questions involved in the analysis of foreign policy topics.

=====THREE=====

The Public

In this chapter, we address three questions about public opinion: What are the patterns and trends in public opinion on foreign policy issues? What are the sources of people's foreign policy opinions? To what extent and in what way does public opinion affect foreign policy?

The analytic models discussed in the previous chapter lead us to expect varied answers to these and other questions about public opinion. On the basis of the rational and democratic models, we expect explicit, specific policy preferences based on information about the problems confronting the country; and we expect those preferences to have a significant impact on policy through elections. The pluralist model emphasizes conflicting policy preferences resulting from the diverse interests and perspectives of varied groups in a pluralistic society; but the policy preferences are not strongly held most of the time, are usually not based on informed analysis, and do not significantly and directly affect policy under normal circumstances. The psychological model assumes that opinions are based to some degree on misperceptions and that they are related to personality traits. The ruling elite model, finally, leads us to expect opinions that are manipulated by the government, especially through the press, and that in any case have little impact on policy.

We are fortunate to have an abundance of public opinion and voting behavior data to help answer these questions and determine the validity of the model's assumptions. However, as we examine these data, we should recognize that we must exercise judgment in interpreting them, and we should also recognize that such data have some inherent limitations.

Poll results on a given topic, of course, depend on the wording of the questions that the interviewers ask the respondents. Although the questions are generally as clear and unbiased as we can reasonably expect, changes in their wording can yield quite different results. For instance, a poll of a sample of fifteen hundred adults asked their evaluations of President Carter on the basis of three different questions.[1] One was the standard Harris Poll question: "How would you rate the job Jimmy Carter is doing as president? Would you say he is doing an excellent, pretty good, only fair, or a poor job?" Another was the standard Gallup Poll question: "Do you approve or disapprove of the way Jimmy Carter is handling his job as president?" Both are reasonable wordings, but they produced different results. The Harris Poll question yielded 48 percent favorable responses of "excellent" or "pretty good" and 49 percent unfavorable responses of "only fair" or "poor"; the Gallup Poll question found that 63 percent "approved" and 29 percent "disapproved." A third question asked the same respondents "to grade President Carter *A, B, C, D,* or *F* for the way he is handling his job as president." They responded with 41 percent *A* or *B,* 35 percent *C,* and 17 percent *D* or *F.* Thus, the president's job performance rating might have been interpreted as somewhere between 41 and 63 percent positive at that time.

Another example is based on five different polling organizations' attempts to measure opinions of President Reagan's handling of foreign policy.[2] All five happened to ask their foreign policy–approval questions within a nineteen-day period, so there would only be small differences in the results because of differences in timing. The results are summarized in Table 3–1. Four of the five polls obtained nearly identical results for favorable responses, but there were sizable differences in the "unfavorable" and "don't know" responses.

TABLE 3–1   Comparisons of Polls on President's Handling of Foreign Policy

	PERCENTAGE OF RESPONSES		
POLL	FAVORABLE	UNFAVORABLE	DON'T KNOW
CBS/New York Times*	37	40	23
Gallup**	36	44	20
Harris†	36	59	5
ABC/Washington Post††	43	45	12
NBC/AP‡	35	58	7

*Question: Do you approve or disapprove of the way Ronald Reagan is handling foreign policy? (asked Mar. 11–15, 1982)
**Question: Do you approve or disapprove of the way Mr. Reagan is handling our foreign policy—that is, our relations with other nations? (asked Mar. 12–15, 1982)
†Question: Now let me ask you about some specific things President Reagan has done. How would you rate him on handling foreign policy matters—excellent, pretty good, only fair, or poor? (asked Mar. 12–16, 1982; favorable = excellent or pretty good; unfavorable = only fair or poor)
††Question: Do you approve or disapprove of the way Reagan is handling foreign affairs? (asked Mar. 18–21, 1982)
‡Question: What kind of job do you think Ronald Reagan is doing in handling our foreign affairs—do you think he is doing an excellent job, a good job, only a fair job, or do you think he is doing a poor job? (asked Mar. 29–30, 1984; favorable = excellent job or a good job; unfavorable = only a fair job or poor job)
Source: Compiled from data in *Public Opinion* 5, 2 (April/May 1982), 35–36.

Lest you become unduly skeptical about poll data, however, you should note that whenever you use such data to make comparisons over time or among presidents on the basis of a single, consistent question, the differences among the questions are not particularly troublesome; the objective is to determine relative rather than absolute levels. But you must be careful to notice the wording of the questions and the response categories whenever you interpret poll results.

Another problem with polls is that they usually only record opinions that are expressed in a superficial manner and in an artificial context. Such recorded opinions are literally only verbal responses to questions posed during interviews. They do not necessarily indicate deeply held or carefully considered opinions. Indeed, of the many dimensions of opinions, polls typically measure only the direction of the opinion and sometimes the intensity. They do not usually determine the salience of the issue for the respondent, nor the level of information or understanding of the implications associated with the opinion. Finally, the place of the opinion in the respondent's belief system and the relationship to other opinions are rarely determined.

In spite of these problems, public-opinion surveys provide us with much more valid and reliable evidence about public opinion than we could obtain without them. In fact, they are nearly always based on sufficiently large and representative samples of the adult population to be virtually certain that the margin of error is only ± 3 percent or less.

PATTERNS AND TRENDS IN OPINIONS

Perceived Importance of Foreign Policy Problems

Figure 3–1 depicts a set of public opinion data that are widely circulated and frequently analyzed. It concerns the *relative* importance that people attribute to various problems in response to the Gallup Poll question: "What do you think is the most important problem facing the country today?" It is apparent that during the past several decades, the public's perception of the relative importance of foreign affairs has fluctuated considerably. Foreign affairs was the dominant concern only during the peak cold war period from the late 1940s to the early 1960s and during the peak of the Vietnam War period in the mid-1960s. During the early and late 1960s, race relations, civil rights, and other social problems were dominant. During the early 1970s, economic and energy problems became the dominant concerns, and relative concern over foreign affairs dipped to extraordinarily low levels—tendencies that continued throughout the 1980s.

By the 1990s, however, the admixture of economic issues and national security–foreign relations issues made it difficult to isolate the relative importance attributed to each issue individually. Indeed, just as the oil price increases of the 1970s represented economic and national security as well as foreign relations issues because of the involvement of the Middle East, so, too, did the issues arising from the Middle East war of 1991. Thus, even as the end of the cold war was lowering people's fears

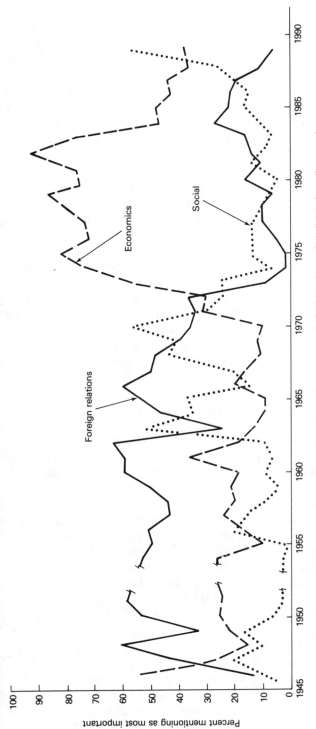

FIGURE 3–1 Public perceptions of relative importance of issues

Question: "What do you think is the most important problem facing the country today?" (Wording varied slightly in earlier years.)

Sources: American Institute of Public Opinion (Gallup Poll) surveys: adapted by the author from data in *Public Opinion* 1, 1 (May/June 1978), 32, and 6, 2 (April/May 1983), 25; *Gallup Report* 219 (December 1983), 6; *Public Opinion* 9, 6 (March/April 1987), 30–31; 11, 2 (July/August 1988), 35; *Gallup Report* 285 (June 1989), 4–5. For years when the question was reported in more than one survey, the mean of all surveys during the year is presented. Question not asked in 1952–1953.

53

about a U.S.–USSR nuclear war, increasing concerns about trade relations with Japan and other countries were making these foreign relations issues more prominent as public concerns.

Although fluctuations in the relative importance attributed to foreign affairs have often been interpreted as evidence of an unstable "moodiness" in the public's orientation to foreign affairs or even as evidence of periodic isolationism, neither of these is an appropriate interpretation.[3] When we consider evidence of the absolute level of public concern about foreign policy issues, we find more nearly stable and higher levels. During the late 1970s, the Gallup Poll's relative importance question indicated that less than one-tenth of the population considered foreign affairs problems "the most important." However, between one-third and one-half believed that the threat of a war involving the United States was a serious problem and indeed "somewhat likely" or "very likely" within a few years.[4] In other words, even though most people believed economic and energy problems to be "the most important," they still recognized important foreign affairs problems.

Consider also the economic and energy problems that were widely perceived by the mid-1970s as the most pressing problems. Increasingly, they were seen as international problems as well as domestic problems, that is, "intermestic" problems. In early 1974, the percentage of the public seeing energy as the most important problem increased from 3 percent to 46 percent. This was a reaction to the temporary Arab embargo of oil deliveries to the United States (a foreign policy problem).[5] The same could be said of international trade in other goods and services during the 1980s and 1990s.

Attention, Information, Understanding, Activity

Being concerned about general foreign affairs problems is one thing; being truly attentive, informed, and knowledgeable about specific problems is another matter. Several polls on opinions about U.S. business investments in South Africa found that one-fourth to one-third of those interviewed said they had not followed the issue closely enough to have an opinion.

In 1978, only one-half of the population knew that the United States imported any oil (when almost half the oil being consumed was in fact imported). In 1983, only 29 percent knew that the United States supported opponents of the Nicaraguan government in the civil war there, although by 1987 the figure was 54 percent.[6] On numerous occasions, the Gallup Poll has asked people whether they have "heard or read about" such topics as the MX missile, the Panama Canal Treaties, and the B-1 bomber, and in earlier years the civil war in China, the United Nations, the Atlantic Alliance, the Marshall Plan, the European Common Market, and tariff legislation.[7] About 25 percent typically reported that they had not (occasionally as many as 50 percent had not, and rarely as few as 5 percent had not). Thus, about one-fourth of the public is normally utterly unaware of specific current foreign affairs topics.

Among the remaining three-fourths who are usually aware of such issues, only about one-tenth are sufficiently attentive to be able to answer accurately several basic informational questions and describe the issue in their own words. The occasional upper and lower limits of this attentive segment are about 25 percent and 5 percent of the population.

Periodically, there have been dramatic examples of active expressions of opinions on foreign policy issues, such as the Vietnam War demonstrations involving tens of thousands of citizens. There is also evidence that the proportion of citizens who express their opinions by writing letters to newspaper editors, members of Congress, and the White House has increased over the past decade or more.[8] Still, typically less than 1 percent of the population actively express their opinions of foreign policy issues in these ways.

Figure 3–2 shows these estimates of public awareness of foreign affairs.

Surveys of college students also reveal a widespread lack of basic information about foreign affairs. For instance, in one national survey only 21 percent of the freshmen and 29 percent of the seniors were able to answer correctly a question about whether OPEC's membership includes countries outside the Middle East.[9] (It does: Venezuela, Nigeria, and Indonesia.)

Somewhat technical issues such as nuclear arms control even elicit inherently contradictory opinions. In a poll about a proposal for a nuclear arms freeze, for instance, 27 percent of the respondents answered two separate questions indicating that they *both* supported *and* opposed the freeze proposal.[10]

FIGURE 3–2 Typical proportions of public according to interest in foreign affairs

Sources: Summary estimates by the author based on data in James N. Rosenau, *Citizenship Between Elections* (New York: Free Press, 1974), pp. 26–29; Hazel Gaudet Erskine, "The Polls: The Informed Public," *Public Opinion Quarterly* 26, 4 (Winter 1962), 669–77; Erskine, "The Polls: Exposure to International Information," *Public Opinion Quarterly* 27, 4 (Winter 1973), 658–62; "Opinion Round Up," *Public Opinion* 1, 1 and 2 (1978); and *Gallup Opinion Index.*

Active: Express opinions by activities such as writing letters
Attentive: Can describe issue in own words and answer few factual questions
Aware: Have heard or read about issues
Unaware: Have not heard or read about issues

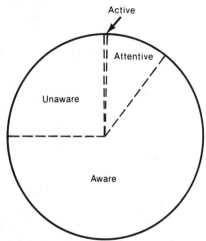

General Policy Preferences

Whether or not individual citizens actively express their opinions and whether or not their opinions have a specific informational basis, they nevertheless do hold opinions. Collectively, those opinions constitute the climate of public opinion concerning foreign affairs. One important component of that climate of opinion is the degree to which the public is isolationist or internationalist.

A commonly used survey item that taps isolationist and internationalist sentiments asks respondents whether they "think it will be best for the future of the country if we take an active part in world affairs, or if we stay out of world affairs." Generally, since the late 1940s, two-thirds to three-fourths of the public have favored an active part, whereas only about one-fourth have wanted the country "to stay out of world affairs." Although there was a slight increase in isolationist sentiment after the Vietnam War, the proportions had nearly returned to their previous levels by the late 1970s.[11] Indeed, in the spring of 1977, 79 percent of the public agreed that "the United States has a real responsibility to take a very active role in the world."[12]

Therefore, there has been a substantial and relatively stable preponderance of internationalist sentiment over isolationist sentiment, but there have been considerable disagreements and changes in opinions about the kinds of American involvement that should be adopted. For example, in 1964 and again in 1976, half of those interviewed agreed that "the United States should maintain a dominant position as the most powerful nation at all costs, even going to the very brink of war if necessary," but about one-third disagreed with such a nationalistic approach.[13]

There is, nonetheless, a clear consensus favoring multilateralism rather than unilateralism. Public support for the United Nations, as a particular multilateral institution, has declined; in its early years, about one-third of the U.S. population said the UN was doing a "good" or "fair" job, but only one-third or fewer were willing to say so by the early 1980s. Support for a multilateral approach to diplomacy has otherwise been consistently supported by substantial majorities of the population. In 1977, for instance, 82 percent agreed that "problems like food, energy, and inflation are so big that no country can solve them alone," and 72 percent agreed that "in deciding its foreign policies the United States should take into account the views of its allies."[14]

There has also been general support for accommodation and cooperation with Communist countries. In the late 1970s, three-fourths said they favored "détente— that is, the United States and Russia seeking out areas of agreement and cooperation," and over half said they favored formal recognition of Communist China, reestablishment of relations with Cuba, and trade with Communist countries.[15] Support for such policies waned during the 1980s, though.[16] At the same time, there has usually been considerable support for maintaining a large and increasing military establishment. Except for the period from the mid-1960s to the mid-1970s and again in the late-1980s, a plurality have generally favored increased military expenditures.

When it comes to the use of military force, however, at least in the hypothetical circumstances presented in public polls, enthusiasm for a military approach to the solution of international problems declines somewhat. Although one-fourth to one-half have said they think that the United States should send troops to Canada, Mexico, or nations in Western Europe if they are "attacked by Communist-backed forces," the proportions supporting such use of the military are much smaller in cases of attacks on other countries. In a late 1977 poll, only 4 percent said they would favor sending troops to Israel if it were attacked.[17] The distribution of opinion on the issue of sending troops to aid countries under attack was only marginally affected by the Vietnam War experience. Its principal effect was to reduce support for military involvement "to prevent the spread of communism" in geographically and psychologically distant areas.[18]

This background conditioned opinions on specific elements of the Reagan administration's policies in Central America. For instance, in the spring of 1984, 67 percent disapproved of American involvement in the mining of Nicaraguan harbors, while only 13 percent approved.[19] As for American policy toward El Salvador, over half the population opposed increasing economic aid, imposing air or naval blockades, or sending troops.[20]

There has also been a marked decline in support for the existing foreign aid programs of economic and military assistance, even though the principle of economic assistance for impoverished people in foreign countries still enjoys considerable support.[21]

Such changes should not lead us to conclude, however, that public opinion on foreign policy issues is constantly changing and unstable. An analysis of the responses to more than three hundred questions on foreign policy that have been repeated in polls at different times found that there was usually considerable stability in the distribution of opinions over time.[22] In fact, the distributions of opinions on foreign policy issues were nearly as stable as the distributions of opinions on domestic policy issues. However, there was a marked tendency for any changes on foreign policy issues to be rather abrupt. That is, the changes that did occur on foreign policy issues took place over a relatively short period of time—usually in response to wars, confrontations, and crises in which major policy changes also occurred.

In sum, the American public has typically overwhelmingly favored internationalism rather than isolationism, and multilateralism rather than unilateralism. Although there has been substantial nationalism as well as support for the maintenance and use of the military, there has also been considerable support for cooperation and accommodation with allies and adversaries. Support for the use of military force has declined since the Vietnam War, as has support for other forms of military and economic assistance. Pluralities or majorities still seem to be willing to send troops in the event of an attack against some countries. The public was evenly divided about whether to undertake military action against Iraq just prior to the initiation of hostilities but became predominantly supportive in the early days of the war.

SOURCES OF OPINIONS

There are important variations in these opinions, not only over time but also among individual members of the public at any one time. Although most Americans may be internationalists, many are isolationists. Although most are multilateralists, many are unilateralists. Although many are willing to be cooperative and accommodating in conflicts with other countries, many others are prone to be implacably hostile when conflicts arise. Although many want more spent on defense, substantial numbers of others want less. Although many are reluctant to resort to the use of force, many others are quite willing to do so. Why do these variations exist? What are the factors (or correlates) that are related to those variations?

Correlates

Numerous studies have shown that there are relationships between certain traits of individuals and their opinions on foreign affairs. We should not assume, however, that such relationships necessarily indicate direct cause-effect relationships. Rather, they only establish the existence of statistical tendencies, which suggest that more complex causal processes are present.

This is particularly true, for example, about age differences. Age differences have often been found to correlate with variations in foreign policy opinions. But it is difficult to determine to what extent the underlying causal factor is differences in the experiences of different age groups (cohorts) or differences in the stages of maturation of individuals. Do younger people tend to have different opinions from older people because they are individually at a different stage in the maturation process or because they have had distinctive experiences as an age group?

Attitudes toward the Vietnam War provide an example. In 1972, about 50 percent of the eighteen-to-thirty-year-olds favored withdrawal from Vietnam, while about 40 percent of those over thirty favored withdrawal. But such differences were probably due to a combination of differences in the life stages and the generational experiences of the respondents. Furthermore, we should note that such differences are not always stable. Indeed, four years earlier, respondents under thirty had been the least likely to favor withdrawal.[23]

Age differences are therefore somewhat unreliable, and the underlying causal dynamics are difficult to disentangle. Nevertheless, a careful study of age differences in foreign affairs opinions suggested that the generation (age cohort) experiencing World War I during their early adult lives tended to be relatively isolationist; the depression-era cohort, relatively pessimistic about peace; and the post–World War II nuclear-era cohort, relatively internationalist.[24]

The Vietnam War era may have produced a relatively antimilitary cohort. Between 1936 and 1973, surveys asked nearly two hundred questions concerning attitudes toward war. A study of the results found that after the mid-1960s, people under thirty years of age were consistently more likely than people over fifty to express antiwar opinions. Prior to that period, the relationship between age and war-related opinions was reversed: Younger people had been less likely to express antiwar opinions.[25] Further, in 1976, one-half of the respondents under thirty wanted less spent on defense, while only one-fourth of those over fifty wanted to spend less.[26] A study of people in *leadership* positions, however, failed to show any substantial evidence of intergenerational differences in their opinions related to the Vietnam War era.[27]

Notable differences have been frequently found in males' and females' opinions on international issues. Questions tapping the relative importance of problems have typically found women to be more worried about war than men have been and less worried about economics. Indeed, one issue on which male and female opinions have consistently differed for several decades is the use of force. Typically, 5 to 15 percent fewer women than men have supported the use of force—whether in actual conflicts such as the Korean and Vietnam wars or in hypothetical situations presented in interviews.[28] Women have also been less supportive of the military draft and increases in defense expenditures. A poll in 1981 found that 67 percent of the women, compared with 80 percent of the men, wanted increased military spending. Finally, women tend to be less internationalist in general in their approach to foreign affairs. In a 1981 poll, 43 percent of the female respondents agreed with the proposition that "the United States should keep to itself and stay out of world affairs," whereas only 31 percent of the males agreed.

A poll in 1984 found about a 10 percent difference in men's and women's opinions of Reagan administration policies in Central America.[29] Whereas 51 percent of the women interviewed found the policies might lead the United States into war there, only 40 percent of the men expressed such fears. Only 22 percent of the women favored attempts to overthrow a "pro-Soviet government" in Nicaragua, while 31 percent of the men did so. A mere 8 percent of the women approved the administration's mining of Nicaragua's harbors, while 19 percent of the men approved. More generally, only 39 percent of the women approved of President Reagan's overall conduct of foreign policy, but 48 percent of the men approved.

Occupation, income, and education are more consistently and more strongly related to foreign policy opinions than age and gender. Individually and collectively, these three factors often account for differences of 10 to 20 percent or more in the distribution of opinions on any given issue. For instance, three-fourths of the college-educated, three-fourths of the higher-income, and three-fourths of the professional, business, and white-collar respondents in one survey expressed internationalist sentiments. But only one-half of the respondents in the least-educated, lowest-income, and other occupational groups expressed internationalist sentiments.[30]

In addition to the age, gender, income, occupation, and education correlates of opinions, other factors are related to opinions in more direct ways. In particular, both personality traits and levels of information have been found to correlate with foreign policy opinions. Studies have found that isolationist and jingoistic attitudes toward foreign affairs are related to generalized feelings of alienation and hostility. Other studies have found that the personality trait of authoritarianism is related to militaristic approaches to foreign policy.[31]

Several polls have found a relationship between levels of information about a specific issue and opinions about it. Although the pattern is mixed, people who are most informed have generally been more likely to take cooperative and conciliatory approaches to the solution of conflicts. For instance, in the autumn of 1977, people's opinions on the Panama Canal Treaties (which will establish full Panamanian control over the canal by the year 2000) were substantially related to the information about the issue. This relationship is evident in Table 3–2. Among those with low or medium levels of knowledge about the treaties, a plurality opposed them; among the highly

TABLE 3–2   Relationship between Information and Opinion on Panama Canal Treaties

OPINION OF TREATIES	INFORMATIONAL LEVEL		
	LOW*	MEDIUM†	HIGH‡
Favored	23%	40%	51%
Opposed	39	48	46
No opinion	38	12	3

Question: "The treaties would give Panama full control over the Panama Canal and the Canal Zone by the year 2000, but the United States would retain the right to defend the canal against a third nation. . . . Do you favor or oppose these treaties between the United States and Panama?"

*Low: Not aware of treaties until interviewer posed question.
†Medium: Aware of treaties prior to interview.
‡High: Correctly answered three factual questions about treaties and canal.

Source: Data compiled from American Institute of Public Opinion (Gallup Poll), September 30–October 3, 1977, reported in *Public Opinion* 1, 2 (March/April 1978), 34.

informed, a majority favored the treaties. Other studies have found the most informed segments of the public to be the most supportive of foreign aid and trade with Communist countries.[32]

The relationship between knowledge and opinion, however, is more complex and less predictable than these examples suggest. Three quite different notions about the relationship between knowledge and opinion are plausible.[33] One is the "enlightenment model," which assumes that relatively knowledgeable people tend to reject simplistic aggressive approaches to international conflict and tend to favor relatively conciliatory approaches instead. The second model is the "mainstream model," which assumes that knowledgeable citizens tend to be more supportive of whatever the government's policy is because they are the most informed about it and the most subject to the influence of official rationales. The third model is the "cognitive consistency model," which assumes that relatively knowledgeable people are more likely than less informed people to adopt positions on specific issues that are consistent with general ideological orientations. Thus, knowledgeable people are prone to be at *either* end of the spectrum of opinions on any given issue because those positions reflect ideological consistency. Less knowledgeable people tend to be more ambivalent about issues, have less strong opinions, and hold opinions that are inconsistent with one another. The available evidence does not conclusively confirm or refute any of the three models. Only further studies will enable us to establish more confidently the nature of the relationship between knowledge and opinion about foreign issues.

The Press

Perhaps the most obvious source of public information on foreign policy topics is the press. From the perspective of the democratic model, we would expect the press to provide detailed, accurate information about foreign policy issues so that the public could develop factually based opinions. We would also expect the press to adopt an independent relationship with the government so that it could play the investigative role that is expected of it in a democratic political system. On the other hand, the ruling elite model depicts the press as merely a transmitter of the facts and opinions distributed by the government or ruling elites for public consumption. The press is presumed to be an instrument used by the elites to manipulate public opinion. The pluralist model leads us to expect a diverse press conveying and representing many opinions. In light of these conflicting assumptions, let us examine the press's relations with the government and the content of its foreign policy coverage.

The government and the press have routinely cooperated during wartime to censor news about military actions. During the Vietnam War, for instance, the press accepted a six-day embargo on any references to an American invasion of Laos and even accepted an embargo on the fact that there was an embargo on news about American action along the Laotian-Vietnamese border. During the American invasion of Granada in late 1983, the press was first banned entirely from on-the-spot reporting and then restricted to a small pool of reporters. Reporting of the Persian Gulf War in 1991 was also severely curtailed.

During the Cuban missile crisis in October 1962, *The New York Times* knew that there were Russian missiles in Cuba and that the American government was deciding on its response, but it agreed not to publish a story about it after President Kennedy asked it to refrain. It also knew that the CIA was planning an imminent invasion of Cuba in 1961 but decided to move the story to an inside page from its tentatively scheduled front-page location, to shorten it, and to remove any indication that it was a definite and imminent CIA operation. The *Times* also knew for over a year that the United States was flying U-2 spy plane missions over the Soviet Union but did not report that fact until one was shot down; even then, it published President Eisenhower's initial denial without mentioning that it knew otherwise.[34]

On other occasions, however, the press's cooperation in keeping government secrets has been less complete. Although several news organizations agreed for several weeks in 1985 to a CIA request that they not publish reports about a salvage operation trying to retrieve a sunken Russian submarine from the Pacific, eventually they did publish those reports.

There are probably many additional instances of complete or partial compliance with government requests to kill stories. But there have also been numerous instances when major stories were published even though they revealed embarrassing and significant information that had been classified "top secret." One such story included verbatim transcripts of a high-level meeting of the National Security Council's crisis decision-making committee. The transcript documented the administration's "tilt toward Pakistan" in its 1971 war with India, thereby giving the lie to the administration's public claim of neutrality in the conflict. In another case, *The New York Times* and several other papers published portions of the Pentagon Papers, a secret government study including revelations about the conduct of the Vietnam War. In that instance, publication was delayed for several days because the administration obtained a court order prohibiting their publication. Then, when the Supreme Court ruled that such prior restraint was a violation of the First Amendment provision for a free press, publication resumed. Other investigative reporting helped reveal the government's involvement in attempts to overthrow the Allende government in Chile and the CIA's domestic spying activities.

On some occasions, the government-press conflict has arisen from a president's objections to a particular reporter's work. President Kennedy tried (unsuccessfully) to have *New York Times* reporter David Halberstam transferred from his Vietnam assignment in the early 1960s because his reports were fostering pessimism and criticism about the American role there. A decade later, the Nixon White House resorted to the more threatening tactic of having CBS reporter Daniel Schorr investigated by the FBI (to no avail) because it was unhappy with his reporting of administration policy.

Although presidents' relations with the press have varied considerably, they have all wearied of what they considered unfair treatment by the press. President Bush occasionally objected to press reports about administration policies. President Reagan frequently contended that the public misunderstood his policies because the press presented distorted stories about his speeches and decisions. President Kennedy ordered the White House subscription to the *New York Herald Tribune* canceled out of pique from its treatment. In answer to a reporter's question about newspaper stories about him, he once responded that he had been "reading them more and enjoying them less." In the Nixon administration, the antagonism toward the press was much more ominous. In an attack spearheaded by Vice-President Agnew, it criticized the press as too powerful in its influence over public opinion and as unfair and irresponsible in its coverage of the administration. It also hinted at further government regulations on the grounds that television networks, in particular, constituted a near monopoly.

Attacks on the press by various administrations, however, have not only focused attention on the press-government relationship; they have raised the issue of whether the content of the news is systematically distorted by a biased press. On the one hand, we would expect that individual journalists' own values and preferences would have some effect on their factual reporting; on the other hand, their sense of professionalism would tend to limit those tendencies.

Fortunately, we can rely on more than general speculation, for we have a substantial amount of detailed empirical evidence. Employing quantitative content-analysis techniques, scholars have tried to determine the nature and degree of any consistent bias in several prominent newspapers and television news programs. *The New York Times,* in particular, has been frequently and thoroughly studied, and its news stories have been consistently found to be more nearly balanced than those of other newspapers.[35]

The New York Times and such other "prestige" newspapers as *The Washington Post,* the *Christian Science Monitor,* and *The Wall Street Journal* may provide generally balanced, factual news reports. But what about the more widely read, heard, and watched mass media? Although the mass-circulation newspapers and radio have not been subjected to extensive careful analysis, they surely provide less balanced, less neutral, less detailed news than the prestige newspapers.

In ownership and editorial opinion, the country's newspapers are overwhelmingly Republican. Except in 1964, when they favored Johnson over Goldwater, a substantial majority of the newspapers have consistently endorsed the Republican candidate in presidential elections since 1932.[36] But they are otherwise so heterogeneous that their biases are probably mixed as well as somewhat responsive to local political opinions. Furthermore, although there has been a tendency toward concentration in the local newspaper and radio industries, most people still have a choice of newspapers; and they probably tend to choose those sources that they perceive as most consistent with their own views. In other words, most newspapers probably serve to reinforce readers' existing opinions as much as they challenge and change them.

In any case, national television news programs are the principal source of information about foreign affairs for most people. Audience and subscription data are not perfect indicators of exposure to foreign affairs news, since the sources contain other news and even much non-news content. Nevertheless, such data do provide clear evidence of the relative importance of the evening national network news programs. The collective audience of the network news programs is typically about one-third of the adult population. Weekly newsmagazines sales represent only about one-twentieth, and prestige newspapers are sold to about 1 percent of the adult population.[37]

Television news content has not been studied as extensively as have the prestige newspapers, but we do have some detailed data on network newscasts. A study of the several hundred news stories on the weeknight network news during several periods totaling seven weeks found that all three networks provided balanced coverage, although with a very slight "liberal" tendency (Table 3–3). It also found considerable similarity in the amount of time devoted to foreign affairs news in general and to particular foreign policy topics. And it found similarity in the placement and treatment of stories concerning the Vietnam War in particular.[38]

Other data based on all CBS nightly news programs during one year indicate some "liberal" bias in the reporting, but they also indicate the considerable extent to which newscasts consist of administration spokespersons and their supporters' expressions.* For example, of the several hundred sentences in stories concerning military spending or the strategic arms control negotiations, 32 percent contained "liberal" criticisms, and 59 percent contained support for the administration's policies.[39]

Aside from questions of bias, there are other concerns about the content of the news—particularly television's ability to inform the public. Television news tends to present a highly disjointed, superficial, and transitory image of foreign affairs. Consequently, it is difficult for people to obtain any substantial understanding of the

---

Liberal in this context includes preferences for defense-spending reductions, more substantial arms control agreements, withdrawal of forces from Vietnam and Europe, recognition of Communist China. *Conservative* means the opposite.

TABLE 3–3   Television Network News Program Content*

TIME DEVOTED TO:	ABC	CBS	NBC
All foreign affairs stories	31%	30%	36%
Europe	2	2	2
Middle East	3	3	3
Asia, except Vietnam	2	—	2
Vietnam	18	18	22
Democratic party	18	17	15
Republican party	19	20	15
Index of favorableness of treatment in:			
McGovern stories	4.54	4.41	4.11
Nixon stories	4.12	4.06	3.87
All stories	4.09	4.16	4.07
(4.00 = neutral; 1.00 = pro Nixon, Republicans, or prevailing policy; 7.00 = pro McGovern, Democrats, or policy change)			
Index of violence-bloodiness in Vietnam stories (1.00 = least violent, 9.00 = most violent)	3.75	3.48	3.87

*Data based on all weeknight broadcasts during seven weeks in 1972.

Source: Extracted by the author from data in Robert S. Frank, *Message Dimensions of Television News* (Lexington, MA: Lexington Books, D. C. Heath and Company, 1973), tables 3–6, 3–8, 3–9, 3–12, 3–13, 3–15, and 3–17, on pp. 48–60.

basic causes or the significance of daily events.[40] Furthermore, in all journalism, there is a tendency to focus on the dramatic, conflictual, personalized aspects of stories. Thus, the images of foreign affairs that the public obtains through the press are undoubtedly similarly distorted.

Prior to the onset of the war with Iraq, studies of TV coverage of the Middle East found an almost exclusive focus on U.S. policy toward the Arab-Israeli conflict with very little attention given to other issues and countries in the area. For instance, until the overthrow of the Shah, Iran received less than five minutes' coverage per year.[41] TV coverage of the war with Iraq, though, was unpreceded in its intensity.

In any case, the effects of TV on people's opinions concerning foreign affairs can be easily exaggerated. In fact, the effect is often much less than is commonly thought. For instance, approximately one hundred million Americans watched a dramatization of nuclear war in the TV movie, *The Day After*. Although nuclear freeze proponents hoped, and the Reagan administration feared, that the program would prompt greater concern about the possibility and the consequences of nuclear war, it apparently had little such impact. Only 11 percent of those who watched the program said that it was thought provoking, and only 27 percent reported that it increased their awareness of nuclear war.[42]

Yet, an administration's ability to use the media to present its views to the public should not be underestimated. The extent to which the media provide channels for the administration to convey its vision of the world can be illustrated by reactions to a key event in the East European revolutionary changes in 1989–1990: the elimination of barriers to emigration by East Germany. On the same day, President Bush was able to meet with the press in the Oval Office to express his immediate reaction (which was actually rather tentative and cautious). Within the next twenty-four hours, Secretary of State Baker expressed a more sanguine and expansive view on no fewer than eight different television news programs: "Prime Time Live," "Nightline," "Good Morning America," "Dan Rather Special Report," "This Morning," "MacNeil/Lehrer News Hour," Cable News Network morning news, and "This Week with David Brinkley" (a day later). Interviews with Secretary Baker also appeared in *The Washington Post* and *The New York Times*. Such access to the public through the media inevitably gives an administration opportunities to shape public opinion.

IMPACT ON POLICY

Elections

Regardless of their nature or sources, citizens' opinions on foreign policy issues can potentially affect policy through many channels. Elections are the most conspicuous channel. A superficial examination of presidential elections since World War II suggests that there were significant foreign policy issues involved in each one. In the 1948 campaign between Truman and Dewey, the American responses to the Berlin crisis, the Communist coup in Czechoslovakia, and other early cold war events were issues. In 1952, the administration's handling of the Korean War was an issue in the Eisenhower-Stevenson campaign; and in 1956, when they ran against one another again, American relations with the Soviet Union were an issue. In 1960, Kennedy and Nixon debated the adequacy of the American nuclear missile program, what to do about the Castro government of Cuba, and how to maintain the security of the islands of Quemoy and Matsu in the Formosa Strait between Nationalist China and Communist China. In 1964, Johnson and Goldwater argued about the best approach to follow in Vietnam. Four years later in 1968, Vietnam was again an issue—this time between Humphrey and Nixon—as it was yet again in the 1972 contest between Nixon and McGovern. Although the American departure from Vietnam removed the Vietnam War from the agenda of issues by 1976, nuclear proliferation, defense spending, and détente were discussed by Ford and Carter. In 1980, 1984, and 1988, defense spending and nuclear arms control were key issues between Reagan and Carter, Reagan and Mondale, and Bush and Dukakis.

Of course, each individual election is held against the background of voters' basic perceptions of the parties and their leaders. An important part of those perceptions is how voters see the parties' tendencies to involve the country in war or to keep it out of war. Figure 3–3 presents data reflecting such perceptions. The fluctuations are evident: In the 1964 election and in 1974–1982, the Republican candidates had to bear the burden of being perceived as relatively war prone; in the other years, the Democratic candidates had to contend with that problem.

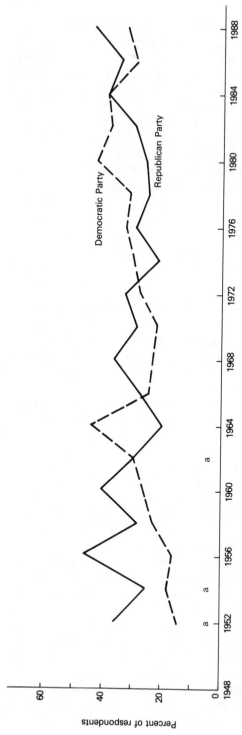

FIGURE 3–3 Public perceptions of parties' relative likelihood of keeping the country out of World War III

Question: "Which political party do you think would be more likely to keep the United States out of World War III — the Republican Party or Democratic party?"

Source: The Gallup Report 217 (October 1983), 28–30; 223 (April 1984), 19; 286 (July 1989), 4. Only election years are included. Polls were taken in August–October, except where indicated by (a).

But how much of an effect do these issues have on people's voting behavior? And does the outcome of the elections affect policy?

Less than one-half of the voting age population vote in congressional elections; only slightly more than one-half vote in presidential elections; and the proportion of voters has generally declined over time. So if public opinion has any impact on foreign policy through elections, it is based on the voting behavior of only about one-half the potential electorate.

The evidence on their voting behavior is summarized in the simple model depicted in Figure 3–4. The first—and correct—impression we get from the figure is that issue variables are only one of many variables that affect voting behavior. Although the relationships are so complex that we cannot be as precise and certain as we would like, we can be more specific about what the evidence indicates about each of the relationships.

The available evidence suggests that the assumptions of the democratic model are highly dubious. Only a small proportion of the population can be considered rational democratic voters for whom specific foreign policy issues are a significant factor in their votes. Such a conclusion may not be very surprising, however, once we recognize how demanding the requirements of rational democratic voting are. They include the requirements that a voter be knowledgeable and concerned about an issue, that he or she formulate a policy preference on the issue, and that he or she perceive differences in the candidates' policy preferences. Although many voters may be somewhat concerned about foreign policy issues in a general way, substantial portions of the population do not have either knowledge or policy preferences on specific foreign policy issues.

Furthermore, they often do not perceive any differences between the candidates or parties on the issues. For instance, in most years, between one-third and one-half of the population have not perceived either the Democrats or the Republicans to be more likely than the other party to keep the country out of World War III. In the elections of 1964, 1968, and 1972, when the war in Vietnam was presumably an

FIGURE 3–4 Voting behavior model

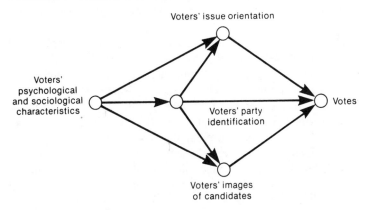

issue, nearly one-half of the respondents in national surveys did not perceive that either party favored a "stronger stand" on Vietnam. During each of the four presidential election campaigns from 1956 to 1968, about two-thirds of the electorate could not say whether the Democrats or Republicans were more supportive of foreign aid.[43] In 1976, a full one-half said they saw no difference in the parties' defense-spending policies. In other words, one of the critical requirements of an issue-based democratic electoral process is frequently not fulfilled: Substantial proportions of the voters do not perceive foreign policy differences between the major parties.

Why is this the case? It is the result of a combination of the voters' behavior and the candidates' behavior. Candidates typically try to appeal to the most voters by expressing "moderate" opinions near the center of the spectrum of opinions, and they try to maintain flexibility by expressing their opinions only in general terms. Even when candidates do express policy positions, they are likely to be perceived inaccurately, if at all, by substantial portions of the electorate.

A study of the 1968 presidential election illustrates both points.[44] A careful analysis of the nearly three hundred major campaign speeches delivered by Humphrey and Nixon revealed that both candidates had consistently opposed an immediate unilateral withdrawal from Vietnam or an escalation of the American involvement. Instead, they both advocated a gradual reduction of the American involvement if and as South Vietnam increased its war effort; but they usually stated this policy preference only in very general terms. And 57 percent of the electorate accurately perceived little or no difference in their stated positions.

Yet there was also a tendency for voters to perceive the candidates' positions as coinciding with their own, particularly among those with strong preferences for either withdrawal or escalation. Among those voters who preferred "immediate withdrawal," three-fourths assumed that Nixon was more "dovish" than "hawkish," and one-half assumed that Humphrey was also. Among those voters who preferred "complete military victory," nine-tenths thought that Nixon was more "hawkish" than "dovish," and seven-tenths assumed that Humphrey was also.

In short, the two major party candidates in 1968 expressed vague, "moderate" positions, which were accurately perceived by most of the electorate. But there was also a pronounced tendency on the part of many voters to perceive the candidates' positions as somewhat similar to their own, regardless of whether they were "hawkish" or "dovish."

In spite of the tendencies toward similarity in candidates' actual and perceived positions and in spite of voters' distorted perceptions, there is nevertheless some relationship between voters' foreign policy attitudes and their votes. Specifically, in the 1964, 1968, and 1972 presidential elections, those voters who favored an escalation of the Vietnam War were more likely to vote for the Republican candidates than were those who favored an immediate or gradual withdrawal—even if we control for other variables, such as party identification.

But in those elections and in the several other presidential elections that have also been carefully analyzed, the evidence indicates that voters' opinions on foreign policy issues have typically accounted for less than 5 percent of the variation in voting behavior. Similarly, although one or the other of the parties has generally been perceived by a somewhat greater proportion of the population as more likely to keep the country out of war, this advantage has been worth only a very few percentage points at the polls (again less than 5 percent). Other issues, such as the state of the economy, typically have a bigger impact on voting behavior than foreign policy issues, and the images of the candidates and the voters' party identifications have still greater effects on votes.

There is evidence, however, of an increase in specific issue voting over the past three decades, and there has been a parallel increase in the proportions of the population identifying themselves as "independents" rather than Democrats or Republicans. But neither of these trends has fundamentally altered the relative insignificance of foreign policy issues in the vast majority of voters' preferences in a presidential election.

Even to the limited extent that foreign policy issues are a factor in elections, it is normally in the form of a retrospective evaluation of the performance of the present administration rather than a prospective prescription of policies that should be adopted by the next administration.[45] The outcomes of presidential elections, there-fore, cannot be reasonably interpreted as an indication of the public's foreign policy preferences. The winner does not receive a clear affirmative mandate to pursue particular policies.

This does not necessarily mean that foreign policy issues have little effect on election outcomes or that election outcomes do not affect foreign policy. Although, as we have seen, foreign policy issues generally account for only a few percentage points in the election outcome, in several recent presidential elections the margin of victory (or defeat) was also only a few percentage points. In fact, in the presidential elections of 1960, 1968, and 1976, it was 2 percent or less. Thus, even though foreign policy issues were not the most significant determinants of people's votes in those elections, they may have had enough net impact to have fundamentally affected the outcome (though, of course, we could make the same point about a lot of other factors as well).

Moreover, election outcomes do have some impact on policy—even though it may not be an impact specifically and explicitly intended by a majority of the voters. Sometimes election returns are interpreted as a rejection of current policy. For instance, the outcome of the 1968 Democratic presidential primary in New Hamp-shire was an important factor in President Johnson's decisions not to run for re-election and to cease bombing much of North Vietnam in an effort to initiate peace negotiations. These results, however, were somewhat paradoxical: President John-son actually received more votes than his antiwar challenger, Senator Eugene McCar-thy, and many of the people who voted for McCarthy favored escalation rather than the withdrawal that he advocated. But the fact that a challenger could obtain as much as 42 percent of the vote against an incumbent president was widely interpreted as a vote of no confidence in the president; and the fact that McCarthy was widely perceived as a single-issue antiwar candidate meant that his "victory" was a defeat for the president's war policy.

Other Channels of Influence

Elections are not the only channel by which public opinion can potentially affect policy. Such an impact can occur through more informal and subtle ways whenever policy makers take into account actual or anticipated public reactions to actual or potential policies.

Although frequent and comprehensive public opinion polling enables policy makers to ascertain public opinion on many foreign policy issues, there are still numerous obstacles to the public's exercise of influence through such means. Poll results are often not sufficiently timely or specific to be very helpful; nor do they always reveal the salience of issues or intensity or stability of opinions about them. The policy choices faced by policy makers are usually much more complex and more specific than the issue prompting the simplified and generalized opinions revealed in public opinion data.

A study of middle-level State Department officials found that they do not pay much attention to public-opinion polls. As a matter of organizational policy, the department has devoted few resources to public-opinion–poll analysis.[46] During some periods, it has not had any staff specifically assigned to monitor relevant poll findings, at other times only a very small staff. In any case, the analysis of poll results that is made available receives little attention from policy makers. Since these bureaucrats individually tend to deal with highly specialized issues and since they are not directly responsible to the public, however, their inattention should not be surprising.

What of the politically responsible officials who deal with issues at a more general level? A study of members of the House of Representatives during an election year found that their opinions on selected foreign policy issues, as revealed in their voting records and in confidential interviews, were essentially uncorrelated with their constituents' opinions. In addition, the members of Congress did not have accurate perceptions of their constituents' opinions.[47]

Again, however, this should not be particularly surprising once we recognize the difficulties confronting individual members of Congress as they try to determine their constituents' opinions. Since public-opinion results are only rarely available by state or congressional district, their results do not tell individual members of Congress what their own state or district constituents' opinions are. Only a few states (such as California) have regular polls at the state level; only specifically commissioned polls are available at the congressional-district level. Furthermore, their formal and informal surveys of constituent opinions as well as the mail and the communications they receive do not provide them with representative samples. Rather, only the most aroused, the most educated, the most wealthy, or the most directly affected segments of a constituency tend to express their opinions to members of Congress.

Yet in spite of difficulties in obtaining an accurate perception of public preferences, members of Congress, the president, and other high administration officials are not indifferent to public opinion. Their perceptions of major shifts in opinion or strongly felt or widely held opinions are all likely to have some impact on their attitudes toward policy alternatives, even though the perceptions may be only approximately accurate and even though they may result from any of several imperfect sources. President Reagan, for instance, moderated at least his public hostility toward nuclear arms control in light of widespread and overt concern about his arms control policies expressed in Europe as well as in the United States.

Furthermore, even in the absence of a perception of what public opinion is, officials occasionally take into account what they assume the public reaction *would be* if they adopted a particular policy, that is, latent public opinion. For instance, during the Cuban missile crisis, President Kennedy was reluctant to adopt policies not involving a show of force for fear of a negative public reaction. Thus, even though public opinion may not normally have an impact on policy through officials' reactions to public expressions of particular policy preferences, the public's reaction *as anticipated by officials* may nevertheless have an impact on policy. Again, however, this impact is normally to proscribe potential policies, particularly those at the extremes of the continuum of policy alternatives. Thus, the anticipated public reaction to policy normally tends to push the consideration of policy alternatives toward the middle (compromise) alternatives. Within the broad spectrum of such alternatives, officials have considerable flexibility.

In fact, presidents can count on public support for many different policy alternatives, even including some that appear to be unpopular before they are adopted. Indeed, the public has sometimes responded favorably to opposite policies—both escalating and de-escalating the war in Vietnam, for instance. It has even gone so far as to respond favorably to policy failure; President Kennedy's performance rating went up after the aborted invasion of Cuba at the Bay of Pigs, for which he publicly accepted responsibility and which he implicitly admitted was a mistake. A few weeks before the Bay of Pigs, 73 percent approved of his performance as president; a few weeks afterward 83 percent approved. A year and a half later, at the time of the Cuban missile crisis, the proportion of the population approving of his performance as president increased by more than 10 percent. President Johnson's approval rating increased by 10 percent when he announced Vietnam bombing reductions in the spring of 1968, as did President Ford's in 1975 when he sent American troops into Cambodia to try to rescue the crew of the merchant ship *Mayaguez*. The greatest short-term increase in presidential popularity in thirty years occurred in 1978 when President Carter's favorable rating increased 13 percentage points in the Gallup Poll after a Camp David summit meeting at which he helped move Egypt and Israel much closer to signing a peace treaty.[48] President Bush enjoyed an unprecedented 92 percent approval for a short time after the Persian Gulf War in 1991.

Such figures do not mean that the public is utterly undiscriminating in their evaluations of presidential performance or that they have unlimited patience with policies that fail. They indicate only that a president can expect a well-publicized event or policy initiative to yield a moderate short-term increase in support for a specific policy or for his presidential performance in general. Over the longer term, the support may stabilize at the new higher level, or it may instead decline to its previous level or perhaps even go lower.

A study of public opinion during the Korean and Vietnam wars provides ample evidence that public support for the wars was at relatively high levels in the early period and periodically increased in response to particular presidential actions.[49] But over the long term, there was increasingly widespread opposition to the president's policy. Just before President Truman left office, only 37 percent of the public thought the United States had not made a mistake by entering the Korean War; by the time President Johnson announced that he would not run for reelection, only 26 percent approved of "his handling of the situation in Vietnam." Their overall presidential-approval ratings, according to the Gallup Poll, were respectively only 31 percent and 43 percent by the end of their terms. Both decided not to run for re-election, partly because they had lost widespread public support; and they had lost it partly because of their war policies.

CONCLUSION

The American public has fluctuated in its perception of the relative importance of foreign policy issues, but it has consistently favored an active role in the world. It has generally supported high and increasing levels of military expenditures, but it has been less supportive of military and economic assistance to other countries. Although substantial portions of the population prefer unilateral, nationalistic, and even jingoistic policies, a majority generally prefer more cooperative bilateral and multilateral diplomacy.

Variations in these and other opinions are often correlated with age, gender, income, occupation, education, personality, and information level. Such correlations indicate, for example, that in recent years young people have been less supportive of military expenditures than have older people. However, these and other correlations are often weak and unstable over time.

Although a few "prestige" newspapers provide the most detailed and balanced journalistic coverage of foreign affairs, local newspapers and television are the most common sources of information for most people.

Foreign policy issues often seem to be prominent in election campaigns, but they are rarely an important factor in voting behavior. The candidates and parties are widely perceived as similar on foreign policy issues. It is difficult to interpret the outcome of an election as a mandate for a particular set of foreign policies. Nevertheless, election outcomes do occasionally have an important impact on policy, particularly when they are interpreted as a lack of support for the previous administration's policies.

Although presidents and other high-level policy makers may feel marginally constrained by their perceptions of public opinion, they still have considerable freedom from public pressures. Indeed, they can rely on the public to acquiesce in most policy initiatives, at least in the short run.

Even though we find little evidence to support the assumptions of the democratic model, we should be careful not to dismiss the public's role entirely. Policy makers' general perceptions of public opinion and occasionally their anticipation of possible public reaction to specific policies often limit their consideration of policy alternatives. They try to mobilize public support, and they are often successful. But they are not able to manipulate public opinion so effectively as the ruling elite model assumes. Sometimes significant shifts in public sentiment change policy, and there are variations in support among different segments of the public at any one time.

The pluralist assumptions of diversity of opinion, as well as relatively low levels of interest and knowledge, are confirmed. For the most part, the public is inattentive, quiescent, and permissive. There have been important exceptions, however, such as the Vietnam War in the 1970s, nuclear arms control in the 1980s, and the Middle East war in 1991.

═══ F O U R ═══════════════════════════════════

Interest Groups

Although the role of the general public may be described as marginal and passive in foreign policy making, this does not necessarily mean that there are not any significant nongovernmental participants actively involved in the policy process. In fact, of course, the opposite is true; for there are numerous nongovernmental groups and organizations that often play a central role.

The terms *pressure groups* and *lobbies* are widely used to refer to such groups and organizations, but it is preferable to think of them as *interest groups,* since that term is more descriptive of their nature and activities. Interest groups do sometimes exert pressure in the policy process, and they do sometimes lobby; however, their nature and activities are not nearly so circumscribed as those terms suggest. When we refer to interest groups, we simply mean a group of people with a common interest that is different from other people's interests; practically any segment of society therefore constitutes an interest group.

Interest groups are particularly important in the pluralist model of the policy process. It assumes that the United States is a pluralistic society consisting of a large number of overlapping interest groups whose interests can be defined by such characteristics as economic position, ethnic background, race, and occupation. The pluralist model further assumes that interest groups are organized for political action and that the struggle among interest-group organizations is central in the policy process. Foreign policy is the compromise outcome of that struggle.

The transnational politics model is also pertinent to a consideration of interest groups, because it suggests that many groups' interests now transcend national boundaries. For instance, because of their transnational economic activities, multinational corporations' interests cannot be defined simply as subinterests of American national interests. Their interests are partially consistent with American national interests and partially consistent with other countries' national interests. But, in essence, they are *transnational corporate* interests. Similarly, labor unions have undertaken transnational political activities, such as assistance to the Solidarity Movement in Poland during the period of the demise of the Communist regime in that country.

Whereas the pluralist and transnational politics models assume that there are competition and a degree of countervailing power among multiple-interest groups, the ruling elite model assumes that there is a single dominant interest group. Multinational corporations are merely another organizational manifestation of elite interests and power, albeit a particularly pernicious one. Also, according to the ruling elite model, there may be other nongovernmental organizations that reputedly represent public interests; but they are actually controlled by a few elites, who use them to promote their own interests rather than public interests.

Again such conflicting assumptions suggest the importance of a careful examination of the available evidence. So let us consider the political activities and resources of interest groups, their impact on policy, and their interests and policy preferences. How do interest groups try to influence government policies, and how much impact do they actually have? What are the key characteristics of multinational corporations? What role do they play in American foreign policy? These are some of the questions that will be addressed in this chapter.

LOBBYING ORGANIZATIONS

The ways in which groups' interests are represented in the policy process are diverse. They include not only the well-known Washington-based professional lobbying staffs of such organizations as the National Association of Manufacturers, the AFL-CIO, and the Veterans of Foreign Wars; they also include numerous Washington law firms, public relations firms, and individual free-lance lobbyists.

There are hundreds of individuals and organizations registered to lobby in Congress under the provisions of the Federal Regulation of Lobbying Act. There are also hundreds of representatives of foreign governments or other foreign interests registered with the Justice Department under the Foreign Agents Registration Act, and they represent clients from nearly every country. But such registration figures indicate only a small fraction of the actual number of individuals and organizations involved in organized interest-group activities. Many active lobbyists are not registered because the legal restrictions are vaguely worded and ineffectively enforced, and many interest-group representatives do not focus their activities on congressional lobbying anyway. Indeed, some are technically only public education organizations, whose presumed principal purpose is to distribute information and otherwise promote greater public understanding of a particular group or issue. In other words, they specialize in "grassroots" lobbying instead of congressional lobbying.

Among the lobbying organizations, there are a large number of "public-interest" organizations. Although many of them have focused their activities on issues that involve foreign policy only marginally or indirectly, some of them have been frequently and directly concerned with foreign policy issues. Common Cause, the "citizens' lobby," has worked for such congressional reforms as the War Powers Act, which affects Congress's role in foreign policy making. Another organization, New Directions, was formed specifically to be a citizens' lobby on such foreign policy issues as nuclear proliferation. Several environmental lobbying organizations have also been active on foreign policy issues. Partly as a reaction to the creation of these "liberal" public-interest organizations, "conservative" public-interest organizations were also formed, among them the Conservative Caucus and the Conservative Political Action Committee. Finally, there have long been many organizations concerned specifically with military issues. These include the Friends Committee on National Legislation and the National Committee for a Sane Nuclear Policy, which have supported arms control measures, and the American Security Council and the Liberty Lobby, which have supported increased military expenditures.

There are also individuals, law firms, public relations firms, and other organizations that represent foreign governments and other foreign groups and organizations in Washington. Many of them represent the governments of South Korea and Israel, which have been highly dependent on continuing American support. Other interest groups are particularly interested in American relations with such countries as Poland and Greece since there are many Americans with personal ties to those countries. Yet other groups are more specialized representatives of commercial interests, particularly of Western European and Japanese governments and corporations. Still others specialize in arms sales and other military equipment transfers.

Some organizations represent transnational interest groups. For example, the United States–Japan Trade Council membership is made up of over a thousand American and Japanese corporations, including General Electric, Standard Oil of California, Japan Airlines, and the Bank of Tokyo.[1] Its annual budget is provided mostly by the Japanese government, and it maintains contact with the Japanese embassy in Washington. It publishes a biweekly newsletter, and its staff members meet frequently with officials in such executive agencies as the State Department, the Commerce Department, the Treasury Department, the International Trade Commission, and the White House—all in an effort to promote trade and cooperative economic relations between Japan and the United States.

Japanese corporations have been especially active in recent years as they try to restrain the movement for more protectionist U.S. trade policies vis-à-vis Japan.[2] Perhaps the most heavily funded of any foreign lobby, the Japanese are estimated to spend over $40 million annually on Washington lobbying activities. They often join forces in transnational coalitions with American organizations that have a common interest in free-trade policies between Japan and the United States. Thus, the Japanese automobile companies have cooperated in antiprotectionist lobbying with American agricultural organizations, longshoremen, and port authorities, all of whom are highly dependent on trade with Japan for their incomes.

Similarly, the Association for Foreign Investment in America is dedicated to opposing movements toward restrictiveness in the traditionally open U.S. policy on foreign investment in the United States. Thus, it has opposed efforts to require the registration and public disclosure of information about foreign-owned firms that buy existing U.S. corporations or otherwise establish new affiliates in this country.

The large array of diverse organizations that actively try to influence American foreign policy is readily apparent in the list of organizations in Table 4–1.

TABLE 4–1   Selective List of Lobbying Organizations*

MILITARY ISSUES

Aerospace Industries Association
American League for International Security Assistance
American Legion
American Security Council
Coalition for a New Foreign and Military Policy
Council for a Livable World
Disabled American Veterans
Federation of American Scientists
Freeze Voter '84
National Association for Uniformed Services
SANE
Veterans of Foreign Wars
Women's International League for Peace and Freedom

TRADE IN MANUFACTURES AND GENERAL TRADE ISSUES

American Chamber of Commerce in Spain
American Federation of Labor–Congress of Industrial Organizations
American Footwear Manufacturers Association
American Importers Association
American Iron and Steel Institute
American Textile Manufacturers Institute
Association on Japanese Textile Imports
Chamber of Commerce
Confederation Européenne de L'Industrie de la Chaussure
Consumers for World Trade
East-West Trade Council
Emergency Committee on American Trade
Footwear Retailers of America
International Association of Machinists and Aerospace Workers
International Union, United Automobile, Aerospace & Agricultural Implement Workers
Latin American Marketing Association
Nation-Wide Committee on Import-Export Policy
National Association of Manufacturers
National Cotton Council of America
Société Nationale Industrielle Aerospatiate
Special Committee for Export Trade
United States–Japan Trade Council
United Steelworkers of America

TABLE 4–1   (continued)

TRANSPORTATION ISSUES

Ad Hoc Committee of Shipbuilders
Air Transport Association
American Institute of Merchant Shipping
Council of European and Japanese National Shipowners' Associations
New York Committee of International Committee of Passenger Lines

AGRICULTURAL ISSUES

American Farm Bureau Federation
American Soybean Association
Bread for the World
National Corn Growers Association
National Farmers Union
National Grange
Swaziland Sugar Association
Wine Institute

ENERGY ISSUES

American Nuclear Energy Council
American Petroleum Institute
Atomic Industrial Forum
National Coal Association
Oil, Chemical and Atomic Workers
Union of Concerned Scientists
United Mine Workers of America

ENVIRONMENTAL ISSUES

Friends of the Earth
League of Conservation Voters
Natural Resources Defense Council
Sierra Club

RELATIONS WITH PARTICULAR COUNTRIES

Action Committee on Arab-American Relations
American Chilean Council
American Committee on U.S.-Soviet Relations
American-Israel Public Affairs Committee
Conference of Presidents of Major Jewish Organizations
Japanese-American Citizens League
National Association of Arab Americans
National Committee on U.S.-China Relations
National Conference on Soviet Jewry
Polish American Congress
Washington Office on Africa

TABLE 4–1 (continued)

GENERAL

American Civil Liberties Union
American Conservative Union
Americans for Democratic Action
Citizens for the Republic
Committee for the Survival of a Free Congress
Common Cause
Congress Watch
Conservative Caucus
Conservative Political Action Committee
Conservative Victory Fund
Friends Committee on National Legislation
Liberty Lobby
New Directions
National Committee for an Effective Congress

*This list does not include any individual corporations or agents of individual foreign governments.
Sources: Compiled by the author from the following Congressional Quarterly publications: *Weekly Report, Annual Almanac, Congress and the Nation,* and *The Washington Lobby*; and from *National Journal.*

Activities

The targets and tactics of these organizations and other interest-group representatives vary. The targets of their activities include not only members of Congress but also officials in executive agencies, the public, and even other interest-group organizations. Their tactics include providing both information and campaign contributions. In 1974, the Federal Election Campaign Act was amended to allow increased activity by political action committees (PACs). By the 1990s, there were thousands of PACs contributing hundreds of millions of dollars to congressional candidates.[3] The PAC sources and the parties of the recipient candidates for one campaign period are indicated in Table 4–2.

TABLE 4–2 Political Action Committee (PAC) Contributions to Congressional Candidates* ($ millions)

PARTY OF RECIPIENT	LABOR	CORPO- RATIONS	TYPE OF PAC[†]	IDEO- LOGICAL	OTHER	TOTALS
Democrats	19	9	9	5	2	45
Republicans	1	18	12	5	1	38
Totals	20	27	21	10	3	83

*1981–1982
†Mostly business
Source: Data compiled from *National Journal* 15, 19 (May 7, 1983), 935, 974.

On major issues, they sometimes organize mass mail campaigns that can implicitly or explicitly threaten elected officials with electoral opposition if they do not adopt a particular position. During the Senate's consideration of the Panama Canal Treaties in 1977–1978, for instance, a coalition of organizations urged voters in the states of ten undecided senators to write their senators to ask them to vote against the treaties. One of the organizations, the American Conservative Union, spent over a million dollars and sent out over two million pieces of mail in an effort to block the treaties.

Interest-group organizations often form ad hoc coalitions with other interest groups, with members of Congress, and with executive agencies to support or oppose particular policy alternatives. Such coalitions are sometimes referred to as *iron triangles*, since the combined forces of interest groups, members of Congress (especially from key committees), and executive agencies pose a formidable obstacle to anyone (such as a president) who prefers a different policy alternative. There are often conflicting coalitions that take opposing sides—with the president and his administration participating in one of the coalitions.

Although there is some stability across issues in these coalitions, there is also considerable shifting. Sometimes business and labor organizations are on opposite sides, but often they are on the same side. Sometimes representatives of groups involved in manufacturing a particular commodity and groups involved in retailing it are on the same side; sometimes they are on opposite sides. Organizations may side with the president on one issue but oppose him on another. Only the more ideologically oriented public-interest groups are consistent coalition partners or adversaries.

This mixed pattern of partly shifting and partly stable coalitions is documented by a tabulation of lobbying activity on selected foreign policy legislation in Congress (Table 4–3). In that table, we can see, for instance, that several citizens' organizations—Common Cause, New Directions, and the Americans for Democratic Action—supported the Carter administration on the Panama Canal, the Ford administration on the embargo of Rhodesian chrome, and the Nixon administration on détente and trade with China. But those organizations were on the opposite side from the administration on other issues, such as funds for the B-1 bomber, the MX missile, and the Sentinel antiballistic missile system. On those issues, the administration was joined by manufacturing organizations and other citizens' organizations (which, however, differed with the administration on the Panama Canal Treaties and the Rhodesian chrome embargo). And, of course, as the administration changes from one party to the other, political alignments with interest-group organizations also shift.

On the trade issues at the bottom of the table, we find an even more complex pattern. The citizens' organizations were not so active here. Instead, those issues engaged commercial organizations, such as the Chamber of Commerce and the retailers of specific commodities, and the administration, which supported lower tariffs on imports. Labor organizations were on the other side, opposing tariff reductions and actively supporting automobile domestic-content legislation that would have severely reduced trade in automobile components as well as fully assembled automobiles. On trade issues, however, it is not unusual to find business organizations and industries divided in their opinions. The interests of many firms

TABLE 4–3 (continued)

CONGRESSIONAL VOTE	LIBERAL CITIZENS' ORGANIZATIONS	LABOR ORGANIZATIONS	ADMINISTRATION	COMMERCIAL ORGANIZATIONS	MANUFACTURING ORGANIZATIONS	CONSERVATIVE CITIZENS' ORGANIZATIONS
			COALITION PARTICIPANTS			
Trade Issues:						
Omnibus Trade Bill (1988)		O	S	S	S	
Automobile domestic content (1982)		S	O	O	O	
Lower tariffs (1974)		O	S	S	S	
Lower tariffs (1970)		O	S	S	O	O
Lower tariffs (1962)	S	S	S	S/O*	S/O*	
Shoe imports (1978)		O	S	S	O	

*Some organizations supported; others opposed.

Sources: Compiled by the author from the following Congressional Quarterly publications: *Weekly Report, Annual Almanac, Congress and the Nation,* and *The Washington Lobby;* and from *National Journal.*

organizations have often been influential on trade issues, such as protective measures for a particular commodity. Defeats and compromise outcomes on protective trade measures, however, indicate the limitations of their influence on those issues. General public-interest organizations have not generally been very influential.

The individual and collective influence of interest-group organizations is marginal on most issues. Generally, the partisan and ideological composition of the Congress, the position of the president, and the preferences and expertise of the bureaucracy all have a greater impact on policy than nongovernmental interest groups and their lobbying organizations. One interest group, however, warrants more detailed analysis in light of its enormous political resources; that interest group is big business, particularly in the form of multinational and global corporations.

GLOBAL CORPORATIONS

Many American businesses have long had major interests at stake in foreign affairs. Manufacturers have relied on imports of raw materials for their production processes; wholesalers and retailers have relied on imports of finished consumer goods for their sales. Exports have been an important source of profits for many corporations. But in the past few decades, there have been important changes in the form, the magnitude, and the scope of the international activities of corporations. Together, these changes have combined to create a significant set of actors comprising a distinctive interest group: large multinational corporations with operations that are global in scope.

Nature and Size

The characteristic feature of these corporations is that they carry on their economic activities through direct investments in more than one country. Altogether, there are approximately three thousand American-based multinational corporations with investments in over ten thousand affiliated foreign firms. The value of their foreign investments is several hundred billion dollars.[5]

Numerous terms and definitions have been used to describe multinational corporations. Among political scientists and most lay people, commonly used terms have been *multinational corporations* or *MNCs* or simply *the multinationals*. Official United Nations usage is *transnational corporations* or *TNCs*. Business practitioners and academics have tended to prefer the term *multinational enterprises* or *MNEs*. A term used frequently now is *global corporations*.

Regardless of the terminology, however, the reference is to the same phenomenon—corporations that own and control production facilities in more than one country and have more or less globally oriented strategies in at least some respects. Thus, they have a headquarters (parent corporation) in one country and affiliates (subsidiary corporations) in other countries. The country where the headquarters is located is called the home country; the countries where the affiliates are located are called host countries. The core trait of multinational corporations is that they engage in foreign direct investment (FDI). That is, they invest in physical facilities in countries other than their own home country.

Foreign direct investment is thus different from another type of foreign invest-ment—often called portfolio investment—that only involves owning shares in a foreign corporation. When an individual investor (or even a corporation) buys a small proportion of the outstanding shares of a foreign corporation, then portfolio invest-ment takes place. On the other hand, when a corporation buys enough shares in a foreign corporation so that it can exercise substantial control over its operations or if it establishes its own new foreign corporation, then foreign direct investment takes place. The essential ingredient in FDI is control—managerial control of a corporation in one country by a corporation in another country.

More than ownership and control usually cross national boundaries, however. For large MNCs have become complex networks of parents and affiliates that engage in numerous and diverse transactions among themselves. Goods, services, funds, technology, and people are all moved around internationally among the various components of a typical large MNC. Goods are traded among MNC components, for instance, because there is commonly a production process marked by considerable international specialization and division of labor. Thus, different phases in the production process for a single final product occur in several countries.

The nature and extent of the trade that accompanies FDI can be illustrated by the automobile industry—which is one of the most highly multinationalized indus-tries. For a single model automobile, Ford Motor Company manufactures (or pur-chases from suppliers): engines in Britain and Spain, wheels in Belgium, transmis-sions in France, fuel tanks in West Germany, and windows and other parts in the United States. Those components are assembled into complete automobiles in three different countries. Another Ford model is also assembled in three different coun-tries—the United States, Britain, and Germany—from components made in Japan, Italy, Brazil, Mexico, Taiwan, Britain, and the United States.

Internationalized production processes are also used by other automobile firms, including many foreign-based firms that now assemble vehicles in the United States—Hondas in Ohio, Mazdas in Michigan, Nissans in Tennessee, Toyotas in Kentucky, Subarus and Izuzus in Indiana, and Mitsubishis in Illinois. In addition, Volvo and General Motors have a joint venture that manufactures heavy duty trucks in North Carolina. Such assembly plants naturally use imported components from their parent corporations in their home countries (e.g., Japan in the case of auto-mobiles) and from affiliated firms in other countries (such as Mexico, Canada, and others).

Because the production process is so widely dispersed among many countries and because so much trade occurs among the parent and affiliates in a large MNC system, there are also many other types of flows across national boundaries. Services, such as design and engineering, are also traded internationally. The automobiles noted above, for instance, are designed in several countries—and not necessarily the countries where they are finally assembled. Technology in the form of knowledge about products and production processes also crosses national boundaries as produc-tion processes are established in foreign countries and as products are traded interna-tionally. Managerial and technical people also become more internationally mobile. Headquarters personnel, for instance, may need to visit affiliates' production facilities for better coordination, or personnel from foreign affiliates may be reassigned to duty at headquarters in the home country. Finally, of course, money is transferred internationally because of the income and expenses associated with activities in the many countries in the MNC system.

Although not all multinational corporations are large, MNCs tend to be very large indeed. A common way to indicate the economic size of MNCs is to compare their annual sales with the gross national products of countries. In recent years, the sales of each of the fifty largest industrial MNCs have been greater than the GNPs of about two-thirds of the 165 countries in the world.

Not only manufacturing industries, such as the automobile industry, and extractive industries, such as petroleum companies, but also service industries, such as banking, have become multinational. The largest American banks have branches and other types of affiliates in numerous countries. They loan large amounts of money to foreign governments, foreign-based firms, and the foreign affiliates of American-based multinationals. They conduct hundreds of billions of dollars of business per day in the foreign exchange markets of New York, Chicago, San Francisco, Tokyo, Hong Kong, Dubai, Paris, Zurich, London, and other cities around the world.

A few selected statistics are suggestive of the extent to which banking in particular has become internationalized. Among the ten largest American-based banks, more than half their income is from foreign activities. About 80 percent of the income of Citibank of New York is from foreign operations. Chase Manhattan Bank has branch offices in more than one hundred foreign countries. There are more than one hundred banks in the United States that are foreign owned. Banks based in the United States, Japan, and Western Europe have outstanding loans of more than $80 billion to the Soviet Union and other countries of Eastern Europe. On a typical day in the foreign exchange markets, banks around the world exchange approximately $1 trillion (equivalent) U.S. dollars and other currencies.

The highly internationalized and even globalized nature of much banking activity is evident despite the partial retreat from cross-border lending to many developing countries on the part of many banks. In any case, the outstanding loans of American-based banks to Third World developing countries remain on the order of hundreds of billions of dollars. Thus, the large "money center" banks as well as some of the large regional U.S. banks continue to have substantial stakes in the economic prospects of countries in Latin America, Africa, Asia, the Middle East, and Eastern Europe.

These facts on the magnitude and global range of large corporations' activities in manufacturing, financial services, and extractive industries implicitly suggest that they are potentially significant actors in world politics. We can also be more explicit about their political significance, including their impact on American foreign policy.

Political Impact and Relations with the Government[6]

    To a degree, multinational corporations have been in at least a tacit cooperative partnership with the American government—a partnership based on the convergence of the corporate officers' perceptions of their interests and government officials' perceptions of the national interest. The multinationals' contribution to the spread of capitalism and American technology and culture has been viewed as an important means of extending American influence. In addition, the oil and mining multinationals have gained access to raw materials that are important for industrial and military activities of interest to government officials, who want to maximize national power capabilities and who want to have strategic materials available in wartime. Furthermore, multinationals' earnings on their foreign investments help alleviate American international balance-of-payments deficits when those earnings are converted back into American dollars. Finally, the multinational corporations contribute to economic development in other countries through their transfers of capital, technology, and training—an important objective of American policy.

As a result of these and other perceived contributions to American security and welfare, American corporations receive subsidies and other forms of government support. One type of subsidy occurs through the government-created Overseas Private Investment Corporation (OPIC), which insures investments against expropriation by foreign governments and other risks. The Export-Import Bank, which is funded and operated by the U.S. government, provides low interest loans to foreign customers of American-based corporations. For instance, the bank has loaned foreign customers billions of dollars for their purchases of nuclear power plant equipment and fuel from American corporations. Also many sales of U.S.-made commercial airplanes are financed by Export-Import Bank loans to foreign airlines.

There have also been instances of American government intervention in countries where American corporations' interests were threatened.[7] In 1954, the United States helped to overthrow the Guatemalan government, an action that was strongly favored by the United Fruit Company, which operated extensive banana plantations in Guatemala. In 1970, American covert activities in Chile were intended first to prevent the election of Marxist candidate Salvador Allende and then to bring about his downfall once he was elected president. These were precisely the objectives of ITT, which feared expropriation of its Chilean investments. Indeed, ITT even offered the American government a million dollars to fund anti-Allende activities. It also maintained close contact with the CIA, through ITT board member John McCone, who had been director of the CIA a few years before.

In these and other instances of American intervention, the government and the multinational corporations shared common objectives, and high-level officials from both were in contact with one another. In some instances—such as the Guatemalan case—there is evidence that the protection of American private investments was one of the motivations for the intervention. In other instances, however, it is not clear from the publicly available evidence that either such motivations or political pressures from the corporations actually had a substantial impact on the decision to intervene.

In any case, multinational corporations and the government have often been at direct odds with one another. Sometimes the government has prevailed in those conflicts, and sometimes the multinational corporations have prevailed. For many years after World War II, the government acquiesced in protectionist West European and Japanese tariffs and quotas, even though they made it more difficult for American corporations to sell exports in those countries. At least until the 1970s, the United States unequivocally supported Israel in its conflict with Arab countries, even though the American oil companies with investments in Arab countries would have preferred otherwise. In 1976, the administration supported the imposition of an embargo on Rhodesian chrome imports, even though the directly affected American corporations disapproved.

In other instances, the multinational corporations have not followed the policies of the government. In 1965, a French subsidiary of Fruehauf sold truck trailers to the Soviet Union at the request of the French government even though the American government had asked it not to do so. In 1982, a British subsidiary of an American firm shipped turbines for the Soviet gas pipeline in spite of the Reagan administration's sanctions that prohibited sales for that project.

In less dramatic, but still important, ways, U.S.-based firms with foreign affiliates are often at odds with the U.S. government over tax issues arising from the prices the related entities of a multinational corporation charge one another for the goods and services they trade among themselves. Corporations are sometimes able to alter such prices on the goods and services that are transferred from the parent to a foreign affiliate in such a way as to reduce their U.S. corporate income tax obligation—clearly a matter of interest to the U.S. Internal Revenue Service. Thus, a particular provision of the tax code (Section 482) establishes criteria and procedures for setting prices on internationally traded goods and services within any given multinational enterprise system. Numerous disputes and court cases have evolved as a result of U.S. government and U.S.-based corporation views on these practices.

In some instances, the interests of different multinational corporations are themselves in conflict, so that the government can only displease some while pleasing others. In 1968, Exxon wanted the U.S. government to threaten to invoke the Hickenlooper Amendment against Peru and thereby threaten to withdraw aid unless Peru paid more compensation for the Exxon facilities it had expropriated. But other American firms opposed such an approach for fear it would jeopardize their own investments; Peru might have retaliated against them if the United States withdrew its aid.

To a considerable extent, however, the multinationals go about their business as they see fit, even though doing so often creates problems for government officials. In 1973 and again in 1978, multinational corporation money managers speculated heavily against the American dollar in international currency markets. In other words, they sold the American dollars they were holding, and they bought money in foreign currencies, especially German marks and Japanese yen. Because their cash assets are so enormous (altogether greater than those of the world's central government banks), their international currency transactions can have a considerable impact on the fluctuations in exchange rates in the currency markets. In the late 1970s and early 1980s, Gulf Oil had operations in Angola and maintained good relations with the Marxist government there even though the American administration was overtly hostile toward that government.

Other examples also demonstrate the impact that multinational firms' activities can have—independent of their relationship with the American government. Acknowledged and alleged bribes by American corporations led to scandals and the resignations of high government officials in Italy, Japan, the Netherlands, and other countries during the 1970s.

The more routine business activities of multinational firms have also created controversies—for example, their business relationships with South Africa. The net impact of these business activities on racial justice inside South Africa is uncertain. But their impact on the military and economic position of the South African government is clear. The several billion dollars in loans to the South African government by American-based banks made it possible for South Africa to acquire the foreign currencies that it uses to buy petroleum and military supplies for its strategic stockpile.

Big corporations, then, individually and collectively do have political and economic impacts that are pertinent to American foreign policy. Sometimes those consequences are ones that are desired or even subsidized by the government; sometimes they are opposed or constrained by the government; and sometimes they are merely tolerated by the government. But in any case they are significant. Their significance, however, lies not only in their economic magnitude; it lies further in their effects on the patterns of interests and power in world politics. Multinational corporations make both more complex, and they therefore make policy makers' calculations about them more complicated.

BUSINESS INTERESTS AND PREFERENCES

A careful study of corporation executives' opinions and political activities concerning tariff legislation found that they sometimes have difficulties themselves determining what is in their best interests.[8] One-third of a representative sample of nine hundred executives who were interviewed expressed no preference for either higher or lower tariffs. Not only did many express uncertainty about which would be better for their firms; they were also in frequent disagreement with independent economists' perceptions of whether firms in their industries would profit more from higher or lower tariffs. Such uncertainty and disagreement about their interests arise precisely from the two characteristics we have emphasized in our analysis: the size and the multinational nature of corporations' activities. In a given corporation, divisions that rely on imports in their production lines or on export sales would profit from low tariffs for cheaper imports and more access to their export markets. But in the same corporation, divisions that rely on domestic sales might profit from higher tariffs, which protect them from foreign competition.

Most of the executives who were interviewed, however, were able to determine whether their interests were in higher or lower tariffs, and many of them became politically active. They formed specialized ad hoc lobbying organizations to try to influence the tariff legislation pending in Congress at the time. But some of them supported liberalized (lower) tariffs, while others wanted protectionist (higher) tariffs. There were even splits within industries. Whereas the large multinational oil companies wanted fewer restrictions on oil imports (so that they could import from their foreign sources more profitably), the small "independent" oil companies wanted more restrictions on imports (so that their domestically produced products would face less competition). There was so much conflict among the industries, in fact, that the major business organization, the National Association of Manufacturers, was not able to take a position on the trade legislation, let alone actively lobby for or against it.

We also have an abundance of survey data from other studies of business executives' opinions on foreign policy issues other than tariffs. In three separate studies, representative samples of nearly fifteen hundred chief executive officers and vice-presidents of the several hundred largest corporations in the country expressed their opinions in face-to-face interviews and in written questionnaires.[9] The results were surprising, at least in light of the assumptions of the ruling elite model. Over half thought the United States had sometimes contributed to the escalation of the cold war; three-fourths thought the United States should be willing to accept socialist governments in Latin America; and between one-third and two-thirds wanted less spent on defense.

Their attitudes toward war were perhaps even more surprising. Comparisons of the business elites' attitudes with those of young people (who were asked the same questions in a separate survey) reveal that the business elites were not more "hawkish" than the self-identified "liberal" college students and were much less so than the noncollege young people.

These business elites were furthermore found to be less hawkish on these and several other issues than Republican political elites and high-ranking military officers, who were asked the same questions in the studies. On the other hand, the business elites expressed somewhat more bellicose opinions than other elite groups: Democratic politicians, labor leaders, high-ranking civil servants, and members of the press.[10] In other words, these elite groups did not express uniform opinions. The corporation executives, in particular, were less hawkish than some groups but more so than others. Yet another study of elite opinions found business leaders to be relatively hawkish on some issues but much less so on others.[11]

These findings are not by themselves conclusive, however, because they are derived from surveys. They therefore inevitably reveal only superficial opinions, which could be highly imperfect indicators of actual or potential political activity. Perhaps, in other words, "dovish" responses to interviews of corporation executives do not reveal their true sentiments or likely political behavior.

Fortunately, we have yet another set of data (concerning stock market trends), which indicate actual behavioral reactions to war.[12] The data are derived from a careful analysis of the relationship of war news during the Vietnam and Korean wars to trends in stock market prices. In sum, the study found that there was little relationship between war news and trends in the stock market. Moreover, those few significant relationships that were discovered were contrary to the ruling elite assumptions that escalation would push market prices up and that conciliatory moves would push them down. The evidence, in other words, indicates that to the extent that American capitalists and their money managers responded to war news, they acted as though war was bad for business and peace would be good for business.

CONCLUSION

Numerous and diverse interest groups are concerned about the effects of American foreign policy on their interests. Those interests are represented by hundreds of organizations, which lobby for special interests and the general public, labor and business, energy producers and environmentalists, food producers and food consumers, and even foreign governments and corporations. Some of them are concerned with American policy toward one country or region; others are concerned with more general American policies. These organizations lobby in the executive branch as well as in Congress. They try to exercise influence by contributing to congressional candidates' election campaigns, by stimulating public mailings to government officials, and by providing information to policy makers on detailed technical questions. They also form coalitions—with one another, with members of Congress, and with executive-branch officials.

An interest group of particular significance is made up of large corporations whose interests transcend national boundaries. Their size and their transnational nature suggest their potential economic and political significance. When we examine the details of particular cases, however, we find a mixed and complex pattern in their relations with American government policy makers. Those relations are often cooperative, but they are also often conflictual. Neither is the pawn of the other. Yet the activities of multinational corporations do have significant economic and political consequences. They have an impact on government policies, and they have an independent impact in other countries through their business activities.

The interests of big business, however, are sometimes ambiguous and often diverse. As a result, their executives' preferences are frequently ambivalent and conflicting. In fact, big businesses are sometimes politically inactive for such reasons. When they are politically active, they often oppose one another. Although they have frequently favored trade liberalization, often the active lobbying of particular business segments, in alliance with labor unions, has successfully supported protectionist trade policies. Individual corporations have encouraged military intervention and covert operations in other countries on many occasions. But the available evidence on attitudes and stock market behavior suggest that as a whole, big-business executives and other capitalists are not highly supportive of war as an instrument of policy.

Thus, the ruling elite model assumptions about the power of multinational corporations and big business are only partially supported by the evidence. They do have significant economic and political consequences; furthermore, those consequences have often included direct or indirect support for repressive foreign governments and for American intervention in foreign countries' internal political processes. Yet neither corporations' power nor their policy preferences are quite what the ruling elite model leads us to expect. Their activities are often restrained by the government; their influence is often countered by other interest groups; their opinions on policy issues are often divided; and their attitudes toward war are not very positive.

The diversity of their interests and preferences and the limits on their power, therefore, tend to conform with the pluralist model. Consistent with the pluralist model, the preferences of key economic interest groups can have significant effects on specific policies, especially in trade. For, as we shall see in a subsequent chapter, those preferences focus on trade issues in particular. Individual industries have been able to influence U.S. policy to their advantage. The steel, textile, footwear, sugar, and automobile industries have all been able to exert influence on U.S. policies that restrict imports in those industries. Yet, even in these instances, their influence has been constrained by other forces in the policy process, and, in fact, those industries have often suffered defeats as well as enjoyed victories in their attempts to protect their interests against the challenge of competitive imports.

Nevertheless, the political resources, activities, and impact of big business are generally far greater than those of any other interest group in American society. There may be some countervailing power because the United States is a pluralistic society with a pluralistic political system. But the political resources are not distributed equally among all the interest groups.

F I V E

Congress

By constitutional design and according to the democratic model, Congress should be responsive to public preferences; and it should have a substantial impact on policy. According to the pluralist model, we expect Congress to represent group interests and to provide a forum where conflicts among those interests are resolved by bargaining and compromising. We also expect power to be decentralized in Congress's internal procedures; and we further expect Congress to be in continual conflict with the executive branch as a result of the constitutional provisions for checks and balances. In contrast, the ruling elite model assumes that Congress is unresponsive to public preferences and interests; that its membership is widely agreed on conservative policies; that it is dominated by a few members; and that it is in a cooperative relationship with the president, the bureaucracy, and big business.

Thus, in this chapter, we are led to ask: What specific roles does Congress play in the policy process? How is Congress related to other participants in the policy process? What internal procedures does it follow? Which members are the most powerful? What impact on policy does it have?

RELATIONSHIP WITH THE PUBLIC AND INTEREST GROUPS

Most of the public chooses not to try to exercise influence on Congress. Half or less of the electorate votes in congressional elections, and only small fractions try to exert influence through other means, such as communicating directly with their representative or senator. Nevertheless, members of Congress are continually sensitive to general trends in public opinion and sometimes acutely sensitive to it on specific issues. Thus, Congress's tendency to cut foreign aid funding is, in part, a result of its perception that the program lacks public support. In 1978, Congress reduced a foreign aid authorization bill by substantial amounts in response to "the taxpayers' revolt" that began with a local property tax referendum in California. Its insistence on important changes in the Panama Canal Treaties in 1978 was also partly a response to public opposition to them. Finally, pertinent members of Congress are also sensitive to the complaints of workers and corporations in industries that claim to be suffering from import competition. Moreover, there is another, less direct, way that Congress can be responsive to public preferences, and that is through political parties.

Parties

The function of political parties in a democratic political system is to provide a means by which the public can influence policy. The public may not be active between elections, and it may not have detailed, informed preferences on specific foreign policy issues at election time; but it can, nevertheless, exercise influence on the general direction of policy through party voting.

However, the fact that many voters do not perceive differences between the two major parties constrains the extent to which the parties can provide a mechanism for representing general public preferences. Moreover, public-opinion studies have usually found only small differences between opinions of Republicans and Democrats on foreign policy issues. One study, conducted during the 1956 election campaign, found nearly identical proportions of Republicans and Democrats favoring increases (or decreases) in foreign aid and support for the United Nations. Democrats, however, were found to be slightly more supportive of defense spending and tariff reductions.[1] Again in 1968 and in 1972, Democrats and Republicans expressed similar divisions of opinion on foreign aid and on trade with Communist countries, although Democrats were slightly more supportive of trade with Communist countries and slightly less supportive of foreign aid. The Vietnam War also prompted only marginal party differences: In 1968, 6 percent more Democrats than Republicans wanted to withdraw from Vietnam. By 1972, however, 23 percent more Democrats than Republicans wanted to withdraw.[2]

The evidence on the attitudes and voting behavior of members of Congress indicates differences between the parties that are typically in the same direction as the differences in public opinion. In other words, the partisan divisions in the Congress tend to parallel the partisan divisions among the public.

A systematic study of dozens of votes in the House and the Senate from the late 1940s to the mid-1970s provides an abundance of pertinent evidence on these party differences.[3] Although there were differences between the House and Senate and there were years when the differences between the parties were small, some basic patterns were evident. Democrats were generally more supportive of the economic aid program, although by the 1970s the two parties were close on that issue. In the early post–World War II years, the Democrats were more supportive of the military assistance program; by the late 1960s and during the 1970s, the Republicans were more supportive. A similar switch occurred on defense spending, with the Republicans becoming more supportive than the Democrats by the early 1960s. For two decades, from the late 1940s to the late 1960s, the Democrats consistently favored low tariffs; the Republicans consistently favored high tariffs. But by 1970, the parties had switched positions on this issue as well, and the new pattern continued into the 1980s and 1990s.

Such instability in partisan voting was partly the result of presidential leadership. Republicans in Congress became more supportive of foreign aid and defense expenditures under the leadership of the Republican presidents Eisenhower, Nixon, and Ford. Northern Democrats followed the opposite pattern, partly in response to Truman's, Kennedy's, and Johnson's presidential leadership. Southern Democrats were usually in between, with a tendency to follow the Republican trend.

Thus, we do find that on these central foreign policy issues, Republicans and Democrats in Congress have typically taken opposite positions. But that conclusion should be qualified in two important respects. First, the party positions reversed on three of the issues and converged on the fourth by the 1970s. Second, there were important intraparty differences. Southern Democrats' votes usually diverged from the rest of the Democrats' votes. Southern Democrats have been more supportive of defense expenditures since the late 1960s and consistently less supportive of economic aid since the late 1940s. They have also generally been less supportive of military aid and free trade, but those differences have been smaller and less consistent. The Republican party has also been split along regional lines: Eastern Republicans often vote with nonsouthern Democrats, and noneastern Republicans often vote with southern Democrats.

Those inter- and intraparty divisions were evident in the 1978 Senate votes on the Panama Canal Treaties. The Democrats voted overwhelmingly in favor of ratifying the treaties, whereas most Republicans voted against ratification. But there were also splits within the parties. Over three-fourths of the eastern Republicans voted yea; nearly three-fourths of the other Republicans voted nay. Two-thirds of the southern Democrats voted in favor; but nine-tenths of the other Democrats did so.

Inter- and intraparty divisions are also often evident in the House, as for example in a 1984 vote on aid to El Salvador. Following President Reagan's lead, only 3 of 159 Republicans voted in favor of making the aid conditional on the Salvadoran government's achievement of certain specified objectives, while 125 of 258 Democrats voted in favor of the conditions. But within the ranks of the Democrats, 69 percent of the northerners voted in favor, but only 7 percent of the southerners voted in favor. Thus, the southern Democrats joined the Republicans in a coalition against the nonsouthern Democrats to defeat the measure and side with the Republican president.[4]

An analysis of fourteen key foreign policy votes in the House during one session found regional differences in the Republican as well as the Democratic party (Table 5–1).[5] Whereas the ideological split among the Democrats tends to pit conservative southerners against liberals from the rest of the country, the split in the Republican ranks tends to place more conservative westerners as well as southerners

TABLE 5–1   House Votes on Key Foreign Policy Issues by Party and Region*

VOTES	ALL DEMOCRATS	EASTERN	MIDWESTERN	WESTERN	SOUTHERN
"Liberal"	63%	74%	72%	77%	37%
"Conservative"	36	25	27	22	62

	ALL REPUBLICANS	EASTERN	MIDWESTERN	WESTERN	SOUTHERN
"Liberal"	32%	44%	39%	18%	19%
"Conservative"	67	56	60	81	80

*Fourteen votes in 1982 concerning: loans to Poland, MX missile (two votes), B-1 bomber, civil defense, Trident missiles, defense authorization, nuclear arms control policy, radio broadcasts to Cuba, NATO contributions, airfield in Honduras, economic sanctions against USSR, tariffs on products from Caribbean countries, and chemical weapons.
Source: Data compiled from *National Journal* 15, 9 (May 7, 1983), 936–52.

at odds with the less conservative eastern and middle-western members. (There are of course many individual exceptions to these tendencies in both parties.)

We find then, that although party differences in Congress have typically been substantial, they have been somewhat unstable over time and diluted by intraparty differences. Yet the congressional party differences on foreign policy issues have been much greater than the differences among the general public. These findings suggest that the two parties in Congress do offer voters a meaningful choice of general policy preferences but that the choice occasionally changes and that it is subject to significant regional variations. However, the shifting distributions in congressional and public opinions over time also suggest that the public partisans are changing their opinions in response to changes in the congressional partisans' opinions as well as vice versa. In other words, there is a mutual relationship: Congressional Democrats and Republicans are responsive to shifts in the opinions of Democratic and Republican citizens, but citizens' opinions are also responsive to shifts in congressional opinions.

Labor and Business

Congressional Democrats and Republicans are also responsive to interest-group preferences. The shifts in congressional voting on trade legislation provide an instructive illustration.[6] In 1962, labor groups supported legislation to lower tariffs; later, in 1970 and again in 1974, they opposed similar legislation. By the 1980s, labor organizations were actively supporting a variety of protectionist measures. The votes of the Democrats in Congress, especially the nonsoutherners, matched the trend. In 1962, approximately 90 percent of the nonsouthern Democratic votes in the House and in the Senate were in favor of trade liberalization; in 1970, half favored trade liberalization; by 1974, less than half were for lower tariffs. By the 1980s, House Democrats in particular were voting heavily in favor of protectionist bills.

Meanwhile, big business and the Republicans in Congress were bec
more supportive of trade liberalization. In 1962, the major business-lobbying orga
zations were divided on the issue; by the 1970s, they were solidly behind trade
liberalization (partly because of the emergence of large multinational corporations
that benefit from free trade). The Republicans in the House and Senate followed the
trend. Whereas they voted overwhelmingly for protectionist trade policies in the early
1960s, they voted overwhelmingly for liberalized trade policies in the 1970s and
1980s (Table 5–2).

TABLE 5–2 Trade Legislation Votes in Congress by Party Affiliation

YEAR/VOTE	DEM.	HOUSE REP.	ALL	DEM.	SENATE REP.	ALL
1930						
Free trade	90%	9%	41%	86%	22%	49%
Restriction	10%	91%	59%	14%	78%	51%
	(147)	(228)	(375)	(36)	(50)	(86)
1936						
Free trade	96%	2%	71%	91%	15%	63%
Restriction	4%	98%	29%	9%	85%	37%
	(280)	(101)	(381)	(56)	(33)	(89)
1945						
Free trade	94%	19%	61%	88%	48%	72%
Restriction	6%	81%	39%	12%	52%	28%
	(217)	(173)	(390)	(43)	(31)	(74)
1949						
Free trade	79%	7%	62%	98%	45%	77%
Restriction	21%	93%	38%	2%	55%	23%
	(297)	(90)	(387)	(48)	(33)	(81)
1958						
Free trade	72%	56%	65%	60%	80%	70%
Restriction	28%	44%	35%	40%	20%	30%
	(221)	(193)	(414)	(45)	(45)	(90)
1962						
Free trade	83%	75%	60%	98%	76%	73%
Restriction	17%	25%	40%	2%	24%	27%
	(254)	(170)	(424)	(57)	(29)	(86)
1970						
Free trade	38%	51%	43%	66%	64%	65%
Restriction	62%	49%	57%	34%	36%	35%
	(220)	(160)	(380)	(53)	(36)	(89)
1974						
Free trade	48%	89%	66%	94%	97%	95%
Restriction	52%	11%	34%	6%	3%	5%
	(233)	(179)	(412)	(48)	(33)	(81)
1982						
Free trade	25%	75%	47%	no comparable		
Restriction	75%	25%	53%	vote		
	(229)	(174)	(403)			

	M.	HOUSE REP.	ALL	DEM.	SENATE REP.	ALL
Free trade	11%	52%	27%		no comparable	
Restriction	89%	48%	73%		vote	
	(217)	(137)	(354)			
1988						
Free trade	1%	61%	26%	2%	76%	36%
Restriction	99%	39%	74%	98%	24%	63%
	(246)	(173)	(419)	(53)	(46)	(99)

Sources: Computed from data in Robert A. Pastor, *Congress and the Politics of U.S. Foreign Economic Policy, 1929–1976* (Berkeley: University of California Press, 1980), pp. 81, 97; Congressional Quarterly, *Congress and the Nation, 1945–1964* (Washington, DC: Congressional Quarterly, 1965), pp. 193–203; *Congressional Quarterly Almanac* 26 (1970), 72-H, 69-S; 29 (1973), 148-H; 30 (1974), 78-S; 35 (1979), 86-H, 36-S; 38 (1982), 128-H; *Congressional Quarterly Weekly Report* 42, 31 (August 4, 1984), 1928; *Congressional Quarterly Almanac* 44 (1988), 26-H, 20-S.

In sum, trends in Democratic and Republican voting in Congress have tended to parallel trends in public and interest-group preferences. Although the congressional party leaders are often leading public and interest-group opinions, they are also often following them.

RELATIONSHIP WITH THE EXECUTIVE BRANCH

Shared Power

Several constitutional provisions give Congress specific functions in foreign policy making: declaration of war, appropriation of funds, ratification of treaties, regulation of foreign trade, and confirmation of appointments to high-level positions in the executive branch. But the executive branch is very much involved in each of these five functions. As commander-in-chief, the president is involved in war making. Requests for funds originate in the executive agencies and are reviewed and decided upon by the president, who recommends them to Congress; and the executive agencies spend the funds that are appropriated by Congress. Treaties are negotiated by the executive branch and then submitted to the Senate for ratification. Foreign trade agreements are negotiated by the executive branch, under authority delegated by Congress. The president nominates ambassadors and cabinet and subcabinet officials, and then the Senate decides whether to confirm those nominations.

Thus, the Congress shares authority in its performance of these functions with the executive branch in general and the president in particular. These facts about congressional-executive relations in foreign policy making require modification of the common notion that their relationship is one of separated powers or functions. In fact, only the institutions are separated; the powers (or functions) are actually shared, not separated.[7]

In any case, a constitutionally based interpretation of congressional involvement in policy making and its relationship with the executive branch provides only a superficial understanding of congressional power. This approach refers only to authority, or formalized potential power, rather than actual power. Furthermore, there is a constant struggle between Congress and the executive branch over authority in foreign policy making. The struggle may wax and wane over time, but there is nevertheless a constant and continuing tension.[8] The tension with the executive branch and the limitations on Congress's power are evident in several congressional roles in policy making.

Declaration of War

Since World War II, there have been two wars and numerous military interventions or other acts of war without any formal congressional declaration. These cases include not only Korea and Vietnam but also Lebanon in 1958, the Congo in 1964 and 1967, the Dominican Republic in 1965, Cambodia in 1970, Lebanon in 1983–1984, Grenada in 1983, Panama in 1989, and the Middle East in 1991. In the case of the Middle East war, however, Congress passed a resolution authorizing the president to use troops in support of the UN resolution—a Congressional measure that was virtually a declaration of war. There have also been cases of direct support of military operations, as in Guatemala in 1954, Cuba in 1961, and Nicaragua in 1984.

In several of these cases and on other occasions, however, Congress did pass joint resolutions that provided support in advance for some kind of presidential action. In the case of Vietnam, Congress passed the 1965 Gulf of Tonkin Resolution, which provided support in advance for administration action. It said, in part, that the Congress approved of the ''determination of the President... to take all necessary measures to repel any armed attack against the forces of the United States and to prevent further aggression.'' In 1955, Congress passed the Formosa Straits Resolution, which authorized the president to ''employ the armed forces of the United States as he deem(ed) necessary'' to defend Formosa. Two years later in 1957, Congress passed a Middle East Resolution, which also authorized the president to ''employ the forces of the United States as he deem(ed) necessary'' to protect the area against ''overt armed aggression from any nation controlled by international communism.''

Furthermore, in the cases of both Vietnam and Korea, Congress passed defense-appropriation bills and supplemental appropriations that included funds specifically for the war, thereby providing at least tacit consent. During the Vietnam War in particular, there was considerable controversy over the legal question of whether these resolutions and appropriations constituted the equivalent of a declaration of war and provided a legal basis for the administration's conduct of it—legal questions that were never resolved by the Supreme Court. However, the practical effect of the Gulf of Tonkin Resolution became clear in 1971, when Congress voted to rescind it. The Nixon administration simply said that the resolution was not necessary to provide a legal basis for the conduct of the war; the president, they argued, had sufficient constitutional authority as commander-in-chief to continue American involvement in it.

Apart from formal congressional declarations or resolutions or appropriations, members of Congress have sometimes become involved in war policy making through consultations with the president. In 1954, when the French were being defeated at Dien Bien Phu, President Eisenhower was considering the possibility of sending American combat troops into Southeast Asia; he solicited the advice of several leaders of Congress before reaching a decision. The congressional leaders advised the president that he should intervene with combat troops only if he could obtain a promise of active support from several other countries. Since that promise was not forthcoming, Eisenhower decided against military intervention. In that particular case, a limited form of congressional involvement clearly had an impact on the decision.[9]

In numerous other instances, however, Congress was not involved even in this limited way. Toward the end of his administration, Eisenhower gave preliminary approval to a CIA plan to support an invasion of Cuba by Cuban refugees in an attempt to overthrow Fidel Castro. Eisenhower gave his approval without consulting with Congress; in early 1961, President Kennedy decided to go ahead with the plan, also without consulting Congress.[10] A year and a half later, in the fall of 1962, President Kennedy and his advisers held highly secret discussions to formulate a response to the placement of Russian missiles in Cuba. The president decided to establish a naval blockade around Cuba without consulting any members of Congress. He merely informed selected members of Congress of his decision a few hours before he appeared on television.[11]

It was the Vietnam War, however, that prompted Congress to define and formalize limits on presidents' authority to deploy combat troops abroad. The War Powers Act of 1973 was the most significant development in this respect, but there were several other congressional moves in this direction starting in the late 1960s.[12] Many times, Congress attempted to pass resolutions that would have required the president to withdraw troops from Southeast Asia; the most prominent among them was the Hatfield-McGovern Resolution. But they all failed to pass.

In 1969, Congress did pass the National Commitments Resolution, with a provision that the United States could undertake a commitment, such as a pledge to provide combat troops to a foreign government, only with the specific approval of Congress. That resolution, though, was only a "sense of the Senate resolution," which simply registered the Senate's majority sentiment; resolutions that only record the "sense of the Senate" have no binding legal effect.

In December 1970, Congress passed the Cooper-Church Amendment, which prohibited the use of American ground troops or American instruction of troops in Cambodia. This action was a reaction to President Nixon's decision to send American troops into Cambodia in the spring of that year. However, by the time the measure was passed in Congress, the administration had already withdrawn the troops, so it did not have any direct effect.

A year later, Congress passed the Mansfield Amendment, which stated that it was the "sense of Congress" that U.S. military operations in Indochina should cease "at the earliest practicable date" and that a "date certain" should be set for troop withdrawal. Neither did this general and nonbinding "sense of Congress" measure have any effect.

In 1973, Congress passed two measures that did impose legal obligations on the president. The first pertained specifically to Southeast Asia. It was the Church Amendment, which prohibited any American combat activity in North Vietnam, South Vietnam, Laos, or Cambodia. Although American ground combat had already ended early in the year, the air combat that was continuing in Laos and Cambodia had to be terminated by August 15.

Later in 1973, Congress passed the War Powers Act (Public Law 93-148) over the veto of President Nixon. This act provides that the president can deploy American combat troops abroad without prior congressional approval such as a declaration of war—but that he can do so only if he finds that the United States is threatened with an attack or that it is necessary in order to protect American troops or citizens abroad. The act also provides that the president must consult with Congress "in every possible instance" before he makes such a decision (a restriction that clearly gives the president an opportunity *not* to consult with Congress in advance). The act also provides that the president has to report to the House and the Senate within forty-eight hours after taking action; he must provide information about the circumstances in which he acted and the nature of the action he took. These provisions, then, clearly provide the president with ample opportunity to take the initiative and allow the Congress only a passive role—at least in the initial stage of an incident.

Other provisions in the War Powers Act, however, enable Congress to restrict the deployment of troops. Within sixty days, it can pass a concurrent resolution prohibiting the continuation of the troop deployment, and this concurrent resolution cannot be vetoed by the president. After a period of sixty days from the time of the initial action, Congress must pass a concurrent resolution to permit the continuation of the troop deployment. In other words, in the first sixty days, Congress must take a positive action to prohibit the president from continuing the deployment, whereas after the first sixty days it must take positive action to allow the president to continue the deployment. There is another provision, though, that qualifies the sixty-day limit; the president can have an additional thirty days to withdraw the troops if he declares that the time is necessary to accomplish their withdrawal safely.

The constitutionality of a portion of the War Powers Act (and many other laws as well) was cast into doubt by a 1983 Supreme Court ruling that legislative vetoes are unconstitutional.[13] As for the War Powers Act in particular, this ruling means that it is doubtful whether Congress can legally pass a concurrent resolution that would force a president to withdraw troops in the absence of specific congressional authorization for their initial deployment.

There has also been considerable controversy about other aspects of the War Powers Act. Many people have contended that it represents an abdication of Congress's authority to declare war rather than a limitation of the president's war-making authority. Senator Thomas Eagleton, one of the original promoters of a restriction on the president's power, voted against the War Powers Act because he thought its effect would be exactly the opposite of his intentions. He and others contended that the act formally conveys war-making authority to the president that did not exist before. Supporters of the act argue that it restricts presidential authority to a short period of time and that it constrains presidents to consider possible congressional opposition to a prospective deployment of troops.

Soon after the passage of the act, there were two occasions when its reporting procedures were implemented. In the spring of 1974, troops were sent to Vietnam to facilitate the withdrawal of the Americans still in Saigon and at other American bases in the face of the imminent defeat of the South Vietnamese government. Technically, the president was not required to implement the reporting procedures of the War Powers Act, since it specifically exempted actions in Vietnam from its provisions. Nevertheless, President Ford sent reports to Congress within forty-eight hours. The second occasion was the late summer of 1975, when Cambodia commandeered the American commercial ship *Mayaguez*. In that instance, President Ford ordered American marines to an island where he thought the *Mayaguez* crew members were being held, and he also ordered attacks on mainland military facilities. Although there was widespread support in Congress for the action, many doubt whether he had abided by the consultation procedures of the War Powers Act. The administration insisted that it had consulted with the Democratic leader in the Senate, Mike Mansfield; but Mansfield said that he had been told of the decision only after it had been made. In any case, the president did submit a report within forty-eight hours.

The most important and interesting case in which the War Powers Act became an issue was the placement of American troops in Lebanon in 1983–1984.[14] The troops were initially sent to Lebanon in August 1983 to provide security for the withdrawal of the Palestinian Liberation Organization (PLO) from Lebanon after their defeat by the Israeli troops that had invaded Lebanon. The U.S. troops were removed within a few weeks. But they were then reintroduced after the assassination of the Lebanese president and the massacre by Lebanese groups of hundreds of Palestinians in refugee camps that were in areas of Beirut controlled by Israeli troops. The Reagan administration explicitly denied that the War Powers Act was applicable, but the president did sign the Lebanon Emergency Assistance Act which included a stipulation that the president should obtain "statutory authorization from Congress" for "any substantial expansion" of the U.S. military presence in Lebanon. The administration also submitted reports acknowledged to be "consistent with" War Powers Act provisions. Though he continued to deny that the War Powers Act was applicable, the president did negotiate and eventually sign a congressional resolution that specifically authorized him to keep the troops in Lebanon for only eighteen months. After 230 of the American marines were killed and as congressional and public opposition to the continued deployment of the troops in Lebanon increased, the president withdrew the troops from Beirut in February 1984 and thus undermined any further moves by Congress to invoke the War Powers Act.

A summary of presidential actions pertinent to the Lebanon case, and other cases as well, is provided in Table 5–3. It is evident that presidents have consistently denied the formal legal applicability of the War Powers Act, while at the same time they have been at least somewhat responsive to the political need to keep Congress informed of their actions.

A parallel relationship between the president and the Congress also exists as a result of the International Emergency Economic Powers Act. That act concerns the imposition of economic sanctions and other economic measures taken during war-

TABLE 5-3 Cases in Which War Powers Act Became an Issue

CASE	PRESIDENT	PRES. ACKNOWLEDGED W.P.A. APPLICABILITY	PRES. CONSULTED WITH CONG.	PRES. INFORMED CONG. IN ADVANCE	PRES. REPORTED TO CONG. AFTER EVENT
Vietnam rescues (1975)	Ford	No	No	Yes	Yes
Mayaguez crew rescue (1975)	Ford	No	No/Yes*	Yes	Yes
Iran hostage rescue (1980)	Carter	No	No	No	Yes
El Salvador advisors (1981)	Reagan	No	Yes†	—	—
Grenada invasion (1983)	Reagan	No	No	Yes	Yes
Lebanon (1983–1984)	Reagan	No	No	No	Yes
Panama (1989)	Bush	No	No	Yes	Yes
Middle East (1991)	Bush	No	Yes	Yes	Yes

*Whether consultation occurred is disputed.
†Presidential-congressional agreement reached that number and role of advisers would be limited and that War Powers Resolution would not apply.

Source: National Journal 16, 20 (May 19, 1984), 989–93; *Congressional Quarterly* 49, 1 (January 5, 1991), 33–44.

time. Thus, section 204 provides that "the President, in every possible instance, shall consult with the Congress before exercising any of the authorities granted by this title and shall consult regularly with the Congress so long as such authorities are exercised."

Treaties and Executive Agreements

In 1920, in a dramatic exercise of its power, the Senate refused to ratify the Versailles Treaty, which included the World War I peace treaty with Germany and the covenant of the League of Nations. But such a dramatic exercise of its power has been a rather rare event. In two centuries, the Senate has failed to ratify only twenty treaties. It has ratified over twelve hundred. Since 1945 alone, it has ratified over five hundred and killed only two. Furthermore, the Senate normally ratifies treaties by substantially more than the necessary two-thirds of those voting. For instance, the 94th Congress ratified all thirty-three treaties submitted to it by favorable votes of more than 80 percent of those voting. All but five of the thirty-three were ratified by unanimous votes. Between ten and twenty are ratified in most sessions.[15]

On the other hand, the Senate has occasionally qualified its ratification by amendments or reservations to treaties. Before it ratified the Panama Canal Treaties in 1978, the Senate adopted twenty-four amendments, conditions, reservations, and understandings. One of them, named after its sponsor, Senator DeConcini, imposed an important change in the terms of the treaty; it provided that the United States could "use military force in Panama" if the canal were closed. Moreover, treaties are sometimes allowed to lie dormant when neither the president nor the Senate is willing to push for their ratification. This inaction occurred for a Genocide Convention, the International Covenant for Civil and Political Rights, and several nuclear arms control treaties.[16]

For the past several decades, the treaty ratification process has been substantially circumvented by memoranda of understanding and by "executive agreements." The Supreme Court has declared that executive agreements have the same legal standing as treaties, even though they are not ratified or otherwise specifically approved by congressional action. The vast majority are "statutory executive agreements" that the executive branch has negotiated with a foreign government on the basis of a congressional statute giving the executive branch the authority to do so. But other executive agreements have been reached without any such congressionally delegated authority. There are typically two hundred or more such agreements per year.[17]

Some of these executive agreements have entailed major policy decisions.[18] They have included, for example, the significant World War II agreements at Cairo, Tehran, Yalta, and Potsdam, and more recent important air-base agreements with Spain, Portugal, and Bahrain. Furthermore, executive agreements have often been kept secret from Congress. An investigation by a subcommittee of the Senate Foreign Relations Committee found that the United States had secret agreements with Ethiopia, Laos, Thailand, South Korea, Spain, and other countries.[19]

As a reaction to the number, importance, and secrecy of executive agreements,

Congress passed the Case Amendment in 1972. It requires the president to send executive agreements to the House Foreign Affairs Committee and the Senate Foreign Relations Committee within sixty days after they are signed. Those committees, however, cannot act on the executive agreements, either to accept them or to reject them; nor can Congress as a whole act on them. Rather, the two committees are given copies of the agreements only for the purpose of being informed about their contents. Furthermore, the president can request that the committees keep the contents of the agreements secret from the rest of Congress. However, there has also been a change in the procedures prior to the initiation of a negotiation that might lead to an executive agreement or a treaty: The State Department consults with the leaders of Congress and the relevant committees in the House and the Senate to determine whether the negotiations will be formalized in an executive agreement or a treaty.

Appropriations

In general, Congress must approve expenditures before executive agencies can make them. Congress passes authorization bills that establish spending limits and appropriations bills that establish funds for agency use. In the exercise of this power, Congress sometimes imposes substantial cuts in the agencies' requests or restricts the kinds of expenditures that are permitted. The budget requests for the operations of the State Department and the Agency for International Development, in particular, have frequently been subjected to careful scrutiny and detailed control in the subcommittees of the House Appropriations Committee.

In contrast, Congress has typically had only a marginal impact on the defense budget. Although it does occasionally make some changes in the total amount (and in the distribution of the total among kinds of expenditures), Congress usually changes the administration's total request by only 1 or 2 percent.[20] Congress as a whole has exercised no direct influence in the appropriations process for the Central Intelligence Agency. The details of the intelligence agencies' budgets are actually kept secret from the vast majority of the members of Congress. Those figures are known only to a few members on the intelligence, armed services, and appropriations committees.

Even when Congress has appropriated money for a specific purpose, an executive agency has sometimes not spent it or has spent it for other purposes.[21] In 1961, when Congress appropriated $700 million for manned bombers that the administration did not want, Secretary of Defense McNamara announced that none of the money would be spent. In the late 1960s, during the height of the Vietnam War, the Pentagon shifted several million dollars of funds appropriated by Congress for Taiwan to Vietnam and then later asked Congress for a supplemental appropriation to replace the funds that had been diverted. In the fiscal years of 1969, 1970, and 1971, the Navy spent $110 million more than its appropriations for personnel moving expenses.

In an effort to gain more control over executive expenditures, Congress passed the Budget Reform Act of 1974.* This law increased congressional control over

---

*The Nixon administration's refusal to spend funds appropriated by Congress for education, health, and pollution control was the immediate catalyst for passage of this act.

expenditures through its provision concerning impoundment (an administration decision not to spend funds appropriated by Congress). Both houses of Congress must now approve of any proposed "rescission" within forty-five days after being notified by the president of his intention not to spend the funds. In the absence of congressional approval, the president must spend the funds.

In another attempt to gain greater control over the appropriations process, specifically concerning weapons development, Congress passed a 1975 amendment to the Arms Control and Disarmament Act. It requires executive agencies to submit "arms control impact statements" to Congress along with their budget requests for weapons development. The initiative for the preparation of these impact statements, however, lies in the agencies that are responsible for the weapons development programs and in the National Security Council. Furthermore, the actual impact statements are prepared by the same agency developing the weapon, and the early impact statements were superficial—in many cases only a few sentences long. As a result, they did not substantially affect the weapons procurement budgeting process.

Oversight

Congress also monitors the actual expenditures of funds and generally oversees the administration of programs and policies by executive agencies. The specific missions of the General Accounting Office (an agency of Congress) are to audit executive agencies' expenditures and to evaluate their programs. It often, however, encounters substantial difficulties as it seeks information from the executive agencies. Table 5–4 contains an account of its attempt to obtain information about a

TABLE 5–4   Chronology of a Congressional Attempt to Obtain Information from Executive Agencies

March 31: Congress's General Accounting Office (GAO) asked the State Department for a copy of an agreement between the American government and the Australian government concerning the delivery of Australian trucks and trailers to Cambodia. The State Department said the request should go to the Defense Department.

April 6: The Defense Department told the GAO that State Department clearance would have to be obtained before it could be released. The State Department said permission from the Australian government would have to be obtained before it could be released.

April 14: The State Department told the GAO that the Defense Department had asked the Australian government for permission to release it. The Defense Department told the GAO it had not asked the Australian government for permission.

April 15: The State Department told the GAO that the Defense Department had received permission to release a copy of the agreement from the Australian government but that the Defense Department had to send a written request to the State Department before it could release it.

April 19: The Defense Department told the GAO that "more internal coordination was needed" before it could release a copy of the agreement.

April 28: The Defense Department told the GAO it had forgotten about the GAO request for the document.

May 5: The Defense Department sent a copy of the agreement to the GAO but said it could not be made public because it was classified (A copy in the Defense Department files was not stamped as classified.)

transfer of trucks and trailers from Australia to Cambodia. Only after repeated inquiries extending over more than a month was it able to obtain a copy of the agreement between the American government and the Australian government, and even then it was not able to make the agreement public because the Defense Department said it was classified.

Another way in which Congress seeks to oversee the administration's implementation of legislation is through committee hearings, but these are not always effective. One problem is that many potential witnesses are prevented from testifying on the basis of executive privilege, the claim that certain communications within the executive branch are privileged and do not have to be divulged. Although the practice of claiming executive privilege extends back to the early period of the country, it has been used more widely in recent years, especially in the area of foreign affairs. It means, for instance, that the special assistant to the president for national security affairs and other high-level presidential advisers do not have to testify before congressional committees and subcommittees.

Furthermore, when officials from executive agencies do testify, their testimony may not be particularly helpful. It may be general or evasive, or it may rely on analysis that is deceptive or irrelevant. Often, witnesses do present candid and even critical testimony about a program within an executive agency. The case of A. Ernest Fitzgerald, however, illustrates the pressures that are sometimes put on witnesses not to be informative. Fitzgerald was a high-ranking civilian cost analyst with the air force who testified before the Subcommittee on Economy in Government about the air force C5-A jet transport plane. He testified that the C5-A program was encountering cost overruns of approximately $2 billion. As a result of this testimony, the air force informed him that his position had been eliminated as unnecessary and that he would be transferred—although the air force planned to hire an outside consultant to replace him. Fitzgerald took the case to the Civil Service Commission, which eventually ruled that his position had to be restored and that he should be granted back pay. A few years later, after he had been reinstated, Fitzgerald was ordered by the air force not to appear before a Senate subcommittee hearing on wasteful military spending and was then subpoenaed by the subcommittee in an attempt to circumvent his air force superiors.[22]

Congressional oversight is also limited by the fact that the committees and subcommittees responsible for oversight are frequently on friendly terms with the agencies whose activities they are overseeing. Perhaps the epitome of this relationship was in the intelligence oversight subcommittees of the armed services committees. The membership of those subcommittees consisted primarily of friends of the CIA, who presumably looked less critically on CIA activities than most other members of Congress would have. Indeed, some people even questioned whether there was genuine oversight of the intelligence agencies, for the subcommittees met to hear testimony from executive agency witnesses only rarely and in some years hardly at all.

This cooperative relationship, however, was altered in 1975, when the House and Senate created select committees to investigate the activities of the CIA and other intelligence agencies and determine if they had abused their power.[23] These select committees were established partly because there was a widespread feeling that the existing intelligence subcommittees were unlikely to conduct thorough investigations (they had been responsible for oversight during the period when the alleged abuses by the intelligence agencies had taken place). In 1984, Senators Goldwater and Moynihan, who were chairman and vice-chairman of the Senate committee, publicly denounced the Reagan administration for failing to inform the committee fully about its involvement in the mining of Nicaragua's harbors. This incident was part of a longer-term dispute between the CIA's Director at the time, William Casey, and key members of Congress, who opposed the general thrust of the administration's policies in Central America as well as the particulars of CIA-supported operations. Eventually, such concerns led Congress to cut off funds for those operations. The subsequent Iran-Contra scandal, involving transfers of funds obtained illegally from arms sales to Iran into support for the contras in Nicaragua, led to extensive congressional hearings into the Reagan administration's handling of covert operations in Central America.

Confirmation of Nominations

The president is occasionally unable to obtain Senate confirmation of a person he has nominated to a high administration position. A notable case was the Senate's refusal to confirm President Bush's nomination of former Senator John Tower to be secretary of defense. Despite his undisputed knowledge of defense issues and his previous membership on the Senate Armed Services Committee, questions about Tower's personal life were enough to cause his defeat in the confirmation process.

Previous administrations also occasionally encountered sufficient opposition for them to withdraw nominations or decide not to submit names for formal consideration. The Nixon administration decided not to nominate Paul Nitze to be the assistant secretary of defense for international security affairs in view of the opposition from Senator Barry Goldwater. Goldwater was a member of the Senate Armed Services Committee, which would have made its recommendation to the full Senate. There have been other occasions when an informal poll or consultations with key committee members have revealed so much opposition that the president decided not to proceed with a formal nomination.

Sometimes a nominee faces considerable opposition in the Senate and is subjected to hostile public scrutiny but is then confirmed anyway, on the assumption that the president should generally be able to appoint whomever he wishes to his administration. William Clark, President Reagan's nominee to be deputy secretary of state, for instance, was given a factual quiz in his confirmation hearings that revealed an almost complete lack of knowledge and experience in foreign affairs; yet, he was confirmed to be the second-ranking State Department official. He was later appointed the president's special assistant for national security affairs, a position not requiring Senate confirmation.

Sometimes the Senate Foreign Relations Committee refuses to support a nomination, but the full Senate confirms it anyway. This was true of President Reagan's nominee to be head of the Arms Control and Disarmament Agency, Kenneth Adelman. Even though the committee found him to be "not qualified" because of a lack of experience and knowledge, the full Senate approved the nomination.

There is rarely sufficient opposition to prevent presidents from obtaining the confirmation of the vast majority of the people they want in their administrations. Confirmation hearings are often rather friendly and uncritical proceedings in which the nominee is not subjected to careful scrutiny and does not have his or her views on policy issues analyzed in any detail. Indeed, except for cabinet-level officials, Congress typically has little interest in the confirmation process. Subcabinet officials and other officials routinely receive *pro forma* confirmation of their appointments. Moreover, many high-level appointments in the executive branch are not subject to Senate confirmation at all. The special assistant to the president for national security affairs and members of the White House staff are not subject to the confirmation process within Congress.

INTERNAL PROCEDURES AND ORGANIZATION

Several characteristics of Congress itself limit its influence in its relations with the executive branch. Other characteristics decentralize influence within Congress.

Voting on Issues

Members of Congress confront an enormous number and variety of issues on which they are expected to vote. Table 5–5 lists the more than one hundred roll-call votes on foreign policy issues during one year in the House of Representatives. That list readily suggests the difficulty in becoming an expert about such a large number of diverse topics. Yet even that long list does not fully indicate the dimensions of the problem, since it includes only roll-call votes on the floor and since it excludes a large number of votes that were at least partly foreign policy votes (such as appropriations for the Agriculture Department).

The formal training and career background of most members inevitably limit their expertise. Few of them have the educational or occupational background that would enable them to deal knowledgeably with international economics, weapons technology, environmental pollution, and energy issues. On the other hand, members

TABLE 5–5 House Roll-Call Votes on Foreign Policy Issues in One Session

Defense Department authorizations and appropriations (65 votes)
Nuclear arms treaties (3 votes)
State Department, Peace Corps, United States Information Agency authorizations and appropriations (4 votes)
Economic and military assistance authorizations and appropriations (5 votes)
Contra aid in Nicaragua (5 votes)
Intelligence authorizations (1 vote)
Trade (13 votes)
South Africa sanctions (6 votes)
U.S.–USSR Fishery Agreement (1 vote)

Source: Compiled by the author from *Congressional Quarterly Almanac* 44 (1988), Appendix, "House Roll Call Votes."

of Congress do acquire a degree of expertise over time as they develop special policy interests and become immersed in committee work. Indeed, policy area specialization—especially through committee assignments—is a major source of influence for individual members of Congress. When particular members gain a reputation in Congress as being relatively expert on specific issues, they become much more influential on those issues than most of their colleagues.

Committees

Many committees have responsibilities in any given issue area. For instance, a dozen Senate committees are involved in foreign economic policy making, and nearly fifty subcommittees are involved in policies affecting the less developed countries. In fact, virtually every committee in Congress is involved in foreign policy issues. An important consequence of the large number of committees and subcommittees involved in issues is a decentralization of authority and influence among many different power centers (Table 5–6).

Furthermore, influence within committees has been decentralized somewhat by a slight erosion in the seniority system. According to the seniority system, the member from the majority party who has been on the committee the longest is normally the chairperson. There have been a few instances in recent years, however, in which some other member of the majority party has been elected chairperson instead. In 1975, the House Armed Services Committee chairman lost his position because many members felt he had abused his power. In the same year, the House Ways and Means Committee chairman lost his position because his public behavior had become an embarrassment to Congress. And in 1977, the House Appropriations Subcommittee chair on military construction was given up when the chairman was censured by the House for unethical conflicts of interest. In 1985, a relatively junior member of the House Armed Services Committee became its chair.

Staffs

Influence is further decentralized because some of the most influential people in Congress are staff members. Many staff members are highly trained experts in complex technical fields. Many have years of experience in Congress or in previous positions in executive agencies or universities working on issues in those fields. Indeed, on many issues a few key staff members are much more influential than most representatives and senators.

Furthermore, Congress has substantially increased its staffs—not only for its individual members and committees but also in the Congressional Research Service (which conducts studies of selected legislative issues) and in the General Accounting Office (which oversees executive operations on behalf of Congress). Congress created two new staff agencies in the early 1970s. One of them, the Congressional Budget Office, provides more detailed analyses of the budget than members of Congress previously had available to them except from the executive branch. The other new staff agency is the Office of Technology Assessment, which provides analyses of technological issues and programs that often concern foreign policy. For

TABLE 5–6   Congressional Committees and Subcommittees Involved in Foreign Policy Making

HOUSE	SENATE
Foreign Affairs (8 subcommittees)	Foreign Relations (7 subcommittees)
Armed Services (7 subcommittees)	Armed Services (6 subcommittees)
Select Intelligence (3 subcommittees)	Select Intelligence
Appropriations (subcommittees: Defense; Foreign Operations; Military Construction; State, Commerce, Justice, and the Judiciary; others)	Appropriations (subcommittees: Defense; Foreign Operations; Military Construction; State, Commerce, Justice, and the Judiciary; others)
Budget	Budget
Ways and Means (subcommittee: Trade)	Finance (subcommittees: International Debt; International Trade)
Interstate and Foreign Commerce	Commerce, Science and Transportation (subcommittee: Foreign Commerce and Tourism)
Banking, Finance and Urban Affairs (subcommittee: International Development, Finance, Trade, and Monetary Policy)	Banking, Housing and Urban Affairs (subcommittee: International Finance and Monetary Policy)
Agriculture (subcommittee: Department Operations, Research, and Foreign Agriculture)	Agriculture, Nutrition and Forestry (subcommittee: Domestic and Foreign Marketing and Product Promotion)
Government Operations (subcommittee: Legislation and National Security)	Governmental Affairs
Judiciary (subcommittee: Immigration, Refugees, and International Law)	Judiciary (subcommittee: Immigration and Refugee Affairs)
Science, Space, and Technology	Energy and Natural Resources
Interior and Insular Affairs	Environment and Public Works
Merchant Marine and Fisheries	
Small Business (subcommittee: Exports, Tax Policy, and Special Problems)	Small Business (subcommittee: Export Expansion)
Veterans' Affairs	Veterans' Affairs
Select Hunger	

Joint Economic Committee
(subcommittees: International Economic Policy; National Security Economics; Economic Growth, Trade and Taxes)

Source: Congressional Quarterly Weekly Report, Supplement to Vol. 47, No. 18 (May 6, 1989), 8–69.

instance, in 1976, it supervised a study for the Senate Foreign Relations Committee of estimates of American casualties in a nuclear war. The study concluded that the Defense Department analysis provided in testimony by the secretary of defense was based on questionable assumptions and methods and that it should be redone; as a result, the estimate was substantially revised. The Office of Technology Assessment has also provided several studies of energy problems bearing on foreign policy, and it sponsored studies of nuclear terrorism and the consequences of nuclear war.[24]

Altogether, these staff additions increased the total number of congressional employees from five thousand in the 1950s to twenty-thousand in the 1970s.

Budget Process

One of the most important changes Congress made in its procedures during the 1970s was in the budget process. Prior to the new budget process, Congress had never explicitly established a total budget with subtotals for categories of expenditures, such as defense. In the new procedures, however, a budget resolution provides a total budget figure and also subtotals for each of a dozen functional categories, including international affairs and national defense.

The budget resolution is formulated in the House and Senate Budget Committees and then submitted to the full House and Senate. Differences in the House and Senate versions are reconciled in a conference committee, as in the regular legislative process, and then resubmitted to the two houses for final adoption. Once the budget resolution is adopted, its total and subtotal figures constitute targets for appropriations in subsequent congressional bills. But this is only a small part of the budget process in Congress, and the budget resolution figures are only nonbinding targets for the authorization and appropriations bills.

The specific and legally binding expenditure figures are contained in authorization and appropriations bills. Authorization bills for several major categories of expenditures go to "legislative" committees in both houses for review and revision before going to the floor for House and Senate action. For instance, the State Department authorization bill goes to the House Foreign Affairs Committee and the Senate Foreign Relations Committee; the weapons procurement authorization bill goes to the Armed Services Committees in both houses. Once an authorization bill passes both houses, its dollar amounts only establish ceilings for expenditures; the bill does not actually enable agencies to spend the money.

An appropriations bill must also be passed. But appropriations bills go to the Appropriations Committees and their subcommittees rather than the legislative committees. For instance, appropriations bills for the State Department go to the appropriations subcommittee for the State Department (and several other agencies) in each house, whereas appropriations bills for the Defense Department go to the defense appropriations subcommittees.

In sum, there are three separate but interdependent budget processes involving three sets of committees in each house: those concerning the budget resolutions, authorization bills, and appropriations bills. Although this complicated process facilitates careful scrutiny of the budget, it also further decentralizes influence in Congress.

CONCLUSION

Congress is clearly a highly decentralized institution. The degree of decentralization is especially apparent in the budget process, but it is also apparent in the large number of committees and subcommittees involved in most foreign policy issues. Variations in expertise also account for a degree of decentralization. Some members are sufficiently expert on one set of issues to be influential in that issue area; other members are relatively expert and hence influential in other areas. Some staff members are also highly influential because of their expertise and experience.

Members of Congress, both as individuals and collectively as an institution, have a conflictual relationship with the executive branch, but there is also a considerable degree of cooperation between them. The mixture of conflict and cooperation is evident in each of the roles Congress plays in the policy process. Congress has generally acquiesced in presidential war policies. But it has occasionally restrained the president in wartime, and it has put him on notice in the War Powers Act that he cannot take congressional support for granted. Although the Senate has ratified nearly all treaties submitted to it, the ratification has sometimes been conditioned on modifications in terms of the treaties. The Congress has furthermore delegated much authority to the president through statutory executive agreements, and it has even acquiesced in executive agreements with other countries in the absence of any explicit congressionally delegated authority. Legislation in the 1970s, however, was designed to enhance Congress's involvement in reaching formal agreements with other countries. Other legislation in the 1970s was designed to increase Congress's control over budget formulation and the expenditures of executive agencies. Therefore, Congress now imposes many more restrictions on executive-branch actions. But this congressional power is likely to continue to be typically negative and passive in the sense that it involves restricting executive actions rather than undertaking initiatives of its own.

Congress often imposes restrictions in response to general public attitudes and specific interest groups' preferences; it remains relatively responsive to the internal political pressures generated by foreign policy issues, especially economic issues. It has become much more assertive on international economic policy matters. But on many issues, Congress continues to follow the lead of the president and the executive agencies. This is true because the information, the expertise, the operational capabilities, and many other sources of influence continue to be found mostly in the executive branch.

In sum, Congress does play some of the roles suggested by the democratic and pluralist models. And it is surely a decentralized institution that shares power with the executive branch, as the pluralist model suggests. There is also much conflict within Congress over policy issues; it is not the monolithic institution that the ruling elite model depicts, nor is it dominated by a cohesive conservative clique.

The Bureaucracy

Both the bureaucratic politics model and the organizational behavior model suggest that American foreign policy is partly the consequence of characteristic tendencies and variations in bureaucrats' behavior. In order to obtain a more detailed understanding of the bureaucrats' role in policy making, this chapter seeks to answer the following questions: What kinds of procedures do they follow? What part does politics play in their policy-making activities? What are the sources of their power? What problems do they pose? How does government reorganization affect policy making?

STRUCTURE

Agencies

The executive agencies involved in American foreign policy making are numerous, large, and varied. It is actually rather difficult to determine the precise number of agencies involved in foreign policy making because many of them are only marginally involved, because the definition of an agency is ambiguous, and because agency responsibilities change periodically. An official commission studying government organization identified over fifty, but that list included executive agencies without major policy-making responsibilities, such as the American Battle Monuments Commission, and it also included congressional agencies.[1]

The list in Table 6–1 includes nearly forty executive agencies, all of them with important policy-making roles. Many of them are the familiar large cabinet departments. Although others are more specialized and perhaps less familiar independent agencies, components of the Executive Office of the President, and other noncabinet agencies, many of them are among the most important agencies in foreign policy making. For instance, the Office of Management and Budget reviews the budget requests of all executive agencies—including the Defense Department, the State Department, and the Central Intelligence Agency—before they are submitted to Congress. The National Security Council is a high-level policy-making group on nearly all foreign policy issues. The International Trade Commission is involved in decisions to raise tariffs for American industries that are threatened by imports. The Nuclear Regulatory Commission is involved in decisions on exports of nuclear reactor fuels.

One of the most striking characteristics of the list is the large number of "domestic" agencies that are involved in foreign affairs.[2] Indeed, most government agencies today have some kind of involvement in foreign affairs; several of them have significant policy-making responsibilities and operate major programs in other countries. Therefore, most agencies have divisions or bureaus that are specifically designated as their international units. Some even have specially designated career groups for their international programs—the Agriculture Department has a Foreign Agricultural Service. Altogether, that department has a thousand or more personnel involved in foreign affairs, and over \$1 billion of its annual budget is devoted to foreign activities, most of it in the form of food assistance. Several "domestic" agencies also play particularly important roles in American relations with the specialized agencies in the United Nations system. The Department of Energy is centrally involved in American relations with the International Atomic Energy Agency, the Agriculture Department in the work of the Food and Agriculture Organization, and the Treasury Department in the activities of the World Bank and the International Monetary Fund.

The multiplicity of agencies involved in foreign affairs is also evident in the personnel rosters of American embassies abroad. A typical embassy includes more than State Department Foreign Service officers serving general diplomatic and consular functions. It also includes military personnel serving in the office of the defense attaché and in the military advisory group, which administers the American military assistance program. There are also Foreign Service information officers from the U.S. Information Service; economic assistance administrators from the Agency for International Development; Foreign Agricultural Service officers; Treasury and Commerce Department representatives in the economic/commercial section; and officers from the FBI, Federal Aviation Administration, and Peace Corps. Finally, of course, there are CIA agents and a CIA station chief, usually under cover in the political, consular, or other sections of the embassy staff.

Many executive agencies have at least a few hundred personnel involved in

TABLE 6-1 Executive Agencies Involved in Foreign Policy Making

TYPE OF AGENCY	MILITARY	ECONOMIC	NATURAL RESOURCES	INTELLIGENCE	OTHER
			POLICY AREA		
Cabinet departments	State Defense Energy	State Treasury Commerce Agriculture Labor Justice	State Energy	State Defense Justice Energy Treasury	State Agriculture Labor Health and Human Services Education Justice Transportation
Executive Office of the President	National Security Council (NSC) Office of Management and Budget (OMB) Office of Science and Technology Policy (OSTP) White House Office	NSC OMB Council of Economic Advisers Office of the U.S. Trade Representative White House Office	NSC OMB Council on Environmental Quality White House Office	NSC OMB White House Office	NSC OMB OSTP White House Office
Other executive agencies	Arms Control and Disarmament Agency	Agency for International Development (AID) Overseas Private Investment Corporation (OPIC) Export-Import Bank	Environmental Protection Agency	CIA	U.S. Information Agency Peace Corps NASA
Independent regulatory agencies		International Trade Commission Securities and Exchange Commission Federal Reserve Board Federal Trade Commission	Nuclear Regulatory Commission		Federal Aviation Administration Federal Communications Commission Federal Maritime Commission

foreign affairs; the central foreign affairs agencies have tens of thousands. The State Department has over twenty thousand employees, the CIA about that many, and the Defense Department one million civilian and two million military personnel.[3] Only a small proportion of these bureaucrats have major policy-making responsibilities, but even they number in the hundreds. For example, there are approximately eighty State Department officials with the rank of undersecretary, assistant secretary, or deputy assistant secretary (the principal levels beneath the secretary of state and the deputy secretary). In addition, there are more than a hundred country directors or equivalent office directors, just below the rank of deputy assistant secretary. In the Pentagon, there are more than twenty civilians at the rank of assistant secretary alone, and there are more than a thousand generals and admirals.[4]

Relationships within and among Agencies

There are two hallmarks of all of these government agencies. One is that they are hierarchical—everyone is in a position of superior or inferior authority in relation to others. People higher up have more authority than people lower down. The second key characteristic of their formal organization is that they are highly differentiated according to functional specialization; that is, each organizational unit has a specific responsibility. The combination of hierarchical authority and functional specialization is the basis for the familiar lines and boxes in organization charts (for example, the State Department's in Figure 6–1).

Such charts, however, usually convey erroneous impressions about the actual responsibilities and relations in organizations. In the first place, although there is a degree of specialization, it is not complete; there is also considerable overlap in the responsibilities of different organizational units. For example, ten agencies are involved in intelligence activities, not counting the National Security Council and its committees. In addition to the Central Intelligence Agency, they are the Defense Intelligence Agency, the National Security Agency, the Departments of State, Treasury, Energy, and Justice, and the army, navy, and air force.[5] Although each one emphasizes somewhat different intelligence activities, there is considerable overlap in their activities. During the Vietnam War, for example, the CIA, the Defense Intelligence Agency, and the air force all analyzed intelligence on the effects of the American bombing of North Vietnam.[6]

Overlapping organizational responsibilities are not limited to intelligence gathering and analysis. At least four departments are involved in international food policy: State, Agriculture, Treasury, and Health and Human Services. Four or more agencies are involved in international nuclear energy issues: the State, Energy, and Commerce departments and the Nuclear Regulatory Commission. Practically every cabinet-level department and several other agencies are involved in development-assistance programs. The names and roles of the agencies involved in trade policy formulation and implementation are indicated in Table 6–2.

Organization charts also convey erroneous impressions because formal authority is not the same as actual power in policy making. Sometimes people higher up, with more authority, have less impact on policy than people lower down. One of the

DEPARTMENT OF STATE

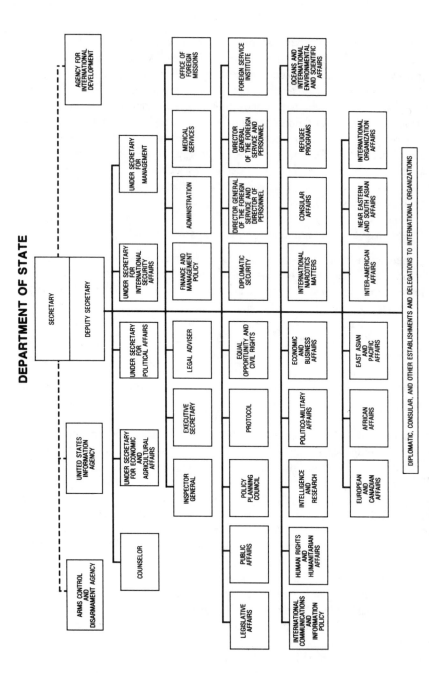

FIGURE 6–1 State Department organization chart

Source: U.S. Organization Manual 1989/90 (Washington, DC: U.S. Government Printing Office, 1989), p. 432.

TABLE 6–2 Executive Agencies Involved in Trade Policy Formulation and Implementation (1990)

INTERAGENCY GROUPS

Cabinet Council on Commerce and Trade—Highest-level trade policy group. Provides general policy guidance. Includes: president, vice-president, counsellor to president, U.S. trade representative, secretary of commerce, secretary of agriculture, secretary of state, secretary of treasury

Trade Policy Committee—Second-level policy group. Focuses on trade negotiations. Associated with it: Trade Negotiation Committee, Trade Policy Review Group, Trade Policy Staff Committee. Chaired by trade representative. Other members from departments of commerce, state, treasury

AGENCIES CENTRALLY INVOLVED

Office of the United States Trade Representative (in Executive Office of the President)—General guidance and coordination of trade policy; especially for negotiations in GATT

Department of Commerce, especially International Trade Administration—Implementation of multilateral trade agreements, antidumping laws, countervailing duty laws, and trade-adjustment assistance; also foreign reporting (by Foreign Commercial Service), statistical services, export promotion services, export controls

Department of State, especially Bureau of Economic and Business Affairs and Bureau of International Organization Affairs—Representation at international organizations, export controls, trade relations with other countries generally

Department of Treasury, especially Office of Assistant Secretary for International Affairs—Trade finance policy, balance-of-payments analysis, foreign direct investment issues. Customs Service administers tariff laws and other import regulations

Department of Agriculture—All aspects of agricultural exports and imports

International Trade Commission—Domestic economic impact of imports

AGENCIES INVOLVED IN SELECTED ASPECTS

Department of Defense—Export controls

Department of Energy—Trade in oil and other fuels

Agency for International Development

Overseas Private Investment Corporation—U.S. private investments in developing countries

Justice Department—Competition in imports and exports

Federal Trade Commission—Competition in imports and exports

Federal Maritime Commission—Shipping industry regulation and subsidies

Nuclear Regulatory Commission—Nuclear power export controls

Civil Aeronautics Board—International competitive practices

Consumer Product Safety Commission

Environmental Protection Agency

Export-Import Bank—Financing for exports

Federal Reserve System

Small Business Administration

reasons for this phenomenon is simply attention. High-level officials with considerable authority frequently do not exercise power over policy on a given issue because they do not devote enough attention to it. Instead, they give higher priority to other matters competing for their attention.

The chart in Figure 6–2 illustrates the common discrepancy between formal authority and actual power. The figure depicts both the formal structure of the

FIGURE 6–2   Formal and actual organization for oil import policy making (1973)

Source: Adapted by the author from Linda Graebner, "U.S. Oil Import Policy: The Decision to Suspend All Quotas on U.S. Imports of Foreign Oil, 1973," in *Report of the Commission on the Organization of the Government for the Conduct of Foreign Policy* (Washington, DC: U.S. Government Printing Office, 1975), vol. III, appendix H, tables II and III, pp. 56 and 64.

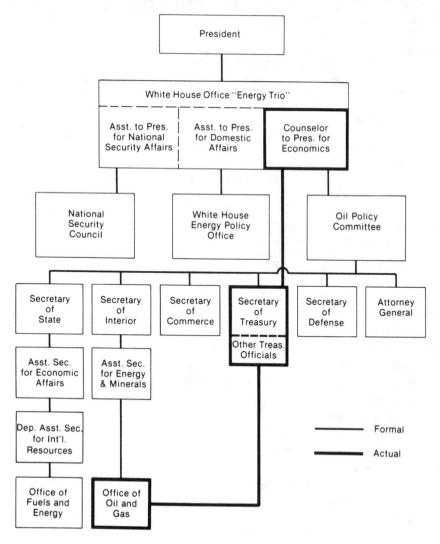

executive branch for oil import policy making at a particular time and the actual relationships among the organizational units and their key personnel. Formally, there were several high-level coordinating units, clear hierarchical relationships among the lower-level units, and specialized areas of responsibility. Actually, however, only a few of the units and the personnel were directly involved and had a major impact on policy. The other participants were distracted by a variety of other foreign and domestic problems, or they lacked special knowledge or interest in oil import policy.

Organization charts, furthermore, are limited by the fact that they provide only a static picture of bureaucratic structure. We also need to consider the procedures followed in government bureaucracies to obtain a more dynamic picture of how they work, as we will do in the following section.

PROCEDURES

Inputs, Decisions, Outputs

For convenience, we can divide the routine processes of organizational policy making into three phases: the input phase, the decision phase, and the output phase.

Information is received and distributed in the input phase. Information comes into the Washington headquarters of government agencies from numerous sources and in many forms: telegrams and dispatches from American embassies in other countries; telephone calls, formal appointments, and casual conversations between U.S. personnel and foreign embassies in Washington; communications from corporation representatives, the press, and other nongovernmental organizations; contacts with officials from other U.S. government agencies and Congress. These messages are also distributed within and among government agencies in a variety of ways. Within the State Department, a telegram coming from an American embassy is received by a message center, which distributes copies of it to bureaus concerned with the kind of issue raised by the telegram. Then each bureau distributes copies to one or more of the offices in that bureau. Often other agencies also get copies, or they receive similar messages through their own channels.

In the decision phase, a response is formulated. Normally, one person is designated as the "action officer" responsible for coordinating the response. But officials at lower and higher levels and in several offices and bureaus within the agency (or even in other agencies) usually become involved in the decision making. In fact, several officials must often indicate their formal clearance of any outgoing messages by "signing off" on them.

Finally, in the output phase, the decision is implemented. This may be as simple as sending a telegram directing the American embassy in a country to give a message to the government there. Or the output phase may involve a variety of government actions: a press release, a meeting between the secretary and the country's ambassador in Washington to discuss a complex issue, and perhaps a presidential speech or news conference.

These organizational procedures were evident in a simple case in which a country asked the American embassy to arrange for an American ship to make a port call.[7] The message from the American embassy went to the State Department bureau concerned with relations with that area of the world and to the specific office within the bureau concerned with relations with that particular country. In that office, the country director responsible for American relations with the country became the action officer for coordinating the U.S. response. He consulted with a naval officer in the Defense Department, and they agreed the response should be positive. The country director then drafted a telegram, which was initialed for clearance by the naval officer and a State Department office director concerned with that country and others in the region. The State Department telegram notified the American embassy that the ship would be sent; the navy sent an order to the ship to pay a port visit to the country.

Another reconstructed case provides a more complicated illustration of organizational procedures.[8] In this case, a telegram to the State Department from a U.S. embassy in Western Europe indicated that the foreign minister of "country X" said that his government would be distressed if the United States did not vote with it on an upcoming UN General Assembly resolution. An action copy of the telegram went to the Bureau of European [and Canadian] Affairs; information copies went to the secretary, the undersecretaries, the Policy Planning Council, the Bureau of African Affairs, the Bureau of East Asian and Pacific Affairs, the Bureau of Near Eastern and South Asian Affairs, the Bureau of Intelligence and Research, and the Bureau of International Organization Affairs—all within the State Department. Other information copies went to the Defense Department and the Central Intelligence Agency.

The same day the issue was discussed at the secretary of state's morning staff conference and in a telephone conversation between officers of the European Affairs and International Organization Affairs bureaus. The country director for country X, the director of the Office of Western European Affairs, and the assistant secretary for European [and Canadian] Affairs then met to draft a telegram to the American embassy in country X. After revision at the request of other offices, the telegram was cleared by three bureaus, signed by the undersecretary for political affairs, and sent to the American embassy in country X.

Since the telegram indicated disagreement with country X on the issue, however, another telegram came from the American embassy the following day. It indicated that country X might make some concessions, but it still expected the United States to vote with it. Since the conflict was then clearly a serious one with a major ally, the secretary of state became more centrally involved. At his next staff meeting, he asked the director of the Policy Planning Staff to evaluate the American alternatives. Those alternatives were discussed the following morning at a meeting among the director of the Policy Planning Staff, the director of the Office of United Nations Political Affairs, the director of the Office for Western European Affairs, the director of the Office of Research and Analysis for Western Europe, the director of the Office of Research and Analysis for Africa, the director of the Office of Research and Analysis for the Near East and South Asia, an official from the Bureau of Public Affairs, and numerous aides to all these officials. They prepared a paper that defined and evaluated the American alternatives. Several days later, after reading their paper, the secretary asked for the advice of four assistant secretaries at his staff meeting. In spite of their disagreements (and disagreements among the president, members of Congress, and American ambassadors, all of which came to his attention), the secretary reached a decision.

His decision was implemented in numerous ways. It was conveyed in telegrams to the American embassy in country X and the American mission to the United Nations. Telegrams also went to American embassies in several other countries instructing ambassadors to present the American position to those governments. After a meeting with officials from the State Department's geographic bureaus and Public Affairs Bureau, officers in the U.S. Information Agency sent guidance to their offices in numerous countries as to how to treat the expected news stories about the issue.

You can easily see from these examples that information processing and problem solving are central to policy making. But you should also recognize that bureaucratic policy making is not nearly so orderly, calm, and controlled as these reconstructions suggest. Policy making from the perspective of the participants who have the burden of responsibility is quite different.

The Burdens of Decision Making

A secretary of state once complained that there were as many as twenty-five items on the agenda for his weekly lunch meeting with the secretary of defense and the special assistant to the president.[9]

During his confirmation hearings before the Senate Foreign Relations Committee, James Baker began to encounter the expanding range of foreign policy issues that he would have to address as secretary of state. They included international narcotics trafficking, global warming and other environmental issues, and the external indebtedness problems of developing countries.[10]

The following detailed account provides a vivid picture of the hectic, pressured circumstances in which policy is often made. The account is from a diary kept by an assistant secretary of state who was responsible for international educational and cultural programs.[11] Although those responsibilities did not involve him in military crises or other issues of "high politics," you can see from his experiences during one day that he was confronted with a constant stream of pressing and diverse problems. You can also see the limited time available to deal with the problems and his limited power as he tried to solve them. His entries for a more or less typical day include the following:

8:00 A.M.   Meeting with immediate staff to review the meeting the previous day of the President's Task Force on International Education, and to [make] follow-up assignments.

8:30   Meeting with staff assistant to go over cables and correspondence. . . .

9:05   Telephone call from Science Adviser to President, related to development of better facilities for research in Asian universities. . . .

9:15   Secretary of State's staff meeting [concerning world situation].

10:00	Meeting with Assistant Secretary of State for Latin American Affairs and Alliance for Progress specialists about educational planning in the Organization of American States.
10:45	Telephone calls, initialing of memoranda, editing of policy statement on exchanges in the arts.
11:15	Meeting with Yugoslav Cabinet Minister and Yugoslav Ambassador.
12:30 P.M.	Lunch with [Chairman of Senate Foreign Relations Committee] concerning the administration's new initiatives in international education.
2:00	Meeting with press officer for preparation of special statement for newspapers to clear up misunderstanding about cultural exchanges with Soviet Union. Clearance requested from Bureau of European Affairs and Bureau of Public Affairs in State Department.
2:30	Conference with counsel of the Kennedy Center for Performing Arts to discuss problems before the Executive Committee of the Trustees.
3:00	Meeting with members of staff to be briefed on the meeting the next day of the Government Advisory Committee on Books and Library programs, related to needs for U.S. textbooks abroad.
3:30	Meeting with U.S. Ambassador to Ghana....
4:00	Two alternative statements on Soviet exchanges received from State Department Bureau of European Affairs and Bureau of Public Affairs. Arguments heard, telephone calls made to each Bureau. Special trouble-shooter assigned to work out or obscure the disagreements.
4:30	Meeting with Assistant Secretary of State for International Organizations to discuss the U.S. position in the coming vote on the countries that should be represented on the UNESCO Executive Board.
5:00	Meeting with representatives of Bureaus of European Affairs and Public Affairs. One sentence and two commas deleted from the joint statement that has been worked out since 4:00 o'clock. Issue settled.
5:30	Meeting with the president of an American university in the Middle East, which needs money.
5:45	Dictation of letters; call to Congressman replying to call he had put in to me; call from Internal Revenue Service about tax status of visiting foreign scholars.
6:10	Call from White House [about] statement that has been prepared for announcement by the President....
6:30	Reception at the Iraqi Embassy for Iraqi Prime Minister and Foreign Minister.
8:00	Dinner at home [with two State Department] colleagues, an Under Secretary from HEW, an editorial writer from the *Washington Post,* and wives.*

The "disagreement" between the European Affairs and Public Affairs bureaus in this account suggests another important aspect of bureaucratic policy making: It involves a struggle among many participants who have power and who have different policy preferences. Former Secretary of State George Shultz once commented on the

*Adaptation of material from *High on Foggy Bottom: An Outsider's Inside View of the Government* by Charles Frankel. Copyright © 1968, 1969 by Charles Frankel. Reprinted by permission of Harper-Collins Publishers.

frustrations he and others experienced: "Nothing ever gets settled in this town. It's not like running a company or even a university. It's a seething debating society in which the debate never stops, in which people never give up, including me, and that's the atmosphere in which you administer." He added that a friend of his, who had been highly successful in business before assuming a high-level State Department position, had said that in the foreign policy-making process "when you decide something, that's just the beginning. Anybody who doesn't like it goes to Congress, goes to the press, or something. It's a different process [from business]."[12] Foreign policy making, in other words, is more highly politicized than business.

POLITICS

Policy making can be conceived as a political game in which participants with conflicting policy preferences use strategies to try to win so that their preferences will prevail.[13] The games are constantly arising because there are always problems needing decisions and because there are usually conflicts over what the decisions should be.

Conflicts

Although all the participants in the policy process may have a conception of the national interest that largely determines their policy preferences, they do not all have the same conception of the national interest. Nor are their organizational interests and their personal interests the same. Such differences in interests and policy preferences originate in the participants' organizational roles, their career groups, and their individual experiences. For instance, if a decision needs to be made concerning strategic arms control agreements with the Soviet Union, we can easily imagine conflicts that would occur as a result of organizational roles. The undersecretary of defense for research and engineering would consider how the issue affects the weapons development programs that he or she oversees. The director of the Arms Control and Disarmament Agency would emphasize the effects on progress toward arms control agreements. The assistant secretary of state for European affairs would take into account the views of Western European governments; the assistant secretary for East Asian and Pacific affairs would consider the implications for American relations with China.

Career-group membership and personal experiences would also affect these and other participants' perspectives on the issue. Career army, navy, and air force officers would view such an issue quite differently. A typical army officer may be relatively uninterested because no prospective decision would directly affect army weapons programs, but the air force and naval officers might be directly involved in the weapons programs that would be affected.

Even within the same organizations and career groups, conflicting preferences sometimes arise from different individual experiences and values. Within the military services, within the State Department, and within the Arms Control and Disarmament

Agency, there are disagreements on nearly any arms control issue. A study of bureaucrats' attitudes toward arms control issues found that there were significant differences in the opinions held within the Arms Control and Disarmament Agency; and those differences were related to differences in career-group membership and to variations in personality type, as determined by standardized psychological tests.[14] A study of State Department officials' opinions on a variety of more general foreign policy questions also found differences in opinions to be related to variations in individual personality types as well as organizational position and career experiences.[15] Yet another study found correlations between variations in military officers' personality traits and variations in their policy preferences on arms control and weapons development issues.[16]

The combination of strong personal views and extensive experience in bureaucratic politics sometimes enables a single high-level bureaucratic official to exercise an unusual degree of influence in the policy process. As an assistant secretary of defense in the Reagan administration, Richard Perle was unusually influential in numerous key nuclear weapons issues, such as the deployment of intermediate range nuclear forces in Europe, the development of the Star Wars nuclear defense program, and strategic arms control negotiations with the Soviet Union.[17]

Conflicts within the bureaucracy are not limited to military issues, however; they also occur on trade issues. Such conflicts have been common on protectionist measures that restrict automobile imports. On one side, the Transportation Department and the Labor Department are prone to be responsive to the interests and pressures of the U.S. automobile industry and thus support protectionist measures. The State Department, on the other hand, worries about the deleterious effects of protectionist measures on U.S. relations with the automobile-exporting countries, which are among the principal allies of the United States. In addition, the Council of Economic Advisers, the Treasury Department, and the Office of Management and Budget worry about the domestic inflationary pressures that result from protectionist trade policies and are also, therefore, inclined to oppose them. The Office of the Trade Representative tends to take a middle position. As part of the Executive Office of the President, it is sensitive about the domestic political implications of the issue and specifically how trade policy can affect key interest groups' support for the president. However, as the office that conducts trade negotiations with other countries, it is also aware of the possible repercussions abroad, such as trade wars, that can be prompted by protectionist policies.[18]

Conflicting preferences and interests are common in the bureaucracy. When policy preferences are strongly held or when important organizational or personal interests are at stake in an issue, bureaucrats are inclined to participate in the decision games concerning that issue. They may employ many strategies once they decide to play.

Strategies[19]

One common strategy is to try to control who else plays. The object of this strategy is to get actual or potential supporters to play and to exclude opponents. CIA officials in American embassies, for instance, have often been accused of reporting their activities directly back to the CIA without keeping the ambassador and other State Department officials informed as well, lest they oppose the CIA's activities.

Informal "back channels" are sometimes used rather than normal organizational procedures. During the Vietnam War, for instance, Pentagon officials sent a message through back channels to the U.S. field commander in Vietnam to tell him the "appropriate" answers he should give through front channels to an inquiry from the White House.

Many strategies rely on manipulating information. Sometimes this involves blatant distortion, but it often involves merely analyzing or distributing information selectively. The press can be used to disseminate information in any of several ways. One way is to communicate with the press on a "background" or "deep background" basis. In the former case, the source of the story is identified only as a government official or a State Department official and not by name; in the latter circumstance, the story is reported without referring to any government source. Finally, there are "leaks" of classified information or other documents. Leaks may be used only to draw attention to an issue or a particular fact, but other times they are used to embarrass opponents, reduce their credibility, or otherwise reduce their effectiveness. Although presidents and other high-level officials frequently condemn leaks as the irresponsible behavior of a disgruntled bureaucrat, many leaks, in fact, come from those very officials. President Johnson, for instance, was a common source of leaks about the Vietnam War.

Power

Who wins these games is partially determined by the participants' power resources and how well they use them. The most obvious power resource, but not necessarily the most important one, is the formal authority conveyed by organizational position. Another is attention, as we noted in our discussion of oil import policy making. People lower down often devote more sustained time and energy to a particular issue and have a greater impact on decisions concerning it than do their superiors. Variations in individuals' and staffs' substantive expertise also affect their power. Particularly on technical issues concerning weapons technology, economic problems, or energy issues, those bureaucrats with specialized training and experience have a great advantage over those who lack technical backgrounds. Some participants, moreover, are skillful at bureaucratic politics; others are not.

At the upper levels of government, some participants have a close personal relationship with the president or a cabinet-level official or at least enjoy their confidence; others are clearly not such insiders. Some high-level administrators enjoy a national reputation or have strong support from an interest group or party faction—or perhaps they have a good relationship with key members of Congress. Other officials are unknown outside their agencies and therefore have no outside supporters.

A few participants may enjoy all these advantages; consequently, they win games regularly over a wide range of issues. But most have only a few resources and occasionally either lose or choose not to play at all.

What is true of individuals is also true of organizations: Power resources for bureaucratic political games are distributed unevenly. But there are discernible patterns in the power resources of the governmental organizations centrally involved in foreign policy making. In particular, when we examine their technical expertise, their operational capabilities, and their support from nongovernmental interest groups, we find that the State Department is relatively lacking in all respects. Most Foreign Service officers are highly educated and have foreign-language skills and extensive experience in dealing with foreign countries; but only a few of them have the technical knowledge of weapons, economics, and technology that would enable them to be as knowledgeable as personnel in the Defense, Treasury, and Energy Departments. As for the operational capabilities for implementing decisions, those are in the Defense Department, the Agency for International Development, the Agriculture Department, and the CIA.

Furthermore, agencies can rely on support for their programs and policy preferences from nongovernmental ''clientele'' groups whose interests are served by the agencies' programs. Thus, Defense Department weapons procurements are supported by the defense industries. The Agriculture Department's subsidy and allotment programs are supported by farmers. The Commerce and Treasury Departments can often call on business and banking support. The Energy Department can call on energy companies for support, particularly for energy research and development program funding. But if the State Department opposes weapons development programs, restrictive agricultural production policies, or nuclear reactor development and export policies, it cannot count on any particular interest group to support it.

Finally, although the CIA enjoys less secrecy, less prestige, and less freedom in the conduct of its covert operations than it used to, it nevertheless continues to have considerable advantages in many bureaucratic struggles. Perhaps its greatest asset is its most obvious: information. For having information and being able to keep others from having it is one of the most precious political assets in the government. If knowledge is power, so, too, is keeping others from being knowledgeable.

These general observations on conflicts, strategies, and power in bureaucratic politics become clearer and more convincing in the details of specific cases.

Vietnam[20]

There were major conflicts over the Vietnam War policy within the government long before the war became a contentious public issue. During the period of the Kennedy administration from 1961 until late 1963, the bureaucratic conflicts generally pitted State Department officials against the military officers on the Joint Chiefs of Staff and on the staff of the Military Assistance Advisory Group in Vietnam. The military officers wanted more American troops to be sent to Vietnam, and they wanted to prosecute the war without regard for the political position or the internal policies of the Diem government of South Vietnam. The State Department officials, in comparison, were more skeptical about the likely effectiveness of a substantial increase in American troops; and they wanted further American military assistance to be conditioned on reforms that would reduce the corruption, inefficiency, and repressiveness of the South Vietnamese government. President Kennedy's response to this conflicting advice was moderate compared with later policies. He increased American troop strength by a few thousand, limited their combat role, and at least paid lip service to the notion that the South Vietnamese government should undergo reforms.

From 1964 until 1968, however, bureaucratic politics and American policies changed under President Johnson. There was relatively little conflict over the air war policy, at least when the United States first began bombing North Vietnam in 1965. A convergence of disparate organizational interests and personal policy preferences led to widespread support within the bureaucracy for the bombing. The air force believed in the effectiveness of strategic bombing, which it saw as its central organizational mission. The navy agreed to the bombing partly because it involved the use of navy aircraft stationed on aircraft carriers. The army also supported it, not because it believed in the effectiveness of strategic or carrier-based bombing but because an enlarged air war would mean more funds for the army's ground forces as well. Civilians in the Defense Department and State Department were not so sanguine about the military effectiveness of strategic bombing, but they did see it in more political and psychological terms as a way to demonstrate American resolve or to impose costs on North Vietnam so that it would stop its struggle against the South Vietnamese government. They also believed an air war was preferable to a land war. Thus, the air war commenced—with little conflict over the decision.

There was more conflict over the introduction and use of ground combat troops, but even that conflict was often muted. When General Westmoreland, the American military commander in Vietnam, began to receive the substantial increases in ground troops that he requested from President Johnson, he decided to use them according to the traditional infantry approach: to conduct "search and destroy" missions designed to kill as many enemy troops as possible. Many civilian and some military officials thought at the time that such conventional military tactics were inappropriate to the circumstances of the particular war in Southeast Asia, but they did not forcefully oppose General Westmoreland's decision. Secretary of Defense McNamara and some of his civilian colleagues in the Defense Department's Office of Systems Analysis and Office of International Security Affairs, as well as a few State Department officials, occasionally expressed their doubts about the Westmoreland search and destroy strategy; they suggested instead an emphasis on territorial control and population defense. But they were in a weak position for any bureaucratic battles over such an issue; an American military field commander is normally granted considerable autonomy in combat strategy decisions. He, after all, is a professional expert in such matters; his judgment is difficult to challenge. Thus, the war was prosecuted with a ground combat strategy that was increasingly perceived as a failure.

Furthermore, as the war progressed, the policy process became more and more closed to anyone with doubts about the policies being pursued. As a result, it was increasingly difficult for bureaucratic dissenters to express their views to high-level officials, especially the president. By 1967, President Johnson made war policy decisions on the basis of direct contact with only a small number of advisers.

By the spring of 1968, however, a coalition of war policy opponents had emerged, especially in the upper levels of the Defense Department. They spent considerable effort trying to persuade the newly appointed secretary of defense, Clark Clifford, of the futility of the prevailing policy. At about the time of a surprisingly strong enemy offensive, Clifford began to express his reservations about policy to the president. Furthermore, former Secretary of State Acheson expressed his doubts about the military's assessment of the situation in Vietnam. Since both men had long experience in foreign policy, since both were widely perceived as "hard-line" cold warriors, and since both had enjoyed President Johnson's respect for many years, their opinions weighed heavily on him. In March 1968, he decided to de-escalate American bombing of North Vietnam and to announce that he would not run for re-election—decisions intended to induce North Vietnam to begin peace negotiations. Although the negotiations and the war lasted for many more years, these decisions marked an important turning point in American policy. And the policy changed at least in part as a result of the political pressures brought to bear on the president, some of them from within the executive branch of the government.

ABM[21]

The decision of the Johnson administration to deploy an antiballistic missile (ABM) system also illustrates the conflicts, strategies, and power involved in bureaucratic policy making. Pentagon strategic weapons experts had been conducting research and development work on an ABM system for many years, but its technical feasibility was doubtful. By 1966, the Office of the Director of Defense Research and Engineering, the Defense Advanced Research Projects Agency, and the army (the Pentagon organizations responsible for development of the ABM system) said that it was technically feasible to defend American cities against a Soviet nuclear attack. In addition, the Joint Chiefs of Staff were asking for funds to begin deployment of a nationwide ABM system. Thus, the prospect of the January 1967 budget proposals to be submitted by the president to Congress provided the occasion for some kind of decision on ABM funds.

But there were substantial conflicts on the issue within the government. The army, the Joint Chiefs, and the weapons research and development scientists all had clear organizational interests for going ahead with ABM deployment and supported it. But Secretary of Defense McNamara opposed it. He argued that its cost would be enormous, that its technical feasibility was still questionable, and, most important, that it would stimulate another round in the Soviet-American arms race. He felt the Soviet Union would increase its offensive weapons capabilities enough to offset any American ABM deployment.

This conflicting advice created a dilemma for the president. If he decided in favor of ABM deployments, he would harm his working relations with his secretary of defense and he would further alienate the opponents of his Vietnam War policies, especially within his own Democratic party. On the other hand, if he decided against ABM deployment, he would face strong criticism from several prominent senators; and their arguments would be bolstered by the fact that the Joint Chiefs were being overruled by the president (always a politically risky position for a president). Furthermore, the president feared that he would be charged in the next election with allowing an "ABM gap" to develop, as the Democrats had charged the Republicans with allowing a "missile gap" in the 1960 campaign.

The participants in the case used several strategies. The president's strategy was to compromise in such a way as to avoid the political costs associated with a decision either for or against deployment. In his budget message, therefore, he asked for funds to begin deployment of an ABM system but noted that he would delay any actual deployment while he tried to get the Soviet Union to begin arms control negotiations. Thus, he protected himself against the criticism by senators and others that he was overruling the Joint Chiefs or allowing an ABM gap, since he was asking for ABM deployment funds. But he was also protecting himself from McNamara's disaffection and increased opposition from the anti-Vietnam faction in the Democratic party, since he was not actually deploying the ABM yet.

But that was not the end of the issue. A decision on whether to go ahead would have to be reached eventually; again, the budget submission (in January of the following year) forced this decision. It became clear after a July meeting between President Johnson and Soviet Premier Kosygin that arms control negotiations would not be underway soon and that an ABM decision would have to be made before the next budget submission. The president thus informed the secretary of defense that some kind of ABM deployment would have to be announced by January.

The nature of the system and the announcement of the decision to deploy it, however, reflected the continuing conflicts within the bureaucracy. Secretary of Defense McNamara was authorized to announce the decision to go ahead with the deployment he had opposed. But his announcement speech emphasized the undesirability of a large-scale anti-Soviet ABM system, in contrast to the limited anti-Chinese function of the smaller-scale system that was to be deployed. In fact, the general tone of the speech was anti-AMB, even though it was presumably part of McNamara's strategy of trying to keep the ABM supporters from successfully pushing ahead for a full-scale ABM system.

But the army and the Joint Chiefs still wanted a full-scale ABM. Furthermore, the director of defense research and engineering and the deputy secretary of defense favored at least keeping that option open. And they were the Pentagon officials largely responsible for implementing the decision. As Vietnam absorbed more of McNamara's and Johnson's time, these implementors of the decision emphasized that the small-scale anti-Chinese ABM authorized by the president and announced by the secretary of defense could be just the initial deployment toward a large-scale anti-Soviet ABM system. In fact, the army's presentation of the ABM program in the congressional budget hearings several months later contained precisely this emphasis.

The outcome of this particular bureaucratic political game was a complex mixture of wins and losses for the participants. The initial presidential decision to ask for deployment funds but to postpone their use was a partial victory and a partial defeat for both the supporters and the opponents of ABM deployment. And so was the "final" decision, because neither the supporters nor the opponents got exactly what they wanted.

Many bureaucrats thrive on such game playing, especially when they are winning. Others find it a distasteful if inevitable part of policy making, which they engage in only reluctantly. In any case, organizational procedures and bureaucratic politics may be inevitable, but they also create problems in policy making. Government reorganization has consequently attracted considerable attention over the years. Although it only occasionally becomes a public issue, organizational reform is continually an issue within the government.

ORGANIZATIONAL REFORM[22]

Several criteria guide organizational reforms. One is that organizations should provide useful analysis for policy making. Thus, executive agencies should produce information and ideas that are helpful in clarifying goals, identifying and defining problems, generating alternative policies, and estimating the consequences of alternatives. Further, the agencies should provide sufficient operational capabilities to implement decisions; their activities should be coordinated; and they should be responsive to the guidance of politically responsible officials: the president, his appointees, and the Congress. Finally, they should be efficient in the sense of providing a high ratio of outputs (services) to inputs (resources).*

In an effort to achieve these objectives, several congresses and presidents have adopted numerous structural, procedural, and personnel reforms.

Defense Department

One of the most significant organizational reforms was the 1947 National Security Act, which established the Department of Defense. That act and subsequent reorganizations attempted to provide greater civilian control over the military, more coordination among the military services, and better coordination between defense policy makers and other foreign affairs policy makers. The two key structural reforms were the creation and development of the Office of the Secretary of Defense and the Joint Chiefs of Staff. Over time, both have evolved into the dominant centers of policy making in the Defense Department; they have become central organizational participants in all major decisions involving the military.

The Office of the Secretary of Defense (OSD) is itself a conglomerate of several offices, each headed by an undersecretary or an assistant secretary. Although their importance changes from time to time depending on the president's and secretary's wishes and the competence of their staffs, some of these offices are noteworthy. One is the Office of the Undersecretary of Defense for Research and Engineering, which is responsible for overseeing weapons development programs. Others are the Office of International Security Policy and the Office of International Security Affairs, which

---

*The services include a vast range of activities from negotiating treaties to fighting wars to issuing passports. The principal resources are personnel and money. The resources are easy to measure, but the services are often not susceptible to meaningful measurement. Hence, most estimates of organizational efficiency are highly intuitive and impressionistic.

maintain liaison with the State Department and generally concern themselves with the political implications of military issues. That office and several others are under the general supervision of an undersecretary of defense for policy. In recent years, the total staff size of all of the components of the Office of the Secretary of Defense has exceeded two thousand people, most of them civilians.

The Joint Chiefs of Staff (JCS) is also a sizable component in the Defense Department. There are only five members of the Joint Chiefs itself: a chairman and the commanding officer of each of the services. But their supporting joint staff has five hundred personnel, most of them in the military services. There are numerous integrated military field commands under their direct control, as well as many integrated support agencies. Both the JCS and the integrated field commands were given greater authority in field operations by recent reorganizations. These include unified commands for various regions of the world, as well as the Readiness Command and Military Airlift Command.

Although the departments of the army, navy, and air force have continued to exist, their responsibilities are largely limited to personnel, weapons development and procurement, and other supply responsibilities. Their roles in major policy decisions are more marginal. Furthermore, weapons procurement decision making, especially for major weapons systems, has been shifted more and more into the Office of the Secretary of Defense and out of the military departments.

The resulting formal organization of the Department of Defense is displayed in Figure 6–3. The appropriateness of these organizational arrangements is a source of continuing controversy. They surely provide greater control and coordination of the military than previous arrangements did—indeed, some would argue that there is too much control and coordination. But there is neither complete civilian control of the military nor coordination among the military services. There is a constant struggle over the policy-making roles of the civilian OSD and the military JCS; and there is considerable interservice conflict. It is also questionable whether the creation of a Defense Intelligence Agency (DIA), for instance, has improved the efficiency or quality of military intelligence. The army, the air force, and the navy all still maintain their own intelligence programs, and the DIA has been frequently criticized for distorting its intelligence reports to suit JCS preferences.

Central Intelligence Agency

Intelligence agencies have undergone several reorganizations over the years. The 1947 National Security Act created a new intelligence agency, the CIA, separate from the military services and separate from any other executive agency. This independence was intended to insulate intelligence gathering and analysis from the influence of policy-making officials who might distort intelligence to suit their needs. Such an organizational strategy may have been partially successful in this respect, but it has not been an entirely satisfactory arrangement. The CIA itself evolved into an agency with programs and policy preferences that sometimes distort intelligence reporting.

The CIA is, of course, a paramilitary covert-operations agency as well as an

DEPARTMENT OF DEFENSE

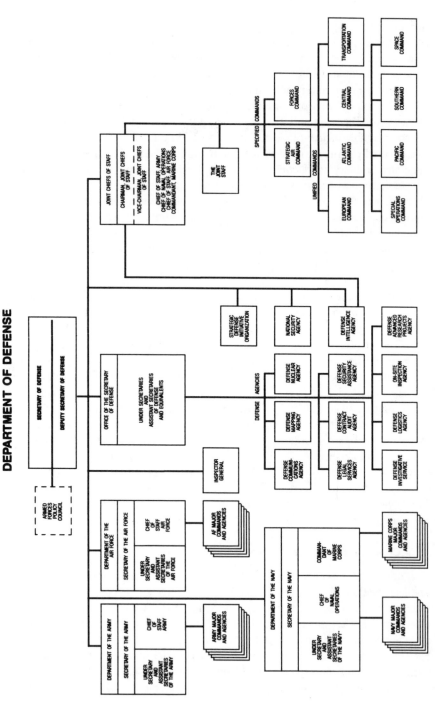

FIGURE 6–3 Defense Department organization chart.

intelligence agency; this dual nature is evident in its basic structure. The two principal organizational units are the Directorate of Intelligence and the Directorate of Operations. Although the two often function independently of one another, covert operations can nevertheless distort the intelligence process. For instance, planning for the CIA-sponsored invasion of Cuba at the Bay of Pigs in 1961 was based in part on the assumption that an invasion would trigger a popular uprising against Premier Fidel Castro inside Cuba. But this assumption was made by the CIA's covert-operations personnel, who were responsible for the invasion plan—not by the intelligence personnel, who were not even informed of the plan. So neither they nor Cuba specialists in the State Department were able to challenge this highly dubious assumption. In the event, other shortcomings in the plan led to its failure, but this Central Intelligence estimate was clearly distorted by the CIA's covert-operations policy.[23] The periodic suggestion that the CIA's two major components should be divided into separate agencies to avoid such contamination of intelligence is consistently resisted on efficiency grounds, however.

State Department

At the State Department, the major structural issues have concerned the desirability of creating new agencies that would provide adequate organizational capabilities in policy areas that did not particularly interest the department. In particular, separate agencies were created for the economic assistance program and for arms control. Thus, the Agency for International Development and the Arms Control and Disarmament Agency are autonomous agencies, although their directors are nevertheless subject to guidance from the secretary of state. In addition, a separate information agency, which is more independent of the State Department, was created so that its public information activities would have more credibility in the countries where its field offices operate. A 1978 reorganization moved the State Department's cultural exchange programs to the U.S. Information Agency and changed its name to the International Communications Agency. Its name has since been changed back to U.S. Information Agency.

The State Department's personnel problems have been more controversial. The controversies have focused on two issues. One is the proportion of ambassadors and other high-level officials who are career Foreign Service officers or noncareer political appointees. The exact proportions have varied, but three-fourths of the ambassadors are typically career diplomats and about one-half of the officials at the assistant secretary level and above are also career Foreign Service officers. Ambassadorial appointments are occasionally patronage payoffs to presidential supporters, but most political appointees are reasonably competent for the job. In some instances, political appointees are highly respected experts on the countries or functional policy areas for which they are responsible; many of them have extensive academic or other nongovernmental backgrounds directly relevant to their official responsibilities. In any event, there is a case to be made for political appointments, since they presumably increase the responsiveness of the department to presidential policies. Nearly all the positions below the assistant secretary and ambassador levels are held by career Foreign Service officers or other career employees.

The Foreign Service has been frequently criticized for being an unusually tradition-bound career group. Even though expertise in economics, energy, weapons, and other scientific and technological areas became more important to foreign policy making many years ago, the Foreign Service demonstrated little interest in recruiting and training personnel in those areas. Instead, it continued to emphasize almost exclusively a general educational background and the development of language skills and geographic-area knowledge.

Yet, recruitment into the Foreign Service is highly competitive. Commonly, more than ten thousand applicants take the Foreign Service exam in hopes of obtaining one of the two hundred or so annual appointments. Competition for promotion to higher levels is stiff, and some officers are selected out if their performance evaluations are not sufficiently favorable.

CONCLUSION

Foreign Service officers, military officers, and other bureaucrats are important participants in the policy process, as both the bureaucratic politics and the organizational behavior models suggest. Bureaucrats are especially important in the implementation of policy decisions; the organizational capabilities that they administer are often essential in this respect. They are also important in defining problems and in generating and evaluating alternatives, for they have the information and the expertise that are critical resources in those policy-making tasks.

The bureaucrats who are important in foreign policy making are not only in the obvious foreign affairs agencies—the State Department, the Defense Department, the Commerce Department, the Agriculture Department, the Energy Department, and most other executive agencies as well. These agencies, however, are not monolithic. Each one is itself a collection of diverse organizational units.

Although each agency and each unit has a specialized function, their responsibilities overlap somewhat. For any given policy problem, there are usually several agencies and parts of agencies with some relevant authority and expertise. Policy making, therefore, often moves slowly as clearances are obtained from numerous units.

Standard operating procedures may be conducive to orderly policy making, but they are not necessarily conducive to timely policy making. Furthermore, organizational routines and tradition-bound career groups often restrain major policy changes. Therefore, organizational policy making tends to be incremental.

Bureaucrats in diverse organizational units often have different values, perceptions, and interests, which lead them to have different policy preferences. And they can try to impose their preferences by resisting clearance or refusing cooperation on decisions they do not like. Before and after decisions are made on conflictual issues, bureaucrats employ many strategies to try to prevail in the conflicts. Which bureaucrats and which organizational units prevail depends partly on the cleverness of their strategies and partly on their political resources.

Bureaucrats in agencies other than the State Department have considerable political resources. They have technical information and expertise, they have operational capabilities for implementing decisions, and they have nongovernmental interest groups who support their programs. The State Department, however, has a central coordinating role in many policy areas in addition to its responsibilities for general, nontechnical diplomacy.

Whatever the distribution of power resources for bureaucratic political games and regardless of who wins or loses those games, they create distortions in the content and flow of information in policy making. Sometimes bureaucrats withhold information, sometimes they leak information, sometimes they even fabricate or destroy information—for information is not a neutral commodity in bureaucratic political struggles; it is a resource to be hoarded or a weapon to be used. Bureaucratic political games impose severe constraints on rational decision making, which depends on comprehensive and accurate information.

Bureaucratic political games also make it difficult to achieve government action that is highly coordinated and directly responsive to high-level policy makers' decisions. Although numerous government reorganization plans have been designed to achieve better coordination and control, they have not been entirely successful.

We should be careful not to conclude, however, that the bureaucracy is utterly irrational and out of control. In the first place, bureaucratic conflicts often contribute to a more rational policy process by ensuring that diverse facts and ideas are brought to light in discussions on a given issue. As in courtroom adversary proceedings, bureaucratic conflicts regularly assure that more than one side to an issue is heard. Furthermore, the expertise and knowledge that bureaucrats bring to policy making routinely improve the analytic basis of decisions. Finally, bureaucrats are, of course, subject to a degree of congressional oversight as well as substantial presidential direction.

══ S E V E N ══

The President

Our examination of the president's role in the policy process in this chapter will be guided by several analytical models. Three of them that are especially relevant—the pluralist, the ruling elite, and the human behavior models—lead to a focus on the following questions: What are the formal and informal sources of presidential power? How much power do presidents and their advisers have? What are the constraints on presidential power? How do a president's background and personality affect policy making?

The president is not only an individual participant in the policy process; he is also part of the institution of the presidency. The presidency is an institution in three respects. First, it is an institution in the sense that any president has certain formal authority conveyed by the Constitution. Second, it is an institution in the tangible form of a specific organization, the Executive Office of the President. Third, it is an institution in the informal behavioral sense that there are widespread expectations about the role the president will play in policy making.

The Constitution specifies several functions for the president in the conduct of foreign policy, but his authority in each area is also limited by constitutionally prescribed congressional authority. The president can negotiate treaties, but the Senate must ratify them. The president is commander-in-chief of the military, but its operations require congressional appropriations of funds. The president can appoint ambassadors and other high-level officials, but the Senate confirms the appointments.

Although these constitutional provisions are important determinants of presidential power, they are not the only ones—and indeed not even the most important ones. The president's power depends to a great extent on other factors, which affect his position in the executive branch, his relations with Congress, and his public standing.

EXECUTIVE OFFICE OF THE PRESIDENT

Within the executive branch, the president's position is substantially strengthened by the staff support he receives from the Executive Office of the President—a large group of people who are individually and collectively among the most powerful participants in the policy process.

The Executive Office of the President was created in the Roosevelt administration to provide more staff assistance so that the president would be better able to control and coordinate the executive branch of the government. Since that time, the size, composition, and responsibilities of the office have changed considerably; these changes have been partly the result of differences in the individual presidents' backgrounds and policy-making styles. Since the Executive Office of the President is intended to serve as the president's own advisory staff, it is altered somewhat by each new president to suit his own preferences. Furthermore, the growth of the rest of the executive branch has also led to a general increase in the size and responsibilities of the Executive Office of the President.

All its major organizational components, as listed in Table 7–1, are involved in foreign policy making. A few of the components, however, are especially important in foreign policy making. One is the White House Office, which includes many of the president's closest advisers. Although their titles and backgrounds usually do not suggest foreign policy interests, they are frequently among the most important participants in foreign policy decision making. This is especially the case when a foreign policy issue has significant political consequences inside the United States.

TABLE 7–1 Components of the Executive Office of the President

COMPONENT	STAFF SIZE
White House Office	338
Office of Management and Budget	570
National Security Council	57
Council of Economic Advisers	34
Office of the U.S. Trade Representative	156
Office of Science and Technology Policy	33
Council on Environmental Quality	20
Office of Policy Development	42

Source: U.S., *The Budget of the United States Government, Fiscal Year 1991* (Washington, DC: U.S. Government Printing Office, 1990), pp. A-389–A-399.

Since most of these senior White House advisers are longtime associates who have advised the president during his campaign for the presidency and even before, they are especially sensitive to the impact of foreign policy issues on the president's domestic political support. For example, when President Carter was trying to build public and congressional support for the Panama Canal Treaties, he assigned the task of coordinating the administration's efforts to Hamilton Jordan, one of his top political advisers. In Reagan's first term, Edwin Meese of the White House Office was a key adviser on many foreign policy issues, even though his background did not include training or experience in foreign affairs. The same was true of John Sununu in the Bush administration. Such other White House staff members as the press secretary, speech writers, and congressional liaison specialists also often become involved in foreign policy discussions.

The Office of Management and Budget is the largest component of the Executive Office of the President. Its director is often a close associate of the president and general purpose adviser on a broad range of issues. Most of its staff, however, are career government employees who specialize in preparing the presidential budget submission to Congress, reviewing other legislative proposals, and providing general managerial oversight of executive-branch agencies. They are especially important in defense-spending issues. Other components of the Executive Office of the President are also regularly involved in particular kinds of foreign policy issues—the Office of Science and Technology Policy, for example, in advanced weapons issues.

The one component that is exclusively and centrally involved in foreign policy making is the National Security Council.

National Security Council

Created by the National Security Act of 1947, the National Security Council proper consists of the president, vice-president, secretary of state, and secretary of defense. In addition, the director of the CIA and the chairman of the Joint Chiefs of Staff regularly participate in its meetings as formal advisers to it, and numerous other officials often participate informally.

The significance of the NSC, as it is commonly called, lies especially in the organization and procedures that have been developed around it. The NSC staff of about sixty is headed by the assistant to the president for national security affairs, who is one of the president's principal advisers on foreign policy. Although several other officials, particularly in the cabinet and the White House Office, have a similar advisory capacity, the NSC staff chief is normally in more frequent contact with the president on foreign policy issues. He usually meets with the president each morning to review the daily intelligence report and discuss pressing problems.

Although they have not usually been so publicly conspicuous as the secretaries of state and defense, several special assistants have become well known outside the government as well as powerful within it. McGeorge Bundy in the Kennedy administration and Walt Rostow in the Johnson administration were particularly influential on Vietnam policy. Henry Kissinger, who held the position in the Nixon administration before he became secretary of state, was much more conspicuous and powerful than was William Rodgers, the secretary of state at the time.[President Carter's assistant, Zbigniew Brzezinski, shared the limelight and the power more equitably with Secretary of State Vance.]Richard Allen, President Reagan's initial assistant, was in office only briefly before allegations of impropriety forced him to leave. William Clark then served inconspicuously for a couple of years before becoming secretary of the interior. He was succeeded by Robert McFarlane, who had had a long military career and NSC staff experience prior to his appointment. Brent Scowcroft, NSC adviser to President Bush, maintained an unusually low profile; yet, the combination of his close relationship with the president, his extensive background in foreign policy, and his previous military positions in the government enabled him to exercise considerable influence.

The NSC staff and its head play supporting and supervisory roles for a large array of NSC committees.[1] There are NSC committees for intelligence, arms control, covert operations, and crisis decision making. The committee members are cabinet- and subcabinet-level officials from executive agencies; they are responsible for providing advice and coordinating the agencies' activities in such policy areas. One of the specific tasks is to oversee the preparation of memoranda that define and evaluate options for policy decisions[Those memoranda cover the entire gamut of foreign policy (for instance, American relations with the Soviet Union, oil imports, the defense budget, and trade with China) (om

We must be careful, however, not to attribute more order or routine to policy making than actually exists. Just as organization charts can create false impressions, so, too, can the formal structure and procedures of the NSC system. The actual functioning of the NSC system depends very much on the particular issues and individuals involved. Even though the Nixon administration proclaimed a commitment to orderly policy-making procedures and had an unusually strong NSC system headed by Kissinger, it made many important decisions on the SALT negotiations with the Russians and trade relations with the Japanese and other countries outside the NSC system. In fact, in August 1971, President Nixon decided on a series of unilateral American actions that fundamentally changed the international monetary system and international trade policies without getting advice through the NSC system. Instead, he relied mostly on the advice of Secretary of the Treasury Connally. Presidents Carter, Reagan, and Bush similarly relied on their own close political advisers from the White House staff, in addition to formal NSC procedures.

Furthermore, the mere existence of an NSC system does not necessarily assure that the president's advisers and the rest of the executive branch will always be responsive to his wishes. Because he cannot devote his undivided attention to any one foreign policy problem and because his advisers and other executive-branch officials often have their own policy preferences, the president is often frustrated by his inability to get the executive branch to implement the policy he prefers.

Presidential frustration is evident in an account of a National Security Council crisis committee meeting during the 1971 Indo-Pakistani war. The meeting was held in the Situation Room in the White House basement on Friday morning, December 3. The participants included: Henry Kissinger, assistant to the president for national security affairs; John Irwin, undersecretary of state; David Packard, deputy secretary of defense; Richard Helms, director of the Central intelligence Agency; Maurice Williams, deputy administrator of the Agency for International Development; Thomas Moorer, chairman of the Joint Chiefs of Staff; and Joseph Sisco, assistant secretary of state for Near Eastern and South Asian affairs.

The minutes, which were prepared by a Defense Department official and marked "secret-sensitive," became public through a "leak" to the press.[2] They read, in part, as follows:

Kissinger:	I am getting hell every half-hour from the President that we are not being tough enough on India. He just called me again. He does not believe we are carrying out his wishes. He wants to tilt in favor of Pakistan. He feels everything we do comes out otherwise.
Helms:	Concerning the reported action in the west wing, there are conflicting reports from both sides and the only common ground is the Pak attacks on the Amritsar, Pathankot and Srinagar airports. The Paks say the Indians are attacking all along the border; but the Indian officials say this is a lie. In the east wing the action is becoming larger and the Paks claim there are now seven separate fronts involved.
Kissinger:	Are the Indians seizing territory?
Helms:	Yes, small bits of territory, definitely.
Sisco:	It would help if you could provide a map with a shading of the areas occupied by India. What is happening in the West—is a full-scale attack likely?
Moorer:	The present pattern is puzzling in that the Paks have only struck at three small airfields which do not house significant numbers of Indian combat aircraft.

• • •

Kissinger:	We have to take action. The President is blaming me, but you people are in the clear.
Sisco:	That's ideal!
Kissinger:	The earlier draft for Bush is too even-handed.
Sisco:	To recapitulate, after we have seen the Pak Ambassador, the Secretary will report to you. We will update the draft speech for Bush.
Kissinger:	We can say we favor political accommodation but the real job of the Security Council is to prevent military action.
Sisco:	We have never had a reply either from Kosygin or Mrs. Gandhi.
Williams:	Are we to take economic steps with Pakistan also?
Kissinger:	Wait until I talk with the President. He hasn't addressed this problem in connection with Pakistan yet.
Sisco:	If we act on the Indian side, we can say we are keeping the Pakistan situation "under review."
Kissinger:	It's hard to tilt toward Pakistan if we have to match every Indian step with a Pakistan step. If you wait until Monday, I can get a Presidential decision.
Packard:	It should be easy for us to inform the banks involved to defer action inasmuch as we are so near the weekend.

Kissinger: We need a [meeting] in the morning. We need to think about our treaty obligations. I remember a letter or memo interpreting our existing treaty with a special
India tilt. When I visited Pakistan in January, 1962, I was briefed on a secret
document or oral understanding about contingencies arising in other than the
SEATO context. Perhaps it was a Presidential letter. This was a special interpretation of the March, 1959, bilateral agreement.

The president may have a dominating position in the executive branch, and he
surely has a substantial power resource in the form of the Executive Office of the
President. Nevertheless, his power is limited. He cannot assume that his preferences
are clear; nor can he assume that his decisions will be implemented without hesita-
tion.

RELATIONS WITH CONGRESS

On many issues, the president encounters considerable congressional resistance to his
wishes. The constituents, responsibilities, and personal political stakes are different
for members of Congress and the president. The president is likely to view tariff
issues, for instance, from the standpoint of their effects on the national economy,
American trade relations with other countries, and, of course, his own political
fortunes. Since tariff increases are inflationary domestically and harmful to American
relations with its trading partners internationally, the president is likely to take these
consequences into account more than most members of Congress do. Although
members of Congress may be concerned about those consequences, they are likely to
be more concerned about the local economic impact and the effects on their own
political standing. If a tariff increase is beneficial to local employment and profits in a
congressional district or state, a representative or senator is likely to support it.
Narrow economic interests are less relevant on other types of foreign policy issues,
such as nuclear arms control or military intervention. Yet different conceptions of the
national interest and varying views about the risks and effectiveness of policy
alternatives can lead to conflict on those issues as well.

Since the president often meets congressional resistance, he must try to persuade members of Congress to help him. His success depends on many factors, but
one of the most important is his professional reputation.[3]

Reputation

Washington is a city of president watchers. If people see a president who knows
what he wants and knows how to get it, they will be relatively easily persuaded to help
him. If on the other hand, they see a president who is not in command, who is unsure
of what he wants or is unwilling to fight for it, they will be reluctant to help him. All
presidents occasionally appear inept, and their professional reputations suffer temporary setbacks. But if they create such an impression very often, their professional

reputations may become permanently damaged and their ability to get what they want diminished. Cases from the Eisenhower and Carter presidencies illustrate the importance of reputation and how it can be damaged.

The Eisenhower case concerns a budget request he submitted to Congress in January 1957.[4] Fresh from a substantial re-election victory two months earlier, Eisenhower was in a strong position to exert leadership on the government spending priorities reflected in his budget proposals. Those proposals included more spending on foreign aid, defense, education, welfare, and natural resources; and the budget total was several billion dollars higher than had been expected. Thus, Eisenhower was offering, in his own words, a "modern" Republican budget.

But his behavior over the next several months cost him much congressional support for his program priorities, and it also cost him dearly in terms of his professional reputation. On the same day the president's budget proposals went to Congress, his secretary of the treasury held a press conference in which he said there were many places where the budget should be cut, and he even implied that increased government spending could lead to a depression. Not only did Eisenhower fail to make it clear that the secretary was not speaking for the president, he even said a few days later that he partially agreed with the secretary's sentiments. A few months later, he went further; he ordered reductions in his own budget.

A year later, an administration official testifying on a budget matter before a congressional committee said his recommendations were essential to the president's program, and everybody laughed. They laughed because the president's own behavior had created widespread doubts about what he actually wanted in his budget, and their laughter indicated how low the president's professional reputation had fallen.

President Carter's professional reputation also suffered when he appeared not to be in command on several occasions.[5] One instance concerned the neutron "bomb," which is a nuclear artillery shell, or a warhead for short-range surface-to-surface missiles. Its specific tactical function is to disable tanks by penetrating their shields with neutron radiation.

In early 1977, a weapons procurement authorization bill submitted to Congress by the outgoing Ford administration contained a request for funds to produce such weapons, which would be deployed in Europe. The Carter administration, which came into office shortly after the Ford budget submission, quickly revised several items in the Ford budget to reflect its own priorities. In June, after *The Washington Post* ran a story about the neutron bomb program, President Carter said that he had not been aware of the program but that he did want the option of making a decision to produce it later in the year. After a move in Congress to cancel the program was defeated, the authorization bill including funds for the program was passed. The president then announced that his decision to go ahead with production would depend on the European NATO members' agreement to have the weapons deployed on their territory.

A major West German party leader, however, said that he strongly opposed the deployment, as did several other political groups in Western Europe. The governments of West Germany and other European NATO countries expressed their reluctance to accept deployment in the face of strong domestic opposition. Over the next several months, the NATO countries indicated that the United States should decide whether to produce the neutron bombs, then try to use them as a bargaining chip in the SALT negotiations with the Soviet Union. If the United States was unable to negotiate a quid pro quo with the Russians that would include cancellation of the U.S. neutron bomb program, West Germany would be willing to accept deployment—but only if Belgium or the Netherlands also agreed to deployment. Meanwhile, the Soviet Union had denounced the neutron bomb as a serious escalation of the nuclear arms race.

President Carter was thus caught in the middle of conflicting political pressures. The Soviet Union was scoring propaganda points against him; European allies were offering only contingent support; and Congress was badly split over the issue. He was also getting conflicting advice from within the executive branch. His national security adviser and secretaries of state and defense were advising him to go ahead; his UN ambassador and White House aides were advising him to cancel the program.

In early April 1978, a *New York Times* article reported that the president had decided to cancel the program. The White House contended that no decision had been reached, but there were strong negative reactions from congressional supporters of the program and from several European governments as well. Moreover, strong domestic criticism of the presumed presidential decision came from several prominent Democrats and Republicans inside and outside Congress. A few days later, the president announced that he had decided only to postpone production, pending a show of reciprocal restraint on the part of the Soviet Union. This compromise decision satisfied neither the supporters nor the opponents of the program in Congress.

Most important, though, it left the impression that the president had vacillated on the issue, that he had been ineffective in his diplomacy with the Soviet Union and the NATO countries, and that he had been inept in his relations with Congress. This impression may have been unfair in view of the complexities of the issue and the conflicting pressures on the president. But the president's reputation is based on impressions and appearances. He appeared not to know what he wanted and not to be in command. His reputation among president watchers in Congress and elsewhere was damaged.

The Carter administration's handling of conflicts with Congress over arms transfers to Turkey and other issues prompted a prominent Democratic leader in the House to remark that "they handled these...incidents with all the finesse of an alcoholic hippopotamus." More generally, a Republican congressional leader noted: "There's great confusion over what the administration really wants. Carter's voice doesn't come through loud and clear on anything." He added that because of the president's low standing in the public-opinion polls at the time, "many Congressmen have concluded that he is a one-term President. So, naturally, they ask themselves why they should go out of their way to help him."[6]

Even so, President Carter enjoyed a reputation for attention to detail and for being well informed about the substance of complex technical issues. President Reagan, however, suffered from an opposite reputation. Indeed, Reagan was widely regarded as being uninterested and uninformed about many issues. (He was reported to have dozed off in cabinet meetings and to have commonly used oral briefings and even videotaped briefings in place of more detailed written reports as a way to follow issues.) Yet, the firmness of Reagan's views and his ability to communicate them effectively to the public contributed to his reputation as a president who could successfully articulate and promote his policy preferences.

PUBLIC STANDING

Although the general public does not scrutinize presidential behavior as closely as the professionals in Washington do, they nevertheless form vague impressions of a president's competence. They also notice whether the general nature and consequences of the president's policies are agreeable to them. Several decades of polls indicate that presidents can expect their public standing to be relatively high at the beginning of their terms. But they can also expect it to decline during their time in office. The uncertainty is over how quickly, how consistently, and how far it will decline—and the causes and consequences of the decline. Presidential experience has varied significantly in these respects.

Trends

The trend lines in Figure 7–1 depict the substantial variations in presidential popularity. Truman's popularity rating reveals the greatest range. His public standing was unusually high just after he entered the presidency at Roosevelt's death in 1945. It declined precipitously, however, as a consequence of a recession, opposition to his civil rights policies, and other problems. Although he was able to win re-election and regain much popularity by the beginning of his second term in 1949, his public standing then plummeted as a result of scandals in his administration, charges of Communist infiltration in the government, the defeat of Chiang Kai-shek's nationalist forces by the Communists in the Chinese civil war, and finally the continuation of the war in Korea. However, neither Truman's conduct of the war nor his other foreign policies were much affected by his declining public support.

Eisenhower's public standing was high at the outset and went even higher during his first term, but it declined during his second term, partly because of a recession. Both Eisenhower and Kennedy, however, enjoyed considerable popularity throughout their presidencies. It was not until Johnson that an erosion in public support clearly undermined the president's ability to conduct foreign policy, particularly the Vietnam War.

Even though Nixon's popularity was lower than other presidents' at the beginning of his time in office and remained barely above 50 percent during his first term, he was not prevented from undertaking major foreign policy initiatives—notably a strategic arms limitation agreement with the Soviet Union and steps toward normalizing diplomatic relations with China.

During his second term, however, as his public standing and his credibility

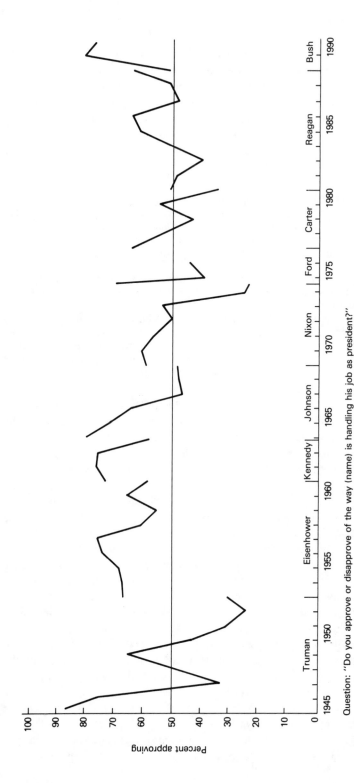

FIGURE 7–1 Trends in presidential popularity. (Data points are the first poll of each year plus the first and last polls for each president.)

Question: "Do you approve or disapprove of the way (name) is handling his job as president?"

Sources: The Gallup Opinion Index; The Gallup Poll: Public Opinion, 1972–77 (Wilmington, DE: Scholarly Resources, 1978); The Gallup Poll: Public Opinion, 1935–1971 (New York: Random House, 1972); Gallup Report 175 (February 1980), 13; 225 (June 1984), 11; 244/245 (January/February 1986), 22–23; 270 (March 1988), 20; 280 (January 1989), 13; 281 (February 1989), 10; The Gallup Poll Monthly 292 (January 1990), 16.

declined because of the various Watergate revelations, his ability to muster public support for foreign policy was impaired. Some observers suggested that he acted impulsively or even disingenuously when he ordered a worldwide alert of American military forces during the 1973 Arab-Israeli war. Secretary of State Kissinger despaired over speculation that the president was trying to divert attention from his Watergate-related problems. The following exchange during a press conference indicates the doubts about the president's motives and Kissinger's concern with maintaining the president's credibility.

> Reporter's question: It seems . . . that you're asking the American people . . . to accept a very dramatic military alert involving nuclear forces on the basis of a kind of handful of snow, without telling them or us exactly why. If I understood you earlier, you said that we had discovered the alert of some Soviet forces and we were disturbed by the behavior, apparently, of some people whom American officials were dealing with. And that's all we really have to justify this alert.
>
> Now this country's pretty badly shaken right now, and I wonder if you can give us any more information that will help convince people that there is some solid basis for the actions that have been taken.
>
> Kissinger's answer: . . . We have tried to give you as much information as we decently and safely and properly can under these conditions. As soon as there is a clear outcome, we will give you the full information . . . we will be prepared . . . to put the facts before you. But there has to be a minimum of confidence that the senior officials of the American government are not playing with the lives of the American people.[7]

President Ford's pardon of Nixon for his role in Watergate reduced his own popularity from its initial high level to below 50 percent, where it stayed for the remainder of his term. That low public standing made it difficult for him to achieve another strategic arms limitation agreement with the Soviet Union. President Carter also faced a similar problem in his presidency, as congressional opponents of further U.S.–USSR arms control agreements were emboldened by his vulnerable public standing. President Reagan's standing at the beginning of his presidency was relatively low, at barely more than 50 percent positive and, after a moderate dip, returned to that level by the end of his first term.

The Reagan presidency also illustrates how opinion on specific foreign policy issues can constrain a president, at least in marginal ways. Polls frequently found a substantial portion of the population that was disquieted by what they regarded as Reagan's almost cavalier approach to nuclear arms control and military intervention.[8] About one-fourth of the public thought Reagan policies were increasing the risk of nuclear war. Slightly more than half thought the administration was too quick to use military forces in its handling of international problems. Half the public said they felt "uneasy" in response to a question about their confidence in Reagan's "ability to deal wisely with a difficult international crisis." Although it would be difficult to document, the administration's approaches to nuclear arms control and intervention in Central America appeared to be responsive to such public concerns, and the hostility in their public posture toward the Soviet Union was reduced, particularly during the 1984 election. Their approach to arms control negotiations with the Soviet Union, in particular, appeared to become less hostile and more receptive.

President Bush enjoyed substantial popularity early in his presidency, after an initially low popularity rating. His own and the public's confidence in his foreign policy management skills, furthermore, enabled him to garner considerable public support for his decision to send U.S. troops to Saudi Arabia in the summer of 1990 and then to employ them against Iraqi troops and other targets in Kuwait and Iraq in early 1991.

Overall, we find that a low standing in the public-opinion polls or public opposition to specific policies or concern about his general approach to foreign policy can restrict a president's ability to pursue his preferred policies. A president may refrain from making some decisions for fear his popularity will decline further, or he may make some decisions in an effort to improve his public standing. Furthermore, variations in his public standing tend to increase or reduce congressional resistance to his wishes. Nevertheless, the president has considerable leeway in his choices. In spite of congressional resistance and declining public popularity, a president normally has several politically acceptable alternatives open to him. And he has enormous political assets to try to make his desires prevail.

The alternatives that he selects, the way in which he decides among them, and his success in gaining support for his decisions all depend on his own personal traits. To gain a better understanding of presidential policies, style, and power, we need to consider the president as a person.

THE PRESIDENT AS A PERSON

We all bring an accumulation of personal experiences and emotions to our decision making, and the president is no exception. As political scientist James David Barber has observed, ''Every story of Presidential decision making is really two stories: an outer one in which a rational man calculates and an inner one in which an emotional man feels. The two are forever connected.''[9]

Much of what a president feels as he makes decisions depends on how he feels about himself—in particular, his self-esteem. Some presidents have had a decent regard for themselves and the self-assurance and security that accompany a strong, healthy ego. Others have been ego-defensive and insecure. The sources of such variations are diverse, complex, and subtle, but the variations are evident, and they affect presidential performance.

The effects on presidential style are the most obvious. Personally insecure presidents—Johnson and Nixon—have been relatively tense, distrustful, secretive, and hostile toward their critics. More personally secure presidents—Truman, Eisenhower, Kennedy, Ford, Carter, Reagan, and Bush—have been more relaxed, trusting, and open, even friendly with their critics. The Nixon administration put its political opponents on an ''enemies list'' to be harassed by the Internal Revenue Service and to be excluded from the White House invitation lists for dinners and other occasions; other administrations have invited their critics to White House functions in spite of their disagreements. Nixon and Johnson saw only a relatively small number of close advisers because their insecurities made it difficult for them to meet with advisers whose loyalties and opinions were less supportive; other presidents have had a larger circle of advisers. Nixon and Johnson demanded extraordinary secrecy and relished surprising their critics; other presidents have expressed their thoughts and plans more publicly.

Personality Differences

Variations in presidential style are also a reflection of differences in personality, that is, basic behavioral and attitudinal tendencies. Barber has identified two dimensions of personality that are particularly important determinants of presidential performance. One is activity or energy. Although all presidents obviously expend great energy as they perform their duties, some do it more compulsively and exhaustively than others. Johnson often spent whirlwind twenty-hour working days as president, and Carter was often directly involved in the highly detailed aspects of policy making. In an earlier era, Coolidge slept eleven hours at night and still took an afternoon nap. This dimension of behavior, however, reflects more than mere variations in physical energy. It also reflects several other active-passive personality contrasts, such as the tendency to be dominant or submissive, extroverted or introverted, aggressive or timid.

The second dimension identified by Barber refers to the president's feelings about his work, whether they are positive or negative. Some presidents (especially Roosevelt, Kennedy, and Reagan, among the recent ones) have clearly enjoyed being president; others have not. All have felt the heavy burdens of presidential responsibilities, but a few have often been gloomy and depressed in the presidency.

These two dimensions—active-passive and positive-negative—can be combined to produce four personality types and four types of presidents: active-positive, active-negative, passive-positive, and passive-negative. Active-positive presidents are the most likely to be effective because they are assertive, persistent, and goal oriented. Passive-positive and passive-negative presidents tend to be ineffective. Their tendency to withdraw from conflict makes it difficult for them to engage in the political battles a president needs to fight to get what he wants; their reluctance to be assertive makes it difficult for them to lead.

Active-negative presidents may be fighters and thus often able to get what they want, but they also tend to be destructive. The energy they put into their presidential roles is a reflection of a compulsive striving for power and status. They need these emotional rewards as compensation for their weak egos and as assurance against their insecurities. They also tend to become inflexible and dogmatic about the policies they adopt. They cannot admit to mistakes or defeats; such admissions would be too threatening to their already low self-esteem.

Johnson's handling of the Vietnam War revealed active-negative tendencies. For five years, he doggedly pursued an increasingly costly and destructive Vietnam War policy in spite of its evident failure. And he did so with great energy, considerable self-doubt, and bitter hostility toward his critics.

The effects of personality on presidential behavior were even more evident in Nixon's case. Before becoming president, Nixon wrote in his book *Six Crises* that "reaction and response to crisis is uniquely personal in the sense that it depends on what the individual brings to bear on the situation—his own traits of personality and character, his training, his moral and religious background, his strengths and weaknesses."[10]

Several of Nixon's Vietnam decisions reflected his own strengths and weaknesses.[11] In November 1969, he prepared a major speech on Vietnam policy without consulting his secretary of defense. He wrote the speech himself, mostly while alone at Camp David (the presidential retreat in the mountains near Washington) with little advice from his speech writers or his national security adviser. Contrary to expectations, he announced there would not be any new troop withdrawals, and he implied that only the domestic critics of his policy could defeat or humiliate the United States in Vietnam. Five months later, however, he announced that 150,000 American troops would be withdrawn—a decision that was made without consulting the secretary of defense or the secretary of state.

A week after that, he decided to invade Cambodia with thousands of American troops. He decided in favor of the invasion even though the secretary of defense, the Joint Chiefs of Staff, the secretary of state, the attorney general, and NSC staff members warned that the military benefits of doing so were uncertain and that a strong negative domestic reaction was likely. Indeed, he made the decision the night after his secretary of state had testified in Congress that the administration would continue to de-escalate in Vietnam and surely avoid any commitment of ground troops in Cambodia. Over the next two days and nights, the president prepared a television address to the nation, mostly working alone at night. His draft of the speech said the operation would enable the United States to capture the Communist headquarters for all of South Vietnam. When the secretary of defense learned of this statement, he suggested taking it out, since no such headquarters even existed. When the president's national security adviser briefed reporters on the speech just before the president appeared on television, he recommended they not expect the military action to lead to the capture of an enemy headquarters. The president's address nevertheless announced that the troops entering Cambodia would "attack the headquarters for the entire Communist military operation in South Vietnam." (He also noted that it "was not an invasion of Cambodia.") The actual consequences of the decision were to increase domestic turmoil over the war, including the killing of student demonstrators by National Guard troops at Kent State University, but not to reduce significantly Communist military operations in Cambodia or South Vietnam.

In short, presidential performance is partly a function of the president's personality. However, the personal sources of a president's style, power, and policies are always operative within the institutional constraints of the presidency. Public, congressional, and even bureaucratic expectations about presidential behavior all restrict an individual president's leeway. An incident toward the end of the Nixon presidency is suggestive. As the prospect of impeachment loomed and as Nixon's political fate and psychological state were increasingly in doubt, the secretary of defense sent an unusual message to American military forces: They were to obey only orders coming through the normal chain of command, which includes the secretary of defense and the Joint Chiefs of Staff. The significance of the message was that the secretary was in effect telling the troops they should not obey an order coming directly from the president, who might have forcibly tried to resist any efforts to remove him from office.

Yet, in spite of institutional constraints, in spite of common congressional resistance, and in spite of the vicissitudes of his public standing, a president is able to adopt his preferred policies and to do so according to his own decision-making style to a great extent. This is particularly true when the security of the country is perceived to be at stake or when policy can be formulated relatively secretly.

Many of the most significant decisions concerning relations with Russia and China have reflected individual presidents' personalities and power. Those presidential decisions include in particular: Truman's decisions that established containment of communism as the guiding principle in American foreign policy; Kennedy's decisions during the confrontation with the Soviet Union over missiles in Cuba; and Nixon's decisions to seek a reduction of tensions (détente) in relations with Russia and China. These presidential decisions determined American policy at important points in the early, peak, and late phases of the cold war era. They are among the most consequential American foreign policy decisions since World War II.

CASES

Truman's Containment Decisions

During the four-year period 1947–1950, President Truman made a series of decisions that reflected his desire to contain the expansion of Soviet and Communist Chinese influence. In the spring of 1947, he decided to provide economic and military aid to Greece and Turkey to help them resist what he perceived as Communist-supported attempts to overthrow their governments.[12] At the same time, he stated more generally that "it must be the policy of the United States to support free peoples who are resisting attempted subjugation by armed minorities or outside pressure." His proposal to provide such countries with economic and military aid became known as the Truman Doctrine, and it also became a key component of the containment policy.

The decision was precipitated by messages from the British government on February 21 that severe economic problems in Britain would prevent it from continuing its support of the Greek and Turkish governments. Within a week, after discussions with Secretary of State Marshall, Undersecretary of State Acheson, and military officials, the president decided to send economic and military aid. Although the president could provide some military supplies on his own authority, he needed congressional legislation authorizing the several hundred million dollars of further aid he wanted to provide.

Both houses of Congress had Republican majorities at the time, and the Republicans had been advocating reductions in government spending. Moreover, Truman's personal popularity was low (48 percent favorable responses in the Gallup Poll in late January). But Truman was able to achieve congressional and public support relatively easily.

At a meeting with key Republican and Democratic congressional leaders on February 27, he had Secretary of State Marshall and Undersecretary Acheson describe the situation they perceived and their rationale for the administration's decision to provide aid. Marshall's focus on the military and economic situation in Greece and Turkey and the humanitarian rationale for the administration's decision did not evoke a positive response from congressional leaders. But Acheson's more apocalyptic description of the conflicts between the world's two dominant countries—Communist Russia and the democratic United States—moved them to be more responsive. Senator Vandenburg, Republican chairman of the Senate Foreign Relations Committee, indicated that he accepted the administration's depiction of the situation and suggested that the president should address Congress and the public to describe the serious threat the administration perceived.

Administration officials then began drafting a presidential speech and giving background press interviews on the situation. The predominant reaction to the president's speech recorded in polls of members of Congress and the general public was favorable; among congressional Republicans, Senator Vandenburg gave his prestigious support. Within two months, the administration's request was approved unanimously by the Senate Foreign Relations Committee and approved by votes of 67 to 23 on the Senate floor, 24 to 1 in the House Foreign Affairs Committee, and 287 to 107 on the House floor. Thus, the president had taken a major policy initiative and achieved widespread congressional and public backing for it—all within three months. (And the president's approval rating had increased by more than 10 percent.)

At the same time, the administration was also formulating a massive economic assistance policy for all of Western Europe.[13] Developed by Undersecretary of State Clayton and Director of Policy Planning Kennan, the policy was a response to the serious economic problems that were retarding the postwar reconstruction of Europe. Those problems were also, in the view of the administration, making Western Europe more vulnerable to increasing Communist influence (for example, through electoral victories).

But again the president would need congressional approval of such a program. The administration began its campaign to prepare the Congress and the public for its European Recovery Program with a speech by Undersecretary of State Acheson in Mississippi. In his speech, Acheson discussed the administration's view of the economic and political problems in Western Europe, their implications for American interests, and the general nature of the American response that was needed. Then on June 5, in a Harvard University commencement address, Secretary of State Marshall reiterated the administration's concern about the economic and political situation in Europe and suggested that the United States would be willing to help the Europeans formulate and fund a recovery plan—the Marshall Plan, as it was eventually called.

During the following months, the administration again sought and received the crucial support of Senator Vandenburg; and it also obtained the support of several labor, industrial, and agricultural groups. The plan also enjoyed considerable press and public support, the latter achieved partly through the work of the Citizens' Committee for the Marshall Plan, which was created at the administration's initiative.

Meanwhile, American and European government officials developed the details of the Marshall Plan. In December, the president proposed to Congress a European Recovery Program of $17 billion (the equivalent of more than $100 billion in 1990 dollars) to be dispensed over several years by a new U.S. Economic Cooperation Administration. After minor differences and compromises over organizational arrangements for the program, a slightly modified bill was passed by votes of 329 to 74 and 69 to 17. Thus, the president had again been able to undertake a major policy initiative with widespread congressional and public approval.

During early 1948, the Truman administration also began to initiate a new Western European military alliance that would include the United States.[14] To prepare congressional sentiment for such a historic decision, Undersecretary of State Lovett worked with Senator Vandenburg in drafting the Vandenburg Resolution for Senate approval. The resolution included a provision that the United States should support the development of "regional collective self-defense" arrangements, that is, military alliances. The Senate Foreign Relations Committee approved it unanimously, and the full Senate approved it 80 to 6.

Lovett and others in the administration had already been conducting secret negotiations with European governments in an effort to formalize an alliance. After a compromise with key senators concerning draft treaty language, the president submitted the North Atlantic Treaty to the Senate for ratification in April. In July, it was ratified by a vote of 82 to 13. Thus, for the first time in its history, the United States became a member of a military alliance during peacetime.

A year later, President Truman decided to send American combat troops into the war between North and South Korea.[15] On Saturday night, June 25, 1950, Secretary of State Acheson informed President Truman that large numbers of North Korean troops had crossed the 38th parallel and attacked South Korean forces in the area. At Acheson's suggestion, Truman authorized him to make plans to call a UN Security Council meeting. A few hours later, Acheson informed Truman that a special Security Council meeting could be called by the United States and that the State Department had drafted a resolution condemning the North Koreans and suggesting that the Security Council take action to restore peace. On Sunday afternoon, the Security Council passed a resolution calling on the North Koreans to withdraw their troops.

On Sunday evening, the president met with the secretary of state, secretary of defense, Joint Chiefs of Staff, and other State and Defense Department officials. The president decided to accept Secretary Acheson's recommendations that he order available military supplies to be sent to South Korea from the U.S. Far Eastern Command, that American air and naval combat units evacuate American civilians from Korea, and that the American Seventh Fleet be sent to the Formosa Straits between mainland Communist China and Nationalist China on the island of Taiwan.

The next day State Department and Defense Department officials discussed the situation briefly before Senate and House committees. There was also brief public discussion—and some criticism—of the administration's handling of the situation by a few members of Congress. But the Senate Republicans as a group formally endorsed providing military supplies to the South Koreans, although they opposed direct American involvement in the fighting. That evening at a meeting with his principal civilian and military advisers, the president accepted Secretary Acheson's recommendation that the United States employ air and naval combat units south of the 38th parallel to try to stop the continuing North Korean advance. He also ordered the Seventh Fleet in the Formosa Straits to protect Taiwan from a possible Chinese Communist attack and to protect China from possible attack by Taiwan as well. He also ordered an increase in American military assistance to the Philippines and to the French in Indochina.

The next morning, the president and several advisers completed a public statement for release at noon to announce that the United States had entered the war with air and naval combat forces. At 11:30, the president met with fourteen congressional leaders of both parties to inform them of his decisions. After Secretary Acheson reviewed the situation in Korea and the American response, President Truman read his public statement to the group. They unanimously approved of his actions, and there was widespread support forthcoming from other members of Congress, the press, and the public.

On Thursday at an NSC meeting, the president accepted a Joint Chiefs recommendation that combat air and naval units be authorized to attack north of the 38th parallel and that ground troops be committed for limited rear-guard duty. On Friday morning, the president approved General MacArthur's request to use army troops in ground combat. Later that morning, the president informed a meeting of fifteen congressional leaders of his decisions; only one objected. Congressional comment later in the day also generally supported the president.

In this case and the others, Truman made his decisions promptly after soliciting numerous advisers' opinions and on the basis of his own rather simple perceptions and preferences. He then sought congressional and public support, which were relatively easy to achieve.

A decade later, President Kennedy approached the problem of Russian missiles in Cuba in a similar manner, although with more caution and less violence.

Kennedy's Cuban Missile Crisis Decisions[16]

On Tuesday morning, October 16, 1962, National Security Adviser McGeorge Bundy informed President Kennedy that the CIA had photographic evidence that the Soviet Union was placing nuclear missiles in Cuba. The president apparently resolved almost immediately that he wanted the missiles removed and that forceful action would be necessary to accomplish their removal.

The precise nature of the American response was discussed and decided in strict secrecy during the following week by the president and sixteen other people. Eventually called the Executive Committee of the National Security Council (ExCom), it was an ad hoc group of officials from several agencies, White House advisers, and former government officials. The group included the usual foreign policy advisers: the secretary and four other State Department officials; the secretary, the chairman of the Joint Chiefs of Staff, and two other officials from the Defense Department; the director of the Central Intelligence Agency; and the assistant to the president for national security affairs. But it also included several others whose advice the president particularly respected: his brother Robert Kennedy, the attorney general; Theodore Sorensen, his special counsel; Douglas Dillon, secretary of the treasury; Dean Acheson, former secretary of state; and Robert Lovett, former secretary of defense.

During a Tuesday morning meeting and at subsequent meetings later in the week, the group considered five basic alternatives: no active response, diplomatic pressures, naval blockade, air strike, invasion. The first alternative was quickly rejected when the president indicated he wanted to take forceful action. In fact, his initial preference was for an air strike that would destroy the missile sites. By the Wednesday ExCom meeting, the choice was effectively narrowed to an air strike or naval blockade, with a clear division of opinion among the president's advisers. The supporters of the blockade alternative included Robert Kennedy, Secretary of Defense McNamara, Deputy Secretary of Defense Gilpatrick, and Special Counsel Sorensen.

On Thursday evening, the president told the group he had tentatively decided in favor of a blockade. During the following two days, however, the Joint Chiefs continued to oppose the blockade and favor an air strike. At a Saturday meeting, the president heard arguments from both the advocates of the air strike and a blockade, and he also heard UN Ambassador Stevenson's arguments in behalf of diplomatic pressure. At that meeting, the president reiterated his preferences for the blockade, but he wanted to discuss the air strike alternative with the air force tactical bombing commander.

His discussion with air force personnel the next day confirmed the previous analysis that an air strike would not necessarily destroy all the missiles and that it would risk massive damage to the areas around the missile sites, where there would be Cuban civilians and Russian technicians. Thus, at a formal NSC meeting on Sunday, the blockade decision was formalized.

By Monday evening, a naval task force of nearly two hundred ships was preparing for a blockade in the Atlantic. In addition, tactical fighter squadrons were moved to airports within range of Cuba, and over two hundred thousand troops were moved to Florida—to be ready for an air strike and/or an invasion in case the blockade failed. These deployments were also over threats of further actions if the missiles were not removed. Also by this time, a television address drafted by Sorensen and revised by the president was ready for the president to deliver on Monday evening.

Until 5 o'clock Monday evening, no member of Congress had been aware of the situation. At a White House meeting at that time, the president informed twenty congressional leaders of both parties about the events of the past several days and of his decision to impose a blockade, which would be announced that evening on television. Although the congressional leaders indicated strong opposition to the decision and a preference for an air strike or invasion, Kennedy gave his speech announcing the blockade, as already decided.

During the next several days, the confrontation became increasingly tense, and the fate of several hundred million people in North America, Europe, and the Soviet

Union was in doubt. After numerous public and private communications between Kennedy and Soviet Premier Khrushchev, the Soviet government said on Sunday that it would remove the missiles. An ExCom meeting had already been scheduled for later the same day to discuss the next American move if a positive Soviet response had not been received by then. In short, the world came perilously close to nuclear war. During the crisis, President Kennedy himself estimated the odds at "between one out of three and even."

Like Truman, Kennedy solicited the opinions of many civilian and military advisers. Although he formulated his own opinion and reached a tentative decision, he carefully considered his advisers' conflicting evaluations of more than one alternative. More sensitive to the complexities and uncertainties in decision making than Truman, he was nevertheless willing to persist in his course of action in spite of more bellicose congressional preferences.

The conflict was ultimately resolved without resort to large-scale violence. But the fear of nuclear war engendered by the confrontation led to renewed efforts to reduce cold war tensions. A decade later, President Nixon decided to speed up this process of détente.

Nixon's Détente Decisions

In his January 1969 inaugural address, Nixon hinted that there would be changes in policy toward Russia and China in his administration. Although he had specifically said he opposed admission of China to the UN during his campaign, he noted more generally in his inaugural speech that "after a period of confrontation, we [were] entering an era of negotiation" and the administration's "lines of communication [would] be open" to all nations.

During the next three and a half years, he communicated openly and secretly with the Chinese and Russian leaders in an effort to improve relations. As he did so, he carefully tried to prepare congressional and public opinion for changes in American relations with the two Communist countries, but he also engineered spectacular surprises. His diplomacy, moreover, combined quiet persistence in gradually making tangible changes in policy with dramatic symbolic gestures. The climaxes were trips to Peking in February 1972 and to Moscow in May of the same year. But he began the work toward those climaxes almost immediately after entering the presidency.

When Nixon became president, American-Chinese relations had been dominated by hostility for twenty years. The United States officially recognized only the government on Taiwan as the government of China; it opposed the admission of Communist China to the UN; it forbade any exports to Communist China; and it maintained a naval patrol in the Formosa Straits. Representatives of the two countries met periodically in Warsaw, Poland, beginning in 1955, but these meetings became less frequent over time, particularly as the Vietnam War became more severe. Only one meeting was held in 1968, and the one scheduled for early 1969 was cancelled.

During February 1969, one month after entering office, Nixon ordered an NSC review of American policy toward China; he renewed contacts with China through third countries; and he renewed offers to begin scientific and cultural exchanges.[17] During the next year, the president on his own authority instituted several changes in policy. In July, restrictions were reduced on tourist travel to China and imports of goods from there. In November, naval patrols in the Formosa Straits were discontinued. In December, the removal of American nuclear weapons from Okinawa (less than five hundred miles from China) was announced. Also in December, import and export restrictions were reduced.

In January 1970, the first meeting of the countries' representatives in two years was held in Warsaw. The Warsaw talks and the pace of further improvement in relations, however, were interrupted by the American invasion of Cambodia in the spring of 1970.

In 1971, there were several important developments. Remaining restrictions on travel and trade were substantially reduced. But the most dramatic and significant events were more symbolic. In July, the president announced that he would visit China within a year "to seek normalization" of relations. The visit had been arranged by Henry Kissinger, his assistant for national security affairs, during a secret trip to China a few days before. The planning for the president's visit had been known only to a handful of people in the White House and State Department. Although there was widespread support, some members of Congress, representatives of the (Nationalist) China lobby, and, of course, the government on Taiwan all expressed their dismay.

Meanwhile, the administration had been reconsidering its policy on Chinese membership in the UN. It announced in August that it was no longer opposed to Communist Chinese membership, though it did oppose expelling Taiwan if Communist China gained admission. In the end, both happened; and there was considerable congressional displeasure with the UN's action and the change in administration policy. The administration said it would continue its recognition and tangible support of the Nationalist Chinese government, but it also successfully resisted a congressional move to cut off American financial support of the UN.

Finally, in February 1972, the president went to China for a dramatic and highly publicized one-week stay. The two countries subsequently established "liaison offices" in the two capitals, one step closer to the full diplomatic relations that were eventually established in early 1979.

During this same period, from early 1969 to early 1972, Nixon and Kissinger were also trying to improve relations with the Soviet Union, although that effort was focused on strategic arms control negotiations.[18] The outgoing Johnson administration had already prepared an American negotiating position in anticipation of the start of strategic arms control negotiations with the Russians. Nixon, however, decided not to go ahead with those plans; instead, he ordered a full review of American policy shortly after he was inaugurated. When the results of that review were found to be unsatisfactory, Kissinger created a new NSC committee for SALT, which he chaired. Because of the policy review and the organizational changes, the first SALT negotiating session was delayed until November 1969. Over the next two and a half years, American and Russian delegations met alternately in Helsinki, Finland, and Vienna, Austria, to conduct the formal negotiations.

Because of the technical complexities of the issues and the basic conflicts in the Soviet and American negotiating positions, only slight progress was made for more than a year. Then in January 1971, a "back channel" was created to facilitate negotiations among higher-level government officials. In particular, Kissinger and Soviet Ambassador Dobrynin began meeting in Washington to represent directly the views of Nixon and Soviet Premier Kosygin. These back-channel negotiations were kept secret from all but a few government officials. After several months of feverish negotiations, Nixon and Kosygin were able to reach tentative agreement on several basic issues. In May, Nixon announced the general nature of the agreement, although the specifics were still known only to Nixon, Kissinger, and a few other officials.

For the next several months, further negotiations were conducted through both the front and back channels. In April 1972, Kissinger took a secret trip to Moscow—unknown even to the chief of the American negotiating delegation—to try to settle the remaining differences. After compromising with the Joint Chiefs of Staff on a critical negotiating point in order to gain their support, the president was ready to go to Moscow for another dramatic and highly publicized summit meeting. With a few issues still unresolved, Nixon went to Moscow in May. Chaotic last-minute negotiations at that summit meeting produced a treaty limiting ABMs and an interim agreement limiting other missiles.

Even though Senate ratification of the treaty was required, only Senators Jackson and Brooke has been consulted during the negotiating period. Furthermore, until the exact terms of the documents were made public in Moscow, not even the formal negotiating delegations knew for certain what their contents would be, since they had been so carefully excluded from the back-channel negotiations.

We can see, then, that unlike Truman, Kennedy, and most other presidents, Nixon often relied on a very few advisers. He often excluded cabinet members from deliberations, made his decisions in seclusion, and then announced them to a surprised public, Congress, and even administration. Ultimately, of course, Nixon's secretive and distrustful tendencies were the source of his own undoing.

In other respects, however, Nixon, Kennedy, and Truman were similar. They were all prone to decide what they wanted first and then solicit congressional and public support. They all, furthermore, skillfully used the enormous potential power of the presidency.

CONCLUSION

The president is almost inevitably at the center of action in the policy process. The Constitution confers considerable authority on the president; the Executive Office of the President provides him with staff support that enhances his position in the executive branch; the Congress and the public look to him for leadership. He is in a strong position to respond to problems and to take the initiative according to his own preferences and style.

The resources of the presidency as an institution, however, provide an individual president with only the potential to exercise power and thereby impose his preferences on policy. The extent to which he actually does so and the way in which he tries to do so depend on his own values, beliefs, background, and personality. Thus, we need to incorporate psychological variables in our analysis of individual presidents to understand their power, policies, and style.

We also need to recognize the limitations on a president's power. As the pluralist model indicates, the president often encounters numerous obstacles as he tries to exercise power over policy. According to constitutional provisions, he shares authority with Congress in several ways; therefore, he needs congressional support or at least acquiescence to play his constitutionally delegated roles. Furthermore, although Congress and the public may look to the president for leadership, they do not necessarily follow his lead. Members of Congress often resist his leadership— sometimes because they think he is encroaching on their institutional prerogatives, sometimes because their personal political interests are different from his, and sometimes because they do not think that his objectives or policies serve the national interest as they see it. Furthermore, sometimes his reputation as an effective president or his standing with the public, or both, are so low that he cannot lead. He can neither persuade people that he knows best, nor bargain with them from a position of strength. Indeed, his political position may become so weakened that he cannot even command his own advisers and the rest of the executive branch.

Yet in times of crisis, when there are widely shared perceptions of a serious threat to common interests, even a politically weak president is likely to become the center of action. Furthermore, Congress and the public are usually inclined to rally around the president—at least for a while.

EIGHT

Defense Spending

One of the most commonly asked questions about American defense spending is: How much is enough? Or alternatively, we might ask: How much is too much? To answer these questions, we need to be explicit and precise about the underlying issues that lead us to ask them. One issue concerns how much should be spent in the pursuit of foreign policy objectives. Thus, we might ask: How much should be spent to try to maintain peace in general or to deter specific potential wars? Other issues related to foreign policy goals include how much to spend in order to minimize losses if war should occur, to support interventions in other countries, to enhance a general political role in the world, to gain bargaining advantages in negotiations, or to achieve status.

Still other issues concern the militarization of American society. Long ago, political scientist Harold Lasswell warned that the United States could become a "garrison state" dominated by military values and institutions that would threaten civil liberties.[1] To what extent has this occurred?

A third set of issues concerns governmental and societal priorities: Does the United States spend too much on the military and too little on education and other social programs? What are America's priorities compared with other countries' priorities?

Finally, the economic implications of military expenditures are an issue: What is the financial burden of supporting the military compared with the past and compared with other countries? What are the employment and other economic effects of increases or decreases in defense expenditures?

HISTORICAL AND CROSS-NATIONAL COMPARISONS

In recent years, American defense expenditures have been over $300 billion per year. How does that compare with the past? Is it relatively high or relatively low? The answers to these questions depend on the indicators and the years used for the comparisons.

In any comparison over time, price changes can create false impressions. As inflation erodes the purchasing power of a given amount of money, the same nominal amount of money does not represent the same amount of goods and services. Thus, the usual unit that is used to indicate monetary values, which is called a *current dollar*, is not a good indicator of trends in defense expenditures.

A better measuring unit is the *constant dollar*. A constant dollar amount is computed rather easily by selecting a base year and using a price deflator such as the consumer price index to convert each year's current dollars into a constant dollar amount. For instance, if we want to compare expenditures in 1990 and 1992, we could use 1990 as the base year, compute the ratio of the consumer price index in 1990 to that of 1992, and divide the 1992 current dollar amount by the change in the consumer price index. We would then have the 1992 amount expressed in 1990 constant dollars.

Consider the data in Figure 8–1, which indicate defense expenditures for the period from 1950 to 1995 (the FY91–95 figures are projections from the FY91 budget proposal). The data there show the difference in time comparisons based on current and constant dollars. The bottom line, which uses current dollars, conveys the impression of large and continual increases throughout most of the period. But since the inflation rate was substantial during part of this period (as much as 12 percent per year), we need to use constant dollars to obtain a more meaningful impression of the real changes in expenditures. And, indeed, the constant dollar figures of the top line convey a different and more complicated trend. By the late 1970s, defense expenditures were more than twice as high as in the early post–World War II years just before the Korean War. But they were much lower than in the peak years of the Korean and Vietnam wars and about the same as the period between those two wars. There were substantial increases in real as well as nominal terms in the 1980s but real decreases in the early 1990s.

How do these U.S. expenditure levels compare with those of other countries? When we compare countries' expenditures, we face two complications. One is that those expenditures are originally expressed in different currencies (U.S. dollars, German marks, French francs, Russian rubles, and so on). But the exchange rates that enable us to convert the amounts into a single currency change over time, and they are not necessarily indicative of comparable purchasing power at any one time.

Another problem is that countries use different definitions of their defense budgets. The official Soviet defense budget figures, for instance, exclude much of its weapons research, development, and procurement expenditures, which would be included in the American budget. The Soviet defense expenditure figures widely used in the United States, therefore, come from CIA estimates, which include a proportion

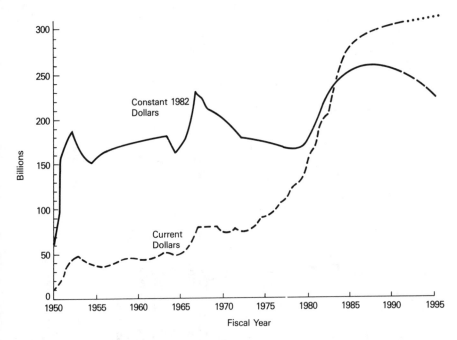

FIGURE 8–1   Trends in U.S. military expenditures

Sources: U.S., *The United States Budget in Brief, Fiscal Year 1979* (Washington, DC: U.S. Government Printing Office, 1978), p. 21; U.S., *The Budget of the United States Government, Fiscal Year 1979,* p. 487; U.S., *The 1957 Federal Budget Midyear Review,* p. 7; U.S., *The Budget of the United States Government, FY 1985,* table 25; U.S., *Statistical Abstract of the United States 1985; The Budget of the United States Government, Fiscal Year 1991,* table 6.1. Figures for FY91–95 are projections ("estimates").

of the official Soviet science budget in their estimates and which use the cost of equivalent U.S. weapons systems when they do not have adequate intelligence on Soviet weapons systems.[2] These estimates indicate that Soviet and American defense spending have been at similar levels for many years, with the Soviet Union spending more in some years and the United States more in others.

Although such basic data help us to have clearer impressions of current American expenditures in relation to both past expenditures and other countries' expenditures, they do not directly provide us with information that enables us to answer the particular questions raised at the outset of the chapter.

For purposes of addressing the specific issues of social priorities, the militarization of American society, and the economic burden of defense, we can use the data in Figure 8–2. Recent American military expenditures have been about 6 percent of the gross national product (or about 25 percent of the federal government's total budget). Compared with the several decades since World War II, we find that these figures are relatively low except in comparison with the immediate postwar period, when they were comparable. On the other hand, if we extend our horizon further back in time, we see that the period since World War II has been an era of high-level commitment of societal and governmental resources to the military.

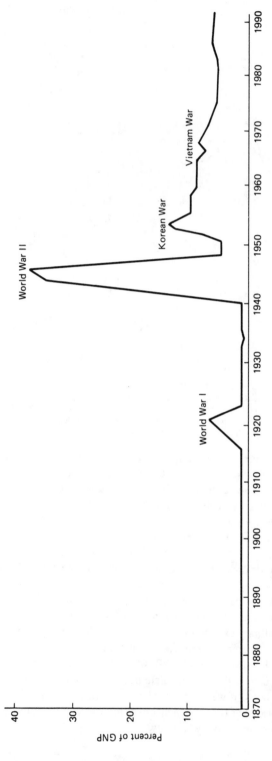

FIGURE 8–2 U.S. military expenditures as percent of GNP

Sources: Stanley Lieberson, "An Empirical Study of Military-Industrial Linkages," in *Testing the Theory of the Military-Industrial Complex,* ed. Steven Rosen (Lexington, MA: Lexington Books, D. C. Heath and Company. Copyright 1973, D. C. Heath and Company), fig. 3–2, p. 74. By permission of the publisher; U.S. Bureau of the Census, *Statistical Abstract of the United States 1977* (Washington, D.C.: US Government Printing Office, 1977), p. 358, table 564; U.S., *The Budget of the United States Government, FY 1985,* tables 24 and 25; U.S., *The Budget of the United States Government, FY 1991,* table 6.2, pp. A-302–A-303.

How do such expenditures for the military compare with expenditures for other purposes? What do they reveal about national priorities? The data in Table 8–1 provide a preliminary answer to this question. They indicate expenditures by category and the proportion of the total government budget represented by each category. Military expenditures clearly constitute a major portion of federal government expenditures—about 25 percent. But income security (unemployment benefits) and Social Security (retirement benefits) have constituted an even greater proportion in recent years. On the other hand, military expenditures have been twice as great as federal government health expenditures and many times greater than federal government education expenditures.

Although these figures provide substantial evidence of the high priority given to military expenditures by the federal government, they do not provide appropriate indications of total societal priorities. Federal government expenditures represent only about one-fifth of total GNP. In some categories, such as education, the federal government expenditures are only a small fraction of total societal expenditures; but nearly all direct societal expenditures for the military are represented in the federal budget. So we need another set of data to obtain a better picture of the entire society's priorities.

Unfortunately, such data are not nearly as abundant or reliable as we would like. The best available data include all public (governmental) expenditures; but they exclude all private expenditures, which are substantial for health and even education

TABLE 8–1   U.S. Federal Government Spending Priorities

FUNCTIONAL CATEGORY	PERCENT OF TOTAL EXPENDITURES
Defense	25
Veterans' Benefits and Services	2
International Affairs	1
Science, Space, and Technology	1
Energy	<1
Natural Resources and Environment	1
Agriculture	1
Community and Regional Development	1
Transportation	2
Education, Training, Employment, Social Services	3
Health	5
Medicare	<8
Income Security	12
Social Security	21
Administration of Justice	1
Commerce and Housing Credit	2
General Government	1
Interest	15

Source: Computed by the author from fiscal year 1990 estimates in U.S., *The Budget of the United States Government, Fiscal Year 1991* (Washington, DC: U.S. Government Printing Office, 1990), table 3.3, pp. A-295–A-297.

in the United States. In any case, they indicate that the United States has recently ranked twenty-sixth in the world in per capita public health expenditures and sixteenth in per capita public expenditures for education.[3] In recent years, the proportion of the American GNP going to defense expenditures has been declining, while the proportion of the GNP and federal government expenditures going for health, education, and other social services has been increasing.

In sum, American military expenditures are high in absolute terms, in relation to pre– and immediate post–World War II expenditures, in comparison with most other categories of government expenditures, and in relation to much of the rest of the world. On the other hand, they are only a small fraction of GNP.

We also want to know whether this is enough or too much in relation to foreign policy goals and how policy makers decide such questions. We therefore turn to a consideration of the analytic techniques used in government budgeting and then to a discussion of the political perspectives and behavior of participants in the defense-spending policy process.

INSTITUTIONALIZED ANALYTIC TECHNIQUES

Over time, the government has employed several different analytic approaches to defense budget decisions.[4] The Truman administration set the defense budget at one-third of the total federal government budget. Thus, defense-spending levels were directly responsive to changes in government revenues rather than changes in world politics. The Eisenhower administration also set defense-spending ceilings on the basis of internal economic conditions, but it set the ceiling at one-tenth of GNP. This Defense Department total was then divided among the services according to constant proportions.

The Kennedy administration considered those approaches arbitrary and not sufficiently related to foreign policy goals. Under the direction of Secretary McNamara, therefore, the Defense Department instituted a set of techniques designed to improve the quality of the analysis for expenditure decisions. Although the novelty, significance, virtues, and limitations of these procedures have been controversial and exaggerated, they do constitute a distinctive and appealing analytic approach to defense-spending questions. They represent an attempt to apply scientific analysis and economic rationality to defense budgeting—that is, to make defense budgeting conform more closely to the rational decision-making model.

There has been a great deal of confusion as well as change in the terminology used to describe these procedures, but the following is typical.

The basic approach to decision making involved in these procedures is called *systems analysis.* Basically, this approach means that budget analysts should be sensitive to the whole problem that they encounter; that they should be aware of the relationships among components of systems; that they should link together the inputs and outputs of any given alternative solution to a problem; that they should make assumptions explicit rather than leave them implicit; and that they should be quantitative to the extent feasible.

One of the implications of this approach has been the emphasis on *cost-effectiveness analysis,* which encourages the use of quantitative measures of both inputs (costs) and the effectiveness of outputs. It also emphasizes comparing alternatives in terms of their relative costs and effectiveness. The analysis of the cost of any given alternative normally involves only the computation of dollar costs. The analysis of the effectiveness of alternatives, however, is more complex.

Two examples will illustrate cost-effectiveness analysis. One concerns a key cold war issue in American defense policy—namely, the force levels to be maintained by the United States and its NATO allies.[5] For many years, the question was commonly answered by the simple statement that it should be as much as could be afforded or at least as many as and preferably more troops than the Soviet Union and its Warsaw Pact allies maintained. There was very rough equality for many years in terms of active duty uniformed military personnel. On the other hand, the Warsaw Pact had more than twice as many tanks as NATO, but NATO had more than twice as many "tactical" nuclear weapons as the Warsaw Pact.

Such simplistic analyses, however, left a great deal to be desired. In the first place, they left implicit the military function or mission of those forces. Moreover, they ignored the foreign policy objectives that they served. If we follow the systems-analysis dictum to be explicit in our assumptions and explicit about objectives, then we need to take into account the fact that the NATO forces presumably exist only to deter or defend against a potential attack. They are presumably not for offensive purposes. Traditional military rules of thumb indicate that defensive forces have a substantial advantage over attacking forces of the same size.

In addition, we need to take into consideration the effectiveness of the troops in their defensive function, not simply their numbers. When we do so, we find the comparative numbers of troops or tanks or "tactical" nuclear weapons are not particularly relevant. A more useful comparison, for instance, is the number of NATO antitank weapons that could be used to defend against an attack by tanks. Such a comparison indicates that the ratio is more than 3:1. NATO forces have more than two hundred thousand antitank missiles that can be launched from land vehicles, helicopters, and other aircraft.

A thorough analysis of the effectiveness of NATO troops as a defensive force would have to take into account many more variables. These would include terrain, other weapons capabilities, and the geographic distribution of forces. Most important in the 1990s, however, such an analysis needs to take into account the revolutionary changes in Eastern Europe and in East-West relations as a result of the end of Communist party domination and the subsequent changes in diplomatic relations and military policies. The simple analysis above, though, does illustrate the limitations of common balance-of-forces comparisons that ignore the purposes and effectiveness of those forces.

Arguments over the balance of naval forces also illustrate the importance of taking into account foreign policy objectives and measures of effectiveness.[6] Many of the simplistic comparisons made in those arguments ignore effectiveness altogether. For instance, those who argued that the development of the Soviet navy in the 1980s was threatening American naval superiority often compared the number of ships in the two navies, since the Russian navy was bigger by this measure. Those who argued that the American navy was superior used tonnage figures, since the American navy was bigger by this measure.

A more appropriate approach is to analyze the effectiveness of American naval capabilities in relation to the missions or functions that those naval forces are intended to serve. Four such missions are commonly cited. One is to "maintain a military presence" in regions where the United States wants to exercise influence. This may occur in peacetime in the form of routine visits, or it may occur in crises to demonstrate concern or even to make visible threats. The United States, for instance, deploys carrier task forces to provide tangible evidence of U.S. support for its allies and to demonstrate its interest in specific regional conflicts. A second naval mission is to "control sea lanes" to try to prevent interruptions in the flow of economic goods and military supplies in wartime. Antisubmarine capabilities are particularly important for this mission. The third mission is to "project power ashore" through air attacks, coastal bombardment, and amphibious assault; such a mission was actively undertaken in the Persian Gulf war as well as the Korean and Vietnam wars. The fourth mission is "strategic deterrence," which entails threatening retaliation with submarine-launched missiles that carry nuclear warheads.

Calculating the effectiveness of American naval forces requires a different analytic approach for each of these missions. For instance, comparisons of naval forces are irrelevant to effectiveness calculations concerning "strategic deterrence" and "power projection." The strategic deterrence effectiveness of American strategic missile-bearing submarines depends instead on the number of targets, the effectiveness of antisubmarine measures, and other factors. Similarly, the "power projection" effectiveness of the American navy depends on the coastal defenses at potential attacking points in other countries.

Thus, only in attempting to determine the American navy's effectiveness in serving its "presence" and "sea control" missions do we need to compare naval forces. And even those comparisons must take into account many factors besides simple quantitative relationships. For instance, because maintaining a military presence is largely a symbolic matter, a large aircraft carrier may be more effective than a small attack submarine in demonstrating a military presence. It is not necessarily more effective than several cruisers, however.

In sum, military effectiveness calculations should be based on indicators that are appropriate to specific missions and objectives.

In the early 1960s, another set of procedures was introduced in the Defense Department to improve the quality of defense-spending decision making. This was *PPBS—Planning, Programming and Budgeting System.* Its purpose is to link defense-budgeting decisions directly to long-term planning and to programs or functions. The emphasis on programs or functions is intended to replace the traditional budgeting focus on military services and inputs. Thus, instead of focusing on the amount and shares of the military budget going to the army, navy, air force, and marines, program budgeting emphasizes the functions of those services' forces.

Accordingly, the Defense Department budget request is divided into "program" categories such as personnel, procurement, construction, and operation and maintenance. Although these and other program categories differ from earlier years, they preserve the emphasis on functions and programs rather than organizational units in the budget process.

In any case, all these analytic techniques—whatever terminology they may employ—often merely provide data to support decisions based to a great extent on other considerations. Such decisions, after all, are not made by disinterested government administrators in a political vacuum. They are the result of a process in which economic and political pressures are brought to bear. To obtain a more thorough understanding of defense-spending decisions, we need to consider them from a broader perspective—one that includes the interests and influence of participants in the policy process.

INTERESTS AND INFLUENCE

The Military-Industrial Complex

We can define the military-industrial complex as (a) high-level military officers and civilians in the Department of Defense and in the parts of the Department of Energy that are concerned with weapons development; and (b) managers, directors, and major stockholders of corporations that are either primarily defense contractors (regardless of size) or partly defense contractors (if they are among the larger corporations in the country). The former category of corporations includes such well-known defense contractors as General Dynamics, Lockheed, McDonnell-Douglas, and North American Rockwell; but it also includes lesser-known corporations that are small but still obtain more than half their sales from defense contracts. The latter category includes such giants as General Motors, which sells thousands of automobiles and trucks each year to the military. Such corporations can appropriately be considered part of the military-industrial complex because the absolute amounts of their defense sales are substantial, even though they are only a small proportion of their total sales.[7]

Together, these participants constitute an interest group. Like participants in all interest groups, they have mixed and even conflicting interests; but they have core interests in common. They all have an interest in a high volume of weapons production and a high level of military expenditures. Moreover, the governmental participants and individual corporations have a common interest in the distribution of the total military budget. Both want to assure the survival of individual corporations, because governmental participants are often dependent on given corporations for continuing to produce weapons. There are also conflicting interests, however. The corporations often compete for the same contracts; and governmental and corporate participants often disagree about quality and prices. But the relationship between governmental and corporate participants is basically one of mutual dependence. One needs the weapons; the other needs the sales. Thus, there is a symbiotic relationship between the governmental and corporate participants in the military-industrial complex.

Furthermore, like other interest groups, they actively promote their common interests in the policy process. Both the corporate and the governmental participants lobby in Congress. Indeed, the Pentagon's congressional-relations expenditures are probably bigger than the lobbying budgets of all of the defense contractors together. The participants in the military-industrial complex also promote their interests through public information and advertising programs. When defense contractors take out newspaper ads touting the desirability of one weapons system or another, they are clearly engaging in a public lobbying effort. But the Defense Department's public affairs activities are also essentially a lobbying effort.

These participants in the military-industrial complex may have common interests, and they may actively promote them. But are they a single, cohesive, organized interest group? The evidence on this point is more circumstantial, but it is highly suggestive.

In the first place, there is substantial overlap and circulation of personnel. Some people are on the boards of directors of several different defense corporations. Hundreds of retired military officers are employed by defense contractors. Numerous corporation executives assume high-level Defense Department positions and then return to defense industries. The career of Malcomb Currie is indicative. After fifteen years at Hughes Aircraft and four years at Beckman Instruments (both defense contractors), he became director of defense research and engineering in 1973. In that position (the third-ranking official of the Defense Department), he successfully supported Hughes Aircraft missile contracts over the objections of the army and the House Armed Services Committee. In 1977, he left his Defense Department position for a vice-presidency at Hughes Aircraft at a very high salary.

Further, corporate personnel have ample opportunities to gain the ears of government officials without going through the revolving doors (a practice which is now limited by conflict-of-interest laws). Several Department of Defense advisory boards provide corporation representatives with direct access to governmental administrators who are centrally involved in the weapons design and procurement process.

Government-corporation linkages are even closer in financial and operational matters. The government guaranteed, for example, a $200 million loan to the Lockheed Corporation to keep it out of bankruptcy. Department of Defense accountants audit the finances of defense contractors. The Department of Defense leases facilities it owns to defense contractors so they can fulfill contracts with the Department of Defense. Defense Department representatives often oversee operations on site at production lines. Such a merging of corporate and governmental involvement in financing and operations suggests that many defense contractors are not, in a true sense, private corporations at all. They can be more accurately described as quasi-private corporations.

The military-industrial complex, even if it is not a completely cohesive interest group, surely contributes to higher defense spending and cost overruns in weapons procurement. But its basic nature is quite similar to interest groups that have developed in the other issue areas.[8] Although their consequences may not be so dramatic or so directly related to foreign policy, there are also agricultural, health care, and educational complexes. That is, in each major policy area there are groups of governmental and nongovernmental participants who share common attitudes, interests, and policy preferences; who maintain close and even cooperative relationships; and who engage in political activities.

This notion of the military-industrial complex as one interest group among many suggests that its existence, its nature, and its consequences are more consistent with the pluralist model than the ruling elite model. It also suggests that although the military-industrial complex may be an unusually large and powerful (and to some, pernicious) interest group, it does not exist in a political vacuum. Its recommendation for defense expenditures must be approved by Congress, and these expenditures must at least be tolerated by the public.

Congress

One assumption commonly associated with the notion of a military-industrial complex is that defense expenditures create interests that lead to political pressures for continued defense spending. As far as Congress is concerned, this assumption implies that members of Congress from areas with relatively high defense spending are likely to support increased military expenditures, because their constituents' economic welfare (and votes) are dependent on them.

We would therefore expect a strong statistical relationship between (a) the amount of dependence of a state or congressional district on defense spending and (b) the voting behavior of the members of Congress on defense-spending issues. Several studies have tried to determine whether such relationships have in fact existed.[9] To the extent that there is a relationship, it seems to be a weak one (the correlation coefficients are often close to zero). Of those correlations that are relatively strong, most are in the expected direction of the hypothesis (although many are in the opposite direction). Finally, the relationship is strongest when military and civilian payrolls at military installations, rather than contracts, are used as an indicator of defense spending.*

We are interested, however, not only in trying to explain the differences in the voting behavior of individual members of Congress on defense-spending issues; we are interested also in the influence of Congress as a whole on defense spending. In most years, Congress imposes a reduction, and since the late 1960s, it has nearly always done so. The data also indicate, however, that the changes have usually been quite small (less than 5 percent). Indeed, Congress often changes the administration's proposal less than the president changes the request the Department of Defense submits to him.

---

*The significance of the studies, however, is limited by their focus on the Senate rather than the House. Since variations in the economic significance of defense spending are clearer and greater among congressional districts than among states, the relationship between defense spending and congressional voting is probably stronger in the House than in the Senate. Furthermore, the studies were conducted in the 1960s, when there was strong congressional consensus supporting military expenditures.

Congress's impact on defense appropriations has tended to be greater on the subtotals than the totals. In addition to a total defense-expenditure figure, the appropriation bills passed by Congress contain expenditure subtotals in each of several categories: research, development, testing, and evaluation; procurement; personnel; and operations and maintenance. One study found that although Congress changed the administration's request in the latter two categories by an average of only 1 percent, it changed the request in the first two categories by an average of 4 percent and in some instances by as much as 15 percent. Furthermore, the first two categories are more central to decisions on weapons systems and strategic decisions; therefore, these findings suggest that Congress has a programmatic impact on defense-spending priorities in addition to its impact on total defense spending.[10] The Congress has also frequently delayed or reduced the level of deployment of individual weapons systems—such as the B-1 bomber, the MX missile, the Stealth bomber, and the Star Wars nuclear defense program.

Public Opinion

The public's role in defense spending is, of course, much less direct than Congress's. Yet over the long run, the acquiescence, if not the active support, of the public is needed for the general levels of defense expenditures. Neither the military-industrial complex nor the Congress nor the two of them together would be likely to sustain highly unpopular defense-spending levels over a long period.

Figure 8–3 presents time-series public-opinion data that reveal substantial shifts and interesting recent trends. First, they reveal that between 30 and 45 percent of the public have consistently considered the levels of defense spending about right. One-third to one-half of the public seem inclined to accept whatever spending levels are adopted. Otherwise, opinion has been divided between those wanting more and those wanting less. In the late 1960s, in the mid-1970s, and in the early 1980s, there were dramatic shifts in the proportions adopting those conflicting perspectives. Prior to the late 1960s, the dissenters from actual spending levels were fairly evenly divided, with a little more than one-fifth wanting more defense expenditures and a little under one-fifth wanting less. There was a consensus supporting the prevailing expenditure levels or more. But from the late 1960s until the mid-1970s, a plurality felt that defense expenditures were too high. Then there was another shift. Beginning in 1977, the number of citizens wanting more defense expenditures again exceeded the number wanting less; but in the early 1980s, there was yet another reversal just as a large build-up of the defense budget was underway.

Although it is difficult to establish any cause-effect relationship between public preferences and actual expenditure levels, there has been a degree of parallelism in the trends of the two. In fact, shifts in public opinion have often preceded changes in defense-expenditure trends.[11] Such a pattern suggests that defense expenditures are at least somewhat consonant with public opinion. Furthermore, the decline in spending (in constant dollar terms) between the late 1960s and the late 1970s was partly a direct result of Congress's consistent and greater reductions in the administration's requests. Although the declines in public and congressional support for defense expenditures are probably linked, it is difficult to determine which led and which

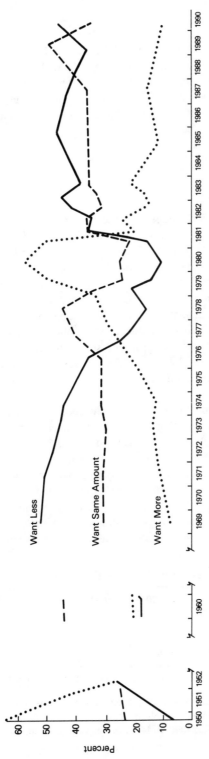

Questions: "There is much discussion as to the amount of money the government in Washington should spend for national defense and military purposes. How do you feel about this? Do you think we are spending too little, too much, or about the right amount?" In 1960, "There is much discussion as to the amount this country should spend for national defense ...?" In 1953, "Do you think too much of the taxes you pay is being spent for defense — or is too little being spent for defense?" In 1978, "Do you think that we should expand our spending on national defense, keep it about the same, or cut back?"

FIGURE 8–3 Public opinion of defense spending

Source: Gallup Poll surveys reported in *Public Opinion* 10, 6 (March/April 1988), 24; 11, 6 (March/April 1989), 25; *The Gallup Poll Monthly* 292 (January 1990), 10.

followed or whether they had mutually reinforcing effects. In any case, the lower levels of public and congressional support were accompanied by lower levels of expenditures in constant dollar terms. The converse could be said about the increases in the 1980s. The coincidence surely does not prove conclusively that defense expenditures are directly responsive to public opinion. But it does suggest that the military-industrial complex, powerful as it is, has not always been able to sustain continuously increasing defense expenditures in the face of congressional and public opposition.

A NEW ERA

President Bush's proposed FY1991 budget was the first manifestation of defense budgeting in the post–cold war era, and it was similarly Congress's first opportunity to express its budget priorities in the new era. The president's overall total for defense in his proposal was $303.3 billion in outlays—which represented a nominal increase of 2 percent but a projected real decrease of 2 percent after adjusting for the (forecasted) inflation rate. Similarly, its proposal of $306.9 billion in new budget authority represented an increase in nominal terms of about 2 percent but a decrease in real terms of about 2 percent. Subsequent real decreases of about 2 percent a year for five years were also envisioned. He also proposed substantial reductions in U.S. troops in Central Europe to less than 200,000. Numerous base closings in the United States were also slated, as were reductions, delays, or terminations of several weapons programs.

However, concerns about domestic economic prospects and a desire to reduce the overall budget deficit were creating additional pressures to reduce defense expenditures—apart from any changes in East-West relations. Moreover, it was unclear whether dramatic shifts in military strategy or spending priorities would be forthcoming. The administration was inclined to continue with prominent weapons programs such as the Strategic Defense Initiative (often referred to as "Star Wars"), for instance, at higher levels than most members of Congress wanted.

In one effort to outline projected force levels for the end of the decade, military analysts have suggested the figures in Table 8–2 as indicative of several sets of

TABLE 8–2   Illustrative Force Levels for the Late 1990s

	1990	PLAN A*	PLAN B†	PLAN C‡
Army divisions (active)	18	14	10–12	7
Aircraft carriers	14	12	10–12	6
Air Force tactical wings	36	28	25	23

*Bush administration preliminary proposal for 2 percent reductions in total defense budget through FY97.
†Composite based on alternative proposals for 25 percent reduction in five years.
‡Proposal for 50 percent reduction by year 2000.
Source: The New York Times, May 20, 1990, p. 14. Copyright © 1990 by the New York Times Company. Reprinted by permission.

possibilities. In any case, the shape of the defense budget in the post–cold war era depends on a complex interaction of strategic thinking, economic constraints, and political relationships that are evolving in the 1990s. The repercussions of the U.S.-Iraqi war can be profoundly important in this respect.

CONCLUSION

Although current dollar figures indicate regularly increasing American defense expenditures for most of the past four decades, more appropriate constant dollar figures indicate a different pattern. In constant dollar terms, American military expenditures were highest during the Korean War and the Vietnam War, and during the 1980s. Between the end of World War II and the Korean War, they were relatively low.

Political discussions about the adequacy of American military expenditures usually rely on simple balance-of-forces figures that compare numerical force levels in terms of the same categories. It would be more appropriate to consider foreign policy objectives, force missions, military effectiveness, and economic costs. The government now uses analytic techniques to focus defense-spending decisions on these considerations. Although these analytic techniques have had an impact on defense decision making, internal political pressures continue to be important determinants of defense-spending levels.

Although the military establishment and the defense contractors have some conflicting interests, they have a common interest in high levels of defense expenditures. They actively lobby in Congress, conduct public information programs, and generally promote increases in defense spending. Those increases have generally been supported by Congress and the public, but there have been periods of opposition as well.

Therefore, the American military and its industrial and commercial suppliers have substantial political resources in American society, as the military-industrial–complex version of the ruling elite model suggests. However, their power fluctuates over time, partly as a result of wars and other external conditions, as the international politics model indicates. Finally, the resources devoted to the military also depend partly on the internal political pressures generated by the public and the Congress, as the pluralist model suggests.

Nuclear Weapons

Nuclear weapons have been a central foreign policy concern since their development in the American Manhattan Project during World War II. Indeed, their potential destructiveness almost inevitably places them at the center of attention on a more or less continuous basis—at least among high-level administration officials, many members of Congress, and portions of the most attentive public. Although the threat of nuclear war and fears of American involvement in such a war have fluctuated over the years, and although there have been only a few occasions when high-level American officials have advocated or expected nuclear war, nuclear weapons policies have remained prominent for more than three decades. They have often been controversial as well. The attention and controversy since the early 1970s have been focused on the periodic strategic arms talks between the Soviet Union and the United States, which we will consider in detail. In the consideration of those talks and other nuclear weapons topics in this chapter, we will try to answer the following questions: What concepts and criteria can be applied to the analysis of nuclear weapons issues? What weapons deployment and arms control policies has the United States adopted? What are the arms control agreements the United States is a party to? What political forces affect U.S. nuclear weapons policies? But first we need to become more knowledgeable about nuclear weapons systems and the criteria we can use to analyze policies concerning their development, deployment, possible use, and control.

TECHNICAL CHARACTERISTICS OF NUCLEAR WEAPONS[1]

The term *nuclear weapon* refers to any weapon whose explosive yield is based on the fission of the nuclei of uranium or plutonium atoms (or, in thermonuclear weapons, the fusion of hydrogen atoms).* They inflict population casualties and property damage through a combination of blast, heat, and radioactivity.

Their energy yields are measured in terms of the amount of conventional non-nuclear explosives that would yield a similar explosion (except for the radioactivity). Since nuclear weapons have much greater blast and heat yields than conventional explosives, we normally express their yields in terms of thousands of tons— kilotons (KT)—or even millions of tons—megatons (MT)—of conventional explosives' yields. A 1 megaton (MT) nuclear bomb or warhead thus has an energy yield similar to one million tons of conventional explosives.

The destructiveness of nuclear weapons, however, is not perfectly proportional to their yield; a 2 MT weapon is less than twice as destructive as a 1 MT weapon. To take into account the fact that the destructive area of nuclear weapons does not increase in direct proportion to their size, we use a more refined measure of yield. Called equivalent megatons (EMT), it can be computed by converting the number of megatons to its two-thirds power; that is, $EMT = MT^{2/3}$. A 2 MT bomb equals 1.6 EMT, and a 0.2 MT (or 200 KT) bomb equals 0.6 EMT.

The extent and nature of the destruction from any one nuclear weapon also depends on several other variables: its design, the amount of radioactivity it releases, the nature of its target, and the weather conditions at the time of detonation. In general, however, greater yields mean more casualties and more destruction. The 15 KT bomb dropped on Hiroshima killed or injured more than half of its three hundred thousand people and obliterated most structures within a few miles; a 1 MT warhead would destroy most of a city of a million or so population; one 10 MT warhead (or a few smaller ones) would destroy most of a metropolitan area of several million people.[2]

Over time, the development of nuclear weapons technology has made it possible to increase the energy yields and decrease the physical size of such weapons. The nuclear bombs dropped on Hiroshima and Nagasaki in 1945 were each about ten feet long and several feet in diameter, and each weighed about ten thousand pounds. Today, weapons with similar or even greater yields can weigh as little as 20 to 30 pounds.

Because of their relatively small size, it is possible to deliver nuclear explosives with a large variety of weapons systems. In fact, many delivery systems are now "dual capable"—meaning that they can be fitted with either nuclear or conventional explosives. Some of these weapons are commonly referred to as "tactical" nuclear weapons, since their ranges are relatively short and they are intended primarily for use

*The terminology concerning such weapons can be confusing. Fission and fusion weapons are physically different; for a given mass, fusion yields are about a thousand times greater than fission yields. The terms *nuclear* and *atomic* commonly refer to both types, and we follow that practice here.

in the immediate battlefield or theater of war. Such weapons include howitzers, short- and medium-range land-based missiles, land-based and carrier-based aircraft, and cruise missiles (pilotless drones) that can be launched from ships, planes, or land. Since the ranges of some "tactical" systems are over a thousand miles, and especially since their yields are sometimes as much as 300 KT, there is no clear and universally accepted distinction between these "tactical" systems and "strategic" systems.

In general, however, "strategic nuclear weapons systems" have ranges of thousands of miles. The term specifically refers to long-range bombers, land-based intercontinental ballistic missiles (ICBMs), and submarine-launched ballistic missiles (SLBMs)—the three weapons systems comprising the so-called triad. The size and form of the payloads of individual delivery vehicles in the triad vary enormously. A single American bomber can carry several bombs of more than a megaton each for a total payload of about 10 MT, plus air-launched cruise missiles (ALCMs) with nuclear warheads. Each ICBM and SLBM has several warheads with yields of tens to hundreds of kilotons per warhead.

The practice of putting multiple warheads on missiles began in the 1960s. Originally, all the warheads on one missile were targeted on one area and were simply called multiple re-entry vehicles (MRVs). By the early 1970s, however, the re-entry vehicles could be independently targeted on separate areas and hence were called multiple independent re-entry vehicles (MIRVs). By the late 1970s, re-entry vehicles that could adjust their flight paths as they approached their targets were developed, and they were named maneuverable re-entry vehicles (MARVs).

The accuracy of strategic nuclear weapons has also substantially increased over the years. The technical term for indicating accuracy is the *circular error probable* (CEP), which refers to the radius of a circle around a target within which one-half of the warheads will fall. If ten warheads are aimed at a particular target, such as the center of a city, five would be expected to strike within a distance from the target equal to their CEP. By the 1980s, the CEP of many American warheads was a few hundred feet, so each such warhead had a 50 percent chance of landing within that short distance from its target. Some cruise missiles have CEPs of approximately ten meters.[3]

These weapons systems, which comprise the American nuclear arsenal, are summarized in Table 9–1. Altogether, that arsenal includes over 20,000 separate explosives. The "strategic triad" includes about 13,000 explosives, with a total yield of more than 4,000 equivalent megatons. Theatre nuclear forces deployed in many parts of the world account for another 9,000 separate explosives.

Since strategic weapons can be targeted on the population, industrial, and military centers in another country, they are often referred to as offensive weapons. But what about defensive weapons that might be used to destroy attacking weapons? For several reasons, defenses against nuclear attack are marginal. Since cruise missiles can fly less than a hundred yards above the surface of the water or land, they are extremely difficult to detect with radar and shoot down. Warheads launched by ICBMs and SLBMs, on the other hand, follow trajectories that take them hundreds of miles above the earth's surface, and they approach their targets at speeds of thousands

TABLE 9–1 United States Nuclear Weapons Arsenal

TYPE OF WEAPONS SYSTEM	LOCATION	APPROXIMATE NUMBER OF INDIVIDUAL WARHEADS, BOMBS*	YIELDS OF INDIVIDUAL WARHEADS, BOMBS (KT = THOUSAND TONS; MT = MILLION TONS)
Submarine-Launched Ballistic Missiles (SLBMs)	Atlantic and Pacific Oceans	5,312	50KT–100KT
Intercontinental Ballistic Missiles (ICBMs)	Continental U.S.	2,450	170KT–1.2MT
Long-range bombers	U.S.	5,238	5KT–9MT
"Strategic Triad"— Subtotal		13,000	
Theatre Nuclear Forces	Europe, Asia Oceans, U.S.	9,093	0.01KT–400KT

*Includes air-to-surface missiles, surface-to-surface missiles, surface-to-air missiles, aircraft, artillery, mines, and depth charges.

Sources: Stockholm International Peace Research Institute, *World Armaments and Disarmament: SIPRI Yearbook, 1989* (London: Oxford University Press, 1989), tables 1.1 and 1.2.

of miles per hour. ICBMs can hit their targets in less than thirty minutes after launch, SLBMs in less than fifteen minutes. Furthermore, there are limitations on antiballistic missile systems (ABMs) in the SALT/START agreements (we will discuss these shortly). Although there are aircraft and missile defenses against attacking bombers, their effectiveness is uncertain and in any case likely to be well below 100 percent. Thus, once an attack is initiated, devastating damage is virtually unavoidable, in spite of such "active" defense measures.

There are also "passive" defense measures, such as civilian shelters. Although these might save lives, at least initially, they cannot prevent property damage; nor can they prevent radioactive contamination that might make the areas around the shelters uninhabitable in any case.

There is another possible defense—using "offensive" weapons to try to destroy potential attacking weapons before they are launched. We discuss this possibility in the next section.

STRATEGIC CRITERIA AND CONCEPTS[4]

Deterrence

One purpose of the American strategic nuclear arsenal is to deter a nuclear attack on the United States itself. In this context, deterrence means minimizing the probability of such an attack, not physically preventing it. Deterrence is based on the threat of launching a highly destructive retaliatory strike on the attacking country. (Although such threats are rarely declared explicitly, they are tacitly recognized.)

The credibility and effectiveness of deterrent threats inevitably depend in part on psychological processes, for they have their impact through the perceptions and behavior of the would-be attacker. They are also partly dependent on the weapons capabilities of the deterrer. The deterrer must have an arsenal with enough destructive potential in a retaliatory (second) strike to do unacceptable damage to the would-be attacker, so that it will not launch an initial (first) strike.

How much destructive potential is that? The direct and simple answer is that nobody knows, except the would-be attacker. Yet, for purposes of the analysis of nuclear weapons deployment policies, policy makers must make an assumption of how much is enough to deter. Although substantially different assumptions are plausible and arguable, the United States has established official criteria. This "assured destruction capability" has been defined as the ability to destroy one-fourth of the Russian population and one-half of their industrial capacity in a retaliatory strike. It was proclaimed to be enough to deter by Secretary of Defense McNamara in 1961 and by many others since. The figures of one-half of the population and three-fourths of the industrial capacity have also been suggested. Early in its tenure, the Carter administration established the criteria as the ability to retaliate and destroy 70 percent of Soviet "recovery resources," that is, its economic, political, and military institutions.

Any assured destruction levels are inherently arbitrary, debatable, and essentially psychological in nature. But the determination of the numbers and kinds of weapons necessary to achieve a given level of assured destruction involves a much more technical and empirical analysis of the targets' and weapons' characteristics. For example, the distribution of the Russian population and industrial installations is such that approximately one-fourth of the population and one-half of the industrial capacity are located in only 100 cities that could be destroyed by 100 EMT.[5] Such a capability exists in a few submarines carrying SLBMs, and they are invulnerable to a disarming first strike.

Therefore, one possible strategic weapons posture—sometimes referred to as a "minimum deterrence" posture—would be to have only a small number of submarines carrying SLBMs, on the assumption that this level of destruction in a retaliatory strike would be sufficient to deter an attack.

Official American doctrine, however, has been to have such a destructive capability in each of several different weapons systems—what we might call an "ample redundant deterrent" posture. In particular, since the early 1960s, the United States has sought to maintain an assured destruction capability in each of the three weapons systems in the triad: SLBMs, ICBMs, and intercontinental bombers.

SLBMs have, in fact, remained secure against a disarming first strike, but bombers in the 1960s and ICBMs in the 1970s became somewhat vulnerable to attack before they could be used in retaliation. Since attacking SLBMs have launch-to-impact times of only 15 minutes and since they can be used effectively against airfields where bombers are stationed, a portion of the bombers might not be able to retaliate. The bombers can be kept airborne to protect against this possibility, but this is a highly expensive practice that has been employed only occasionally. American ICBMs became somewhat vulnerable to being destroyed in their silos by the 1980s because of the deployment of large, accurate, multiple warheads on Soviet ICBMs. Similarly, Soviet ICBMs are also somewhat vulnerable to being destroyed in their silos by American ICBMs.

The question of vulnerability of each type of weapons system to a disarming first strike has been subjected to extensive analysis, which raises numerous complex technical issues. And there is still uncertainty about the exact number of American bombers and ICBMs that would survive for a retaliatory strike. Nevertheless, many probably would survive to retaliate. In short, an ample redundant assured destruction capability remains.

Stability

An additional qualification is often employed to determine how much is enough for deterrence—namely, that the deterrence be stable. This requirement of stable deterrence has two components. One is that the deterrent capability be stable against the possibility of technological breakthroughs. This is precisely the rationale for the redundance represented by the triad. If a technological breakthrough in antisubmarine warfare, for instance, rendered a substantial portion of SLBMs vulnerable to a disarming first strike, other weapons systems would still have a deterrent capability.

Another form of stability is crisis stability. This kind of stability exists only so long as neither country involved in a crisis could plausibly believe that it would be better off (that is, less worse off) if it launched the first strike than if it waited to be attacked before launching a retaliatory strike. Imagine, for instance, a severe confrontation in which fears of a nuclear war were substantially heightened. Imagine further that those fears progressed to a point at which nuclear war seemed likely or even imminent. If either country's or both countries' leaders believed that they would be able to inflict much more damage on their adversary and/or suffer much less damage in their own country if they launched first rather than waited to retaliate, then deterrence could fail. It could fail because the leaders would have an incentive to strike first. Furthermore, if the leaders of both countries believed that the leaders of the other country were thinking such thoughts, there would be reinforcing, reciprocal fears of surprise attack, which could lead to a preemptive first strike.

Many strategists argue that one way to protect against the reciprocal fear of surprise attack and hence to achieve stable deterrence is to maintain "mutual assured destruction" capabilities (a condition in which both countries can inflict unacceptable damage on the other in a retaliatory strike). We have already observed that having invulnerable retaliatory weapons facilitates this objective. There is a second—and much more controversial and paradoxical—way to try to meet this objective, and that is to keep populations vulnerable to attack. As long as both populations are vulnerable to devastating retaliatory strikes, both countries' leaders will be deterred from launching a first strike. Both sets of leaders will know that the other is also deterred; therefore, they will not fear a strike. Thus, there is a "mutual hostage" relationship, which presumably contributes to stable deterrence. Such a reliance on a *m*utual *a*ssured *d*estruction relationship has been labeled MAD by its critics. For, according to them, it leads to a politically and/or morally unacceptable policy that assures the destruction of one's own country in the event of a nuclear war. Regardless, it is widely agreed that the United States and the Soviet Union have been in a relationship of relatively stable deterrence based on mutual assured destruction for many years now.

Damage Limitation

We need to consider another possible function of nuclear weapons in addition to deterrence of nuclear war. If deterrence fails, nuclear weapons might be used for damage limitation purposes. Critics have labeled those strategists who emphasize the damage limitation function of nuclear weapons (and hence dwell on nuclear war fighting scenarios) as *nuclear utilization theorists*, or NUTS. The nuclear strategy debate thus pits those who are MAD against those who are NUTS! The debate was fueled and made into a much more salient public issue by the Reagan administration proposal for a "Star Wars" defense system based in space and designed to defend against a full-scale nuclear attack. Subsequently named the Strategic Defense Initiative (SDI), the program became an expensive and controversial project throughout the 1980s and into the 1990s.

There are three basis ways to try to limit damage in nuclear war. As we have indicated, neither active defense against attacking weapons nor passive defense with shelters offers more than marginal protection. However, the possibility of using offensive weapons to destroy potential attacking weapons before they are launched has been a central issue in the nuclear strategy debate in the United States for many years. Referred to as a counter-force strategy, as distinguished from a deterrent counter-population strategy; it places priority on trying to achieve a capability and adopting a targeting strategy that would enable the United States to destroy an adversary's ICBMs and airfields with highly accurate ICBMs and SLBMs. In fact, the combination of large and/or numerous warheads with increased accuracy has given both the Soviet Union and the United States partial hard-site kill capabilities against ICBMs; this marginally reduces their retaliatory damage-inflicting potential. One controversial alternative for reducing this vulnerability is to make ICBMs mobile so that they are difficult to locate and hit.

However, some observers see this development as destabilizing, because it might create an incentive to launch a first strike—not on the basis of an illusion of invulnerability to retaliation but on the grounds that the damage might be at least somewhat less than if they wait to retaliate. In the extreme, the leaders of one country might believe that the other country has achieved a partial disarming first strike capability against ICBMs and bombers before they could be launched. Such a development would mean that the damage-inflicting capabilities of the surviving SLBMs would become a key deterrent factor.

Relative Advantage

Yet a third set of criteria is sometimes employed in strategic weapons analysis (in addition to deterrence and damage limitation). It combines a concern with minimizing damage to oneself with a desire to inflict maximum damage on the adversary so one's own country will have a relative advantage in the postwar situation. Relative advantage acquired official status as a strategic objective during the Nixon administration, but this was probably only a nominal criterion, rather than an operational goal that effectively determined policy. Yet the Carter administration also appeared to adopt postwar relative advantage as a strategic objective, as did the Reagan and Bush administrations.

Status and Influence

Quite apart from issues concerning the utility of nuclear weapons for nuclear war-winning, war-fighting, or war-deterring purposes, however, there are also a variety of issues concerning their more general political value.

On the one hand, there is the argument that nuclear weapons convey status in a general way and even provide influence in specific instances. Perhaps it was American strategic nuclear superiority that induced the Soviet leaders to withdraw their missiles from Cuba, as President Kennedy demanded. On the other hand, there is the argument that because nuclear threats lack any credibility except against a nuclear attack, nuclear weapons have little influence value in any other kind of political relationship. Nuclear superiority did not enable the United States to achieve its objectives in Central Europe in the late 1940s or in Southeast Asia in the 1960s and 1970s or in several other instances.[6]

Regardless of the merits of either argument, the fact is that the relative quantitative and qualitative characteristics of the U.S. and USSR nuclear arsenals have been a central American foreign policy issue. Thus, it behooves us to consider some comparative data so that we can better understand the issue. As we do so, however, we should keep in mind that it is arguable whether comparative capabilities have much significance in terms of their political consequences in international politics.

Furthermore, as the comparative data in Table 9–2 indicate, the pattern is mixed and varied. Whereas the United States had nearly comprehensive quantitative and qualitative superiority until the early 1970s, since then the Soviet Union has acquired numerical superiority in missile launchers (ICBMs and SLBMs). The throw-weight and therefore payload yield of Soviet ICBMs is also greater than that of American ICBMs. Thus, to the extent that large, numerous missiles convey status and influence, the Soviet Union has an advantage. However, other commonly used comparisons indicate an American superiority—either quantitative or qualitative. This is particularly true of the total number of deliverable warheads and bombs and the accuracies of the weapons, although the degree of American superiority in these respects has been declining. Because of the combination of partial Soviet superiority by some measures and the partial American superiority by other measures, it is now common to refer to the U.S.–USSR strategic relationship as one of "parity," or "essential equivalence."

In any case, these comparisons do not by themselves directly indicate anything conclusive about the absolute or relative deterring, damage-limiting, or even damage-inflicting capabilities of the two countries. Any conclusions about these capabilities must be based on much more complicated and detailed analyses; they must take into account a variety of esoteric technical issues as well as the conceptual issues we

TABLE 9–2 Comparisons of U.S. and USSR "Strategic" Nuclear Weapons*

	U.S.	USSR
Submarine-Launched Ballistic Missiles		
Submarines	36	63
Missiles	640	942
Independent Warheads	5,312	3,602
Individual Warhead Yield (maximum)	100KT	1.5MT
Intercontinental Ballistic Missiles		
Missiles	1,000	1,386
Independent Warheads	2,450	6,860
Individual Warhead Yield (maximum)	1.2MT	1.1MT
Long-Range Bombers		
Number	337	175
Bombs, SRAMs, ALCMs	5,238	1,100
Total Number of Missiles and Bombers	3,427	2,503
Total Number of Bombs and Warheads	13,000	11,562

*These data are the strategic triad forces only; they do not include theatre or tactical nuclear forces. Data are for 1989.

Sources: Same as Table 9–1; and International Institute for Strategic Studies, *The Military Balance 1988–89,* pp. 13–44.

have discussed. For example, to compare the damage-inflicting capabilities of American and Soviet SLBM forces, one must consider the proportions of SLBM-carrying submarines that are on-station and therefore in position to launch their missiles at any one time, their missile and warhead reliabilities, their accuracies, their individual warhead yields, the nature and location of their targets, their targeting strategies, the numbers of missiles and warheads, and their yields.

Clearly, we should be wary of conclusions about superiority or inferiority based on simple numerical comparisons. However, we should also be wary of conclusions about "overkill" based on simple ratios of megatonnage-to-population. An assertion that the Russians have achieved nuclear superiority is not very meaningful; but neither is an assertion that the United States could kill every Russian ten times.

Casualty Estimates

In spite of all of the complexities and technicalities, we can make some informed estimates of the consequences of nuclear war. If there were a large-scale nuclear war involving about ten thousand megatons, human life would probably survive. But the casualties would be on the order of hundreds of millions or even billions, and life might end altogether.[7] Smaller-scale nuclear wars would be much less catastrophic, although still horrendous by any historical or humanistic standards. Although some studies have estimated that American casualties might be as low as a few million in a limited Russian counterforce strike against American ICBMs, such estimates are based on controversial war-fighting scenarios that assume remarkable human restraint in dire circumstances.[8]

Because of the destructiveness, cost, and tension-producing consequences of nuclear weapons, several countries have shown considerable interest in seeking arms control agreements. Much of that interest has focused on the Strategic Arms Limitation Talks (SALT) between the United States and the Soviet Union, which were renamed the Strategic Arms Reduction Talks (START) in the 1980s.

SALT/START[9]

The initial incentives for entering into the Strategic Arms Limitation Talks were similar to incentives for most arms control agreements—namely, to increase security, to save money, and to improve political relations generally. Indeed, the objectives of nuclear arms control agreements include many of the same objectives of other forms of strategic nuclear weapons policy—for instance, security through stable deterrence. The negotiations are therefore an integral part of the strategic weapons policies of the two countries. The characteristics that distinguish the talks from other types of weapons policy are (a) the explicit attempt to negotiate agreements based on common interests, (b) the cooperation involved in that process, and (c) the mutual restraints that result.

By the late 1960s, several developments in weapons technology gave an extra impetus to the interest in seeking U.S.–USSR strategic arms limitation agreements. An ABM system was being deployed around Moscow, and one was planned in the United States as well. The USSR was preparing to deploy much larger ICBMs, and the United States was nearing the deployment phase of highly accurate MIRVs. Many government policy makers and experts outside the government felt that these developments would threaten stable deterrence. The ABMs would create doubts about the ability of incoming warheads to penetrate to targets in a retaliatory strike; therefore, they would create doubts about the vulnerability of populations. The large and MIRVed ICBMs would threaten the survivability of the retaliatory ICBMs they would be targeted against.

Thus, these impending weapons deployments seemed to threaten the central requirements of stable deterrence: vulnerable populations and invulnerable retaliatory weapons. Furthermore, they threatened to mark the beginning of a new weapons deployment cycle in which additional weapons would be deployed as countermeasures to offset one another's ABMs and ICBMs. Not only would stable deterrence be threatened, but the costs of the strategic arsenals would escalate.

Other factors also added impetus to U.S.–USSR strategic arms control by the late 1960s. The Soviet Union had achieved rough parity in strategic arms by then, and it would not have to negotiate from a position of relative weakness. The United States wanted to restrain additional Soviet deployments at the rate then prevailing. Finally, several previous arms control agreements had created a climate of opinion that was conducive to achieving more such measures. These included the limited test ban treaty signed in 1963, the nonproliferation treaty in 1968, and treaties prohibiting nuclear weapons in outer space and on the seabed in 1967 and 1971. Thus, by the time the American and Soviet negotiating delegations first met in Helsinki, Finland, in

November 1969, arms control had become a widely accepted foreign policy objective.

The negotiations have become an ongoing process; and they have produced many formalized, temporary, and tentative agreements. To simplify, we can focus our attention first on the SALT I ABM treaty signed in 1972 and then on the series of agreements in SALT I and SALT II to limit offensive weapons.

ABM Treaty

By the time the ABM treaty was signed and ratified in 1972, both the Soviet Union and the United States were deploying ABM systems. The Soviet Union already had a few in operation near Moscow, others were under construction, and still others were presumably planned for deployment around different cities. The United States had two ABM sites under construction, one in North Dakota and one in Montana. Named Safeguard, the U.S. system was designed principally to protect ICBM sites from attacking warheads, but if all twelve of the planned sites had been deployed, it would have provided some population defense as well (each site was to have one hundred ABMs).

The SALT I ABM treaty limited each country to two widely separated sites of one hundred missiles each, one site at the national capital and a second site near ICBM silos.* The basic strategic rationale was to promote stable deterrence by ensuring that each country would be equally vulnerable to retaliatory strikes. In other words, its purpose was to ensure that the two countries would maintain mutual assured destruction retaliatory capabilities.

In the United States, a consensus of support for the ABM treaty soon developed, and it has persisted. But since the treaty reinforces and perpetuates a strategic relationship based on mutual assured destruction, it has also been criticized for preventing damage limitation. In fact, it does ensure that both populations will continue to be defenseless against nuclear attack. In other words, the ABM treaty represents a trade-off that emphasizes stable deterrence at the price of foregoing damage limitation measures. The critics of the treaty object to such a trade-off. The supporters of the treaty defend it on the grounds that making the trade-off in the opposite direction would mean a greater risk of war; as we have noted, damage-limiting strategies tend to undermine stable deterrence.

By other criteria, the ABM treaty has been less controversial. Not building a full-scale Safeguard ABM system saved the United States tens of billions of dollars. Further, the treaty's provisions were symmetrical; they imposed identical limits on both countries. Thus, there were few objections that it was a poor bargain or that it created any politically disadvantageous asymmetries.

However, key provisions of the treaty were the subject of intense debate and serious conflict between the Reagan administration and many members of Congress

---

*In a subsequent supplementary agreement, the two countries further agreed that they would deploy only one site, and the United States eventually dismantled its one site at Grand Forks, North Dakota, as an economy measure.

during the 1980s. The conflict was prompted by Reagan's Strategic Defense Initiative (SDI) and his associated reinterpretation of the ABM treaty's restrictions on testing. In particular, the traditional interpretation of the treaty was that tests of all existing or future antimissile systems were prohibited. Reagan's new interpretation, by contrast, was that space-based systems such as SDI could be tested without violating the treaty. In the end, Congress sustained the traditional interpretation as part of a defense authorization bill, although without explicitly mentioning the ABM Treaty and with the provision that the administration could *plan* such tests (but not actually conduct them). The Congress continued to preclude the new interpretation of the treaty through the annual defense authorization process into the 1990s, and the issue was still alive in debates over the START treaty in the early 1990s.

Limits on Offensive Weapons

The other major SALT agreements were also controversial. The agreements themselves and the issues surrounding them are also more complex. When the American and Russian leaders signed the ABM treaty in 1972, they also signed an interim agreement on the limitation of strategic offensive arms, which imposed a temporary freeze on the number of ICBMs and SLBMs each country could deploy. Ceilings were set at the numbers of ICBMs and SLBMs in operation or under construction at the time.

This agreement became controversial for two reasons. One was that the ceilings were asymmetrical, since the Soviet Union had more ICBMs and more SLBMs in operation or under construction than the United States did at the time. The other was that the limits did not reduce any weapons below their existing number. Furthermore, the limits did not include bombers; they did not prohibit increasing the number of warheads on missiles by MIRVing them; nor did they preclude deployments of such other weapons systems as intercontinental bombers or cruise missiles. Over the next several years, the SALT negotiations focused on issues concerning limits on MIRVs, bombers, and cruise missiles—limits that would be symmetrical for the two countries, and limits that would be below existing deployment levels.

SALT II limits impose the same ceilings on both countries, thereby avoiding the politically sensitive asymmetries of the SALT I interim agreement. The limits furthermore impose ceilings slightly below the Soviet deployment levels at the time and hence constitute partial disarmament, albeit in a marginal form. They also specifically include ceilings on MIRVed missiles and long-range cruise missiles. As Table 9–3 shows, these ceilings are imposed through a series of sublimits on increasingly specific categories of weapons systems.

Within these limits, however, each country has some "freedom to mix" its particular weapons systems. For instance, either country can have any proportion of its weapons in the form of MIRVed SLBMs, as long as they do not exceed 1,200 in combination with MIRVed ICBMs, or 2,250 in combination with all ICBMs and bombers. This approach is a compromise between the internal political demands for equal limits on both countries and the technical and negotiating difficulties that would be involved in reaching equal limits in every weapons system category.

TABLE 9–3   SALT II Limits

WEAPONS	LIMITS
Total ICBMs plus SLBMs plus heavy bombers	2,250
MIRVed ICBMs plus MIRVed SLBMs plus heavy bombers with long-range cruise missiles	1,320
MIRVed ICBMs plus MIRVed SLBMs	1,200
Fixed heavy ICBMs	existing numbers
Warheads on a single ICBM	10
Warheads on a single SLBM	14
Cruise missiles per airplane	28 (avg.)
ICBMs on mobile launchers	0*
Ground-launched cruise missiles	0*
Sea-launched cruise missiles with ranges over 360 miles	0*

*Protocol limits—expired in 1981 (cruise missile testing was not limited).

The SALT II limits also maintain essential equivalence, at least in the short run. By imposing ceilings on the numbers of highly accurate MIRVs and cruise missiles, SALT II limits both countries' counterforce capabilities. To the degree that it thereby limits retaliatory forces' vulnerability, it contributes to the continuation of mutual assured destruction capabilities. In other words, it promotes stable deterrence.

The SALT II limitations also reveal that each country achieved some but not all of its objectives in the negotiations. The terms represent a compromise outcome, which is precisely what we would expect in negotiations. The United States obtained limits on large, MIRVed, Russian ICBMs, although at a higher level than the United States wanted and at a lower level than the Soviet Union wanted. The Soviet Union obtained limits on American cruise missiles, although less comprehensive ones than the Soviet Union wanted and more extensive ones than the United States wanted.

The SALT II limits became highly controversial, even before being formally announced. Some critics contended that the terms were a poor bargain for the United States, that the American negotiators had yielded more and gained less than the Russian negotiators. Other critics assailed it in strategic terms for perpetuating the mutual assured destruction relationship. Still others were disappointed that it did not establish lower numerical ceilings or more effective limits on future technological developments on new types of weapons or qualitative improvements in existing types of weapons. These and other problems were placed under temporary limits and postponed for further negotiations.

The SALT II treaty was never ratified; President Carter discontinued his attempt to secure ratification after the Soviet invasion of Afghanistan in 1979. However, both the American and Soviet governments announced they would infor- mally observe the treaty's limits—a policy in effect until 1986. In that year, the Reagan administration announced that it would no longer observe the limits in light of what it considered Soviet violations of SALT II and other arms control agreements. The same year, the American administration exceeded the treaty limits when it deployed long-range cruise missiles on a B-52 bomber. However, the Congress subsequently imposed limits on the defense budget that kept U.S. forces generally within the SALT II limits.

START Treaty

In 1990, following the revolutionary changes in the Soviet Union, President Bush and President Gorbachev agreed on the outlines of a treaty resulting from the strategic arms limitation talks (START). This first START treaty reflects a compromise between each side's central concerns. For its part, the United States sought a reduction in ICBMs because that is where the Soviet Union has had numerical superiority over the United States. For its part, the Soviet Union sought reductions in SLBMs because that is where the American forces have had numerical superiority over Soviet forces. The agreement provides for reductions in both categories of weapons in both countries, although the resulting numbers are asymmetrical across countries and across weapons systems. Thus, the United States is allowed more SLBMs while the USSR is allowed more ICBMs. In terms of the numbers of weapons given up by each side, compared with current force levels, the United States gave up approximately 1,000 ICBMs and about 1,500 SLBMs, while the USSR gave up about 3,500 ICBMS and 1,800 SLBMs. The resulting limits on these and other weapons systems, which are presented in Table 9–4, still leave many nuclear weapons issues remaining. These include such strategic/technical issues as: limits on large Soviet ICBMs; how to incorporate mobile ICBM launchers being deployed by the United States; whether further limits should be placed on testing in both countries; and whether Soviet Backfire bombers should be considered strategic long-range weapons, as the United States contends, or not counted, as the USSR contends.

Although the SALT/START agreements have been by far the most conspicuous arms control agreements, the United States is also a party to numerous other nuclear arms control agreements with the Soviet Union and other countries as well.

TABLE 9–4 START Treaty Limits

WEAPONS	U.S.	USSR
Intercontinental ballistic missiles	1,444	3,060
Submarine-launched ballistic missiles	3,456	1,840
Submarine-launched ballistic missiles in overhaul	576	528
Submarine-launched cruise missiles	880	880
Air-launched cruise missiles	1,840	1,350
Short-range attack missiles	3,440	2,000

Source: Data compiled from government sources and reported in *The New York Times,* June 2, 1990, p. 4.

Other U.S.–USSR Arms Control Agreements

The Intermediate Nuclear Force (INF) Treaty of 1987 broke new ground—it provided for the destruction of all existing U.S. and USSR missiles with ranges of 300 to 3,400 miles, and it prohibited future deployments of such weapons. The treaty enjoyed widespread (although not universal) support in Congress and among arms control specialists and lobbying organizations. It was approved by the Senate (93–5) and led to the destruction of 859 U.S. missiles and 1,836 Soviet missiles. The treaty also provided for unusually thorough and intrusive verification through on-site visits as well as satellite monitoring.

There are also agreements designed to reduce the chances of inadvertent nuclear war from accidental, unauthorized, or misunderstood developments. During the Cuban missile crisis in October 1962, the Soviet-American communications required as much as several hours transmission time from one head of government to the other. To facilitate communications in any future crisis, the United States and the USSR signed an agreement in 1963 to establish a direct communications link, or "hot line," based on telegraph circuits between Washington and Moscow. A 1971 agreement, reached in the context of the SALT negotiations, provided for technically improved telecommunications channels. The "hot line" has been used on several occasions during Middle East crises. A Nuclear Accidents Agreement provides that the two countries will notify one another of accidental, unauthorized, or unexplained incidents possibly involving a nuclear explosion that would risk nuclear war; unexplained signals or interference detected by their warning systems; and all planned missile tests.

The United States and the Soviet Union also signed a second group of agreements, which imposed limits on nuclear explosives tests. In 1963, along with the United Kingdom, they signed a Limited Test Ban Treaty prohibiting nuclear weapons tests in the atmosphere, outer space, or the oceans. One of its principal objectives was to avoid further radioactive fallout from atmospheric weapons tests. Although it did substantially reduce that fallout, it did not eliminate it altogether because France and China are not parties to it. In addition to the health-related incentive, the limited test ban was also viewed by some as an initial step toward ultimately banning all weapons tests; the intention was to slow or even stop their spread and to improve the political climate in general. It was not until more than a decade later, however, that another step in that direction was taken: A Threshold Test Ban Treaty was signed initially in 1974 and then in revised form in 1976. It prohibits underground nuclear weapons tests over 150 KT, and it also prohibits "peaceful nuclear explosions" (as for canal or underground storage excavation) over 150 KT unless provisions are made in advance for on-site inspection. Since nearly all nuclear weapons tests were already substantially less than 150 KT and since both countries had lost interest in peaceful nuclear explosion applications, this agreement had little practical effect. But it did have some symbolic significance; it was the first time the Soviet Union agreed in principle to any on-site inspections inside the Soviet Union.

In 1988, the United States and the USSR agreed to a Joint Verification Experiment (JVE), whereby each country could undertake on-site monitoring of the other's nuclear explosions. The purpose of the agreement was to enable the two countries' scientists to find mutually acceptable ways to verify compliance with the Threshold Test Ban Treaty and the Peaceful Nuclear Explosion Treaty, which had been signed more than a decade earlier but not ratified at the time because of concerns about verification. In 1988, as a result of the JVE, underground nuclear explosions were in fact monitored on-site in each country by scientists from the other country in an unprecedented show of cooperation.

Whatever the merits of the various arms control agreements, compliance with them can generally be reliably verified by each country's own verification measures.[10] The SALT agreements contain explicit recognition that national means of verification will be used. Both countries have also agreed not to interfere with one another's verification procedures. There is also a Standing Consultative Commission, where compliance and verification issues can be discussed.

A diverse array of surveillance systems provides an impressive capability to detect noncompliance. The surveillance systems depend on several different kinds of instruments located in many parts of the world, and high above it as well. They include satellites in orbit 22,000 miles above the Indian Ocean in a synchronous orbit with the revolving earth. Such satellites can survey the Soviet Union (and China) with infrared detectors, which can detect the heat generated by the firing of missile rocket engines. Although this system is principally an early warning system to detect missile attacks, it can also be used to monitor weapons tests.

Another set of satellites follows polar orbits at more than 100 miles in altitude. These satellites, which circle the earth every ninety minutes, carry cameras providing wide-area surveillance pictures that are transmitted back to the United States continuously and also detailed high-resolution photographs that are periodically returned to earth in recoverable capsules. The latter are precise enough to be able to detect objects as small as several inches across. Such photographs make it possible to monitor weapons deployments with considerable accuracy on a continuous basis. Several short-range (line-of-sight) and long-range (over-the-horizon) radar systems are also used to monitor weapons tests.

More important than the specific issues about features of particular weapons and how they are treated in the provisions of arms control agreements, however, are the larger strategic/political issues about nuclear weapons and arms control in the post–cold war era: Should the United States and the USSR worry less about nuclear threats from one another and more about nuclear threats from third countries? Should more emphasis be placed on avoiding accidental nuclear war? Should economic constraints, or even mutual economic interests, become more important considerations in arms control negotiations?

In any case, it seems likely that there will be further arms control agreements between the two countries—and that nuclear weapons issues such as proliferation will continue to be key issues.

NUCLEAR PROLIFERATION

Other arms control agreements seek to limit the spread of nuclear weapons to new areas of the world. In 1959, in the first postwar arms control agreement, the United

States, the Soviet Union, and eventually seventeen other countries agreed not to place any weapons in Antarctica. A 1967 treaty, signed by the United States, the Soviet Union, and seventy other countries, prohibits the placement of weapons of mass destruction in outer space; a 1971 treaty signed by over sixty countries does the same for the seabed. There are also treaties designed to limit the proliferation of nuclear weapons to countries not previously possessing them. The 1967 Treaty of Tlatelolco established much of Latin America as a nuclear-free zone, although Brazil and Argentina are conspicuously absent from its list of parties. The more nearly global Non-Proliferation Treaty (NPT) of 1970 obligates its one hundred signatories not already having nuclear weapons not to acquire them. Nuclear weapons countries that are parties, including the United States, agree not to help any country acquire nuclear weapons. However, many countries, including Israel, Egypt, South Africa, India, Pakistan, Brazil, and Argentina, have not become parties to the NPT.

A more detailed understanding of nuclear weapons proliferation requires an analysis of the relationship between civil and military applications of nuclear energy.

Nuclear Energy

Since the discovery of nuclear fission in Europe in the 1930s and the development of nuclear bombs in the United States in the 1940s, the possibility of using nuclear energy for peaceful purposes as well as for war has been well known. And in fact, the United States has actively promoted civil nuclear energy since the late 1940s.[11] For several years after World War II, however, research and development work on nuclear technology for electricity production was restricted to government laboratories. Then in the 1950s, the American government began to encourage private industry to participate in nuclear energy development, and it began to encourage other countries' interest in peaceful applications of nuclear energy.

In the mid-1970s, when the oil embargo, oil price rises, and the prospect of further energy shortages motivated governments and industry to consider alternative energy sources, nuclear energy was a technically feasible and economically viable alternative. By the 1980s, there were over seventy nuclear power reactors in the United States producing electricity, and there were more than 170 reactors in operation in twenty-some countries in the rest of the world.[12]

The same basic materials, facilities, and knowledge are involved in both military and peaceful applications of nuclear energy, although there are some important differences as well. These similarities and differences can best be understood in terms of the civil nuclear fuel cycle, the technical phases in the utilization of nuclear energy for electricity production.[13]

There are several basic fuel cycles, depending on the kind of fuel used in the reactor, but nearly all begin with the mining of uranium ore.* Uranium ore contains 0.7 percent of the uranium isotope U-235 and 99.3 percent of the uranium isotope U-238. Only the U-235 can create the chain reaction fission process that fuels a nuclear reactor.

*Some fuel cycles use thorium rather than uranium, but they have only progressed to the research and development stage, not commercial application.

In a natural uranium fuel cycle, uranium containing these natural proportions of U-235 and U-238 is sent to a fuel fabrication facility where it is made into reactor fuel rods. Since uranium containing only 0.7 percent of the isotope U-235 cannot be used to make a bomb—which requires about 80 percent or more U-235—such a fuel cycle does not involve a direct weapons proliferation potential.

There are, however, other civil fuel cycle phases that do involve a direct weapons proliferation potential. One is the uranium enrichment phase, which is part of the fuel cycle for enriched uranium reactors that need fuel with 3 to 5 percent of the U-235 isotope. An enrichment process is therefore necessary to increase the proportion of U-235 from 0.7 percent in ore to 3 percent or more for reactor fuel. But an enrichment facility can be operated so that it continues to enrich uranium beyond the small percentage of U-235 necessary for reactor fuel to the much higher percentage necessary for weapons material. An enrichment facility, in other words, can be used to produce reactor-grade uranium for peaceful purposes or weapons-grade uranium for military purposes.

Another nuclear fuel cycle phase, the reprocessing phase, can also serve military as well as civil purposes. After uranium fuel is "burned up" in a reactor, the spent fuel rods contain a variety of elements that can be separated from one another in a chemical separation reprocessing plant. In particular, the spent fuel contains the element plutonium, which itself can cause chain reactions and thus fuel reactors. Separated plutonium can be taken to a fuel fabrication facility where it is mixed with uranium to form new fuel rods. However, separated plutonium can also be used to make bombs.

Spent fuel, in other words, contains a material that can be used to fuel reactors or to make bombs. However, the plutonium has to be separated from the other elements in the spent fuel to be used for either reactor fuel or bomb material. Thus, a chemical separation plant designed for reprocessing plutonium for reactor fuel is potentially not only a civil nuclear facility but a military nuclear facility.

Plutonium reprocessing is not a necessary phase for either the natural uranium or the enriched uranium reactors that are now widely used in the world. Although plutonium reprocessing increases energy efficiency in those reactor fuel cycles, its use is optional. It can remain mixed in with other spent fuel elements when they are sent to waste disposal sites.

On the other hand, plutonium reprocessing is an integral phase in the breeder reactor fuel cycle. A breeder reactor is designed specifically to produce large quantities of plutonium as it burns up uranium and then to use plutonium as fuel after it is separated in a spent fuel reprocessing plant. An advantage of the breeder reactor is that it is highly energy efficient, since it utilizes a high proportion of the energy potential in uranium and plutonium. On the other hand, since the plutonium breeder reactor inevitably involves plutonium recycle, it involves a greater weapons proliferation potential as well.

In short, the uranium enrichment and plutonium reprocessing phases of civil nuclear fuel cycles represent nuclear weapons proliferation potentials. If a country has either uranium enrichment facilities or plutonium reprocessing facilities, together with the nuclear materials and skilled personnel that normally accompany them, it has the basic capability to manufacture nuclear weapons. These phases and proliferation possibilities in civil nuclear fuel cycles are depicted in Figure 9–1.

Several countries already have a nuclear weapons manufacturing capability, and many more may acquire it over the next decade or two.[14] As of 1991, at least eleven countries had such a capability: Japan, Belgium, West Germany, South

FIGURE 9–1   Basic nuclear fuel cycles

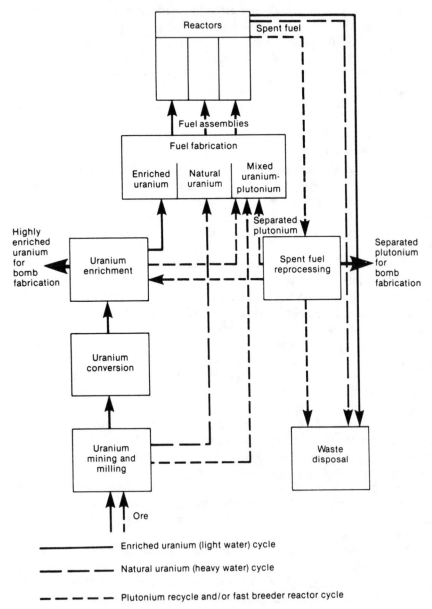

Africa, Israel, and the countries that had actually exploded nuclear devices—the United States, USSR, U.K., France, China, and India. It was widely assumed that Israel had nuclear weapons and that South Africa either already had or could soon have them. However, a country must have more than a technological capability to produce nuclear weapons; it must also have sufficient incentives to acquire them.[15] In fact, several countries that could have developed nuclear weapons have not done so, and this is likely to be the case in the future.

An antiproliferation policy can therefore try to influence technological capabilities and/or political motivations. Although American policy has involved a mix of both, it has put principal emphasis on trying to limit capabilities. It has specifically tried to restrain the spread of the most sensitive facilities in the civil nuclear fuel cycle, enrichment and reprocessing plants. American law prohibits the export of such facilities, and the United States opposed a German sale of enrichment and reprocessing facilities to Brazil and French sales of reprocessing facilities to Pakistan and South Korea. It was able to convince France and South Korea to rescind their prospective sale, and it was also able to obtain German and French commitments not to sell any further enrichment or reprocessing plants. But Brazil and Pakistan were nevertheless obtaining facilities during the 1980s.[16]

The United States has also tried to discourage the adoption of plutonium reprocessing, and it has expressed skepticism about breeder reactors. In an effort to exert leadership on those two scores, the United States first announced that it would not adopt plutonium recycle in its own nuclear industry—a decision made initially by the Ford administration and then reiterated by the Carter administration. The Carter administration's attempt to slow down and redirect the American breeder reactor development program encountered severe opposition in Congress, however, as did its attempt to discourage Western European breeder development programs. Although the Reagan administration was more supportive of the breeder program, opposition in Congress has continued to cast doubt on its future in the 1990s.

The other major component of American nuclear weapon antiproliferation policy has been to try to verify that civil nuclear facilities are not used for weapons fabrication. Such attempted verification occurs through the "safeguards" program of the International Atomic Energy Agency.[17] Although a few civil nuclear facilities have remained outside this international safeguards regime, and although there are some significant loopholes in the safeguards system, it nevertheless provides a substantial degree of verification. The system is subject to periodic review under the terms of the Non-Proliferation Treaty.

EVALUATION OF ARMS CONTROL AGREEMENTS

If we evaluate the NPT and other arms control agreements, as summarized in Table 9–5, in terms of their security-enhancing, money-saving, and conflict-reducing effects, we find that they have some value individually and collectively, in spite of their shortcomings. The hot-line and accidental-measures agreements help reduce the risk of inadvertent nuclear war between the Soviet Union and the United States. They

TABLE 9–5   Nuclear Arms Control Agreements Involving the United States

Antarctic Treaty (December 1, 1959; June 23, 1961)*

"Hot Line" Agreement (June 20, 1963; June 20, 1963)

Limited Test Ban Treaty (August 5, 1963; October 10, 1963)

Outer Space Treaty (January 27, 1967; October 10, 1967)

Latin American Nuclear-Free Zone Treaty (February 14, 1967; April 22, 1968)

Non-Proliferation of Nuclear Weapons Treaty (July 1, 1968; March 5, 1970)

Seabed Arms Control Treaty (February 11, 1971; May 18, 1972)

Agreement on Measures to Reduce the Risk of Outbreak of Nuclear War between the United States of America and the Union of Soviet Socialist Republics (September 30, 1971; September 30, 1971)

"Hot Line" Modernization Agreement (September 30, 1971; September 30, 1971)

Salt I—ABM Treaty (May 26, 1972; October 3, 1972)

Salt I—Interim Agreement (May 26, 1972; October 3, 1972)

Agreement between the United States of America and the Union of Soviet Socialist Republics on the Prevention of Nuclear War (June 22, 1973; June 22, 1973)

Salt I—ABM Protocol (July 3, 1974; May 24, 1976)

Threshold Test Ban Treaty (July 3, 1974; June 1, 1989; NIF)

Peaceful Nuclear Explosion Treaty (May 28, 1976; June 1, 1989; NIF)

U.S.-IAEA Safeguards Agreement (November 18, 1977; December 9, 1980)

Salt II—Offensive Arms Treaty (June 18, 1979; NIF)†

Intermediate Nuclear Forces (December 7, 1987; June 1, 1988)

Joint Verification Experiment Agreement (June 1, 1988).

*First date is date of U.S. signing; second date is date agreement entered into force. NIF means not in force.

†Technically not in force. However, informal agreement and implicit policies have maintained limits, with marginal exceptions.

Source: U.S. Arms Control and Disarmament Agency, *Arms Control and Disarmament Agreements* (Washington, DC: U.S. Government Printing Office, 1982); *The Arms Control Reporter* (Brookline, MA: Institute for Defense and Armaments Studies).

also serve as reminders not to undertake actions that could be misinterpreted or perceived as threatening nuclear war. They may also have helped to facilitate the achievement of other arms control agreements, particularly in SALT/START, by contributing to a more cooperative negotiating atmosphere. Although neither the test ban agreements nor the INF treaty nor the other agreements prohibiting nuclear weapons from various areas seem to reduce the risk of nuclear war in any very direct way, they do contribute to American and world security by symbolizing cooperation and recognition of common interests.

It is doubtful whether these measures have saved the United States (or any other country, for that matter) significant amounts of money. Indeed, the Limited Test Ban Treaty led to an increase in the American weapons-testing program. Although all tests after the treaty were (legally) conducted underground, they were much more numerous during the years after the treaty than during the period before the treaty. The rationale for such an active testing program was that the United States should remain ready to resume atmospheric testing on short notice in case the Soviet Union violated the treaty. The internal political reality was that President Kennedy agreed to an expanded testing program to obtain support for the treaty from senatorial and other critics.

More generally, none of the various arms control agreements, except the SALT ABM treaty, has had more than marginal direct effects on the resources devoted to nuclear weapons research, development, testing, and deployment. To be sure, arms control agreements have sometimes led to a change in emphasis in the nuclear weapons programs, but the aggregate effort remained fairly stable throughout the 1970s, and increased substantially in the 1980s. The INF Treaty and the START Treaty, however, in combination with new international political relations and national economic constraints, seem to offer the prospect of more significant changes in U.S. and USSR nuclear weapons policies.

EXPLANATIONS OF NUCLEAR WEAPONS POLICIES

Part of the explanation for the continuing development of American nuclear weapons lies in the attempt to maintain the capabilities required for deterrence, damage limitation, and damage infliction. But this rationalistic analysis does not fully explain nuclear weapons policy. For a more adequate understanding, we need to take into account the nature of the international political system and the internal political pressures impinging on nuclear weapons policy.

International Politics

International politics provides the underlying incentives that lead countries to acquire nuclear weapons in the first place and then to continue to add to their nuclear arsenals. International political competition leads them to deploy nuclear weapons in the pursuit of status and influence. Furthermore, the combination of the lack of a centralized world authority and the presence of distrust, suspicion, and fear of one another creates a sense of insecurity.

The anarchic tendencies of the international political system produce a ''security dilemma.'' In the case of nuclear armed countries that are adversaries, the dilemma consists of two particularly unattractive unilateral policies that each country can follow.[18] One policy is not to increase the nuclear arsenal—to save resources and avoid the tensions that increasing the arsenal engenders. But this alternative entails the risk that the other country will build up its arsenal and thereby eventually threaten the first country's security even more. The other alternative is to increase the nuclear arsenal to try to achieve greater security through superiority. But this alternative prompts the other country to react to the increased threat that it perceives. Since both countries increase their nuclear arsenals, neither is more secure. They are perhaps even less secure, and they are surely poorer for having spent scarce resources on more weapons. Nevertheless, it may be better than the other alternative, and it is the alternative that the United States and the Soviet Union chose for many years.

But there is another alternative for such countries—namely, to recognize that they have a mutual interest in agreeing that neither will acquire more weapons. Thus, both can be better off if they cooperate through arms control agreements than if they separately seek to achieve superiority. In essence, arms control represents an attempt to avoid both the alternatives posed by the security dilemma. By the late 1960s, this alternative had acquired considerable appeal in both countries. By the 1990s, its appeal was much greater.

The simple matrix in Figure 9–2 summarizes these possibilities. Arms control enables the countries to move to the upper left cell of the matrix, where they are both better off than they would be in the lower right cell, in an arms race.

Thus, the basic structure of the international political system accounts for both the interactions in arms races and the rationale for arms control. But to understand the specific weapons and arms control policies adopted at particular times, we also need to consider the policy preferences and influence of the participants in the national policy process.

National and Bureaucratic Politics

The American public is generally inattentive and uninformed on nuclear weapons and arms control issues.[19] Several surveys during the 1960s and 1970s indicated that one-half to three-fourths of the adult population paid very little or no attention at all to such issues. For example, in 1976 when the B-1 bomber program and the SALT negotiations were central preoccupations of foreign policy makers, 71 percent of the public reported they had heard or read "nothing" or "very little" about the B-1 bomber; 49 percent said they had not been "paying much attention at all" to SALT. Furthermore, polls over the years have consistently shown that about half the population, even in major cities, does not expect its cities to be attacked in a nuclear war.

FIGURE 9–2   Matrix of basic nuclear arms policy alternatives and outcomes

U.S. POLICY ALTERNATIVES

		Restraint	Deployment
OTHER COUNTRY'S POLICY ALTERNATIVES	Restraint	Arms control. Relatively stable parity at relatively low deployment levels	U.S. superiority
	Deployment	Other country's superiority	Arms race. Relatively unstable parity/superiority/ inferiority at relatively high deployment levels

To the extent that people hold opinions about nuclear weapons issues, those opinions have shifted some over time. During the 1940s and 1950s, one-fourth to two-thirds favored arms control agreements in principle. By the 1970s, after the SALT I agreements had been signed, three-fourths approved of specific actual or prospective SALT agreements. In 1968, only four in ten respondents agreed that the "United States and Russia can reach agreements to keep the peace"; by 1973, seven in ten agreed.[20] During the 1980s, there was increased skepticism, but renewed enthusiasm appeared in the early 1990s.

This substantial public support for nuclear arms control has not meant, however, that policy makers have been able to reach arms control agreements without considerable domestic opposition. Nor has it meant that the public has opposed the development and deployment of new nuclear weapons systems. In late 1976, for instance, 64 percent said they agreed when asked, "Do you agree or disagree with the Department of Defense that we need the B-1 bomber to keep our strategic defenses equal to Russia's?[21] There was also much public support for the large number of nuclear weapons development and deployment programs undertaken by the Reagan administration.

As the military-industrial complex model and the pluralistic-bureaucratic politics model remind us, policy is often made without much direct public impact. In contrast, throughout the arms negotiations with the Soviet Union, there has been considerable active opposition to presidential policy preferences from the American military. During SALT II, after President Ford and Secretary of State Kissinger reached a tentative agreement on the provisions for a treaty, the American military objected to the treaty's including American cruise missiles and excluding the Russian Backfire bomber. It thereby contributed to a postponement in formalizing the agreements for the remainder of Ford's tenure as president.[22]

During the SALT I negotiations, President Nixon and Henry Kissinger decided to go ahead with deployment of MIRVed ICBMs partly to placate the American military and to gain its acquiescence in the SALT I agreements. Nixon and Kissinger also resorted to the use of secret "back-channel" communications with the Soviet leaders, lest their negotiating position as revealed in the formal negotiations through "front channels" be undermined by bureaucratic opposition.[23] Indeed, the conflicts among the executive agencies represented on the American formal negotiating delegation were so severe that the American negotiators joked after negotiating with the Russians that they had to go back to the harder negotiations—which were among themselves as they tried to determine the American position.

During the Reagan administration, there were frequent conflicts between the Defense and State Departments over interpretations of the ABM treaty, the Strategic Defense Initiative, and START negotiating positions.

Such bureaucratic conflicts were not limited to the American side. During one negotiating session, it became apparent that the chief of the Russian delegation did not know the precise number of Russian submarines in operation or under construction because the Russian military had not told him. He later found out—from the chief of the American delegation.[24]

This event provides a vivid example of a transnational bureaucratic process.

Indeed, the SALT negotiations can be thought of as a complex mixture of three different kinds of overlapping negotiations. There are the formal international negotiations between the United States and the USSR. There are the informal but often explicit and overt intranational negotiations within the American government and within the Russian government. Finally, there are the informal and normally tacit and unspoken transnational negotiations between the arms control advocates in the United States and the USSR and the arms control opponents in the two countries.

CONCLUSION

Because of their catastrophic potential, nuclear weapons create many central foreign policy issues. Those issues inevitably involve a diverse variety of technological, psychological, strategic, and political facts and concepts.

One of the central strategic concepts is deterrence—minimizing the probability of attack. A stable mutual deterrent relationship presumably exists between the United States and the USSR on the basis of mutual assured destruction capabilities, which in turn depend on invulnerable retaliatory weapons and vulnerable populations. The advisability of such a strategy as well as of damage-limiting and damage-inflicting strategies based on counterforce weapons is a central question in nuclear policy making.

The principal purposes of the SALT agreements and other arms control agreements are to maximize security and/or reduce the costs of maintaining security. The SALT agreements presumably stabilize deterrence by limiting antimissile defenses (ABMs) and offensive missiles (ICBMs and SLBMs) and bombers. The arms control agreements reached to date have imposed some restraints on American, Russian, and other countries' nuclear weapons policies, but they have not prevented the continued development of nuclear weapons in the United States, the USSR, and several other countries. Although there is a compelling rationale for arms control, given the nature of the international political system, and although there is now widespread support inside and outside the United States for arms control, certain political conditions pose serious obstacles to it. These include the interests and policy preferences of influential groups inside the United States and other countries. They also include the basic nature of the international political system, which fosters competition and the pursuit of status, influence, and even security through nuclear weapons.

The net result of these many forces has been a world in varying degrees of jeopardy from the threat of nuclear war. One popularly noted method of tracing the variations in the threat has been the clock on the front of the *Bulletin of the Atomic Scientists*. Although it represents the assessment of only a few (albeit expert) observers of nuclear issues, and although its use of the minutes to midnight should not be taken too literally or precisely, the history of the clock's position does convey strong impressions of the history of nuclear weapons issues. That history has been plotted in Figure 9–3. The large jumps up in the late 1980s and early 1990s marked the beginning of a new era in nuclear weapons issues.

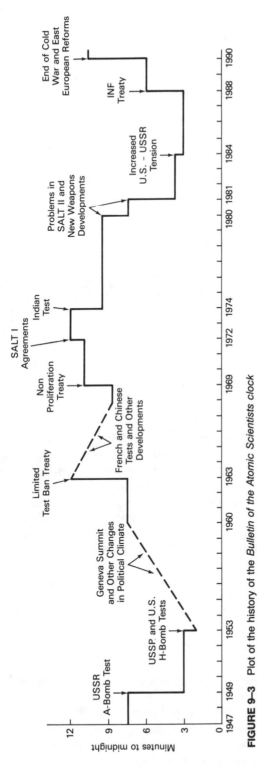

FIGURE 9–3 Plot of the history of the *Bulletin of the Atomic Scientists* clock

Source: Adapted from Stephen Meyer and Thomas L. Brewer, "Monitoring Nuclear Proliferation," in J. David Singer and Michael Wallace, eds., *To Auger Well: Early Warning Indicators in World Politics*, p. 205, Figure 6–3. Updated from the *Bulletin of the Atomic Scientists*, various issues.

Military Intervention and Assistance

The United States uses its military, paramilitary, and economic resources to try to influence the policies of foreign countries, the internal political support for their leaders, the composition of their governments, and the activities of groups in their political processes. The United States sometimes engages in covert actions inside other countries; it has frequently intervened with combat military forces in internal and international conflicts; and it routinely transfers military and economic goods and services to many other countries. This chapter addresses several questions concerning those activities: What is the nature of covert paramilitary actions? Where have they been employed? In what countries and for what reasons has the United States intervened with troops? What kinds of military assistance does the United States provide foreign governments?

COVERT ACTION

Although covert actions are often conducted by government "intelligence" agencies, they are not intelligence activities in the most precise sense: the collection and analysis of information. Whereas the purpose of intelligence is to find out what is happening or might happen, the purpose of covert action is to influence what happens. Therefore, American covert actions involve direct, active American participation in foreign countries' political processes.

Because of the secretive nature of covert actions, detailed and reliable information about them is difficult to obtain. Indeed, for many years very little was known about covert actions and the government organizations that conduct them. Eventually, however, a few serious studies became available; in addition, investigative journalists, congressional committees, and former government employees began to provide accounts of covert actions.[1] As a consequence, we now know a good deal about many past covert activities. On the other hand, public information about thousands of past covert projects is still not available; nor is there public information about continuing covert projects in most instances.

Several American government agencies have been involved in covert actions. The CIA is regularly involved in covert action projects, and military units are also occasionally active, either as direct participants in paramilitary units or as supporting groups providing transportation, supplies, and other services. In addition, military units, the Agency for International Development, the State Department, and other government agencies regularly provide "covers" for CIA agents in American embassies.

These undercover agents and their associates have engaged in a wide range of activities—from the dissemination of propaganda to the attempted assassination of political leaders. A former CIA deputy director who had been in charge of the agency's clandestine services once summarized the diverse forms of covert actions as follows:

> (1) political advice or counsel; (2) subsidies to an individual; (3) financial support and technical assistance to political parties; (4) support of private organizations, including labor unions, business firms, cooperatives, etc.; (5) covert propaganda; (6) "private" training of individuals and exchange of persons; (7) economic operations; and (8) para-military or political action operations designed to overthrow or to support a regime. . . .[2]

The United States has employed these forms of covert actions in scores of countries. A Senate committee report indicates that there were major covert operations in forty-eight countries during 1953 and that there were "several thousand covert action projects" between 1961 and 1975.[3]

Covert actions began in Europe immediately following World War II. The CIA supported underground and guerrilla organizations in Poland, Albania, and the Soviet Union.[4] Cash subsidies were paid to the two major parties of West Germany and many of their leaders.[5] For three decades, the CIA subsidized several Italian politicians.[6] In 1967, a CIA-supported colonel led a coup in Greece.[7]

Covert actions were also undertaken in Asia soon after World War II. From 1949 until 1961, the CIA supported several thousand Chinese Nationalist troops who had fled into Burma during the Chinese civil war. From their bases in Burma, they launched guerrilla attacks back across the border into China.[8] From 1958 until 1961, the CIA trained Tibetan guerrillas to fight against the Chinese. In 1974, when the "cultural revolution" involving rival party factions in China began to calm down, the CIA tried to exacerbate the conflict by distributing leaflets that appeared to be from one of the factions and that condemned the other faction.[9]

In 1954, the United States sent saboteurs into North Vietnam to try to undermine the Geneva Accords providing for French withdrawal from Southeast Asia.[10] Covert activities in Southeast Asia were later expanded considerably; they included cooperating with the generals who overthrew the South Vietnamese government in 1963 and supervising a large-scale program of guerrilla warfare in which more than thirty thousand suspected Viet Cong were killed. In Laos, the CIA supported an army of tens of thousands of Meo tribesmen from 1960 to 1973.[11] In Cambodia, it assisted a coup against Premier Sihanouk in 1970.[12] In Indonesia, the CIA provided air support for a coup attempt against President Sukarno in 1958.[13]

In the Middle East, the CIA helped overthrow Iranian Premier Mossadegh in 1953 after he nationalized the oil industry.[14] In Somalia in the 1960s, the CIA funded a candidate who eventually became premier but was then overthrown in a coup.[15] During the early 1960s, the CIA provided propaganda, cash, and bombing missions in support of the central government of the Congo (now Zaire), which was suppressing a revolt in its Katanga province.[16]

American covert actions have also been common in Latin America. In 1964, the CIA provided air attacks against the palace of Guatemalan President Arbenz in support of a successful coup against him by Colonel Armas.[17] A short time later, the CIA helped establish a police force in Cuba so that Premier Batista could better fight guerrillas led by Fidel Castro. Once Castro became premier, the United States organized an invasion by Cuban refugees at the Bay of Pigs in 1961. After the invasion failed, the United States made numerous attempts to assassinate Castro over several years.[18]

American government opposition to Castro also led to covert attempts to influence other Latin American countries' policies toward Castro. The CIA spent over $10 million between 1960 and 1963 in an effort to overthrow the government of Ecuador because it would not break diplomatic relations with Cuba.[19] In Brazil, the United States made election contributions to opposition candidates and helped organize antigovernment labor groups from 1962 to 1964 because of that government's relations with Cuba and the Soviet Union; Brazilian President Goulart was eventually the victim of a military coup.[20] Also in Latin America, in 1962–1963, the CIA helped labor unions in British Guiana organize a general strike and overthrow the government.[21]

Perhaps one of the most intense programs of covert actions took place in Chile.

Chile

For over a decade, the United States actively opposed the election of President Salvadore Allende and then his continuation in office once he was elected. The United States successfully opposed his election in 1964, when it spent more than $3 million to support his opponent. Six years later, Allende was elected in spite of a concerted American attempt to defeat him. The following specific measures against Allende have been documented by congressional committee staff investigations.[22]

March 25, 1970   [NSC] 40 Committee [approved] $125,000 for a "spoiling operation" against Allende's Popular Unity Coalition (UP).

June 27   40 Committee [approved] $300,000 for additional anti-Allende propaganda operations.

August 18   National Security Study Memorandum (NSSM) 97 [was] reviewed by the Interdepartmental Group; the Group [considered] options ranging from efforts to forge amicable relations with Allende to opposition to him.

September 4   Salvadore Allende [won] 36.3 percent of the vote in the Presidential election. Final outcome [was] dependent on October 24 vote in [Chile's] Congress between Allende and the runner-up, Jorge Alessandri, who received 35.3 percent of the vote. . . .

September 8   40 Committee [discussed] Chilean situation. The Committee approved $250,000 for the use of Ambassador Korry to influence the October 24 Congressional vote [in Chile].

September 15   President Nixon [instructed] CIA Director Helms to prevent Allende's accession to office. The CIA [was] to play a direct role in organizing a military coup d'état. This involvement [came] to be known as Track II.

October [c.7]   CIA [contacted] Chilean military conspirators; following a White House meeting, CIA [attempted] to defuse plot by retired General Viaux, but still to generate maximum pressure to overthrow Allende by coup; CIA [provided] tear gas grenades and three submachine guns to conspirators.

October 14   40 Committee [approved] $60,000 for Ambassador Korry's proposal to purchase a radio station. The money [was] never spent.

October 24   The Chilean Congress [voted] 53 to 35 in favor of Allende over Alessandri.

After Allende was inaugurated, the United States stepped up the covert actions directed against him:

November 13, 1970   40 Committee [approved] $25,000 for support of Christian Democratic candidates.

January 28, 1971   40 Committee [approved] $1,240,000 for the purchase of radio stations and newspapers and to support municipal candidates and other political activities of anti-Allende parties.

March 22   40 Committee [approved] $185,000 additional support for the Christian Democratic Party (PDC).

April 4   Allende's Popular Unity (UP) coalition [garnered] 49.7 percent of the vote in 280 municipal elections.

May 10   40 Committee [approved] $77,000 for purchase of a press for the Christian Democratic Party newspaper. The press [was] not obtained and the funds [were] used to support the paper.

May 15   40 Committee [approved] $100,000 for emergency aid to the Christian Democratic Party to meet short-term debts.

May 26   40 Committee [approved] $150,000 for additional aid to Christian Democratic Party to meet debts.

July 6   40 Committee [approved] $150,000 for support of opposition candidates in a Chilean by-election.

September 9   40 Committee [approved] $700,000 for support to the major Santiago newspaper, *El Mercurio*.

November 5   40 Committee [approved] $815,000 support to opposition parties and to induce a split in the Popular Unity Coalition.

December 15   40 Committee [approved] $160,000 to support two opposition candidates in January 1972 by-elections.

April 11   40 Committee [approved] $695,000 for additional support to *El Mercurio.*

April 24   40 Committee [approved] $50,000 for an effort to splinter the Popular Unity Coalition.

June 16   40 Committee [approved] $46,500 to support a candidate in a Chilean by-election.

September 21   40 Committee [approved] $24,000 to support an anti-Allende businessmen's organization.

October 26   40 Committee [approved] $1,427,666 to support opposition political parties and private sector organizations in anticipation of March, 1973, Congressional elections.

February 12, 1973   40 Committee [approved] $200,000 to support opposition political parties in the Congressional elections.

March 4   In the Congressional elections, Allende's Popular Unity Coalition [won] 43.4 percent of the vote.

August 20   40 Committee [approved] $1 million to support opposition political parties and private sector organizations. This money [was] not spent.

September 11   The Chilean military [overthrew] the government of Salvador Allende. Allende [died] during the takeover, reportedly by suicide.

American intervention has not always been so covert or so focused on the electoral politics and the economies in the target countries. Sometimes American intervention has involved overt military operations.

OVERT MILITARY INTERVENTION

The United States has intervened with military logistical support in many conflicts. For example, it provided air transport for Indian supplies and troops during a 1962 border war with China.[23] It also conducted patrols in the Formosa Straits between China and Taiwan for many years.

In addition, there have been several cases of direct intervention with combat troops: Korea in 1950; Lebanon in 1958 and in 1983; the Dominican Republic in 1965; Vietnam, Laos, and Cambodia during the 1960s and 1970s; Grenada in 1983; Panama in 1989; and the Persian Gulf in 1990.

Korea[24]

Korea was still occupied by Japanese troops at the end of World War II. The Soviet Union and the United States agreed that Soviet troops would supervise the withdrawal of the Japanese troops north of the 38th parallel and that American troops would supervise their withdrawal south of that line. When subsequent attempts to reunify Korea and hold nationwide elections were unsuccessful, the country became effectively divided into two parts, each with a separate regime. The U.S. recognized the South Korean regime and provided it with economic and military assistance.

After several years of animosity and occasional border clashes between the two

Korean regimes, in June of 1950 the North Koreans invaded the South across the 38th parallel.

The United States responded by sending several thousand troops (in addition to the few thousand already in South Korea). The United States was also able to get the United Nations—whose membership was dominated by American allies at the time—to authorize a UN military action against the North Koreans. The direction of the troops was still clearly under the American president and American officers, however, and nearly all of the troops were Americans and South Koreans.

The initial American objective was only to restore South Korean control below the 38th parallel and thus contain the expansion of Communist countries' influence. But after several months of fighting, the American policy became more ambitious; the stated objective was then to "liberate" North Korea and to reunify the entire peninsula under one government. As a consequence of that decision and the subsequent northward movement of the troops beyond the 38th parallel, the Chinese entered the war.

Although the American–UN troops were pushed back, nearly to defeat, after a few months they were able to regain control over virtually all the territory south of the 38th parallel and a small portion north of it as well. As they reached the area of the 38th parallel, the issue of whether to try to gain control over the entire northern section arose again, as did the issue of whether to attack China. The president and the Joint Chiefs of Staff, as well as the British and French governments, all opposed these possibilities; but the American field commander, General MacArthur, strongly supported them. When MacArthur openly solicited public and congressional support for his position, he was fired for insubordination by President Truman.

Truce talks began in the summer of 1952, and an armistice was finally signed in July 1953. A demilitarized zone at approximately the 38th parallel has since separated the two areas controlled by the North and South Korean governments.

Lebanon: The First Time[25]

A series of complex events in the Middle East led to the dispatch of American troops to Lebanon in 1958.

Prior to the intervention, Egypt, Syria, and other Arab countries had developed closer diplomatic relations with the Soviet Union. When a civil war erupted in Lebanon over the composition of its government and its relations with the United States, Moslem partisans in Lebanon received verbal and material support from Syria and Egypt, which were joined together as the United Arab Republic at the time.

The Eisenhower administration became concerned about the fate of Lebanon and its Christian president, who favored close relations with the United States. A coup in Iraq and reports of a coup attempt in Jordan reinforced American fears that Lebanon and other Middle Eastern countries might become more hostile to the United States and more friendly with the Soviet Union. In July 1958, when Lebanon's president asked the United States to intervene with troops to help restore order, the United States obliged by sending fourteen thousand marines.

There was actually relatively little fighting in Lebanon at the time. Moreover, the political factions inside Lebanon were working out a compromise settlement on the composition of a new government. Three months later, when a new Lebanese president (who was acceptable to both Egypt and the United States) had been elected and the fighting had ended, the American troops left without having done much except demonstrate American concern about political trends in the Middle East.

Dominican Republic[26]

Seven years later, in 1965, civil war in the Dominican Republic prompted the Johnson administration to intervene with American troops.

During the early 1960s, there were numerous changes in the Dominican government as a result of coups by various military and political factions. Although the United States had provided support to some leaders and their factions, it had been unable to achieve a stable, friendly government.

In April 1965, there was another coup and an ensuing struggle for power. One participant in the struggle and prospective winner of it was former President Juan Bosch, whom the United States had supported for a while during his previous time in office. But the American ambassador and military attachés in the Dominican Republic suspected Bosch and some of his colleagues of Communist sympathies. When the ambassador called President Johnson in Washington to ask for American troops (to "prevent another Cuba," in his words), President Johnson responded by sending twenty-three thousand marines.[27]

During the next several months, the American troops tried to separate the rival Dominican forces and occasionally engaged in combat themselves. Eventually, peace was restored, and an election was held; the American-supported candidate won the election.

Southeast Asia[28]

American involvement in Southeast Asia began in 1950 when the United States started a program of substantial military assistance to the French, who were fighting Communist Viet Minh revolutionaries in an attempt to retain control over the Indochina portion of the French empire. After World War II, the French created the three Associated States of Laos, Cambodia, and Vietnam in Indochina, but the French maintained effective control for several years. France's control was eventually undermined, however, when its troops lost a crucial battle at Dien Bien Phu in 1954.

The United States nearly intervened in support of the French at the time of Dien Bien Phu. The secretary of state, the chairman of the Joint Chiefs of Staff, and several members of Congress were so inclined. But when the British prime minister refused to support the idea, President Eisenhower decided not to intervene.

Instead, the United States participated in negotiations at Geneva to arrange a French withdrawal. The Geneva agreements provided for independence and neutrality for Laos and Cambodia, and they divided Vietnam into two "zones," which were to be united in one Vietnam after elections in 1956. The provisions for all three countries eventually collapsed as a result of a combination of internal and international factors.

In Laos, the United States supported some political factions, while the North Vietnamese and Russians supported others. The United States also provided military assistance to the central Laotian government, including advisers and reconnaissance flights, in its fight against guerrilla troops. In 1961 and again in 1962, the United States came close to overt intervention but was able to achieve a temporary settlement of the conflict each time.

Several years later, the war in Vietnam spilled over into Laos and Cambodia as well. One of the most dramatic episodes of the long American intervention of Southeast Asia was the invasion of Cambodia in the spring of 1970. The longest and most massive American intervention in Southeast Asia, however, was in Vietnam.

When the Vietnamese national elections and reunification scheduled for 1956 did not occur, the country became effectively divided at the 17th parallel—the north controlled by Communists led by Premier Ho Chi Minh and the south eventually controlled by President Ngo Dinh Diem. The United States provided military assistance to the South Vietnamese government from the outset. By 1960, the Eisenhower administration had sent over a thousand American advisers to help the South Vietnamese government in its fight against guerrillas, some of whom were trained in North Vietnam. The Kennedy administration increased the number of advisers to more than ten thousand, and they occasionally engaged in limited combat operations as well. The phase of large-scale overt U.S. military intervention did not begin until 1964, when the Johnson administration initiated air strikes against North Vietnam and began to increase substantially the number of American ground troops.

Several years later, in spite of the presence of over half a million American troops and the massive, sustained bombing of North Vietnam, there was a widespread perception that the American military position in South Vietnam was still vulnerable. During the Tet offensive by the Viet Cong and North Vietnamese in early 1968, it was clear that neither the cities nor the countryside of South Vietnam was secure from attack. Thus, the United States was not achieving its stated objective, the reestablishment of the South Vietnamese government's effective control over the territory south of the 17th parallel. In the aftermath of the Tet offensive and in the face of increasing internal American opposition to the war, President Johnson agreed to begin peace negotiations. While the peace negotiations continued, so did the war.

The Nixon administration changed the military strategy in 1969 to try to make it more politically acceptable. Although it reduced the numbers of American ground troops, it increased the intensity of the air war. Neither did this strategy, however, enable the United States to achieve its objective.

By 1973, the administration agreed to a peace settlement that provided for the continued presence of several thousand North Vietnamese troops in South Vietnam. Two years later, in 1975, the South Vietnamese government collapsed in military defeat. While the city was being captured, the few hundred remaining American advisers and other embassy personnel in the South Vietnamese capital city of Saigon were evacuated by helicopter from the lawn and rooftop of the American embassy. Saigon was subsequently renamed Ho Chi Minh City.

Lebanon: The Second Time

The American troops in Lebanon in 1983–1984 were formally designated as part of a multilateral peacekeeping force. The specific purpose of the troops, however, was similar to their role in other military interventions—namely, to support the government in the midst of civil strife. In this instance, though, the role was largely symbolic since the number of troops was limited to a few hundred and since they were mostly restricted to the occupation of a small area near the Beirut airport. Along with the other nations' contingents in the force, they were there purportedly to try to separate the warring Christian and Moslem factions. In the event, the troops did become directly involved in the fighting, and in particular they engaged Lebanese Moslems and also Syrian troops with periodic artillery barrages.

From the American perspective, the most dramatic and tragic development was the deaths of 241 American marines from a suicide attack with explosives at their compound. This event reinforced public and congressional concern about the Reagan administration's decision to employ troops in Lebanon. In a poll taken in late 1983, for instance, only 45 percent of the respondents with minimal knowledge of the situation approved of the decision to send U.S. troops there.[29] Eventually, such concerns as well as other considerations prompted the administration to withdraw the troops and rely instead on bombardment of Syrian and Lebanese Moslem positions by naval guns to signal the continuing American interest in the Lebanese government's fate.

CENTRAL AMERICA AND THE CARIBBEAN IN THE 1980s

The Reagan administration sent American military personnel into Central American and Caribbean countries in the early 1980s—although for quite different reasons. An invasion of the small Caribbean island nation of Grenada in October 1983 was undertaken specifically as a rescue mission on behalf of American students who were attending a medical school in Grenada and whose lives may have been endangered by civil strife. The American troops not only rescued the students but also defeated the troops of the Marxist government, which was subsequently replaced by a government more friendly to the United States and to its Caribbean neighbors.

More significant and controversial interventions concerned El Salvador and Nicaragua. In El Salvador, the Reagan administration substantially increased U.S. military assistance to the Salvadoran government to help it combat a widespread guerrilla movement trying to overthrow the government. The amounts of U.S. military assistance to El Salvador increased from practically none in 1979 to $6 million in 1980 to more than ten times that amount in 1984.

One controversial aspect of that aid was that most of it was being provided without specific congressional approval by "reprogramming" funds that had been appropriated for aid to other countries and by the use of "emergency" funds. A more salient controversy, though, concerned the use of American military advisers. Inasmuch as the introduction of U.S. advisers in 1981 reminded people of the seemingly similar evolution of American policy in Vietnam in the early 1960s, there was considerable public and congressional opposition to increased American involvement in Central America. For example, a 1983 Gallup Poll asked the following question: "Some people say that the United States should give military assistance to governments in Central America that are friendly to us. Others say we should not get involved in the internal affairs of these nations. Which point of view comes closer to the way you feel—that we should give military assistance to these nations or that we should not get involved?" Of those responding, 55 percent said not to get involved, and 35 percent favored military assistance. A year later in April 1984, the proportions were 49 percent and 39 percent respectively. Numerous repeated polls during those same years found that only one-fifth to one-third of the population said that they approved of the way President Reagan was "handling the situation in Central America," while nearly half disapproved. About one-fourth did not express an opinion one way or the other.[30]

American involvement in Nicaragua also caused concern and became a central issue in the administration's relations with Congress. In Nicaragua, the United States supported the rebels who were trying to overthrow the Sandinista government. Through an openly acknowledged and widely reported program of "covert" aid, the United States provided bases in neighboring Honduras from which the guerrillas launched operations; the United States also supplied a wide array of weapons, supervised the mining of Nicaraguan harbors and other commando operations, and perhaps flew air-support missions. The revelation that the CIA had been involved in the mining of the harbors, which threatened the ships of many friendly as well as unfriendly countries, created much dismay in Congress in particular since there had been little, if any, notice given to the intelligence committees of the plan for such an action.

Even more damaging to the administration's efforts, however, were revelations that administration officials had used funds from sales of arms to Iran to support the contra rebels in Nicaragua. In what came to be known as the Iran-Contra scandal, NSC staff member Col. Oliver North became a controversial national figure. Condemned by some as a reckless and dangerous zealot and praised by others as a heroic fighter for freedom, Col. North was questioned in congressional hearings and eventually tried in federal courts for his role in the Iran-Contra affairs. Former NSC director Adm. John Poindexter was similarly subjected to legislative and judicial proceedings concerning his role in the affair. Although there were many questions about the possible knowledge of President Reagan, Vice-President Bush, and CIA Director Casey about the Iran-Contra connection, those questions were never completely resolved to everyone's satisfaction.

In any case, the eventual partial resolution of the armed conflicts in Nicaragua and El Salvador through elections marked the end of U.S. intervention in Central America as a salient foreign policy issue, at least for a while.

THE MIDDLE EAST IN 1990–1991

In August 1990, President Bush sent hundreds of ships and aircraft as well as hundreds of thousands of troops into the Persian Gulf and Saudi Arabia in response to the Iraqi invasion of Kuwait. As Iraq consolidated its military occupation of Kuwait and deployed troops near the border with Saudi Arabia, Bush ordered a large-scale deployment of air, ground, and sea forces along with a dozen Arab and other countries that also dispatched thousands of troops to deter further Iraqi moves in the area.

Bush also imposed a naval blockade in the Persian Gulf to prevent exports of Iraqi oil through the Straights of Hormuz to the rest of the world, and he prohibited the importation of Iraqi oil into the United States. The United Nations called for economic sanctions against Iraq, and scores of countries responded by suspending arms sales and other exports to Iraq, prohibiting oil imports from Iraq, freezing Iraqi assets held in bank accounts in their countries, and imposing diverse other forms of economic sanctions. The ensuing war against Iraq was also authorized by the UN.

The military and economic reactions by the United States and the rest of the world were notable for their swiftness and the extent of their support. There was also a dramatic symbol of the newly transformed Soviet-American relations: The Soviet foreign minister and the American secretary of state issued a joint communiqué condemning Iraq—despite the fact that the USSR had been a major supplier of military equipment to Iraq for many years. The USSR also supported economic sanctions as part of the worldwide effort to isolate Iraq.

The Persian Gulf war thus marked a new era in military intervention for the United States—one in which the cold war tensions between the United States and the Soviet Union did not play a role. That case also reflected the strong sense of economic interdependence felt by leaders in most of the world and their willingness to use multilateral economic and military measures to intervene along with the United States. The Gulf war also renewed interest in arms transfer issues.

ARMS TRANSFERS

Soon after World War II, the United States government began exporting military supplies to other countries, and such government-sponsored arms transfers have continued at several billion dollars per year since. However, those arms transfers occur in several forms, and the mix of types of transfers has changed over the years. When the postwar American arms transfer program began in 1950, the principal form of assistance was government grants under the Military Assistance Program (MAP). Such grants were made mostly to Western European countries, and they were made in large amounts. During the early 1950s, as much as $30 million (in constant 1990 dollars) in U.S. military grants was provided to the NATO countries.[31] During the next decade, arms transfers through grants-in-aid diminished; they were less than $1 billion per year by the late 1970s.

While arms transfers funded by government grants were decreasing, arms sales were increasing. The Foreign Military Sales (FMS) program of government-to-government sales began in the early 1950s, but it did not become a major component of American arms transfer policy until the early 1960s.[32] The principal factor prompting the change in emphasis from grants to sales was concern about the economic consequences of arms transfers and the cost of stationing American troops abroad, especially their effects on the American balance of payments.

In the early 1960s, the United States began to pressure West Germany for financial reimbursement for the cost of maintaining American troops in that country. When the West German government balked at this suggestion, a compromise was reached whereby West Germany bought several hundred million dollars of American arms over a few years. Such purchases partially offset the costs and the balance-of-payments problems caused by the large numbers of American troops stationed there.

Subsequent developments reinforced the increasing emphasis on sales. As American weapons costs increased, foreign arms sales came to be viewed as one way to help pay for research, development, and production-overhead expenses.[33] Also, disenchantment with the Vietnam experience, together with the "Nixon Doctrine" emphasis on increased burden sharing by American allies, made arms sales a more politically acceptable form of military assistance than grants. Furthermore, the OPEC oil-price increases and American oil imports during the 1970s gave Middle Eastern oil-producing countries the dollars with which they could purchase American military supplies and services. Finally, the Middle East war of 1973 destroyed large amounts of Israeli military equipment.

Deliveries of military supplies and services under the government's Foreign Military Sales program are well over $10 billion per year. Although private commercial sales under government license are at much lower levels, they exceed $2 billion annually.[34] Surplus government military supplies were also transferred at nominal cost or no cost to the recipient.

The United States exports more than $10 billion annually in military supplies and services, which is about 5 percent of the total value of all American exports and about 0.3 percent of GNP.[35] These supplies and services include not only weapons and ammunition but also spare parts, supporting equipment, training, and construction.

Such levels of arms transfers make the United States the world's leading arms exporter, though the USSR has exported arms at similar levels. France, West Germany, and Great Britain have also claimed substantial shares of the export market. Altogether, these five countries account for four-fifths of the world total.[36]

These high and increasing levels of arms transfers by the United States and other countries raise many issues, but the central one is their effects.[37] As far as the United States is concerned, arms transfers are intended to serve several purposes. The American transfers to its European and East Asian allies in the past were primarily for anti-Soviet and anti-Chinese strategic deterrence and regional defenses.

Transfers to most other countries, however, are intended to increase American influence over their foreign policies or to strengthen a particular regime against internal or external opponents. The United States has used military assistance to participants in the Arab-Israeli conflict partly to try to gain their support for American peace efforts. It has used military assistance to African and Latin American governments to try to strengthen their position in relation to internal and external foes. More generally, the United States has used military assistance to try to maintain friendly relations with countries.

Sometimes it is successful in terms of these objectives; sometimes it is not. But the actual consequences of these arms transfers include several undesirable effects. They exacerbate regional arms competition, for instance. This has been true especially in the Middle East, where American, Soviet, and European arms supplies have reinforced the Middle East's highly militarized status. Furthermore, if war breaks out, American weapons may make it more destructive, and they may be used to fight the "wrong war," at least from the American perspective. For example, Turkey used American weapons in its invasion of Cyprus in 1974, and Argentina used American-supplied ships in its war against Britain in 1982 over control of the Falkland/Malvinas Islands. Iraq used Soviet and American weapons in its 1990 invasion of Kuwait and its attacks on coalition forces.

Weapons may also be used by authoritarian regimes to repress internal dissidents. During 1978, the Somoza government of Nicaragua used American-supplied small arms and riot-control equipment against internal opponents.[38]

CORRELATES OF POLICIES

There are several plausible explanations for the central tendencies and variations in American intervention and assistance policies. One common one, which has been subjected to careful, quantitative analysis, is a variant of the ruling elite model. It suggests (a) that the United States has been particularly prone to intervene in less developed countries where there were American economic interests at stake, and (b) that the United States has also used assistance programs to promote these American economic interests in foreign countries. It is sometimes argued, for instance, that American sugar interests in the Dominican Republic and banana interests in Guatemala led to American interventions in those countries. It has been similarly argued that potential American oil interests off the coast of Vietnam led the United States to become actively involved in political conflicts there. The role of oil in the 1991 Persian Gulf war was clearly evident.

These arguments are supported by further documentary or circumstantial evidence in some cases, but we would like to have more systematic evidence to test these assumptions. Several studies have tried to do precisely that, and they have produced pertinent findings. Two studies tried to determine whether there was a relationship between variations in American economic interests in foreign countries and variations in American military intervention policy.

One study used levels of American trade with countries as an indicator of American economic interests.[39] The study compared American trade with countries where the United States intervened militarily between 1950 and 1967 and American trade with other countries in the same regions where the United States did not intervene. The study also made similar comparisons among regions and countries in terms of the levels of direct American investment. The principal finding was that there was only a slightly greater tendency for the United States to intervene in countries with substantial trade and investment interests than in countries where such interests were minimal.

Another study also tried to determine whether American interventions were related to economic interests.[40] It included ninety-one countries and covered the two decades from 1948 to 1967. It used not only the levels of direct American investments in the countries and trade with them but also the importance of their raw materials in American imports. The study found that the relationships between variations in these indicators of American economic interests and variations in American intervention in those countries were generally positive but weak. In other words, this study also found only a slightly greater tendency for the United States to intervene in countries where its economic interests were relatively substantial than in countries where its economic stakes were relatively small. Among the least stable countries, however, there was a somewhat stronger relationship between American economic interests and interventions. Moreover, when U.S. investments and trade in the region around the countries were taken into account, the relationships between American economic interests and intervention were yet stronger.

In general, however, the findings from these studies suggest that factors other than American economic interests were more important determinants of American military *intervention* policy. American support through the military *assistance* programs, on the other hand, has been found to be more strongly related to American economic stakes in the recipient countries.

A study of 119 recipients of U.S. military assistance between 1950 and 1965 found that variations in the levels of assistance were related to variations in the importance of the countries' raw materials to the United States, the amount of U.S. direct private investments in the countries, and the countries' shares of U.S. trade.[41] The correlations between the recipient countries' rankings on the economic variables and their rankings on the military assistance variable were 0.29 for raw materials, 0.48 for investment, and 0.46 for trade. These relationships, furthermore, were evident even when variations in the economic size (GNP) of the recipient countries were taken into account by using normal statistical-control techniques. Another study found similar results for the Latin American countries in particular.[42] Between 1960 and 1969, the value of American military assistance to those countries varied according to the value of American exports to them, the value of imports from them, and the value of investments in them, especially during the early part of the decade.

There is evidence that changes in the levels of American military and economic assistance have also been related to changes in regimes. One study traced the levels of American aid from 1954 to 1972 for five countries: Brazil, Indonesia, Chile, Greece, and Peru.[43] In each of those countries, there was at least one change in the government that represented a major political shift—from ''leftist'' civilian regimes to ''rightist'' military regimes in the first four countries and from a ''leftist'' civilian to a ''leftist'' military regime in the fifth (Peru). In every case except Greece, American aid increased after the military regime gained control. (Greece's position as a NATO member may account for its aberration from the pattern.)

We should note, however, that none of the relationships in any of these studies is perfect. Clearly, other factors have also affected the distribution of American military assistance.[44] Each of the following has been at least partially involved on some occasions: a generalized capitalistic ideological hostility toward socialist governments; internal pressures generated by a large American military establishment; politicians' catering to perceived public preferences and fear of electoral punishment for "losing" countries to communism; bureaucratic-organizational tendencies to try to impose control on their environments; and great-power rivalry in a competitive, anarchic international system.

CONCLUSION

The American foreign assistance policies that have been operative since the late 1940s have undergone important changes over the past several decades. The military assistance program has been shifting away from a reliance on government grants to an emphasis on sales of arms; the levels of those sales increased substantially during the 1970s.

It is more difficult to detect trends in covert and overt intervention policies. The publicly available data on covert operations are simply not adequate to make an informed statement in this regard, except to note that they presumably continue to be undertaken on an occasional basis.

As for overt military interventions, the American involvement in Southeast Asia may represent a long-term peak. The United States did send troops into Lebanon and Grenada in the early 1980s and into Panama in 1989, but the numbers of troops, the scope of their missions, and the duration of their stays were all quite limited. The intervention in the Middle East in 1990 was a significant departure from the trend.

═══ E L E V E N ═══

Trade

One of the most significant developments in American foreign policy since the mid-1970s has been the increased salience and controversy around economic issues. To a considerable extent, this increased prominence of foreign economic policy issues has been the consequence of developments in domestic economic issues. Periodic concerns about recession, inflation, and unemployment in the domestic economy naturally spill over to include greater interest in international economic relations. Domestic economic conditions and international economic relations are, after all, inevitably and intimately related to one another. Indeed, one of the themes of this chapter is that international economic interdependence is an important fact of life for the American public and government alike. International economic issues are important not only because they are related to domestic economic conditions, but also because they are related to international politics. Quite apart from domestic economic conditions, many international economic issues have become central foreign policy issues. Economic issues dominate American relations with many countries, and the revolutionary changes in East Europe have made U.S. economic relations with those countries major items on the foreign policy agenda.

In this chapter, we focus our attention on international trade issues. The discussion will be organized around the following questions: What are the main patterns and trends in the international trade system and in American trade? What are the domestic economic consequences of trade? What are the central elements of

American trade policy, and how has it been changing in recent years? What about the use of trade sanctions in international political conflicts—when, why, and with what effects has the United States used trade as an economic weapon? Finally, how do domestic political processes affect American trade policy?

PATTERNS AND TRENDS IN TRADE

An overview of the entire world trade system is presented in Figure 11–1. That figure highlights several important characteristics of the contemporary world trade system. First, trade among the industrialized countries of North America, Western Europe, and Japan comprises about one-half of the total monetary value of world trade. A second principal set of trading relationships consists of trade between those same industrialized countries and the oil-exporting countries of the Middle East, Africa, Latin America, and Asia. The third principal trading relationship is between the industrialized countries and the other developing countries. The oil-exporting coun-

FIGURE 11–1 International trade system (merchandise exports/imports, US $ billions, 1988). Space within each rectangle and square reflects approximate proportion of total world exports/imports. Middle East in original source is used as the country grouping.

Source: Adapted by the author from data in General Agreement on Tariffs and Trade, *International Trade, 1988–89* (Geneva: GATT, 1989), table A3.

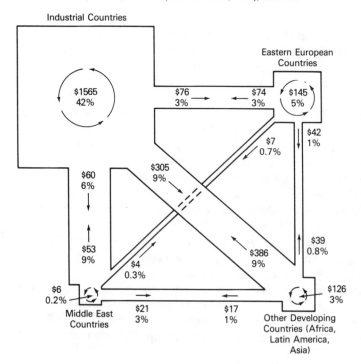

tries and other developing countries trade very little among themselves. Nor is trade among the countries of Eastern Europe and Asia at very high absolute levels in comparison with the three principal trading relationships. Finally, trade among the three sets of non-Western, nonindustrialized countries is also at relatively low levels.

An understanding of specific trade issues, however, requires a much more detailed analysis of trade patterns; in particular, we often need to focus on individual countries' trade relations. For many countries, especially relatively small ones, trade is centrally important to their economies; indeed, exports constitute much more than half of the gross national product of some countries, such as Belgium and Singapore. We also often need to focus on a specific industry or commodity; steel, automobiles, and textiles, for instance, have all been at the center of major international trade issues in recent years because changes in those industries have left some countries' producers unable to compete effectively in the international trade system.

A few key patterns of U.S. trade are readily apparent if we look at the structure of trade as reflected in the commodities being traded and the foreign countries involved in the trade. Table 11–1 presents summary data according to a commonly used format that enables us to combine two dimensions of trade: commodity composition and country groups. The data in the right-hand columns indicate the dominance of food and chemicals in U.S. exports, and the dominance of fuels and motor vehicles among imports. It can also be noted that the United States is both an exporter and importer in each commodity group; a more refined breakdown of the commodity categories reveals, for instance, that the United States exports wheat, corn, soybeans, and other grains but imports sugar, cocoa, and other tropical agricultural products.

As for geographic patterns, the fact that about 50 percent of U.S. trade is with other industrial countries is central to the structure of U.S. trade; furthermore, American trade with those countries extends across all of the broad categories of commodities represented in the table. By contrast, trade with the East European countries is highly concentrated in a few goods. The vast majority of U.S. trade with the former group of countries is in oil, of course, with modest amounts of machinery being exported from the United States to those countries. About half of U.S. exports to Eastern Europe is in food, mostly wheat and corn, although the commodity composition of those trade relations is changing rapidly. American trade with the non–oil-developing countries is relatively diversified, although two-way trade in agricultural commodities is especially important; in addition, the United States exports substantial amounts of machinery and chemicals to those countries and imports many consumer goods from them. In total, American trade with these developing countries constitutes about one-fourth of the total dollar value of all U.S. trade.

ECONOMIC CONSEQUENCES

The importance of international trade to any country's economy is commonly gauged by the ratio of its exports and/or imports of goods and services to its gross national product. American exports were about 10 percent of GNP by the mid-1980s, and the

TABLE 11–1 Structure of U.S. Merchandise Trade by Country Groups and Selected Commodity Groups (US $ billions)*

COMMODITY GROUPS	INDUSTRIAL		DEVELOPING		EAST EUROPEAN		TOTALS**	
	EXP.	IMP.	EXP.	IMP.	EXP.	IMP.	EXP.	IMP.
Food	21	13	15	14	3	1	39	27
Minerals, ores	13	10	7	4	1	—‡	21	14
Fuels	5	12	2	31	—	1	8	44
Iron and steel	1	9	1	3	—	—	15	12
Chemicals	19	17	12	3	2	1	33	20
Office, telecommunications equipment	28	32	15	25	—	—	44	57
Motor vehicles	25	70	5	8	—	—	30	78
Totals†	205	286	107	162	9	12	320	460

*Data are for 1988.
**Includes Australia, New Zealand, and South Africa, which are not classified in country groups.
†Includes commodities not classified in commodity groups.
‡——indicates less than $0.5 billion.

Source: Adapted by the author from General Agreement on Tariffs and Trade, *International Trade, 1988–89* (Geneva: GATT, 1989), table A7. Data have been rounded to nearest billion.

ratio of imports to GNP was slightly greater. Both ratios are increasing gradually over time, despite year-to-year fluctuations.[1]

However, such figures provide only general indications of the increasing importance of international economic relations to the American economy. If we consider the relationship of international trade to other economic indicators as well, and if we focus on the effects of changes in trade on those economic indicators, we find that the American economy is quite sensitive to changes in the rest of the world economy. In particular, changes in exports and imports affect all three of the principal indicators of economic conditions: income, employment, and prices.

The most obvious and familiar of these effects is that increases in exports lead to higher employment and income; but since increased demand for a good or service may increase its price, exports also sometimes have an inflationary impact. Imports tend to have the opposite effects. Although increasing imports may reduce domestic incomes and employment in the short term they also tend to reduce prices. Imports have anti-inflationary tendencies, since foreign products are presumably purchased because they are available at lower prices than comparable domestic products. At the aggregate level, therefore, both imports and exports involve trade-offs; both have a variety of effects on the national economy.

When we disaggregate these national effects, we find an even more complex mixture of effects. For instance, exports of American automobiles may increase profits and employment in the automobile industry and generally increase incomes in areas around automobile plants. Increased imports of shoes may be detrimental to incomes and employment in the American shoe industry, but, on the other hand, they are beneficial to American shoe retailers and consumers. Inexpensive imported steel may be costly to American steel industry workers and owners, but it is beneficial to American automobile and appliance manufacturers because their production costs are lower; and it is beneficial to the consumers of the products because their purchase price is lower. The economic effects of trade, therefore, vary among sectors of the economy.

The effects of trade also vary over time; what is detrimental in the short run may be beneficial in the long run and vice versa. Although increased demand for exports of a product may increase its price in the short run, its price may be reduced in the long run if unit production costs are lowered through economies of scale. Imports that reduce incomes and employment in a particular industry in the short run will lead to higher employment and income in the long run, as workers and capital move into more productive industries.

Relationships between trade and internal economic conditions are also evident in the balance of payments and in the foreign exchange markets.

Balance of Payments

A country's balance-of-payments accounts provide a statistical summary of its economic transactions with the rest of the world during a given period of time, such as a year, quarter, or month. The accounts are based on information about the payments by American residents to foreign residents and the receipts by Americans from foreign residents, as well as other transactions. Although it is difficult to determine the precise causes and consequences of balance-of-payments conditions, an analysis of the balance of payments can nevertheless be helpful for gaining an understanding of the basic patterns and trends in American economic relations with foreign countries. Furthermore, an understanding of a few of the basic concepts of balance of payments will enable you to understand better the politics as well as the economics of foreign trade.

Table 11–2 contains U.S. balance-of-payments figures for one year. The first two main sections at the top reflect exports and imports of goods and services. Within those two main categories, trade in merchandise is by far the largest subcategory; this refers to trade in tangible goods and is what most people have in mind when they speak of trade. However, there are three other important subcategories. One subcategory refers to exports/imports of military equipment, which are separated out

TABLE 11–2   U.S. Balance-of-Payments Summary

	U.S. $ BILLIONS
Exports of goods and services (excl. military grants)	+600
Merchandise, excl. military	+362
Military sales	+9
Receipts of income on U.S. assets abroad	+125
Other services	+114
Imports of goods and services	−692
Merchandise, excl. military	−475
Direct defense expenditures	−14
Payments of income on foreign assets in U.S.	−124
Other services	−193
Unilateral transfers, excl. military (net)	−14
U.S. government	−10
Other	−4
U.S. assets abroad (net increase)	−126
U.S. official reserve assets	−25
Other U.S. government assets	+1
Direct investments abroad	−32
Other private investments	−69
Foreign assets in U.S. (net increase)	+197
Foreign official assets	+7
Direct investments in U.S.	+61
Other foreign assets	+128
Allocation of IMF special drawing rights	0
Statistical discrepancy	+35
Balance on merchandise trade	−113
Balance on goods and services	−92
Balance on goods, services, and remittances	−96
Balance on current account	−106

Source: "Current Business Statistics" *Survey of Current Business* 70, 3 (Washington, DC: U.S. Government Printing Office, March 1990), p. 48. Data are for 1989.

from other goods since they do not represent normal commercial trading relations. The other two subcategories reflect trade in intangible services rather than tangible goods.

One type of service item reflects the income of foreign affiliates of firms that is remitted back to the parent firm in the home country. For instance, when a General Motors subsidiary in Brazil transfers profits back to its American headquarters, this receipt by an American corporate resident shows up in the export accounts of the U.S. balance of payments. On the other hand, when an American subsidiary of a firm with headquarters in a foreign country transfers income abroad to its headquarters, this transaction by an American corporate resident to a foreign corporate resident shows up in the U.S. balance of payments as an import. Services such as shipping fees, air fares, tourists' hotel accommodations, and students' tuition are also recorded in the balance of payments—as "other services."

Government and private grants, gifts, and other payments such as retirement payments to people living overseas are recorded as "unilateral transfers." Such unilateral transfers, together with exports and imports of goods and services, are considered "current account" items, as distinguished from the "capital account" items in the lower section of the table.

Capital accounts are grouped into the "U.S. assets abroad" and "foreign assets in U.S." categories. Those items reflect international investments and transfers of funds between the United States and foreign countries. Thus, if a foreign resident buys a U.S. Treasury bond or stock in an American corporation, there would be an increase in foreign assets in the United States; there may also be an inflow of funds into the United States. Or when a foreign-based corporation loans funds to its American subsidiary, this would also be an increase in foreign assets in the American balance-of-payments accounts, but it would be accompanied by an inflow of funds into the U.S. On the other hand, when an American buys stock in a foreign corporation or when an American corporation invests in a new facility in a foreign country and transfers funds to it from the United States, those transactions increase U.S. assets abroad, but they also represent outflows of funds in the U.S. balance of payments. The subsequent receipts of stock dividends by the individual investor or income remittances to the U.S. corporation, however, would later appear as services exports in the current account, and they would also be recorded as short-term funds inflows in the capital account.

Line items in the balance of payments can be combined in several ways to arrive at the balances noted at the bottom of Table 11–2. Thus, the "balance on merchandise trade" is simply merchandise exports minus merchandise imports. If exports exceed imports, we speak of a trade *surplus;* if imports exceed exports, we refer to a *deficit.* Although that balance is an important and interesting number that is frequently cited in the press, the other balances are also indicative of basic relationships between the U.S. economy and the rest of the world. The other balances include not only merchandise trade but also the service items noted above. In recent years, the United States has tended to run large deficits on the merchandise trade balance, the goods and services trade balance, and the current account balance.

The significance of these balances is that they have other economic repercussions—in the foreign exchange markets and in the domestic economy. The effects on domestic economic conditions can be briefly summarized as follows: A balance-of-payments current account surplus will tend to increase incomes and employment. A balance-of-payments deficit will tend to reduce incomes and employment. The extent and timing of these consequences depend on a large number of other factors, and an analysis of those factors would take us far beyond the scope of this elementary discussion. However, we do need to note briefly the role and importance of foreign exchange rates and markets.

Foreign Exchange Markets

International trade and other types of international economic transactions lead to sales and purchases of foreign currencies in foreign exchange markets. When an American buys a new foreign-made car, for instance, normally the dollars paid are eventually exchanged for the currency of the country where the car was manufactured—perhaps German marks, Japanese yen, British pounds, French francs, or Italian lira. The amount of each currency involved in the exchange depends on its relative values—that is, its exchange rate. If the German mark/American dollar exchange rate is 2.0 German marks/U.S. dollar, a German-made automobile with a price tag of 80,000 German marks would cost 40,000 U.S. dollars; however, if the exchange rate is 2.5 marks/1 dollar, the 80,000 deutsch mark automobile would cost only 32,000 American dollars. The exchange rate is a direct determinant of the prices of goods and services in international transactions.

Until the early 1970s, currency exchange rates were "fixed," at least over the short term. Most governments, including the United States, guaranteed that they would convert their own currencies into gold or other currencies within a small margin of a fixed (or "pegged") rate of exchange. Between 1971 and 1973, however, this long-standing international monetary system based on fixed exchange rates was abolished. It was abolished when the United States announced that it would no longer guarantee the convertibility of the dollar into gold or other currencies at a fixed rate. Since that action, exchange rates between the U.S. dollar and other principal international currencies have generally been allowed to "float" in the foreign exchange markets with periodic government interventions.[2]

For a country such as the United States that allows its currency to float, the exchange rate of its currency at any given time is determined by the supply-and-demand relationship for that currency. When the demand for American dollars increases in relation to their supply, the exchange rate of the American dollar with other currencies changes so that the dollar becomes more valuable; conversely, when the supply of American dollars increases in relation to demand for them, their value declines in exchanges with other currencies. Those supply-and-demand conditions are in turn affected by the balance of trade, investors' expectations about future economic conditions in the United States and other countries, relative interest rates in numerous countries, and other factors as well.

The value of the dollar in the foreign exchange markets and the levels and trends of exports and imports in international trade are often related. For instance, an increasing U.S. trade deficit may lead to a declining value of the dollar, which makes imports more expensive to Americans and makes U.S. exports cheaper to foreigners. These price changes may then tend to decrease imports and increase exports and thus offset the original trade deficit. (The reader may want to trace through the opposite sequence of events to check his or her understanding of those relationships.)

Government policies also have important effects on the dollar's value in the foreign exchange markets. During the late 1970s, when the Congress was at an impasse on policies to restrain energy consumption and oil imports, the value of the dollar declined because international financial experts expected the substantial American trade deficits to continue. During the early and mid-1980s, on the other hand, government monetary policies that produced high interest rates also attracted foreign funds into the United States and thereby pushed up the value of the dollar. Furthermore, governments sometimes try to affect exchange rates directly by entering the foreign exchange markets themselves; American, Japanese, British, German, and other governments periodically buy and sell currencies in an effort to influence exchange rates. During 1978, when the American dollar was under severe pressure and its value was declining in relation to other currencies, several governments bought dollars to try to counter the antidollar selling pressures. They were only partially successful, however, even though they bought billions of dollars.

Why would foreign governments want to buy American dollars, especially when their value is declining? Because the exchange rate between the U.S. dollar and their own currencies affects their trade as well as American trade. As the dollar declines in value and foreign currencies rise in value, American exports become cheaper to foreigners, and foreign countries' exports concomitantly become more expensive to Americans. American exports increase, and foreign exports decrease. As foreign countries' exports decrease, their employment and income also decrease. So, paradoxically, foreign countries enjoy some benefits from having a currency that is low in value relative to such other currencies as the American dollar. (They enjoy different benefits from having a currency that is high in value relative to the American dollar.) Americans—particularly those whose employment or income depends on exports—benefit from a declining or devalued dollar. Once again, however, the economic consequences are more complicated. A declining dollar—which leads to more American exports and hence to greater American employment and income— also creates inflationary pressures as a result of the greater foreign demand for American goods and services and the increased dollar prices of imports.

In the mid-1980s, on the other hand, the high American interest rates and the consequent high value of the dollar were creating problems for U.S. exporters whose prices to foreign purchasers were high in terms of their currencies and hence less competitive. The high U.S. interest rates, moreover, were leading to high interest rates in Europe as well and were depressing their economies. As a result, at economic summit meetings among the heads of government of the seven largest industrial countries, President Reagan was under pressure to lower U.S. interest rates. The fact that U.S. interest rates affect other countries' interest rates is but one of many indications of the existence of international economic interdependence. In a further manifestation of interdependence, several governments agreed to try to push down the value of the dollar through intervention in foreign exchange markets (the Plaza Accord) beginning in 1985 and then stabilized it in 1987 (the Louvre Accord).

International Economic Interdependence

The many relationships among internal economic conditions, trade conditions, foreign exchange markets, and government policies are summarized in Figure 11–2. That figure also indicates how trade and other international economic transactions link economies together in complex interdependent relationships. As a consequence of these international economic interdependencies, there must be some kind of adjustment process linking changes in the American economy to changes in economic conditions in the rest of the world. That adjustment process entails a combination of changes in exchange rates; changes in domestic incomes, employment, and prices; changes in interest rates; and changes in the balance of payments. Changes in such key economic variables, however, do not merely create economic issues; those changes also create domestic political issues and domestic political pressures.

FIGURE 11–2   The role of international trade and the foreign exchange markets in international economic interdependence

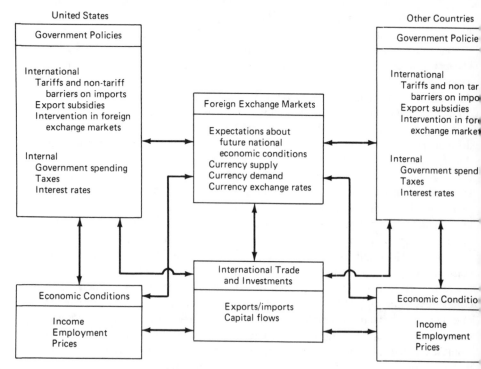

APPROACHES TO TRADE POLICY

American trade policy on specific issues usually represents a compromise between two general conflicting approaches: a "mercantilist," or "protectionist," approach, and a "laissez-faire," or "liberal," approach. (The terms *liberal* and *liberalism* have precise meanings in this context, which are quite independent of any other meanings they may have on other issues.)

The mercantilist approach focuses on the benefits to be gained from exports. It views exports as good because they contribute directly to domestic income and employment; it views imports as undesirable because they directly threaten domestic income and employment. Thus, in the mercantilist view, a surplus balance of payments is desirable. Such an approach to trade issues quite naturally leads to protectionist policies that restrict imports—and to subsidies for exports. The questionable economic reasoning implicit in such an approach to international trade has long been recognized by economists. It ignores, for instance, the inflationary consequences of restricting imports. It ignores the problem that if other countries also impose restrictions on their imports, then the first country will not be able to export. The mercantilist approach also neglects to consider how foreigners will be able to buy American exports if Americans are not able to buy the foreign countries' exports.

The laissez-faire, or liberal, approach to trade issues takes a broader and a longer term view of trade. It is based in particular on the recognition that total welfare will be maximized if trade is allowed, so that countries can specialize in producing and exporting those goods and services in which they have a "comparative advantage." Thus, a country will be best off if it tends to produce and export goods and services that use its relatively abundant resources. For instance, a country such as the United States has relatively abundant fertile farmland for growing grains, and so it can produce those crops relatively efficiently. It also has the highly skilled technical personnel for making computers. On the other hand, other countries may have a relative abundance of the resources needed to produce sugar and shoes relatively efficiently. Thus, it is not only in the American economic interest to export grains and computers, it is also beneficial economically for the United States to import sugar and shoes.

The highly protectionist mercantilist policies that were adopted by the United States and other countries in the 1920s and 1930s were substantially discredited when it was realized that they had contributed to the severe decline in economic activity during the Great Depression. Thus, during most of the past five decades, the consensus among government policy makers and informed segments of the public has generally been that American policies should be based on a laissez-faire, or liberal, approach. Off and on during those years, however, and especially since the mid-1970s, there have been substantial protectionist elements in American trade policy; and of course at any given time in those industries and firms that feel particularly threatened by imports, there are strong protectionist sentiments—as unemployment rates increased in the textile, steel, automobile, and shoe industries, they sought greater protection against imports.

These conflicting approaches to trade policy and the associated domestic political pressures shape American policy in several international trade policy-making arenas. Those policies, however, are also shaped by the distinctive international economic and political relations between the United States and each of three different groups of countries—the industrial countries, the developing countries, and the East European countries.

INDUSTRIAL COUNTRIES

American policy toward the industrial, market-economy countries of Western Europe, Canada, and Japan has been fundamentally affected by its acceptance of the General Agreement on Tariffs and Trade (GATT).[3] When the United States and other industrialized countries signed GATT in 1947, they committed themselves to the principle of trade liberalization—that is, reducing tariffs and other obstacles to free trade. This agreement was the culmination of American efforts to avoid the protectionist beggar-thy-neighbor trade policies and trade wars that prevailed prior to World War II and contributed to the world depression of the 1930s. The American government, however, was not only interested in avoiding a repetition of that global catastrophe; it was also interested in increasing its own exports by obtaining lower tariffs in other countries.

The United States and more than a hundred other national governments have met periodically to negotiate lower tariffs within the framework of GATT. At those negotiating rounds, the participants have negotiated on the basis of two principles: "most favored nation" and reciprocity. The most favored nation principle means that each country agrees to extend to all GATT countries the same (lowered) tariff level on a given item that it extends to any one other GATT country. Thus, the phrase actually means that no one nation is the most favored; all are similarly favored. The principle of reciprocity means that each nation is expected to reciprocate when another nation lowers its tariffs.

As a result of numerous rounds of negotiations, tariff levels among GATT members have declined substantially. By the 1990s, American tariff levels averaged less than 5 percent, compared with 25 percent in 1945 and 60 percent in 1934. Tariff levels in other GATT countries have also been reduced substantially. On some items, tariffs have been eliminated altogether. Agreements on further tariff reductions were reached during the Tokyo round of GATT negotiations completed in 1979. When those agreements were implemented during the 1980s, the tariff levels on trade in industrial goods among the industrialized countries became even lower (Table 11–3). Those substantial mutual tariff reductions are an important achievement of American trade policy objectives. They have facilitated trade among GATT countries and thus generally contributed to higher incomes and employment, and lower prices, in the United States and the other industrialized countries.

However, GATT tariff reductions have not eliminated all obstacles to trade. Several obstacles to free trade still exist, and they take many forms. Japan, for

TABLE 11-3   **Tariff Levels on Raw Materials and Manufactured Goods Traded among Industrialized Countries**

	TRADE WEIGHTED AVERAGE PERCENT*			
	ALL INDUSTRIAL PRODUCTS	RAW MATERIALS	SEMIMANUFACTURED PRODUCTS	FINISHED PRODUCTS
United States	4.4	0.2	3.0	5.7
European Community†	4.7	0.2	4.2	6.9
Japan	2.8	0.5	4.6	6.0

*Tariff levels in effect in mid-1980s after full implementation of Tokyo Round GATT agreements.
†The countries of the European Community (EC) are Belgium, Denmark, Germany, France, Greece, Ireland, Italy, Luxembourg, Netherlands, Portugal, Spain, United Kingdom.
Source: GATT, as reported in Chemical Bank, *Report from Europe* 7, 5 (May 1980), 11.

instance, has employed complicated customs administration procedures, which make it difficult for importers to gain access to Japanese markets. The European Economic Community, the United States, and other GATT countries have retained high tariff levels on many agricultural imports. Beginning in the late 1960s, moreover, the American government adopted several protectionist measures. Those measures were partly a response to continued elements of protectionism in European and Japanese trade policies and partly a reaction to American economic problems. The Johnson administration pressured European countries and Japan to adopt "voluntary" controls on their steel exports to the United States; and, a few years later, the Nixon administration did the same for textiles from Japan and other Asian countries. In 1971, when American imports exceeded exports for the first time in the twentieth century, the United States unilaterally imposed a 10 percent surcharge on its tariffs. Two years later, in response to unusually heavy foreign demand for American grain exports, which was creating inflationary pressures on American food prices, the administration imposed grain export quotas. By the mid-1980s, the United States had adopted protectionist policies that limited automobile imports from Japan as well as steel imports from Japan, Brazil, and West Germany. It also continued to provide considerable protection for textiles, numerous agricultural products, and the shipping industry. There has been mounting concern that protectionist trade policies in the United States and other industrialized countries might become even more common and thus exacerbate long-term income, employment, and price problems.

On the other hand, the United States and other countries in GATT have expanded their agenda to try to reduce nontariff barriers to trade (NTBs). They agreed on codes to reduce the use of customs procedures, technical standards, and government procurement regulations as means to restrict imports. In the 1980s, the GATT countries also began to consider reductions in barriers to trade in service industries, such as banking and insurance. During the Uruguay Round of GATT negotiations, which began in the mid-1980s and ended in 1991, nontariff barriers to trade, agricultural trade, and trade in services were all central items on the agenda. At the annual economic summit meetings of the heads of government of seven industrial countries (and the president of the European Community), conflicts over agricultural import restrictions and export subsidies have been among the main concerns.

In any case, the focus of GATT's activities has been trade among the non-Communist industrialized countries of Western Europe, North America, and Japan, although special provisions for trade with developing countries have been made. Agreements within GATT have frequently not been well received by the developing countries, however.

DEVELOPING COUNTRIES

The developing countries have never been very happy with GATT trade liberalization policies. During the 1980s and 1990s, however, those attitudes softened as many developing countries reconsidered and revised their protectionist import substitution economic policies and adopted more open, liberal international trade and investment policies. Mexico, for example, changed its policies and became a member of GATT.

When planning was underway in the 1940s for a new international trading system, the less developed countries lobbied for a system that would give them preferential treatment. They felt that protectionist measures would enable them to develop their "infant industries," thus contributing to their economic development plans. In fact, the Havana Charter signed in 1947 provided for such preferential treatment for developing countries.* Furthermore, the industrial countries adopted a Generalized System of Preferences (GSP) of lower tariff levels for poor countries.

The developing countries' disenchantment with the GATT-dominated international trade system eventually led to the formation of a new international organization in 1964—the United Nations Conference on Trade and Development (UNCTAD). It is essentially a lobbying organization that is trying to change the international economic order. In 1974, at a special session of the UN General Assembly, UNCTAD members successfully lobbied for a resolution titled "Declaration and Action Program on the Establishment of a New International Economic Order," or NIEO. The resolution included demands that the industrialized Western countries reduce tariffs on imports from developing countries on a preferential, nonreciprocal basis.[4]

The resolution also called for the establishment of commodity price stabilization arrangements. Because agricultural products and raw materials are subject to unusually large price fluctuations in international trade and because the developing countries' exports are highly concentrated in these commodities, the economies of those countries are particularly vulnerable to international trade fluctuations. In principle, there are several ways that such fluctuations can be reduced—for example, by establishing international buffer stocks of commodities. Buffer stocks can be built

---

*Although the American administration had been instrumental in formulating that agreement, it was opposed by so many members of Congress that it never became a functioning system; instead, it was quickly replaced by GATT.

up by purchasing commodities when their prices are low; such purchases would generate more demand and thus counter declining prices. When prices are high, the buffer stocks can then be used to sell the commodity, thus increasing the supply and countering the price rise. Although there are some obstacles to the effective operation of buffer arrangements, they have been established for tin and sugar, and they are being developed for additional commodities. Other price stabilization arrangements already exist for wheat and coffee.

Oil[5]

When the Arab members of the Organization of Petroleum Exporting Countries (OPEC) embargoed oil shipments to the United States and the Netherlands in retaliation for their support of Israel in the 1973 Middle East war, and then all OPEC members increased the price of their oil exports by more than 300 percent, they focused world attention on a variety of energy problems. The most obvious and immediate problem was that the United States and the other industrialized countries were vulnerable to interruptions in imported oil supplies. Because such supply interruptions could cause economic disruptions, the threat of them could be used effectively for political purposes. Thus, oil reserves and oil production became significant political as well as economic resources in international relations, and dependence on foreign energy supplies became a major foreign policy issue.

During the two-decade period from the late 1940s to the late 1960s, the oil consumed by Americans was almost entirely from domestic sources. Although the United States became a net importer of oil as early as 1947, the level of imports remained low for many years. As late as 1969, crude-oil imports were still at a rate of only about one million barrels per day, or about one-tenth of consumption. In fact, import quotas imposed from 1959 until the early 1970s limited foreign-oil imports into the eastern half of the United States to 12 percent of domestic production.

The prices of both imported and domestically produced oil were low and stable throughout this period. Between 1950 and 1968, the average price of domestic crude oil increased from $2.51 to $2.94 per barrel, an increase of only 17 percent over nearly two decades. Foreign oil prices remained even more stable and at lower prices. The posted price of Saudi Arabian crude oil in the Persian Gulf was $1.80 per barrel in 1960, and it was still the same price in 1970. (By comparison, the U.S. Consumer Price Index increased by 24 percent from 1950 to 1960 and by another 30 percent from 1960 to 1970.)

There were important changes in oil-supply trends during the 1970s. Domestic production of crude oil reached a peak in 1971 and then began to decline. At the same time, imports began to increase much more rapidly. Whereas imports had been averaging only slightly over one million barrels per day for a decade, they increased to more than three million per day by 1973. By 1990, imports were about 8 million barrels a day, or almost 50 percent of U.S. consumption.

In late 1973 and early 1974, the Organization of Petroleum Exporting Countries substantially increased their prices for exports to all countries. Persian Gulf crude oil went from less than $3 per barrel to nearly $12 per barrel in a few months.

Further increases in the late 1970s put prices in the $30 range, but they declined during the global recession in the early 1980s. Oil prices jumped up again and became more volatile in the summer of 1990 when Iraq invaded Kuwait and the United States and many other countries sent troops to Saudi Arabia to protect it from further Iraqi military action. After the war broke out, oil prices actually declined substantially and remained at relatively low levels because the oil market participants expected the war to be short and because Saudi Arabia substantially increased its production to offset the decline in production in Iraq and Kuwait. Oil prices, however, have remained volatile relative to most other traded items and will continue to be so. These basic supply and price trends are summarized in Figure 11–3.

FIGURE 11–3 Petroleum sources and prices

Source: Monthly Energy Review, various issues; IEA Statistics 1989; Quarterly Oil Statistics and Energy, New York Times, January 18, 1990, pp. 1, D5; IAE Statistics 1989: Energy Prices and Taxes, 3.

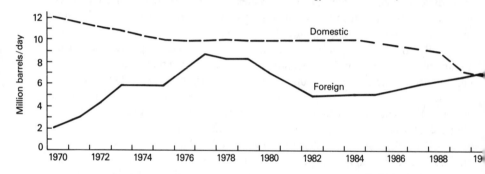

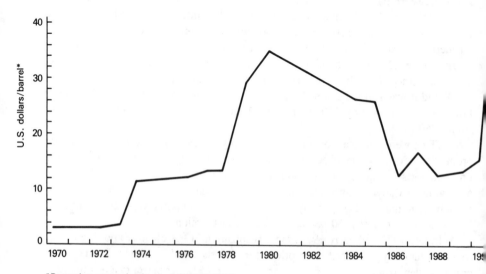

*Rotterdam spot price for Arab Light APT 34.

It should aiso be noted that at any given time, oil prices are spread over as much as a ten-dollar-per-barrel range. Price variations depend on the geographic location and hence transportation costs of the oil, its gravity (quality), the government that is selling it, and whether it is being sold at a previously set contract price or at a current spot-market price. For instance, the contract price of Saudi Arabian 34°, which is commonly used as a benchmark oil price, was $32 per barrel at the official price at the same time Algerian 44° was selling for over $40 per barrel in the European spot market.

In the aftermath of the 1974 OPEC price increases, the immediate U.S. response was to impose price ceilings on domestic oil in order to prevent further inflationary increases. Thus, a complicated two-tier system of price regulations distinguished between "old" and "new" oil. To encourage production, oil from the new wells or increased production from old wells could be sold at close to the new OPEC prices. To prevent windfall profits, oil from existing wells could be sold only at about half that price. In addition, extra import tariffs were imposed to reduce imports.

For several years, however, any more substantial American policy response to changes in energy supplies and prices was marked by conflict, delay, and indecision. The main directions of American policy did not become apparent until 1978, when a complex package of energy bills was passed. After a year and a half of work on the Carter administration's legislative proposals, Congress passed a series of energy bills. Among them, an energy conservation bill established mandatory energy efficiency standards for home appliances and heating and cooling equipment, and it provided for government financial aid to low-income families for home insulation improvements. It also required public utilities to provide informational and financial services to encourage their customers' energy conservation efforts, and it established programs for solar demonstration projects and energy efficiency measures in public buildings. Finally, it raised the fuel consumption standards for new automobiles.

Another element of the American response to the 1973–1974 oil embargo was to begin to establish a Strategic Petroleum Reserve of millions of barrels of crude oil stored underground. By the time of the Middle East crisis prompted by Iraq's invasion of Kuwait in August 1990, there was enough oil stored to provide the equivalent of several months' imports.

Additional legislation provided for gradually raising government-controlled natural gas prices and eliminating the controls altogether in 1985. The rationale for allowing substantial natural gas price increases and greater reliance on market price mechanisms is to encourage greater exploration and development of natural gas resources by its producers, on the one hand, and to encourage more efficiency in its use by consumers on the other.

The Reagan administration's commitment to a reliance on market forces led it to continue the deregulation of energy prices. It also scaled back many government energy conservation programs and R&D programs for the development of non-nuclear alternatives to fossil fuels. Furthermore, the recession and accompanying energy price declines in the early 1980s made oil a much less salient issue in American foreign policy and domestic policies—until the 1990 Middle East crisis.

In any case, there were important shifts in oil consumption and trade following the oil embargo and price rises of 1973–1974. The major industrial countries reduced their oil consumption in general and their dependence on imported oil, including oil from the volatile and vulnerable Persian Gulf area in particular (Table 11–4). Yet an important difference between the United States and the other industrial countries remained: The United States was still much less dependent on imported oil.

However, the basic patterns in oil reserves, production, and consumption remained essentially the same. The United States and the other industrial countries are drawing upon their domestic oil resources relatively rapidly and at the same time continuing to be substantial net importers. The Soviet Union is also drawing down its quite sizable domestic sources, and exporting substantial amounts to East European countries and other countries. Meanwhile, the yet greater reserves in the Middle East, Africa, and Latin America are largely being drawn upon for export to the industrial countries. Table 11–5 gives summary statistics.

Metals and Other Raw Materials

Supply and price problems in oil have periodically focused attention on the possibility of similar problems occurring in metals and other raw materials that are important in industrial processes.[6] World reserves of most metals seem less scarce than oil, although reserves of aluminum, copper, gold, lead, mercury, silver, tin, tungsten, and zinc would last only a few more decades at most if their exploitation continued to increase at the rates of the 1980s. Even if exploitation continued at a constant rate, several of these metals might approach exhaustion of world reserves by the end of the century. In any case, the generally increasing scarcity and extraction costs are expected to lead to substantial long-term price increases.

In the short term, concern is focused on the possibility of supply interruptions and on the actuality of highly unstable prices. The data in Table 11–6 suggest the origins of the concern about supply interruptions. The eighteen raw materials listed there are all significant inputs in various industrial processes. The United States, Western Europe, and Japan depend on imports of most of them.

TABLE 11–4   Industrial Countries' Oil Consumption and Imports from Persian Gulf: Cross-National and Longitudinal Comparisons

	CONSUMPTION (MILLION BARRELS PER DAY)		IMPORTS FROM PERSIAN GULF (PERCENT OF CONSUMPTION)	
	1973	1983	1973	1983
United States	16.7	15.2	6	3
France	1.9	1.6	96	36
West Germany	2.6	2.0	49	13
United Kingdom	1.7	1.3	75	14
Japan	4.8	4.2	68	56

Source: The New York Times, May 27, 1984, sec. 4, p. 1. Copyright © 1984 by the New York Times Company. Reprinted by permission.

TABLE 11–5   Oil Reserves, Production, and Consumption (billions of barrels)

	RESERVES	PRODUCTION PER YEAR	CONSUMPTION PER YEAR	NET EXPORTS (X) OR IMPORTS (M) PER YEAR
United States	36.9	3.7	5.4	1.7 (M)
Canada	7.0	0.6	0.5	0.1 (X)
Western Europe	23.5	1.1	4.6	3.5 (M)
Subtotal	67.4	5.4	10.5	5.1 (M)
Soviet Union	63.0	4.5	3.3	1.2 (X)
Eastern Europe	2.4	0.1	0.8	0.6 (M)
Subtotal	65.4	4.6	4.1	0.6 (X)
Middle East	369.0	4.7	0.6	4.1 (X)
Latin America	78.5	2.4	1.8	0.6 (X)
Africa	57.8	1.7	0.6	1.1 (X)
China	19.5	0.7	0.6	0.1 (X)
Other Asia	19.8	1.0	3.1	2.1 (M)

Source: Computed by the author from data in *The New York Times,* October 7, 1983, p. 35. Data are for year end 1982 and were originally taken from *British Petroleum Statistical Review* of *World Energy, 1982.* Minor discrepancies are due to rounding.

Several additional considerations, however, suggest that the United States and other industrial countries may not in fact be so vulnerable to supply interruptions in most of those materials. In the first place, there are substantial stockpiles of several of these materials; the United States has stockpiled a year's supply or more of aluminum, chromium, tin, manganese, cobalt, tungsten, and columbium.[7] Moreover, there are several short-term substitution possibilities, although some of them would be costly. Synthetic rubber, for instance, can be substituted for natural rubber; and numerous metals are at least partially interchangeable in stainless steel and other metal alloys. Furthermore, the heterogeneity among the exporting countries decreases the likelihood that they could effectively cooperate in a cartel.

Yet, there have been attempts to form mineral exporters' cartels. Several bauxite-aluminum–exporting countries joined Jamaica in 1974 in imposing substantially greater taxes and royalties on the mining companies operating in their countries. They also formed the International Bauxite Association, which has tried to exert collective control over world supplies and prices, but it has enjoyed only slight success. Also in 1974, the Intergovernmental Council of Copper Exporting Countries tried to impose greater controls over copper supplies and prices, but it was unsuccessful. The increased exploitation of copper reserves in other countries and the recession in the industrialized countries reduced the demand for copper exports and actually led to a reduction in price.

The prices of most raw materials exports have been highly unstable. These price fluctuations are a function of the economic cycles of growth and recession in the

TABLE 11–6   Minerals-Import Dependence in the United States and Other Industrialized Countries

RAW MATERIAL	PRINCIPAL USES	PERCENT OF IMPORT DEPENDENCE (IMPORTS/CONSUMPTION)			PRINCIPAL U.S. SUPPLIERS
		U.S.	EEC	JAPAN	
Aluminum-bauxite	Construction, transportation, containers, electricity	91	97	100	Jamaica, Australia, Surinam
Chromium	Stainless steel	91	100	98	USSR, S. Africa, Turkey
Platinum	Chemical and petroleum processes	87*	na	na	U.K., USSR, S. Africa
Iron	Steel	46	82	100	Canada, Venezuela
Nickel	Steel alloys	76	100	100	Canada, New Caledonia, Dominican Republic
Manganese	Steel production processes	98	100	99	Gabon, Brazil
Zinc	Galvanizing, die casting	57	91	74	Canada, Mexico
Tin	Solder, tinplating	84*	93†	97†	Malaysia, Thailand
Titanium	Aerospace construction, paint	47*	na	na	Australia, Canada, South Africa
Cobalt	Metal alloys	97	100	100	Zaire, Zambia, Finland
Mercury	Electrical equipment, chemical processing	49*	na	na	Spain, Algeria, Italy, Canada, Yugoslavia
Tungsten	Steel alloys	54*	100†	100†	Canada, Peru
Lead	Batteries, plumbing	13	76	78	Canada, Peru, Australia, Mexico
Columbium	Stainless steel, metal alloys	100*	na	na	Brazil, Canada
Vanadium	Metal alloys	15*	na	na	S. Africa, Chile
Fluorspar	Chemical and steel processing	84*	na	na	Mexico, Spain
Copper	Electricity, plumbing	13	100	97	—
Phosphate	Fertilizer	0	99	100	—

Source: U.S., Congress, Congressional Research Service, *A Congressional Handbook on U.S. Materials Import Dependency/Vulnerability* (Washington, DC: U.S. Government Printing Office, 1981), p. 30. Data (*) are for 1980, (†) for 1975, otherwise for 1977. Source of (†) data is U.S., President, *International Economic Report of the President* (Washington, DC: U.S. Government Printing Office, 1977), p. 187, table 78.

industrialized countries, whose imports determine the demand for the raw materials. Although such price fluctuations are somewhat disruptive for industrialized countries, they are much more disruptive in the developing countries. The LDCs' earnings from these exports are their principal source of foreign exchange assets, which are necessary to buy the imported oil, manufactured goods, and services that are important to their economic-development plans. Their earnings from these exports are often a major component of their GNPs.

Exports of Manufactured Goods

Several developing countries have also become significant exporters of heavy industrial goods (e.g., steel), automobile components and assembled vehicles, and a variety of consumer goods such as clothing and electronic items. Commonly referred to as NICs (Newly Industrializing Countries), they include important U.S. trade partners: Taiwan, South Korea, Singapore, Malaysia, Hong Kong, Mexico, Argentina, and Brazil.

In some instances, these countries' exports have become serious competition for U.S. manufacturers, and their trade policies have become sources of tension. Brazil, for example, is a major exporter of steel and of commuter airplanes to many countries, including the United States. Brazil is also a potential large market for U.S. exports of such products as computers. For many years, however, the Brazilian government restricted imports of computers; in retaliation, the U.S. government imposed 100 percent duties on imports of Brazilian commuter airplanes into the United States. Also, the United States imposed special duties and quotas on imported Brazilian steel in retaliation for the Brazilian government's subsidies of its steel exports.

There have also been conflicts between the United States and many developing countries over restrictions on trade in services, such as insurance, and over the failure to provide adequate legal protection for intellectual property rights, such as patents, trademarks, and copyrights.

These and other issues in U.S. trade relations with developing countries have in fact become key items on the U.S. trade policy agenda—and they will inevitably become increasingly important and salient as developing countries' economies continue to evolve and as their populations continue to grow.

EAST EUROPEAN COUNTRIES

U.S. trade relations with East European countries have many of the same features as trade with the developing countries of Africa, Latin America, and Asia. At the same time, U.S. trade relations with Eastern Europe are changing dramatically as a result of *glasnost* and *perestroika*—the political and economic liberalization of those countries.

For several decades prior to the 1990s, U.S. trade relations with Eastern Europe were dominated by the cold war. Thus, the United States imposed numerous obstacles to economic relations with Communist countries after World War II.[8] Under the provisions of the Export Control Act of 1949, the Commerce Department maintained a list of items that could not be exported to Communist countries—a list that was maintained for twenty years and had as many as a thousand items on it. The United States also exerted pressure on Western European countries not to trade with Communist countries by threatening to withdraw economic and military assistance if they did; this threat was embodied in the Mutual Defense Assistance Control Act of 1951. Other legislation prohibited American loans to most Communist governments. The United States also imposed much higher tariffs on imports from Communist countries (except Yugoslavia). As a result of these restrictions, there was virtually no trade between the United States and the Communist countries for many years.

Détente

In 1963, however, the Kennedy administration began to change American trade policy. Increasing trade with Communist countries offered the usual economic benefits, especially increased income from exports. But it also offered the potential of contributing to a general improvement in political relations. This latter incentive was particularly important as the administration began to try to reduce cold war tensions in the aftermath of the Cuban missile crisis. The new policy allowed a large sale of American wheat to the Soviet Union; it allowed private financing of the sale; and it guaranteed repayment of the loan through the government-subsidized Export-Import Bank. No trade with China was allowed, however.

A decade later, the Nixon administration incorporated trade policy in its rapprochement with the Soviet Union and China. In 1972, the administration negotiated an agreement to allow private American institutions to loan money to the Soviet government. The United States also agreed to provide government guarantees of loans for exports to the Soviet Union; it allowed a large Soviet purchase of American wheat and other grains; and it agreed to extend most favored nation tariff status to the Soviet Union. All the agreements except the grain sales were aborted, however, because of congressional opposition. After the Vanik-Jackson Amendment made congressional approval of the changes in trade policies conditional on a relaxation of Soviet restrictions on Jewish emigration, most of the trade agreements were nullified.

Nevertheless, large Russian purchases of American wheat were arranged in 1972 and subsequent years. By the early 1980s, U.S. trade with the Soviet Union had reached an annual level of more than $4 billion, mostly U.S. exports of grain. Trade with the other Eastern European Communist countries also increased considerably during this period. Trade with China also increased; agricultural products, high-technology items, and other exports totaled more than $1 billion per year by the 1980s. Imports from China, however, were still at low levels and limited to textiles and a few other items.

The most notable development in American trade with Communist countries during the 1980s, though, was the use of trade sanctions.

Sanctions

After the Soviet Union invaded Afghanistan during the winter of 1979–1980, the United States imposed an embargo on grain sales to the USSR.[9] The embargo, however, did not eliminate U.S. grain sales to the Soviet Union; it only reduced the amount of grain exports that could be implemented during the remaining two years of a five-year grain trade agreement. The embargo specifically limited sales to the guaranteed level of eight million tons less than anticipated sales during the 1979–1980 year. The embargo also limited soybean sales.

The impact of the embargo on the Soviet economy included reduced meat production, higher prices and less attractive financing for imported grain, and complications in economic planning. However, the Soviet Union was able to mitigate substantially the impact of the embargo, since it was able to draw on its own stockpiles of grain and import millions of tons of grains from alternate sources, such as Argentina. The USSR was also able to import more grain from its own East European allies, which in turn imported more from the United States. Finally, the Soviet Union was able to import more meat to compensate for the declining domestic meat production resulting from the lower levels of feed grains available.

As for the domestic impact in the United States, there was some initial decline in grain prices for American farmers resulting from the greater than expected available supply. However, that price trend was reversed as the Agriculture Department bought up supplies to compensate the American farmers. Moreover, increased U.S. grain exports to Eastern European countries and to the former Argentine customers in Latin America, Western Europe, and Japan made up for most of the lost exports to the Soviet Union. In short, the net effect was that world trading patterns in grain shifted in response to the embargo; but neither the levels of grain consumed in the USSR nor the amount of grain produced and exported by U.S. farmers changed very much.

Nevertheless, there was widespread opposition to the embargo among American farmers, and candidate Reagan announced his own opposition during the 1980 presidential campaign. Shortly after becoming president, Reagan ended the embargo in the spring of 1981.

A year later, the Reagan administration imposed a series of lesser economic sanctions on the Soviet Union and Poland, when the Polish government imposed repressive measures on its blossoming trade union movement. Those sanctions included closing the Russian purchasing mission in the United States, suspending export licenses for high-technology items going to Russia, postponing discussions on a new grain trade agreement, denying U.S. landing rights to Russian and Polish airlines, and otherwise reducing trade and exchanges in selected areas.

An additional element in the Polish sanction case, however, was the issue of Polish debt owed to American and other Western banks—some of it guaranteed by the U.S. government. By 1981, Poland owed approximately $26 billion to Western banks and governments from a decade of borrowing for industrial-development projects and trade financing. Since Poland was running a substantial trade deficit with the non-Communist industrial countries, it had to borrow to pay for its rising imports of food and industrial equipment. But its ability to repay those debts was undermined by a declining economy, including the economic problems created by the political turmoil in 1980–1982.

Private banks and government agencies negotiated rescheduling agreements with the Polish government so that it could avoid defaulting on its debt. Even so, in February 1982, the Polish government informed the U.S. government that it could not make $17 million in payments due to American banks. Since the credit had been extended to finance American agricultural exports to Poland, and since the loans had been guaranteed by the U.S. Agriculture Department, the U.S. government paid the U.S. banks on behalf of the Polish government. Otherwise, the Polish government would have been in default on those loans—and all other loans from Western banks as well.

The American government decided to take the rather unusual step of covering a Communist country's debt because it wanted the political leverage provided by the continuing indebtedness of the Polish government to Western lenders. Such indebtedness created an influence relationship between the U.S. government and the Polish government. This situation entailed an influence relationship between the Soviet government and the U.S. government as well, since the Soviet government would be widely regarded as implicitly responsible for part of Poland's indebtedness.

Economic dependence, trade, financing arrangements, and sanctions have also been central to Western countries' involvement in a large gas-pipeline project in the Soviet Union.[10] The project is a $10 billion, three-thousand-mile-long pipeline that carries natural gas from Siberian gas fields to Western Europe. There was some support within the American administration for trying to undermine the Soviet project by refusing to export construction equipment and other technology from the United States and other Western countries; there was also U.S. opposition to the granting of credits by Western European banks to finance the project. The Reagan administration's concern about the pipeline was that it would create substantial West European dependence on Soviet energy sources and thus perhaps increase Soviet influence over those European allies of the United States. The Soviet Union will ultimately supply Western Europe with about 20 percent of its natural gas and about 5 percent of its total energy consumption. In the face of strong European support for the project, however, the Reagan administration moderated its opposition and withdrew its sanctions.

The Post–Cold War Era

By the time of the Houston economic summit of industrial countries' heads of government in the summer of 1990, economic relations with Eastern Europe were at the center of the U.S. foreign policy agenda. By this time, though, the issues were the speed and the extent of efforts to enhance those economic relations. The United States found itself somewhat isolated on these issues from the other industrial countries, which tended to favor more rapid and more massive efforts to increase trade—and aid—vis-à-vis the East European countries.

However, the administration and the Congress did undertake numerous important policy changes in the early 1990s in an effort to expand East-West economic relations. These measures included reductions in U.S. tariffs on imports from Eastern Europe, opening more U.S. ports to Soviet shipping, increasing Soviet and American commercial passenger and cargo flights, and increasing export credits to East European customers of U.S. firms.

The array of barriers to increased U.S. economic relations with Eastern Europe is still formidable, however. As of 1990, the list of U.S. policy issues needing attention in the effort to remove such barriers was long and complex (Table 11–7).

TABLE 11–7   U.S. Policy Issues in Reducing Barriers to Enhanced Economic Relations with East European Countries

---

Export-Import Bank—The 1974 Stevenson amendment prohibits loans or loan guarantees in excess of $300 million to the Soviet Union. Other provisions of law prohibit loans or guarantees of any amount for fossil-fuels production. The president may waive those limits, if Congress agrees by adopting a concurrent resolution. Current law also specifically bans loans and guarantees to Estonia, Latvia, Lithuania, Czechoslovakia, Hungary, Bulgaria, Romania, Yugoslavia and the Soviet Union. The Ex-Im Bank is controlled by Jackson-Vanik restrictions.

Overseas Private Investment Corporation (OPIC)—Insurance against losses by U.S. investors abroad due to political upheaval is denied by current law in countries that do not adhere to internationally recognized workers' rights or make progress on human rights. The recently enacted Poland-Hungary aid bill lifted OPIC restrictions for both those countries.

International Monetary Fund (IMF)/World Bank—Under current law, the U.S. executive directors of these agencies are ordered to oppose loans and other credits to communist dictatorships unless the assistance would benefit the population, improve the country's balance of payments and improve market forces.

Bank Loans/Security Holdings—The 1934 Johnson Debt Default Act prohibits U.S. bank loans to countries whose governments have defaulted on loans from the U.S. government. The law also prohibits purchases of securities from such a country by U.S. citizens. The law applies to the Soviet Union, which defaulted on $188 million in pre-communist debt in 1917. The law does not apply to loans made by foreign branches of U.S. banks, to loans made explicitly for purchase of U.S. exports and to countries that are members of the IMF and World Bank.

Export Controls—Current law prohibits sales of certain high-technology goods to the Soviet Union and certain Eastern European countries, unless the sales are specifically authorized. U.S. law is tied to an international agreement among 17 Western countries, enforced by the Paris-based Coordinating Committee on Multilateral Export Controls.

Most-Favored-Nation Status (MFN)—This system of normalized tariffs for most industrial-country exports to the United States is prohibited for certain countries by the 1974 Jackson-Vanik amendment if those countries deny their citizens free emigration and other basic human rights. The president may waive Jackson-Vanik if Congress agrees by adopting a concurrent resolution. Jackson-Vanik also restricts the president's ability to negotiate trade agreements and loans and guarantees from the Ex-Im Bank. Hungary, Poland and Yugoslavia currently have MFN status; the Soviet Union, Bulgaria, Czechoslovakia, East Germany and Romania do not.

Generalized System of Preferences (GSP)—These special reduced tariffs for developing-country exports to the United States are denied by law to Czechoslovakia and the Soviet Union. GSP benefits also are denied to communist countries unless they are members of the General Agreement on Tariffs and Trade and the IMF and they are eligible for MFN status. The recently enacted Poland-Hungary aid bill lifted GSP restrictions for both those countries.

Source: John R. Cranford, "Cold War Barricades Remain As East Bloc Crumbles," *Congressional Quarterly Weekly Report,* 48, 1 (January 6, 1990), 29. Used with permission.

DOMESTIC POLITICS

Domestic conflicts over American trade policy are common. Policy responses typically involve a compromise between the long-term national interest in increased wealth that would come from open trade policies and the short-term profits and employment in certain industries that would come from protectionist policies.

These conflicting pressures, as well as the interests and power of the participants in the policy process, can be illustrated by a case concerning ad hoc measures imposed to protect the sugar industry.[11] At the May 4, 1982, meeting of his cabinet-level Council on Commerce and Trade, President Reagan decided to limit sugar imports into the United States to their average level during several preceding years. These quotas were imposed in addition to an existing tariff of 2.8 cents per pound plus extra import fees.

The adoption of such a protectionist measure by an administration nominally committed to laissez-faire trade policies can be explained partly by an agreement made the previous year by President Reagan with southern members of Congress. In particular, he agreed to increase domestic price supports for sugar if they would vote in favor of his tax reduction bill. However, when the world price of sugar fell substantially over the next year, the administration was faced with the prospect of having to pay an additional $800 million to American sugar growers through the price-support program. Since this would have imposed additional pressures on the federal government's budget, the president decided instead to raise domestic sugar prices indirectly by limiting the amount of imported sugar. Thus, this particular decision on trade policy reflected the outcome of executive-congressional bargaining on an unrelated tax issue the previous year.

The decision also highlighted a rich mixture of converging and conflicting preferences among many institutional participants in the policy process. There were splits within the executive branch, within the Congress, and within the pertinent interest groups. The principal lines of conflict cut across institutional associations. On the one hand, there was an "iron triangle" favoring protection. It consisted of the Agriculture Department, southern members of Congress from sugar-growing states, and the sugar producers' lobby. On the other hand, the State Department was sensitive to the fact that the quota violated the spirit of America's GATT agreements and that it was contrary to the interests of several countries in the Caribbean area, where the United States was trying to improve relations through a series of recently announced economic-development measures. Thus, the presidential decision entailed some special consideration for sugar imports from Caribbean countries. Members of Congress from states where the interests of sugar consumers (not sugar producers) were at stake also did not favor the quotas; there was even an attempt by some northern members of Congress to kill the quota through legislative action. In addition, the quota was opposed by industrial users of sugar, represented by the Sugar Users Group and Cane Sugar Refiners Association who faced higher prices for the raw sugar that they bought.

The general public was not actively involved in the politics of this particular trade policy decision, as is typical for all but the most conspicuous trade issues. Yet, this particular policy decision was consistent with prevailing public opinion. Repeated polls have found that about two-thirds of the public favor restrictions on imports if they are "priced lower than American-made goods of the same kind."[12] Indeed, even during the highly inflationary period of the late 1970s and early 1980s, a substantial majority of Americans supported trade policies that exacerbate inflation. Public-opinion polls have also found that although two-thirds of the American population recognize that the United States is economically "somewhat dependent on other countries," about one-third thinks the United States is "nearly" or "completely" self-sufficient economically.[13]

CONCLUSION

Regardless of some segments of the public's perceptions, international economic interdependence exists, and it is increasing. Although it is at lower levels for the United States than for many other countries, although it is less extensive in some sectors of the economy than others, and although it may not be at historically high levels, economic interdependence does exist—and it does affect American foreign policy. If we focus on trade in particular and examine its implications for American interests, power, policies, and politics, we find that the transnational politics and the pluralistic politics models of American foreign policy are especially helpful in our analysis.

Trade creates *interests* that do not necessarily converge with the interests involved in military issues; on many issues, national security interests and group economic interests may be at odds. Security considerations and economic welfare considerations will in any case often lead to conflicting policy preferences and conflicting political pressures.

Trade also creates new *power* relationships. Economic interdependence provides "levers" that may be used by American diplomats as they seek to influence other countries' policies in many areas. Similarly, economic interdependence constrains American power in some respects. Allied and domestic interest-group opposition can impose significant limitations on American use of economic resources and relationships for international political purposes.

Finally, the active pursuit of narrow economic interests by numerous interest groups together with their advocates in Congress and the executive agencies creates a highly pluralistic domestic political *process* that produces compromise policies on commercial trade issues. There is a continuing tension between the laissez-faire and mercantilist approaches to trade policy—a tension that is resolved on an ad hoc basis among continually shifting coalitions of executive, congressional, and nongovernmental participants in the policy process.

Human Rights

Only occasionally have human rights been a salient foreign policy issue. There was considerable interest in the issue while the UN Charter was being drafted in 1945 and while the Universal Declaration of Human Rights was being drafted in 1948. But the promulgation of additional human rights documents during the 1950s and 1960s attracted only slight further attention, and human rights did not become a major concern of high-level American foreign policy makers again until the 1970s.

In spite of the absence of sustained, serious attention to human rights problems by the principal policy makers in the United States and other countries, however, a substantial body of international human rights law has been developed. In this chapter, we consider the following questions: What human rights are prescribed by legal norms and documents? What are the actual conditions, compared with the norms? What policies has the United States adopted on human rights issues?

LEGAL NORMS

Americans and others from the Western legal tradition tend to define human rights as being limited to civil and political rights, but other legal cultures place considerable emphasis on social and economic rights. As a consequence, the human rights documents of international law include provisions that define and protect both kinds of rights.[1] The UN Charter states in its preamble that the signatories reaffirm ''their faith in fundamental human rights, in the dignity and worth of the human person and in the equal rights of men and women''; and it also says that the signatories will ''promote social progress and better standards of life in larger freedom.'' Other provisions of the UN Charter are also intended to protect and promote human rights.[2]

The single most extensive and conspicuous international legal document on human rights is the Universal Declaration of Human Rights, which specifies many social, economic, civil, and political rights. The civil and political rights include the right to life; the right not to be discriminated against; the right not to be subjected to slavery or torture; the right to equal protection of the law as well as other rights in legal proceedings; and the rights of free thought, speech, assembly, and political participation. The social and economic rights specified in the Universal Declaration include the right to marry, own property, and form unions; they also include the right to adequate food, clothing, housing, and medical care; and they assert the right to special assistance for the unemployed, the sick, the aged, the young, and mothers. (The full text of the declaration is reprinted in the appendix to this chapter.

International law not only protects individual rights and imposes concomitant obligations on governments to honor them; it also specifies the collective group right of self-determination. All people have a right to national independence and sovereignty and, therefore, freedom from foreign dominance and intervention.[3] All these rights, and others as well, are proclaimed in the major international human rights documents listed in Table 12–1.

In addition to these universally applicable documents, there are also regional human rights international laws—for instance, the European Convention on Human Rights, the Inter-American Convention on the Granting of Civil Rights to Women, and the Helsinki Agreements of the Conference on Security and Cooperation in Europe.

CIVIL AND POLITICAL RIGHTS

An analysis of elections in all countries of the world between the late 1950s and late 1960s found that only about 40 percent were free and competitive.[4] In 30 percent of the countries, the most recent election had deviated significantly from the free and competitive ideal as a result of violence, fraud, intimidation, boycott by a major electoral group, or the outlawing of major parties. In about 25 percent of the countries, elections were rendered virtually meaningless by racial discrimination against most potential voters, the existence of single parties without any local initiative in candidate selection, or the simple annulment of the results. In the remaining 7 percent of the countries for which information was available, elections had not been held for a decade. Furthermore, during the two decades from 1948 to 1967, executive authority had changed hands 147 times in thirty-three countries as a result of actual or threatened violence.[5]

Freedom of the press is also rare. A study by journalism specialists rated countries in terms of twenty-three legal restrictions that affect freedom of the press.[6]

TABLE 12–1   International Legal Documents on Human Rights

United Nations Charter
Universal Declaration of Human Rights
International Covenant on Civil and Political Rights
International Covenant on Economic, Social and Cultural Rights
Declaration on the Rights of the Child
Declaration on the Granting of Independence to Colonial Countries and Peoples
Convention on the Prevention and Punishment of the Crime of Genocide
International Convention on the Elimination of All Forms of Racial Discrimination
International Convention on the Suppression and Punishment of the Crime of Apartheid
Declaration on Elimination of Discrimination against Women
Convention on the Political Rights of Women
Convention on the Nationality of Married Women
Convention on Consent on Marriage, Minimum Age for Marriage, and Registration of Marriages
Convention relating to the Status of Stateless Persons
Convention relating to the Status of Refugees
Geneva Convention relative to the Protection of Civilian Persons in Time of War
Geneva Convention relative to the Treatment of Prisoners of War
Geneva Convention for the Amelioration of the Condition of the Wounded and Sick in Armed
    Forces in the Field
Geneva Convention for the Amelioration of the Condition of the Wounded and Sick Shipwrecked
    Members of the Armed Forces at Sea
Slavery Convention
Supplementary Convention on the Abolition of Slavery, the Slave Trade, and Institutions and
    Practices Similar to Slavery
International Labor Organization (ILO) Convention concerning the Abolition of Forced Labor
ILO Convention concerning Freedom of Association and Protection of the Right to Organize
ILO Convention concerning Employment Policy
ILO Convention concerning Equal Remuneration for Men and Women Workers for Work of Equal
    Value
UNESCO Convention Against Discrimination in Education

The results were summarized on a scale ranging from $+4$, indicating the absence of any restrictions, to -4, indicating no freedom. Slightly more than a third of the countries fell below the 0 midpoint. Only three countries—the Netherlands, Switzerland, and Norway—received ratings of 3.0 or better. The United States received a 2.7 rating. The movement by many developing countries to legitimize government control of the press through international agreements in the 1980s further threatened freedom of the press.

Other surveys have also found widespread denial of political rights.[7] In Cambodia, after a new government came to power in 1975, as many as several million inhabitants were forced to leave the cities and relocate in rural areas. Even though many of the people were old and sick, they were required to travel many miles by foot, and they were subjected to forced labor. Hundreds of thousands died from the ordeal, and thousands more were executed.

In Indonesia, after an unsuccessful coup attempt in 1965, more than 100,000 people were killed because they were presumed to be coup sympathizers; 50,000 more were imprisoned without trial for a decade. In Vietnam, tens of thousands of former South Vietnamese government officials, military officials, and others were put in "re-education" camps after the end of the war in 1975. In the Philippines, after martial law was declared in the mid-1970s, 50,000 people were detained without charges for as long as several years. In Burundi, after an attempted coup in 1972, 150,000 people were killed, and another 150,000 fled the country. In Malawi, the Jehovah's Witness religious group was outlawed in 1967; a few years later, persecution of the group produced scores of deaths and more than 15,000 refugees. Some were forced to return to the country to be imprisoned.

In Iran, after twenty-two years of autocratic rule, the shah outlawed all parties except one in 1975. He observed that

> A person who does not enter the new political party and does not believe in the three cardinal principles which I referred to will have only two choices. He is either an individual who belongs to an illegal organization, or is related to the outlawed Tudeh Party, or in other words is a traitor. Such an individual belongs in Iranian prison or if he desires, he can leave the country tomorrow, without even paying exit fees and can go anywhere he likes, because he is not an Iranian, he has no nation, and his activities are illegal and punishable according to the law.[8]

(The shah himself was forced into exile four years later.)

Even torture is widely practiced in much of the world. Amnesty International, an independent organization that works to achieve the release of political prisoners in all countries, has collected evidence of torture as a matter of policy in numerous countries.[9]

U.S. Policy

The American response to violations of civil and political rights has generally been to ignore them. In fact, the United States has been reluctant to give even its nominal and formal approval to human rights documents. Although the United States voted in favor of the Universal Declaration of Human Rights in 1948, along with nearly all other UN members, it did not sign or ratify any of the additional human rights documents during the 1950s.

This formal American opposition was largely a result of the Eisenhower administration's agreement with the American Bar Association (ABA) position that human rights should be treated as domestic affairs not subject to international law.[10] The ABA did not favor American approval of any international human rights document until 1967, when an ABA convention supported American ratification of the Slavery Convention. However, it still opposed American ratification of other international human rights documents, such as the conventions on Forced Labor and Political Rights of Women. Because of internal opposition, the United States has still not ratified many of the human rights documents listed in Table 12–1.

Nevertheless, civil and political rights have periodically been a major foreign policy issue in the 1970s and 1980s. Most of the consideration of the issue has focused on the question of whether the United States should make other countries' respect for such rights a prerequisite for American aid or trade. The question first emerged when Congress passed the Vanik-Jackson Amendment, which required a change in Russian policies on Jewish emigration before the USSR could enjoy the same most favored nation trade status that most other countries have with the United States.

The question also arose later during the 1970s, when the Carter administration suggested that it would reduce American military and/or economic aid to countries with poor human rights records. Although U.S. aid to a few countries was subsequently reduced, most countries' aid from the United States was not adjusted according to their human rights practices.

As another move in the direction of taking human rights more seriously, the Congress instructed American representatives to such international organizations as the Inter-American Development Bank and the African Development Bank to vote against loans to countries where the government seriously violates human rights, unless the loans are for projects that are directly beneficial to the most needy people in the country.

Yet, American human rights policy has continued to focus narrowly and almost exclusively on political and civil rights and ignore social and economic rights. Human rights issues are normally obscure and secondary in foreign policy. Instead, economic and military considerations are typically given preponderant emphasis in American relations with other countries. In late 1978, for instance, when the widespread internal opposition to the shah of Iran became overt and active, the Carter administration publicly supported the shah in spite of his human rights record.

The Reagan administration generally disregarded human rights issues in American relations with foreign countries. But human rights in Central America and El Salvador in particular became a major issue—in part because Congress predicated further American aid to the Salvadoran government on its making progress in human rights. The administration was thus required to certify officially that such progress was being made.

SOCIAL AND ECONOMIC RIGHTS

One way to express disparities of wealth in the world is to note the following contrast: The half of the world's population living in the poorest countries produces and consumes only about one-eighth of the world's gross product each year; at the other extreme, the one-eighth of the population in the wealthiest nations produces and consumes half of the gross world product. Such comparisons, however, are based on data that have been aggregated at the national level, and this aggregation obscures the substantial inequalities that exist within countries. When disaggregated (individual level) data are available, the inequalities within countries become readily apparent. The cumulative distribution (or Lorenz) curves in Figure 12–1 show the distribution of income within selected countries. None of the countries' distributions approaches the line of equality; but the distributions in the developing countries, India and Peru, are more unequal than the U.S. distribution.

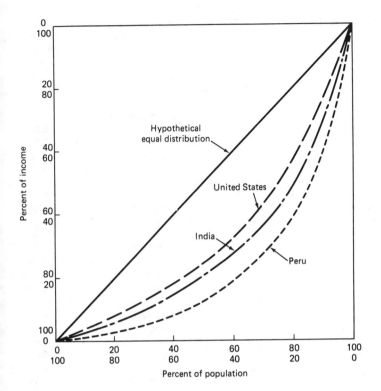

FIGURE 12–1   Distribution of income within selected countries (Lorenz curves)

Source: Derived from data originally published in World Bank, *World Development Report, 1983* (New York: Oxford University Press, 1983), pp. 200–201, table 27.

Although discrepancies in life expectancy and literacy are not so great, they are substantial. Life expectancy at birth in the poorest countries is less than fifty years; in the most affluent countries, life expectancy is seventy years. Only about one-half of the two billion people in the poorest countries of the world can read and write; all but a small fraction of the one billion people in the wealthiest countries can do so.

Life expectancy and literacy can be combined with per capita income to produce a single index of the level of "human development" in each country. As reported in Table 12–2, the results contain some surprises. In particular, eighteen countries rank higher than the United States—mostly because of higher literacy rates and, to a lesser extent, longer life expectancy. The vast majority of countries, however, experience much lower levels of development.

If people in all countries in the world enjoyed a life expectancy of seventy-five years, as in some Scandinavian and northern European countries, there would be approximately twenty million fewer deaths per year.[11] One of the principal causes of the short life-expectancy figures is inadequate food. In fact, starvation and malnutrition cause over ten million premature deaths each year.[12] A nutritionally adequate

TABLE 12–2   Countries' Level of Human Development according to UN Index*

COUNTRY RANK		HUMAN DEVEL-OPMENT INDEX	COUNTRY RANK		HUMAN DEVEL-OPMENT INDEX
Low human development			Medium human development		
1	Niger	0.116	45	Egypt	0.501
2	Mali	0.143	46	Lao P.D.R.	0.506
3	Burkina Faso	0.150	47	Gabon	0.525
4	Sierra Leone	0.150	48	Oman	0.535
5	Chad	0.157	49	Bolivia	0.548
6	Guinea	0.162	50	Myanmar	0.561
7	Somalia	0.200	51	Honduras	0.563
8	Mauritania	0.208	52	Zimbabwe	0.576
9	Afghanistan	0.212	53	Lesotho	0.580
10	Benin	0.224	54	Indonesia	0.591
11	Burundi	0.235	55	Guatemala	0.592
12	Bhutan	0.236	56	Viet Nam	0.608
13	Mozambique	0.239	57	Algeria	0.609
14	Malawi	0.250	58	Botswana	0.646
15	Sudan	0.255	59	El Salvador	0.651
16	Central African Rep.	0.258	60	Tunisia	0.657
17	Nepal	0.273	61	Iran, Islamic Rep. of	0.660
18	Senegal	0.274	62	Syrian Arab Rep.	0.691
19	Ethiopia	0.282	63	Dominican Rep.	0.699
20	Zaire	0.294	64	Saudi Arabia	0.702
21	Rwanda	0.304	65	Philippines	0.714
22	Angola	0.304	66	China	0.716
23	Bangladesh	0.318	67	Libya	0.719
24	Nigeria	0.322	68	South Africa	0.731
25	Yemen Arab Rep.	0.328	69	Lebanon	0.735
26	Liberia	0.333	70	Mongolia	0.737
27	Togo	0.337	71	Nicaragua	0.743
28	Uganda	0.354	72	Turkey	0.751
29	Haiti	0.356	73	Jordan	0.752
30	Ghana	0.360	74	Peru	0.753
31	Yemen, P.D.R.	0.369	75	Ecuador	0.758
32	Côte d'Ivoire	0.393	76	Iraq	0.759
33	Congo	0.395	77	United Arab Emirates	0.782
34	Namibia	0.404	78	Thailand	0.783
35	Tanzania	0.413	79	Paraguay	0.784
36	Pakistan	0.423	80	Brazil	0.784
37	India	0.430	81	Mauritius	0.788
38	Madagascar	0.440	82	Korea, Dem. Rep. of	0.789
39	Papua New Guinea	0.471	83	Sri Lanka	0.789
40	Kampuchea, Dem.	0.471	84	Albania	0.790
41	Cameroon	0.474			
42	Kenya	0.481			
43	Zambia	0.481			
44	Morocco	0.489			

TABLE 12–2 (continued)

COUNTRY RANK	HUMAN DEVELOPMENT INDEX	COUNTRY RANK	HUMAN DEVELOPMENT INDEX
High human development			
85 Malaysia	0.800	108 Hong Kong	0.936
86 Colombia	0.801	109 Greece	0.949
87 Jamaica	0.824	110 German Dem. Rep.	0.953
88 Kuwait	0.839	111 Israel	0.957
89 Venezuela	0.861	112 United States	0.961
90 Romania	0.863	113 Austria	0.961
91 Mexico	0.876	114 Ireland	0.961
92 Cuba	0.877	115 Spain	0.965
93 Panama	0.883	116 Belgium	0.966
94 Trinidad and Tobago	0.885	117 Italy	0.966
95 Portugal	0.899	118 New Zealand	0.966
96 Singapore	0.899	119 Germany, Fed. Rep. of	0.967
97 Korea, Rep. of	0.903	120 Finland	0.967
98 Poland	0.910	121 United Kingdom	0.970
99 Argentina	0.910	122 Denmark	0.971
100 Yugoslavia	0.913	123 France	0.974
101 Hungary	0.915	124 Australia	0.978
102 Uruguay	0.916	125 Norway	0.983
103 Costa Rica	0.916	126 Canada	0.983
104 Bulgaria	0.918	127 Netherlands	0.984
105 U.S.S.R.	0.920	128 Switzerland	0.986
106 Czechoslovakia	0.931	129 Sweden	0.987
107 Chile	0.931	130 Japan	0.996

*The human development index (HDI) is constructed in three steps. The first step is to define a measure of deprivation that a country suffers in each of the three basic variables—life expectancy, literacy, and real GDP per capita. A maximum and a minimum value are determined for each of the three variables given the actual values. The deprivation measure then places a country in the range of zero to one as defined by the difference between the maximum and the minimum. The second step is to define an average deprivation indicator. This is done by taking a simple average of the three indicators. The third step is to measure the human development index as one minus the average deprivation index.

Here is how this formula would apply to Kenya:

Maximum life expectancy	=	78.4
Minimum life expectancy	=	41.8
Maximum adult literacy rate	=	100.0
Minimum adult literacy rate	=	12.3
Maximum real GDP per capita (log)	=	3.68
Minimum real GDP per capita (log)	=	2.34
Kenya's life expectancy	=	59.4
Kenya's adult literacy rate	=	60.0
Kenya's real GDP per capita (log)	=	2.90

Kenya's life expectancy deprivation
$$= (78.4 - 59.4)/(78.4 - 41.8) = 0.519$$
Kenya's literacy deprivation
$$= (100.0 - 60.0)/(100.0 - 12.3) = 0.456$$
Kenya's GDP deprivation
$$= (3.68 - 2.90)/(3.68 - 2.34) = 0.582$$
Kenya's average deprivation
$$= (0.519 + 0.456 + 0.582)/3 = 0.519$$
Kenya's human development index
$$= 1 - 0.519 = 0.481$$

Source: United Nations Development Program, *Human Development Report,* 1990, as reported in *IMF Survey,* 19, 12 (June 18, 1990), 183, 186.

diet includes about 70 grams of protein per day and between 2,200 and 3,000 calories per day (depending on body size). The actual per capita daily consumption rates in South Asia are about 50 grams of protein and 2,000 calories. In most of Africa, the figures are similarly low, in some areas even lower. In contrast, daily per capita food consumption in North America includes more than 90 grams of protein and 3,000 calories.[13]

Socioeconomic conditions are particularly harsh in two areas of the world. One is the northern portion of sub-Saharan Africa, an area that includes Mauritania, Gambia, Guinea-Bissau, Guinea, Mali, and Burkina Faso in the west; Niger, Chad, and the Central African Empire in the central portion; and Ethiopia and Somalia in the east. Among the more than sixty million people living in this area, the infant mortality rate is close to 20 percent, the literacy rate is under 10 percent, and life expectancy is forty years or less.

Another particularly impoverished area is South Asia. Although life expectancy in India and Pakistan is about fifty years and more than half of the adult population in India can read and write, conditions are otherwise harsh. Per capita income in South Asia is low—a little more than $200 per year; the infant mortality rate is high—between 10 and 20 percent. The literacy rate is low; in Nepal, it is only 5 percent. And life is short: an average of about forty years in Bangladesh, Afghanistan, and Nepal.

In short, tens of millions of people are deprived of social and economic well-being. They are not able to satisfy even the most basic human need for adequate nourishment. They do not have adequate shelter or health care to enable them to live much beyond forty or fifty years. Nor do they have the educational backgrounds or economic means to satisfy their desires for more than mere subsistence.

U.S. Policy

The United States has conducted an economic assistance program for more than three decades, but this program has also undergone significant changes. During the late 1940s and early 1950s, foreign aid was mostly Marshall Plan aid for postwar reconstruction in Western Europe. From the mid-1950s until the present, however, the emphasis has been on development in the less industrialized countries of Asia, Africa, and Latin America.

The United States has used economic assistance to try to achieve several economic and political objectives. The most obvious and direct objective has been to increase incomes and otherwise improve the standard of living in other countries. The pursuit of that objective, however, has been essentially a means to other·economic and political ends. For one thing, increasing prosperity in other countries has commonly been viewed as a way to increase American exports. Indeed, the foreign aid program not only serves this purpose indirectly by raising incomes in other countries (and ultimately their demand for imports of American goods and services); it also has a more direct impact through the use of aid funds themselves to buy American goods and services. Economic aid also tends to create more favorable economic conditions for American investments, and it facilitates access to foreign fuel and mineral deposits.

Political objectives, however, have been more important. An underlying assumption of the economic assistance program throughout its history has been that increasing prosperity would make people more content with socioeconomic conditions and less vulnerable to Communist appeals. The United States has also used economic aid to try to achieve specific political objectives in individual cases— sometimes to solicit support for a particular diplomatic initiative, sometimes to strengthen or weaken a particular government's internal political position, sometimes to try to change a government's internal or foreign policies.

In 1978 and 1979, the Carter administration used the promise of economic assistance to Israel as an inducement for the acceptance of a peace treaty with Egypt. In 1974, after negotiating a disengagement of Syrian and Israeli troops and before a presidential trip to the Middle East, the Nixon administration asked Congress for hundreds of millions of dollars in economic assistance appropriations for Israel, Syria, Jordan, and Egypt.[14] It also offered (or at least appeared to offer) economic aid to North Vietnam in 1973 as an incentive to agree to peace terms. It used promises of increased aid and/or threats of reduced aid to try to influence the policies of South Vietnamese regimes during American involvement in the war there. In other instances, the United States has used economic aid to strengthen governments faced with economic crises: Iran in 1961, Columbia in 1962, the Dominican Republic in 1962, Brazil in 1964.[15]

Regardless of the objectives, however, American economic aid programs have emphasized investment and industrialization as the keys to development. For many years, American aid was used primarily to fund capital-intensive industrialization projects, such as factories, mines, and highways. American aid has been used to provide foreign-currency credits so that the recipients can buy machinery, transportation equipment, construction equipment, and other goods and services from the industrialized countries. The underlying assumption of this strategy was that increasing investments, industrialization, and international trade would lead to increasing employment and eventually to self-sustaining economic growth. Furthermore, the economic benefits of growth were expected to "trickle down" from the immediate beneficiaries of the industrialization projects to the other sectors of the population.

By the late 1970s, however, this trickle-down strategy had fallen into disrepute among aid specialists, who felt it had failed on several grounds. In the first place, it had not led to much economic growth, except in a few countries. Some countries, such as Brazil, Taiwan, South Korea, and Nigeria, did enjoy substantial increases in their per capita GNPs during the 1960s and 1970s. In addition, most of the oil-exporting countries had dramatic increases in their GNPs after the oil price increases of the mid-1970s. In fact, by the late 1970s, per capita GNPs in Kuwait, the United Arab Emirates, and Qatar were among the highest in the world; and the other OPEC countries—Algeria, Ecuador, Gabon, Indonesia, Iran, Iraq, Libya, Nigeria, Saudi Arabia, and Venezuela—all enjoyed rapidly increasing per capita GNPs.

However, most of the "developing" countries were not experiencing much growth, and some were actually experiencing declining per capita GNPs. Moreover, the economic development that was occurring in less developed countries was not trickling down very much, for the inequalities in the distribution of wealth within less developed countries remained substantial and even increased. Even to the limited extent that economic development has occurred and even to the limited extent that it has spread among populations, it has not necessarily led to much improvement in living conditions and the quality of life.

Economic development, defined in terms of per capita GNP and based on capital-intensive industrialization projects, does not necessarily lead to a more equitable distribution of available wealth or to improved living conditions for most of the people. Many aid experts now prefer a "human needs" development strategy that is more directed to the health, educational, and employment needs of the poorest people within countries. This means a development strategy that is more rural, agricultural, and human-services oriented rather than urban, industrial, and manufactured-goods oriented. But such a strategy is often resisted by elites within countries because they prefer aid that is more directly beneficial to them.

The economic assistance program's failure to achieve widespread improvements in incomes and living conditions is a function not only of its basic strategies but also of its funding levels. The American resources put into economic assistance have been generally small since the end of the European Recovery Program in the early 1950s, and they have been declining.

In current dollar terms, American economic assistance funding levels have been relatively stable at $2 billion to $5 billion per year. But in constant dollar terms, they have declined considerably since their peak in the Marshall Plan years of 1948–1952. The $5 billion per year in the late 1940s was the equivalent of more than $20 billion in 1990 dollars; the actual current dollar figure was still only about $5 billion.[16] The level of economic assistance has been consistently lower than the level of military assistance. The FY91 budget proposal provided for outlays of $6.3 billion for military assistance and $4.9 billion for economic assistance. The projections for FY95 were, respectively, $9.2 billion and $6.5 billion.

Official American economic assistance has declined as a proportion of American GNP—from 2.8 percent in 1949 to 0.5 percent in 1960 to less than 0.2 percent by the early 1990s. Although the total dollar value of U.S. official economic aid has remained much higher than other industrialized countries' aid programs, its aid has been relatively low in terms of its relation to national population and income. Most Western European countries have been higher than the United States by both measures.

CONCLUSION

The vast majority of humankind does not enjoy the security, the freedom, the economic welfare, or the social justice that allows people a sense of human dignity. In view of these conditions, a central and continuing issue of American foreign relations can be posed as follows: Should American policy seek to promote the human dignity of the many or merely try to protect the interests of the few—at the price of the indignity of the many?[17] Or is there a conflict between the interests of the few and the dignity of the many?

Appendix to Chapter 12

UNIVERSAL DECLARATION OF HUMAN RIGHTS

Preamble

Whereas recognition of the inherent dignity and of the equal and inalienable rights of all members of the human family is the foundation of freedom, justice and peace in the world,

Whereas disregard and contempt for human rights have resulted in barbarous acts which have outraged the conscience of mankind, and the advent of a world in which human beings shall enjoy freedom of speech and belief and freedom from fear and want has been proclaimed as the highest aspiration of the common people,

Whereas it is essential, if man is not to be compelled to have recourse, as a last resort, to rebellion against tyranny and oppression, that human rights should be protected by the rule of law,

Whereas it is essential to promote the development of friendly relations between nations,

Whereas the peoples of the United Nations have in the Charter reaffirmed their faith in fundamental human rights, in the dignity and worth of the human person and in the equal rights of men and women and have determined to promote social progress and better standards of life in larger freedom,

Whereas Member States have pledged themselves to achieve, in cooperation with the United Nations, the promotion of universal respect for an observance of human rights and fundamental freedoms,

Whereas a common understanding of these rights and freedoms is of the greatest importance for the full realization of this pledge,

Now, Therefore,

The General Assembly

Proclaims this universal declaration of human rights as a common standard of achievement for all peoples and all nations, to the end that every individual and every organ of society, keeping this Declaration constantly in mind, shall strive by teaching and education to promote respect for these rights and freedoms and by progressive measures, national and international, to secure their universal and effective recognition and observance, both among the peoples of Member States themselves and among the peoples of territories under their jurisdiction.

Article 1
All human beings are born free and equal in dignity and rights. They are endowed with reason and conscience and should act towards one another in a spirit of brotherhood.

Article 2
Everyone is entitled to all the rights and freedoms set forth in this Declaration, without distinction of any kind, such as race, colour, sex, language, religion, political or other opinion, national or social origin, property, birth or other status.

Furthermore, no distinction shall be made on the basis of the political, jurisdictional or international status of the country or territory to which a person belongs, whether it be independent, trust, non–self-governing or under any other limitation of sovereignty.

Article 3
Everyone has the right to life, liberty and security of person.

Article 4
No one shall be held in slavery or servitude; slavery and the slave trade shall be prohibited in all their forms.

Article 5
No one shall be subjected to torture or to cruel, inhuman or degrading treatment or punishment.

Article 6
Everyone has the right to recognition everywhere as a person before the law.

Article 7
All are equal before the law and are entitled without any discrimination to equal protection of the law. All are entitled to equal protection against any discrimination in violation of this Declaration and against any incitement to such discrimination.

Article 8
Everyone has the right to an effective remedy by the competent national tribunals for acts violating the fundamental rights granted him by the constitution or by law.

Article 9
No one shall be subjected to arbitrary arrest, detention or exile.

Article 10

Everyone is entitled in full equality to a fair and public hearing by an independent and impartial tribunal, in the determination of his rights and obligations and of any criminal charge against him.

Article 11

1.   Everyone charged with a penal offence has the right to be presumed innocent until proved guilty according to law in a public trial at which he has had all the guarantees necessary for his defense.

2.   No one shall be held guilty of any penal offence on account of any act or omission which did not constitute a penal offence, under national or international law, at the time when it was committed. Nor shall a heavier penalty be imposed than the one that was applicable at the time the penal offence was committed.

Article 12

No one shall be subjected to arbitrary interference with his privacy, family, home or correspondence, nor to attacks upon his honour and reputation. Everyone has the right to the protection of the law against such interference or attacks.

Article 13

1.   Everyone has the right to freedom of movement and residence within the borders of each state.

2.   Everyone has the right to leave any country, including his own, and to return to his country.

Article 14

1.   Everyone has the right to seek and to enjoy in other countries asylum from persecution.

2.   This right may not be invoked in the case of prosecutions genuinely arising from non-political crimes or from acts contrary to the purposes and principles of the United Nations.

Article 15

1.   Everyone has the right to a nationality.

2.   No one shall be arbitrarily deprived of his nationality nor denied the right to change his nationality.

Article 16

1.   Men and women of full age, without any limitation due to race, nationality or religion, have the right to marry and to found a family. They are entitled to equal rights as to marriage, during marriage and at its dissolution.

2.   Marriage shall be entered into only with the free and full consent of the intending spouses.

3.   The family is the natural and fundamental group unit of society and is entitled to protection by society and the State.

Article 17
1. Everyone has the right to own property alone as well as in association with others.
2. No one shall be arbitrarily deprived of his property.

Article 18
Everyone has the right to freedom of thought, conscience and religion; this right includes freedom to change his religion or belief, and freedom, either alone or in community with others and in public or private, to manifest his religion or belief in teaching, practice, worship and observance.

Article 19
Everyone has the right to freedom of opinion and expression; this right includes freedom to hold opinions without interference and to seek, receive and impart information and ideas through any media and regardless of frontiers.

Article 20
1. Everyone has the right to freedom of peaceful assembly and association.
2. No one may be compelled to belong to an association.

Article 21
1. Everyone has the right to take part in the government of his country, directly or through freely chosen representatives.
2. Everyone has the right of equal access to public service in his country.
3. The will of the people shall be the basis of the authority of government; this will shall be expressed in periodic and genuine elections which shall be by universal and equal suffrage and shall be held by secret vote or by equivalent free voting procedures.

Article 22
Everyone, as a member of society, has the right to social security and is entitled to realization, through national effort and international co-operation and in accordance with the organization and resources of each State, of the economic, social and cultural rights indispensable for his dignity and the free development of his personality.

Article 23
1. Everyone has the right to work, to free choice of employment, to just and favourable conditions of work and to protection against unemployment.
2. Everyone, without any discrimination, has the right to equal pay for equal work.
3. Everyone who works has the right to just and favourable remuneration ensuring for himself and his family an existence worthy of human dignity, and supplemented, if necessary, by other means of social protection.
4. Everyone has the right to form and to join trade unions for the protection of his interests.

Article 24
Everyone has the right to rest and leisure, including reasonable limitation of working hours and periodic holidays with pay.

Article 25

1.   Everyone has the right to a standard of living adequate for the health and well being of himself and his family, including food, clothing, housing and medical care and necessary social services, and the right to security in the event of unemployment, sickness, disability, widowhood, old age or other lack of livelihood in circumstances beyond his control.

2.   Motherhood and childhood are entitled to special care and assistance. All children, whether born in or out of wedlock, shall enjoy the same social protection.

Article 26

1.   Everyone has the right to education. Education shall be free, at least in the elementary and fundamental stages. Elementary education shall be compulsory. Technical and professional education shall be made generally available and higher education shall be equally accessible to all on the basis of merit.

2.   Education shall be directed to the full development of the human personality and to the strengthening of respect for human rights and fundamental freedoms. It shall promote understanding, tolerance and friendship among all nations, racial or religious groups, and shall further the activities of the United Nations for the maintenance of peace.

3.   Parents have a prior right to choose the kind of education that shall be given to their children.

Article 27

1.   Everyone has the right freely to participate in the cultural life of the community, to enjoy the arts and to share in scientific advancement and its benefits.

2.   Everyone has the right to the protection of the moral and material interests resulting from any scientific, literary or artistic production of which he is the author.

Article 28

Everyone is entitled to a social and international order in which the rights and freedoms set forth in this Declaration can be fully realized.

Article 29

1.   Everyone has duties to the community in which alone the free and full development of his personality is possible.

2.   In the exercise of his rights and freedoms, everyone shall be subject only to such limitations as are determined by law solely for the purpose of securing due recognition and respect for the rights and freedoms of others and of meeting the just requirements of morality, public order and the general welfare in a democratic society.

3.   These rights and freedoms may in no case be exercised contrary to the purposes and principles of the United Nations.

Article 30

Nothing in this Declaration may be interpreted as implying for any State, group or person any right to engage in any activity or to perform any act aimed at the destruction of any of the rights and freedoms set forth herein.

Notes

CHAPTER 1

[1]Chadwick F. Alger, *Columbus in the World; The World in Columbus*, Brief Reports 1–13 (Columbus, OH: Ohio State University, Transnational Intellectual Cooperation Program, 1973–74).

[2]*The Europa Yearbook, 1978* (London: Europa Publications, 1978); UN, *Yearbook of the United Nations* (New York: United Nations, 1978).

[3]*Yearbook of International Organizations*, 16th ed. (Brussels: Union of International Associations, 1977); *The Europa Yearbook*.

[4]U.S., Bureau of the Census, *Statistical Abstract of the United States, 1977* (Washington, DC: U.S. Government Printing Office, 1977), p. 852, table 1455; UN, *Statistical Yearbook, 1976* (New York: United Nations, 1977), p. 820, table 201.

[5]U.S., Department of State, *Foreign Policy and the Department of State* (Washington, DC: U.S. Government Printing Office, 1976), p. 29; U.S., Department of State, *The Department of State Today*, Bicentennial Notes no. 2 (Washington, DC: Department of State, Bureau of Public Affairs, 1981), p. 1.

[6]J. David Singer and Melvin Small, *The Wages of War, 1816–1965* (New York: Wiley, 1972), p. 48.

[7]Congressional Quarterly, *Congress and the Nation*, IV, 1973–76 (Washington, DC: Congressional Quarterly, 1977), pp. 908–10; and volume III, 1969–72 (1973), pp. 935–38.

[8]U.S., Bureau of the Census, *Statistical Abstract of the United States, 1977* (Washington, DC: U.S. Government Printing Office, 1977), p. 361, table 570; and *Historical Statistics of the United States* (1975), p. 1140.

[9]*The Defense Monitor* 12, 1 (1983).

[10]U.S., Arms Control and Disarmament Agency, *World Military Expenditures and Arms Transfers* (Washington, DC: U.S. Government Printing Office, 1983).

[11]Ibid.

[12]International Monetary Fund, *International Financial Statistics* (Washington, DC: IMF, 1990).

[13]Ibid.

[14]Robert O. Keohane and Joseph S. Nye, *Power and Interdependence* (Boston: Little, Brown, 1977); Richard N. Cooper, *The Economics of Interdependence* (New York: McGraw-Hill, 1968); Cooper, "Economic Interdependence and Foreign Policy in the Seventies," *World Politics* 24, 2 (January 1972), 159–81; Robert D. Tollison and Thomas D. Willett, "International Integration and the Interdependence of Economic Variables," *International Organization* 27, 2 (Spring 1973), 253–71; Edward L. Morse, "Transnational Economic Processes," in *Transnational Relations and World Politics,* eds. Robert O. Keohane and Joseph S. Nye, Jr., *International Organization* 25, 3 (Summer 1971), 373–97; Kenneth N. Waltz, "The Myth of National Interdependence," in *The International Corporation,* ed. Charles P. Kindleberger (Cambridge, MA: MIT Press, 1970), pp. 205–23; Karl W. Deutsch and Alexander Eckstein, "National Industrialization and the Declining Share of the International Economic Sector, 1890–1959," *World Politics* 13, 2 (January 1961), 267–99; Peter J. Katzenstein, "International Interdependence: Some Long-Term Trends and Recent Changes," *International Organization* 29, 4 (Autumn 1975), 1021–34; Richard Rosecrance and Arthur Stein, "Interdependence: Myth or Reality?" *World Politics* 26 (October 1973), 1–27; Richard Rosecrance and others, "Whither Interdependence?" *International Organization* 31 (Summer 1977), 425–72.

[15]*International Financial Statistics.*

[16]Ibid.

[17]U.S., *International Economic Report* 187, table 78.

[18]Keohane and Nye, *Power and Interdependence.*

[19]Donella H. Meadows, Dennis L. Meadows, Jorgen Randers, and William W. Behrens III, *The Limits to Growth,* 2nd ed. (New York: Universe Books, 1972; New American Library, 1974).

[20]Mihajlo Mesarovic and Eduard Pestel, *Mankind at the Turning Point* (New York: E.P. Dutton, 1974; New American Library printing, 1976).

[21]*Oil and Gas Journal* 12, 31 (1973); U.S., *International Economic Report.*

[22]Ervin Laszlo, "Toward an Early Warning System at the UN," *Technological Forecasting and Social Change* 8, 2 (1975), 157; U.S., *International Economic Report.*

[23]Karl W. Deutsch, *The Analysis of International Relations,* 2nd ed. (Englewood Cliffs, NJ: Prentice Hall, 1977); Harold D. Lasswell, *Power and Society* (New Haven: Yale University Press, 1950); Lasswell, *Politics: Who Gets What When How* (New York: New American Library, 1958); David Easton, *The Political System,* 2nd ed. (New York: Knopf, 1971); Robert A. Dahl, *Modern Political Analysis,* 3rd ed. (Englewood Cliffs, NJ: Prentice Hall, 1976); Klaus Knorr, *The Power of Nations* (New York: Basic Books, 1975); Keohane and Nye, *Power and Interdependence*; Jeffrey Hart, "Three Approaches to the Measurement of Power in International Relations," *International Organization* 30, 2 (Spring 1976), 289–305.

CHAPTER 2

[1]Graham Allison, *Essence of Decision* (Boston: Little, Brown, 1971).

[3]Robert L. Rothstein, *Planning, Prediction, and Policy-Making in Foreign Affairs* (Boston: Little, Brown, 1972).

[3]Karl W. Deutsch, *The Nerves of Government,* 2nd ed. (New York: Free Press, 1966); Lloyd S. Etheredge, *Can Governments Learn?* (Elmsford, NY: Pergamon, 1983).

[4]David Braybrooke and Charles E. Lindblom, *A Strategy of Decision* (New York: Free Press, 1963).

[5]Herbert C. Kelman, *International Behavior: A Social-Psychological Analysis* (New York: Holt, Rinehart, and Winston, 1965); Margaret G. Hermann and Thomas W. Milburn, eds., *A Psychological Examination of Political Leaders* (New York: Free Press, 1977); Lawrence S. Falkowski, ed., *Psychological Models in International Politics* (Boulder, CO: Westview, 1979); Hermann, "Explaining Foreign Policy Behavior Using the Personal Characteristics of Political Leaders," *International Studies Quarterly* 24, 1 (March 1980), 7–46.

[6]Irving L. Janis, *Groupthink: Psychological Studies of Policy Decisions and Fiascoes,* 2nd ed. (Boston: Houghton Mifflin, 1982).

262   *Notes*

[7]Robert Axelrod, ed., *The Structure of Decisions* (Princeton: Princeton University Press, 1976), especially Ole Holsti, "Foreign Policy Formation Viewed Cognitively," Chapter 2.

[8]Allison, *Essence of Decision;* John D. Steinbruner, *The Cybernetic Theory of Decision* (Princeton: Princeton University Press, 1974).

[9]Kenneth N. Waltz, *Foreign Policy and Democratic Politics* (Boston: Little, Brown, 1967); John Spanier and Eric M. Uslaner, *Foreign Policy and the Democratic Dilemmas*, 3rd ed. (New York: Holt, Rinehart, and Winston, 1982).

[10]Roger Hilsman, *The Politics of Policymaking in Defense and Foreign Affairs* (New York: Harper & Row, 1971); Hilsman, *To Move a Nation* (New York: Doubleday, 1967).

[11]Allison, *Essence of Decision*; Morton H. Halperin, *Bureaucratic Politics and Foreign Policy* (Washington, DC: Brookings Institution, 1974); Morton H. Halperin and Arnold Kanter, eds., *Readings in American Foreign Policy: A Bureaucratic Perspective* (Boston: Little, Brown, 1973).

[12]Steven Rosen, ed., *Testing the Theory of the Military-Industrial Complex* (Lexington, MA: D.C. Heath-Lexington, 1973), especially the contribution by Jerome Slater and Terry Nardin, "The Concept of a Military-Industrial Complex," pp. 27–60.

[13]Hans J. Morgenthau, *Politics Among Nations* (New York: Knopf, 1973).

[14]Robert O. Keohane and Joseph S. Nye, eds., *Transnational Relations and World Politics* (Cambridge, MA: Harvard University Press, 1973); Keohane and Nye, *Power and Interdependence* (Boston: Little, Brown, 1977).

[15]Jay W. Forrester, *World Dynamics* (Cambridge, MA: Wright-Allen, 1971); Donella H. Meadows, Dennis L. Meadows, Jorgen Randers, and William K. Behrens, *Limits to Growth* (New York: Universe Books, 1972); M. Mesarovic and E. Pestel, *Mankind at the Turning Point* (New York: Dutton, 1974); Barry B. Hughes, *World Modelling* (Lexington, MA: Lexington, 1980); Richard A. Falk, *A Study of Future Worlds* (New York: Macmillan, 1975); Karl W. Deutsch, Bruno Fitsch, Helio Jaguaribe, and Andrei S. Markovits, eds., *Problems of World Modeling* (Cambridge, MA: Ballinger, 1977); *International Studies Quarterly* 25, 1 (March 1981), entire issue on "World System Debate."

[16]Thomas L. Brewer, *Foreign Policy Situations,* Sage Professional Papers in International Studies 1, 02–006 (Beverly Hills, CA, and London: Sage, 1972); Brewer, "Issue and Context Variations in Foreign Policy," *Journal of Conflict Resolution* 17, 1 (March 1973), 89–114; Theodore J. Lowi, "Making Democracy Safe for the World," in *Domestic Sources of Foreign Policy,* ed. James N. Rosenau (New York: Free Press, 1967); Lowi, "American Business, Public Policy, Case Studies, and Political Theory," *World Politics* 16 (July 1964), 677–715; Charles F. Hermann, "International Crisis as a Situational Variable," in *International Politics and Foreign Policy,* ed. James N. Rosenau (New York: Free Press, 1969); William C. Potter, "Issue Area and Foreign Policy Analysis," *International Organization* 34, 3 (Summer 1980), 405–27.

CHAPTER 3

[1]*Public Opinion* 1, 2 (May/June 1978), 35.

[2]*Public Opinion* 5, 2 (April/May 1982), 35–36; also see John R. Robinson and Robert Meadows, *Polls Apart* (Cabin John, MD: Seven Locks Press, 1982).

[3]Gabriel A. Almond, *The American People and Foreign Policy* (New York: Praeger, 1960); William R. Caspary, "The Mood Theory: A Study of Public Opinion and Foreign Policy," *American Political Science Review* 64, 2 (June 1970), 536–47; Tom W. Smith, "America's Most Important Problem: A Trend Analysis, 1946–1976," *Public Opinion Quarterly* 44, 2 (Summer 1980), 164–80; Everett C. Ladd, "The Nation's Most Important Problem," *Public Opinion* 1, 2 (May/June 1978), 30–32.

[4]*Public Opinion* 1, 2 (May/June 1978), 32.

[5]Gallup Poll, reported in *Public Opinion* 1, 2 (May/June 1978), 32.

[6]*New York Times,* April 29, 1984, p. 21.

[7]Hazel Guadet Erskine, "The Polls: The Informed Public," *Public Opinion Quarterly* 26, 4 (Winter 1962), 669–77; and Erskine, "The Polls: Exposure to International Information," *Public Opinion Quarterly* 27, 4 (Winter 1963), 658–62.

[8]James N. Rosenau, *Citizenship Between Elections* (New York: Free Press, 1974), pp. 67–86.

[9]Thomas S. Barrows, *College Students' Knowledge and Beliefs: A Survey of Global Understanding* (New Rochelle, NY: Change Magazine Press, 1981), p. 67.

[10]*New York Times,* May 5, 1982, p. 2.

[11]Caspary, "Mood Theory"; John E. Mueller, "Changes in American Public Attitudes toward International Involvement," in *The Limits of Military Intervention,* ed. Ellen P. Stern (Beverly Hills, CA: Sage, 1977), pp. 323–44; Daniel Yankelovich, "Cautious Internationalism," *Public Opinion* 1, 1 (March/April 1978), 15, *Public Opinion* 5, 3 (June/July 1982), 37; Michael Mandelbaum and William Schneider, "The New Internationalisms: Public Opinion and American Foreign Policy," in *Eagle Entangled: U.S. Foreign Policy in a Complex World,* eds. Kenneth Oye, Donald Rothchild, and Robert Lieber (New York: Longman, 1979); John E. Reilly, "The American Mood: A Foreign Policy of Self-Interest," *Foreign Policy* 34 (Spring 1979), 74–86; John E. Reilly, ed., *American Public Opinion and U.S. Foreign Policy* (Chicago: Chicago Council on Foreign Relations, 1979).

[12]Harris Survey, reported in *Current Opinion* 5, 9 (September 1977), 100.

[13]William Watts and Lloyd Free, "Nationalism Not Isolationism," *Foreign Policy* 24 (Fall 1976), 3–26.

[14]Yankelovich, "Cautious Internationalism," p. 14.

[15]Ibid.

[16]*Public Opinion* 7, 2 (April/May 1984), 33.

[17]NBC News survey, reported in *Public Opinion* 1, 1 (March/April 1978), 32.

[18]Mueller, "Changes in American Public Attitudes toward International Involvement."

[19]*New York Times,* April 29, 1984, p. 1.

[20]*Public Opinion* 5, 2 (April/May 1982), 16–17.

[21]Yankelovich, "Cautious Internationalism," p. 14.

[22]Benjamin I. Page and Robert Y. Shapiro, "Changes in Americans' Policy Preferences, 1935–1979," *Public Opinion Quarterly* 46, 1 (Spring 1982), 24–42.

[23]Survey Research Center National Election Studies of 1968 and 1972, reported in Barry B. Hughes, *The Domestic Context of American Foreign Policy* (San Francisco: Freeman, 1978), p. 54, table 2–12.

[24]Davis B. Bobrow and Neal E. Cutler, "Time-Oriented Explanations of National Security Beliefs: Cohort, Life-State and Situation," *Peace Research Society Papers* 8 (1967), 48.

[25]Hazel Erskine, "The Polls: Pacifism and the Generation Gap," *Public Opinion Quarterly* 36, 4 (Winter 1972–73), 616–27.

[26]Gallup Poll, reported in *Current Opinion* 4, 4 (April 1976), 33.

[27]Ole R. Holsti and James N. Rosenau, "Does Where You Stand Depend on When You Were Born? The Impact of Generation on Post-Vietnam Foreign Policy Beliefs," *Public Opinion Quarterly* 44, 1 (Spring 1980), 1–22.

[28]Several Harris Poll surveys, reported in Hughes, *The Domestic Context,* pp. 52–53, tables 2–10 and 2–11; Milton J. Rosenberg, "Images in Relation to the Policy Process," in *International Behavior,* ed. Herbert C. Kelman (New York: Holt, Rinehart and Winston, 1966), pp. 277–344; Marjorie Lansing and Sandra Baxter, *The Political Behavior of Women,* 2nd ed. (Ann Arbor: University of Michigan Press, 1984); *Public Opinion* 5, 2 (April/May 1982), 21–32.

[29]*New York Times,* April 29, 1984, p. 21.

[30]Lloyd Free and Hadley Cantril, *The Political Beliefs of Americans* (New Brunswick, NJ: Rutgers University Press, 1967), pp. 226–28, reprinted in Hughes, *Domestic Context,* p. 40, table 2–6.

[31]Rosenberg, "Images in Relation to the Policy Process."

[32]Survey Research Center National Election Study, 1968, reported in Hughes, *Domestic Context,* p. 68, table 3–3.

[33]William A. Gamson and André Modigliani, "Knowledge and Foreign Policy Opinions: Some Models for Consideration," *Public Opinion Quarterly* 30 (1966), 187–99; Lee Sigelman and Pamela Johnston Conover, "Knowledge and Opinions about the Iranian Crisis: A Reconsideration of Three Models," *Public Opinion Quarterly* 45, 4 (Winter 1981), 477–91.

[34]Peter M. Sandman, David M. Rubin, and David B. Sachsman, *Media,* 2nd ed. (Englewood Cliffs, NJ: Prentice Hall, 1976).

[35]William A. Gamson and André Modigliani, *Untangling The Cold War* (Boston: Little, Brown, 1971), appendix B; Bernard C. Cohen, *The Press and Foreign Policy* (Princeton: Princeton University Press, 1957); Bernard C. Hennessy, *Public Opinion* (Belmont, CA: Wadsworth, 1965), chapter 18.

[36]Milton C. Cummings, Jr., and David Wise, *Democracy under Pressure*, 3rd ed. (San Diego, CA: Harcourt Brace Jovanovich, 1977), p. 280, table 8–2.

[37]Cummings and Wise, *Democracy under Pressure*, pp. 126–27.

[38]Robert S. Frank, *Message Dimensions of Television News* (Lexington, MA: D.C. Heath-Lexington, 1973).

[39]Ernest W. Lefever, *TV and National Defense* (Boston, VA: Institute for American Strategy, 1974), p. 88, table 4–3.

[40]Robert M. Batscha, *Foreign Affairs News and the Broadcast Journalist* (New York: Praeger, 1975).

[41]William C. Adams, "Middle East Meets Middle West," *Public Opinion* 5, 2 (April/May 1982), 51–55.

[42]*New York Times,* November 21, 1983, p. 1; *Ann Arbor News,* January 14, 1984, p. B1.

[43]Michael Margolis, "From Confusion: Issues and the American Voter (1956–1972)," *American Political Science Review* 71, 1 (March 1977), 31–43.

[44]Benjamin I. Page and Richard A. Brody, "Policy Voting and the Electoral Process," *American Political Science Review* 66, 3 (September 1972), 979–95.

[45]V.O. Key, *The Responsible Electorate* (Cambridge, MA: Harvard University Press, 1966).

[46]Bernard C. Cohen, *The Public Impact on Foreign Policy* (Boston: Little, Brown, 1973).

[47]Warren E. Miller and Donald E. Stokes, "Constituency Influence in Congress," *American Political Science Review* 57 (March 1963), 53–54.

[48]*Gallup Opinion Index* 160 (November 1978), 3.

[49]John E. Mueller, *War, Presidents and Public Opinion* (New York: Wiley, 1973).

CHAPTER 4

[1]Congressional Quarterly, *The Washington Lobby* (Washington, DC: Congressional Quarterly, 1971), pp. 92–96; *National Journal* 10, 11 (March 18, 1978), 427.

[2]*New York Times,* April 9, 1984, p. 26; David Osborne, "Lobbying for Japan Inc.," *New York Times Magazine,* Dec. 4, 1983, pp. 133–39. Cf. "Japanese Lobbyists at Capitol Forming Political Coalitions to Combat Protectionist Bills," Congressional Quarterly, *Guide to Current American Government,* Spring 1984.

[3]*Christian Science Monitor,* August 12, 1982, p. B8.

[4]Christopher Madison, "Rapidly Changing Times Keep Central America Lobbyists on Their Toes," *National Journal* 16, 32 (August 11, 1984), 1517.

[5]Obie G. Whichard, "U.S. Direct Investment Abroad in 1982," *Survey of Current Business* 63, 8 (August 1983), 14–30. Also see Whichard, "Trends in the U.S. Direct Investment Position Abroad, 1950–79," *Survey of Current Business* 61, 2 (February 1981), 39–56; and Ned G. Howenstine, "Growth of U.S. Multinational Companies, 1966–1977," *Survey of Current Business* 62, 4 (April 1982), 34–46. We unfortunately do not have reliable and valid data available to indicate all of the patterns and trends in foreign direct investment (FDI) that are of interest to us. Although governments, international organizations, private associations, and scholars have put much effort into the process of collecting and analyzing the basic data, we still do not have an entirely satisfactory indicator of the amount of foreign direct investment. One problem is that we normally trace only international financial flows associated with foreign direct investment. But such flows represent only a portion of the total investment made in international direct investment; this is so because many funds for FDI projects are borrowed in the host country where the affiliate is established and thus do not involve fund flows across national borders. The available data on international *flows* of funds for foreign direct investment are therefore only roughly indicative of the relative magnitudes of FDI across countries and over time. Similarly, data on the cumulated *stocks* of FDI for each country at a given point in time are also only roughly indicative of relative differences among countries (such data are based on the book value of FDI as recorded according to certain

accounting rules). The aggregate present market value or replacement cost of the FDI projects would therefore be quite different.

[6]Raymond Vernon, *Storm Over the Multinationals* (Cambridge, MA: Harvard University Press, 1977); Robert Gilpin, *U.S. Power and the Multinational Corporation* (New York: Basic Books, 1974); Abdul A. Said and Luiz R. Simmons, eds., *The New Sovereigns* (Englewood Cliffs, NJ: Prentice Hall, 1974); Richard J. Barnet and Ronald E. Muller, *Global Reach* (New York: Simon & Schuster, 1974); Joan Edelman Spero, *The Politics of International Economic Relations* (New York: St. Martin's, 1977); David H. Blake and Robert S. Walters, *The Politics of Global Economic Relations* (Englewood Cliffs, NJ: Prentice Hall, 1976); U.S., Congress, Senate Committee on Foreign Relations, Subcommittee on Multinational Corporations, *Multinational Corporations and U.S. Foreign Policy*, vols. 1–15 (1973–76). Particular topics are included in the following volumes: ITT in Chile, 1–2 (1973); Overseas Private Investment Corporation, 3 (1973); oil corporations, 5–9 (1974); East-West trade, 10 (1974); Arab boycott of corporations doing business with Israel, 11 (1976); foreign arms sales, 12 (1976); currency exchange, income, employment 13 (1976); Lockheed corporation payments to agents and government officials in Europe and Japan, 14 (1976); banks, 15 (1976).

[7]Richard J. Barnet, *Intervention and Revolution*, rev. ed. (New York: New American Library, 1972).

[8]Raymond A. Bauer, Ithiel de Sola Pool, and Lewis Anthony Dexter, *American Business and Public Policy* (New York: Atherton, 1963).

[9]Bruce M. Russett and Elizabeth C. Hanson, *Interest and Ideology: The Foreign Policy Beliefs of American Businessmen* (San Francisco: Freeman, 1975); Allen H. Barton, "Consensus and Conflict among American Leaders," *Public Opinion Quarterly* 38, 4 (Winter 1974–75), 507–30; "What Business Thinks: The Fortune 500 Yankelovich Survey," *Fortune*, October 1969, 196.

[10]Barton, "Consensus and Conflict."

[11]Ole R. Holsti and James N. Rosenau, "Does Where You Stand Depend on When You Were Born? The Impact of Generation on Post-Vietnam Foreign Policy Beliefs," *Public Opinion Quarterly* 44, 1 (Spring 1980), 1–22; Holsti and Rosenau, "Vietnam Consensus, and the Belief Systems of American Leaders," *World Politics* 32, 1 (October 1979), 1–56.

[12]Betty C. Hanson and Bruce Russett, "Testing Some Economic Interpretations of American Intervention," in *Testing the Theory of the Military-Industrial Complex*, ed. Steven Rosen (Lexington, MA: D.C. Heath-Lexington, 1973), pp. 225–46.

CHAPTER 5

[1]Herbert McCloskey, Paul J. Hoffman, and Rosemary O'Hara, "Issue Conflict and Consensus among Party Leaders and Followers," *American Political Science Review* 54, 2 (June 1960), 406–27.

[2]Barry B. Hughes, *The Domestic Context of American Foreign Policy* (San Francisco: Freeman, 1978), p. 125, table 5–1.

[3]Hughes, *Domestic Context*, pp. 130–44, figures 5–1 to 5–8.

[4]*Congressional Quarterly Weekly Report*, (May 12, 1984), 1148, note 124.

[5]*National Journal* 15, 9 (May 7, 1983), 936–52.

[6]Hughes, *Domestic Context*, pp. 136, 143, figures 5–4, 5–8; Raymond A. Bauer, Ithiel do Sola Pool, and Lewis Anthony Dexter, *American Business and Public Policy* (New York: Atherton, 1963); Congressional Quarterly *Annual Almanac*, 1970–76 (Washington, DC: Congressional Quarterly, 1971–77).

[7]Richard E. Neustadt, *Presidential Power* (New York: Wiley, 1976).

[8]Louis Fisher, *President and Congress* (New York: Free Press, 1972); Bob Eckhardt and Charles L. Black, *Tides of Power* (New Haven: Yale University Press, 1976).

[9]Morton Berkowitz, P.G. Bock, and Vincent J. Fuccillo, *The Politics of American Foreign Policy* (Englewood Cliffs, NJ: Prentice Hall, 1977), pp. 59–61.

[10]Irving Janis, *Victims of Groupthink* (Boston: Houghton Mifflin, 1972).

[11]Graham Allison, *Essence of Decision* (Boston: Little, Brown, 1971); Berkowitz, Bock, and Fuccillo, *American Foreign Policy*, p. 149.

[12]Congressional Quarterly, *Congress and the Nation,* III, 1969–1972 (Washington, DC: Congressional Quarterly, 1973), chapter 14.

[13]Congressional Quarterly, *Guide to Current American Government* (Spring 1984), pp. 31–32; *New York Times* (June 24, 1983), p. 1.

[14]Christopher Madison, "Despite His Complaints, Reagan Going Along with Spirit of War Powers Law," *National Journal* 16, 20 (May 19, 1984), 989–93.

[15]Congressional Quarterly, *Guide to Congress,* 3rd ed. (Washington, DC: Congressional Quarterly, 1982), pp. 291–93.

[16]*The Interdependent* 8, 6 (October/November 1982), 5.

[17]Congressional Quarterly, *Guide to Congress,* 3rd ed., pp. 291–93.

[18]Loch Johnson and James M. McCormick, "Foreign Policy by Executive Fiat," *Foreign Policy* 28 (Fall 1977), 117–38.

[19]Congressional Quarterly, *Congress and the Nation,* III, 1969–72 (Washington, DC: Congressional Quarterly, 1973), pp. 866–68.

[20]Arnold Kanter, "Congress and the Defense Budget, 1960–1970," *American Political Science Review* 66, 1 (March 1972), 129–43.

[21]Congressional Quarterly, *Congress and the Nation,* I–IV: Congressional Quarterly, *Guide to Congress,* 2nd ed. (Washington, DC: Congressional Quarterly, 1976), pp. 129–36.

[22]*New York Times,* May 25, 1984, p. 8.

[23]Loch K. Johnson, "Controlling the Quiet Option," *Foreign Policy* 39 (Summer 1980), 143–53.

[24]U.S., Congress, Senate Committee on Foreign Relations, Subcommittee on Arms Control, International Organizations, and Security Agreements, *Effects of Limited Nuclear War,* hearings (Washington, DC: U.S. Government Printing Office, 1975); U.S., Congress, Office of Technology Assessment, *Nuclear Proliferation and Safeguards* (New York: Praeger, 1976).

CHAPTER 6

[1]U.S., *Report of the Commission on the Organization of the Government for the Conduct of Foreign Policy* (Washington, DC: U.S. Government Printing Office, 1975).

[2]Raymond F. Hopkins, "The International Role of 'Domestic' Bureaucracy," *International Organization* 30 (Summer 1976), 405–32; U.S., *The Budget of the United States Government, Fiscal Year 1979, Appendix* (Washington, DC: U.S. Government Printing Office, 1978).

[3]U.S., *The Budget of the United States Government, Fiscal Year 1979;* Henry T. Nash, *American Foreign Policy,* rev. ed. (Homewood, IL: Dorsey, 1978), p. 208.

[4]U.S., *Government Manual, 1977/78* (Washington, DC: U.S. Government Printing Office, 1977).

[5]Nash, *American Foreign Policy,* p. 208.

[6]Robert L. Gallucci, *Neither Peace Nor Honor* (Baltimore: Johns Hopkins University Press, 1975), pp. 61–71; Patrick J. McGarvey, "DIA: Intelligence to Please," *Washington Monthly* (July 1970); and Morris J. Blachman, "The Stupidity of Intelligence," in *Inside the System,* ed. Charles Peters (New York: Praeger, 1970), both reprinted in *Readings in American Foreign Policy,* eds. Morton H. Halperin and Arnold Kanter (Boston: Little, Brown, 1973), pp. 318–34.

[7]Dean G. Pruitt, *Problem Solving in the Department of State,* Monograph Series in World Affairs 2 (Denver: University of Denver, 1964–65), 9.

[8]Charlton Ogburn, Jr., in H. Field Haviland, Jr., and others, *The Formulation and Administration of United States Foreign Policy* (Washington, DC: Brookings Institution, 1960), pp. 172–77; reprinted in Burton M. Sapin, *The Making of United States Foreign Policy* (New York: Praeger, 1966), pp. 384–88, appendix A. Used with permission. Some titles have been slightly altered to reflect organizational changes since the original account was written.

[9]*New York Times,* August 17, 1980, sec. 4. p. 4E; the comment was by Secretary of State Muskie.

[10]*The Wall Street Journal,* January 30, 1989, p. 1.

[11]Charles Frankel, *High on Foggy Bottom* (New York: Harper & Row, 1968), pp. 208–10.

[12]Jim Naughton, "George Shultz in Myriad Detail," *Washington Post,* March 19, 1989, p. F4.

[13]Morton H. Halperin, *Bureaucratic Politics and Foreign Policy* (Washington, DC: Brookings Institution, 1974); Halperin and Kanter, *Readings in American Foreign Policy;* Graham T. Allison, *Essence of Decision* (Boston: Little, Brown, 1971).

[14]Thomas L. Brewer, "Personality and Policy Preference," *International Interactions* 3, 1 (1977), 83–89; Brewer, "Bureaucratic Correlates of Arms Control Policy Perspectives," unpublished manuscript.

[15]Bernard Mennis, *American Foreign Policy Officials* (Columbus, OH: Ohio State University Press, 1971).

[16]Thomas L. Brewer, "Military Officers and Arms Control," *Journal of Political and Military Sociology* 3, 1 (Spring 1975), 15–25.

[17]James Gerstenzang, "Richard Perle Reaches 'Bureaucratic Hall of Fame,' " *Ann Arbor News,* December 25, 1985, p. B10.

[18]*New York Times,* May 24, 1984, p. E3; March 5, 1981, p. 27; March 20, 1979, p. D1.

[19]Halperin, *Bureaucratic Politics,* chapters 6–12.

[20]Gallucci, *Neither Peace Nor Honor;* Townsend Hoopes, *The Limits of Intervention* (New York: David McKay, 1969).

[21]Halperin, *Bureaucratic Politics,* chapters 1 and 16; Halperin, "The Decision to Deploy the ABM," *World Politics* 25 (October 1972), 62–95.

[22]U.S., *Report of the Commission on the Organization of the Government for the Conduct of Foreign Policy;* Graham Allison and Peter Szanton, *Remaking Foreign Policy* (New York: Basic Books, 1976); I.M. Destler, *Presidents, Bureaucrats, and Foreign Policy* (Princeton, NJ: Princeton University Press, 1972); John F. Campbell, *The Foreign Affairs Fudge Factory* (New York: Basic Books, 1971).

[23]Irving L. Janis, *Victims of Groupthink* (Boston: Houghton Mifflin, 1972), pp. 24–26; Arthur M. Schlesinger, Jr., *A Thousand Days* (Boston: Houghton Mifflin, 1965), pp. 238–47; Theodore C. Sorensen, *Kennedy* (New York: Harper & Row; Bantam, 1966), pp. 332–39.

CHAPTER 7

[1]John P. Leacacos, "Kissinger's Apparat," *Foreign Policy* 5 (Winter 1971–72), 3–27; I.M. Destler, "Can One Man Do?" *Foreign Policy* 5 (Winter 1971–72), 28–40; Alexander L. George, "The Case for Multiple Advocacy in Making Foreign Policy," *American Political Science Review* 66, 3 (September 1972), 751–85; also Destler, "Comment," and George, "Rejoinder," in same issue; Destler, "A Job That Doesn't Work," *Foreign Policy* 38 (Spring 1980), 80–88; Robert E. Hunter, *Presidential Control of Foreign Policy* (New York: Praeger, 1982).

[2]*New York Times,* January 6, 1972, p. 6. The documents were made available to the *Times* by columnist Jack Anderson. ©1972 by The New York Times Company. Reprinted by permission.

[3]Richard E. Neustadt, *Presidential Power* (New York: Wiley, 1976), chapter 4.

[4]Neustadt, *Presidential Power,* chapters 4 and 6.

[5]*Congressional Quarterly Weekly Report* 36, 15 (April 15, 1978), 885–86; and 36, 20 (May 20, 1978), 1262.

[6]*New York Times,* August 7, 1978, p. D10.

[7]*New York Times,* October 26, 1973, p. 19.

[8]*Public Opinion* 7, 2 (April/May 1984), 33; *New York Times,* January 25, 1984, p. 1.

[9]James David Barber, *The Presidential Character* (Englewood Cliffs, NJ: Prentice Hall, 1972) p. 7.

[10]Richard M. Nixon, *Six Crises* (New York: Pyramid Books, 1968), p. xxv; quoted in Barber, *Presidential Character,* p. 354.

[11]Barber, *Presidential Character,* 430–35.

[12]Joseph M. Jones, *The Fifteen Weeks* (New York: Viking, 1955); Seyom Brown, *The Faces of Power* (New York: Columbia University Press, 1968), pp. 39–42; H. Bradford Westerfield, *Foreign Policy and Party Politics* (New Haven: Yale University Press, 1955), pp. 221–26; Richard J. Barnet, *Intervention and Revolution* (Cleveland: World, 1968), pp. 97–131.

[13]Jones, *Fifteen Weeks*; Brown, *Faces of Power*, pp. 42–45; Westerfield, *Foreign Policy and Party Politics*, pp. 274–320; Morton Berkowitz, P.G. Bock, and Vincent J. Fuccillo, *The Politics of American Foreign Policy* (Englewood Cliffs, NJ: Prentice Hall, 1977), pp. 20–38.

[14]Westerfield, *Foreign Policy and Party Politics*, pp. 330–32.

[15]Glenn D. Paige, *The Korean Decision* (New York: Free Press, 1968).

[16]Graham T. Allison, *Essence of Decision* (Boston: Little, Brown, 1971); Ellie Abel, *The Missile Crisis* (Philadelphia: Lippincott, 1966); Robert Kennedy, *Thirteen Days* (New York: Norton, 1971); Roger Hilsman, *To Move a Nation* (Garden City, NY: Doubleday, 1967); Arthur Schlesinger, *A Thousand Days* (Boston: Houghton Mifflin, 1965); Theodore Sorensen, *Kennedy* (New York: Bantam, 1966); Berkowitz, Bock, Fuccillo, *Politics of American Foreign Policy*, pp. 134–57; Stephen D. Krasner, "Are Bureaucracies Important?," *Foreign Policy* 7 (Summer 1972), 159–79; Jack L. Snyder, "Rationality at the Brink: The Role of Cognitive Processes in Failures of Deterrence," *World Politics* 30, 3 (April 1978), 345–65.

[17]Congressional Quarterly, *China and U.S. Foreign Policy*, 2nd ed. (Washington, DC: Congressional Quarterly, 1973); Kwan Ha Yim, *China & The U.S., 1964–72* (New York: Facts on File, 1975).

[18]John Newhouse, *Cold Dawn: The Story of SALT* (New York: Holt, Rinehart and Winston, 1973); Alton Frye, "U.S. Decision Making for SALT," in *SALT*, eds. Mason Willrich and John B. Rhinelander (New York: Free Press, 1974; first paperback ed., 1974), pp. 66–100.

CHAPTER 8

[1]Harold D. Lasswell, "The Garrison State Hypothesis Today," in *Changing Patterns of Military Politics*, ed. Samuel P. Huntington (New York: Free Press, 1962), pp. 51–70.

[2]William T. Lee, *Understanding the Soviet Military Threat*, Agenda Paper 6 (New York: National Strategy Information Center, 1977).

[3]Ruth L. Sivard, *World Military and Social Expenditures, 1983.* (Leesburg, VA: World Military and Social Expenditures Publications, 1983).

[4]Lawrence J. Korb, "The Budget Process in the Department of Defense," *Public Administration Review* 37, 4 (July/August 1977), 334–46.

[5]Robert Lucas Fischer, "Defending the Central Front," *Adelphi Papers*, 127 (London: International Institute for Strategic Studies, 1976); U.S., Congressional Budget Office, *Assessing the NATO/ Warsaw Pact Military Balance* (1977); Alain C. Enthoven and K. Wayne Smith, *How Much Is Enough?* (New York: Harper & Row, 1971); International Institute for Strategic Studies, *The Military Balance 1983–84* (London: International Institute for Strategic Studies, 1984); *The Defense Monitor* 7, 5 (June 1978); U.S., Congress, Senate Committee on Armed Services, *Fiscal Year 1978 Authorization for Military Procurement, Research and Development, and Active Duty Reserves*, part 2 (Washington, DC: U.S. Government Printing Office, 1977), p. 1128.

[6]Admiral Stansfield Turner, "The Naval Balance: Not Just a Numbers Game," *Foreign Affairs* 55, 2 (January 1977), 339–54; U.S., Congressional Research Service, *Means of Measuring Naval Power with Special Reference to U.S. and Soviet Activities in the Indian Ocean*, Report Prepared for the Subcommittee on the Near East and South Asia of the House Committee on Foreign Affairs (Washington, DC: U.S. Government Printing Office, 1974); U.S., Congress, Senate Committee on Armed Services, *Fiscal Year 1978 Authorizations for Military Procurement, Research and Development, and Active Duty Reserves*, part 2 (Washington, DC: U.S. Government Printing Office, 1977).

[7]Stanley Lieberson, "An Empirical Study of Military-Industrial Linkages," in *Testing the Theory of the Military-Industrial Complex*, ed. Steven Rosen (Lexington, MA: D.C. Heath, 1973), pp. 61–83.

[8]Samuel P. Huntington, "The Defense Establishment," in *The Military-Industrial Complex and U.S. Foreign Policy*, ed. Omer L. Carey (Seattle: Washington State University, 1969).

[9]Bruce M. Russett, *What Price Vigilance?* (New Haven: Yale University Press, 1970); Stephen A. Cobb, "Defense Spending and Foreign Policy in the House of Representatives," *Journal of Conflict Resolution* 13, 3 (September 1969), 358–69; Cobb, "The United States Senate and the Impact of Defense Spending Concentrations," in *Theory of the Military-Industrial Complex*, pp. 197–223; Charles Gray and Glen Gregory, "Military Spending and Senate Voting," *Journal of Peace Research*, 1968, pp. 44–54.

[10]Arnold Kanter, "Congress and the Defense Budget, 1960–1970," *American Political Science Review* 66 (March 1972), 129–43.

[11]Barry B. Hughes, *The Domestic Context of Foreign Policy* (San Francisco: Freeman, 1978), pp. 111–13.

CHAPTER 9

[1]Herbert F. York, ed., *Arms Control: Readings from Scientific American* (San Francisco: Freeman, 1973); Norman Polmar, *Strategic Weapons* (New York: Crane, Russak, 1975).

[2]Albert Legault and George Lindsey, *The Dynamics of the Nuclear Balance* (Ithaca, NY: Cornell University Press, 1974), pp. 32–38.

[3]Kosta Tsipis, "Cruise Missiles," *Scientific American,* February 1977, pp. 20–29.

[4]U.S., Arms Control and Disarmament Agency, *SALT Lexicon,* rev. ed. (July 1975); Barry M. Blechman, ed., *Rethinking the U.S. Strategic Posture* (Cambridge, MA: Ballinger, 1982); Samuel P. Huntington, ed., *The Strategic Imperative* (Cambridge, MA: Ballinger, 1982).

[5]Alain C. Enthoven and K. Wayne Smith, *How Much Is Enough?* (New York: Harper & Row, 1971), p. 207, table 11; Polmar, *Strategic Weapons,* p. 60.

[6]Alexander L. George and Richard Smoke, *Deterrence in American Foreign Policy* (New York: Columbia University Press, 1974).

[7]U.S., Arms Control and Disarmament Agency, *Worldwide Effects of Nuclear War* (Washington, DC: U.S. Government Printing Office, 1975); U.S., National Academy of Sciences, *Long-Term Worldwide Effects of Multiple Nuclear Weapons Detonations* (Washington, DC: U.S. Government Printing Office, 1975); Eric Chivian et al., eds., *Last Aid: The Medical Dimensions of Nuclear War* (San Francisco: Freeman, 1982).

[8]U.S., Congress, Senate Committee on Foreign Relations, Subcommittee on Arms Control, International Organizations, and Security Agreements, *Effects of Limited Nuclear War,* hearings (Washington, DC: U.S. Government Printing Office, 1975).

[9]Mason Willrich and John B. Rinelander, eds., *SALT* (New York: Free Press, 1974); Herbert Scoville, Jr., "The SALT Negotiations," *Scientific American,* August 1977, pp. 24–31; Thomas W. Wolfe, *The SALT Experience* (Cambridge, MA: Ballinger, 1979).

[10]Stockholm International Peace Research Institute, *World Armaments and Disarmament: SIPRI Yearbook, 1977* (Cambridge, MA: MIT Press, 1977), chapter 3; Ted Greenwood, "Reconnaisance and Arms Control," *Scientific American,* February 1973.

[11]Clarence D. Long, "Nuclear Proliferation," *International Security* 1, 4 (Spring 1977); Arnold Kramish, *The Peaceful Atom in Foreign Policy* (New York: Harper & Row, 1963).

[12]Thomas L. Brewer, "Nuclear Energy Forecasts and the International Safeguards System," *Technological Forecasting and Social Change* 11, 1 (1977), 9–23; U.S., Congress, Senate Committee on Governmental Affairs, *Nuclear Proliferation Factbook* (Washington, DC: U.S. Government Printing Office, 1977).

[13]U.S., Congress, Office of Technology Assessment, *Nuclear Proliferation and Safeguards* (New York: Praeger, 1977); Ted Greenwood, George W. Rathjens, and Jack Ruina, "Nuclear Power and Weapons Proliferation," *Adelphi Papers,* 130 (1977); Nuclear Power Study Group, *Nuclear Power* (Cambridge, MA: Ballinger, 1977).

[14]Albert Wohlstetter, "Spreading the Bomb Without Quite Breaking the Rules," *Foreign Policy* 25 (Winter 1976–77).

[15]George H. Quester, *The Politics of Nuclear Proliferation* (Baltimore: Johns Hopkins University Press, 1973); Ted Greenwood, Harold A. Feiveson, and Theodore B. Taylor, *Nuclear Proliferation* (New York: McGraw-Hall, 1977); Richard K. Betts, "Paranoids, Pygmies, Pariahs and Non-Proliferation," *Foreign Policy* 26 (Spring 1977); Stephen Meyer and Thomas L. Brewer, "Monitoring Nuclear Proliferation," in *To Augur Well: Early Warning Indicators in World Politics,* eds. J David Singer and Michael Wallace (Beverly Hills, CA: Sage, 1979).

[16]Karl Kaiser, "The Great Nuclear Debate," *Foreign Policy* 30 (Spring 1978).

[17]Lawrence Scheinman, "The International Atomic Energy Agency," in *Anatomy of Influence,* eds. Robert W. Cox and Harold K. Jacobson (New Haven: Yale University Press, 1973); Thomas L. Brewer, "The International Atomic Energy Agency," *Armed Forces and Society* 4, 2 (Winter 1978); Benjamin Sanders, *Safeguards Against Nuclear Proliferation* (Cambridge, MA: MIT Press, 1975).

[18] Glenn H. Snyder, *Deterrence and Defense* (Princeton: Princeton University Press, 1961).

[19]Gallup Poll and other surveys, reported in Hazel Erskine, "The Polls," *Public Opinion Quarterly* 27, 2 (September 1963), 158–71, and in *Current Opinion* 3, 11 (November 1975), 93.

[20]Harris Survey and others, reported in *Current Opinion* 2, 2 (February 1974), 19–20; *Current Opinion* 4, 3 (March 1976), 28; *Current Opinion* 4, 5 (May 1976), 45; *Current Opinion* 4, 11 (November 1976), 116; *Current Opinion* 5, 5 (May 1977), 58; and Erskine, "The Polls."

[21]Opinion Research Corporation Survey, December 1976, reported in *Current Opinion* 5, 1 (January 1977), 4.

[22]Luncheon remarks of President Gerald Ford, University of Michigan, Ann Arbor, April 5, 1977.

[23]John Newhouse, *Cold Dawn: The Story of SALT* (New York: Holt, Rinehart and Winston, 1973).

[24]Newhouse, *Cold Dawn,* p. 218.

CHAPTER 10

[1]Harry Howe Ransom, *The Intelligence Establishment* (Cambridge, MA: Harvard University Press, 1970); David Wise and Thomas B. Ross, *The Invisible Government* (New York: Random House, 1964); Philip Agee, *Inside The Company: CIA Diary* (New York: Bantam, 1975); Victor Marchetti and John D. Marks, *The CIA and the Cult of Intelligence* (New York: Dell, 1974); Robert L. Borosage and John Marks, eds., *The CIA File* (New York: Grossman, 1976); Morton H. Halperin and others, *The Lawless State* (Harmondsworth, England, and New York: Penguin, 1976); U.S., Congress, Senate Select Committee to Study Governmental Operations with Respect to Intelligence Activities, Final Report, *Covert Action* (Washington, DC: U.S. Government Printing Office, 1976); Ronald M. DeVore, *Spies and All That: Intelligence Agencies and Operations: A Bibliography* (Los Angeles: California State University, Center for the Study of Armament and Disarmaments, 1977); Frank Snepp, *Decent Interval* (New York: Random House, 1977).

[2]Richard Bissell's comments recorded in minutes of Discussion Group on Intelligence and Foreign Policy, Council on Foreign Relations, January 8, 1968, quoted in *The CIA's Global Strategy: Intelligence and Foreign Policy* (Cambridge, MA: The Africa Research Group, 1971), 13, cited in David Wise, "Covert Operations Abroad," in Borosage and Marks, *CIA File,* p. 20.

[3]Senate Select Committee, Final Report, vol. 1, pp. 108–9, 128, cited in Halperin and others, *Lawless State,* pp. 38, 40.

[4]Marchetti and Marks, *The CIA,* p. 46, cited in Halperin and others, *Lawless State,* p. 39.

[5]Halperin and others, *Lawless State,* p. 37.

[6]Ibid., pp. 37–38.

[7]Wise, "Covert Operations," p. 23.

[8]Ibid., p. 20.

[9]Halperin, "Covert Operations," in Borosage and Marks, *CIA File,* p. 167.

[10]Richard A. Falk, "CIA Operations and International Law," in Borosage and Marks, *CIA File,* p. 46.

[11]Fred Branfman, "The President's Secret Army: A Case Study—The CIA in Laos, 1962–1972," in Borosage and Marks, *The CIA File,* pp. 46–78.

[12]Falk, "CIA Operations."

[13]Roger Morris, "The Aftermath of CIA Intervention," *Society* 12, 3 (March/April 1975), 76–80.

[14]Falk, "CIA Operations."

[15]Morris, "Aftermath."

[16]Ibid.

[17]Falk, "CIA Operations."

[18]Ibid.

[19]Morris, "Aftermath."

[20]Ibid.

[21]Halperin and others, *The Lawless State,* p. 48.

[22]U.S., Congress, Senate Select Committee on Intelligence, Staff Report, *Covert Action in Chile, 1963–1973* (Washington, DC: U.S. Government Printing Office, 1975).

[23]Leo Hazelwood, John J. Hayes, James R. Brownell, Jr., "Planning for Problems in Crisis Management," *International Studies Quarterly* 21, 1 (March 1977), 75–106; Frederic S. Pearson and Robert Baumann, "Foreign Military Intervention and Changes in United States Business Activity," *Journal of Political and Military Sociology* 5, 1 (Spring 1977), 799–97.

[24]Charles L. Robertson, *International Politics Since World War II*, 2nd ed. (New York: Wiley, 1975); John Spanier, *American Foreign Policy Since World War II*, 9th ed. (New York: CBS, 1983); Paul Y. Hammond, *Cold War and Detente*, rev. ed. (San Diego, CA: Harcourt Brace Jovanovich, 1975).

[25]Richard J. Barnet, *Intervention and Revolution* (Cleveland: World-Meridian, 1968), pp. 132–52; Morton Berkowitz, P.G. Bock, Vincent J. Fuccillo, *The Politics of American Foreign Policy* (Englewood Cliffs, NJ: Prentice Hall, 1977).

[26]Barnet, *Intervention and Revolution*, pp. 153–80; Jerome Slater, *Intervention and Negotiation* (New York: Harper & Row, 1970); Theodore Draper, *The Dominican Revolt* (New York: Commentary, 1968); Berkowitz, Bock, Fuccillo, *American Foreign Policy.*

[27]John Bartlow Martin, *Overtaken by Events* (New York: Doubleday, 1966), pp. 656–57; cited in Barnet, *Intervention and Revolution*, p. 171.

[28]Berkowitz, Bock, Fuccillo, *American Foreign Policy*; Roger Hilsman, *To Move a Nation* (New York: Doubleday, 1964; Dell-Delta edition, 1967), pp. 91–155, 413–523; Townsend Hoopes, *The Limits of Intervention*, rev. ed. (New York: MacKay, 1974).

[29]*New York Times*, September 30, 1983, p. 8.

[30]*Gallup Report* 223 (April 1984), 15–16.

[31]U.S., Congress, House Subcommittee on International and Scientific Affairs of the Committee on International Relations, Hearings, *Review of the President's Conventional Arms Transfer Policy* (Washington, DC: U.S. Government Printing Office, 1978), p. 39.

[32]David J. Louscher, "The Rise of Military Sales as a U.S. Foreign Assistance Instrument," *Orbis* 20 (Winter 1977), 933–64.

[33]U.S., Congressional Budget Office, *Budgetary Cost Savings to the Department of Defense Resulting from Foreign Military Sales* (Washington, DC: U.S. Government Printing Office, 1976).

[34]Congressional Quarterly, Weekly Report, April 1983, p. 82.

[35] U.S., Arms Control and Disarmament Agency, *World Military Expenditures and Arms Transfers, 1967–1976* (Washington, DC: U.S. Government Printing Office, 1978), p. 153, table VI.

[36]U.S., *World Military Expenditures*, p. 10.

[37]Caesar D. Sereseres, "U.S. Military Assistance to Non-industrial Nations," in *The Limits of Military Intervention*, ed. Ellen P. Stern (Beverly Hills, CA: Sage, 1977), pp. 213–36.

[38]U.S., *Foreign Assistance Legislation*, pp. 30–31.

[39]Frederick S. Pearson, "American Military Intervention Abroad," in *The Politics of Aid, Trade and Investment*, eds. Satish Raichur and Craig Liske (New York: Wiley-Halsted, 1976), pp. 37–62.

[40]John S. Odell, "Correlates of U.S. Military Assistance and Military Intervention," in *Testing Theories of Economic Imperialism*, eds. Steven J. Rosen and James R. Kurth (Lexington, MA: D.C. Heath, 1974), pp. 150–54.

[41]Odell, "Correlates of U.S. Military Assistance," pp. 147–50, table 7–3.

[42]John H. Peterson, "Economic Interests and U.S. Foreign Policy in Latin America," in Raichur and Liske, *Politics of Aid*, p. 76, table 1.

[43]Steven J. Rosen, "The Open Door Imperative and U.S. Foreign Policy," in Rosen and Kurth, *Testing Theories*, pp. 117–42.

[44]James R. Kurth, "Testing Theories of Economic Imperialism," in Rosen and Kurth, *Testing Theories*, pp. 3–14.

CHAPTER 11

[1]For these purposes, the most indicative ratios of exports and imports to GNP are based on goods-and-services trade, excluding military sales/purchases and excluding receipts/payments of income on foreign investments.

[2]Useful discussions of American policy and other issues concerning international monetary relations and the foreign exchange markets are Robert Soloman, *The International Monetary System, 1945–1976* (New York: Harper & Row, 1977); Tom deVries, "The Inconstant Dollar," *Foreign Policy* 32 (Fall 1978), 161–83; deVries, "Jamaica, or the Non-Reform of the International Monetary System,"

Foreign Affairs 54, 3 (April 1976), 577–605; Benjamin J. Cohen, "Balance of Payments Financing: Evolution of a Regime," *International Organization* 36, 2 (Spring 1982), 457–78; John S. Odell, "The U.S. and the Emergence of Flexible Exchange Rates: An Analysis of Foreign Policy Change," *International Organization* 33, 1 (Winter 1979), 57–81.

[3]Jock A. Finlayson and Mark W. Zacher, "The GATT and the Regulation of Trade Barriers: Regime Dynamics and Functions," *International Organization* 35, 4 (Autumn 1981), 561–602; Thomas R. Graham, "Revolution in Trade Politics," *Foreign Policy* 36 (Fall 1979), 49–63; Stephen D. Krasner, "The Tokyo Round: Particularistic Interests and Prospects for Stability in the Global Trading System," *International Studies Quarterly* 23, 4 (December 1979), 491–531.

[4]Richard N. Cooper, "A New International Economic Order for Mutual Gain," *Foreign Policy* 26 (Spring 1977), 66–139; Robert K. Olson, *U.S. Foreign Policy and the New International Economic Order: Negotiating Global Problems, 1974–1981* (Boulder, CO: Westview, 1981).

[5]Robert Stobaugh and Daniel Yergin, "After the Second Shock: Pragmatic Energy Strategies," *Foreign Affairs* 57, 4 (Spring 1979), 836–71; Joseph A. Yager, Eleanor B. Steinberg, and others, *Energy and U.S. Foreign Policy* (Cambridge, MA: Ballinger, 1974); Raymond Vernon, ed., *The Oil Crisis* (New York: Norton, 1976), especially James W. McKie, "The United States," pp. 73–90; David Howard Davis, *Energy Politics,* 2nd ed. (New York: St. Martin's, 1978), chapter 3; Robert S. Pindyck, "OPEC's Threat to the West," *Foreign Policy* 30 (Spring 1978), 36–52; S. Fred Singer, "Limits to Arab Oil Power," *Foreign Policy* 30 (Spring 1978), 53–67.

[6]U.S., Council on International Economic Policy, *Critical Imported Materials* (Washington, DC: U.S. Government Printing Office, 1974), pp. 13–15; Donella H. Meadows and others, *The Limits to Growth,* 2nd ed. (New York: New American Library, 1974), pp. 64–67, table 4; Yuan-li Wu, *Raw Material Supply in a Multipolar World,* 2nd ed. (New York: Crane, Russak, 1979); U.S., Congress, Congressional Research Service, *A Congressional Handbook on U.S. Materials Import Dependency/ Vulnerability* (Washington, DC: U.S. Government Printing Office, 1977).

[7]U.S., *Critical Imported Materials,* p. 22, table II.

[8]Good discussions of East-West trade relations are available in Jozef Wilczynski, *The Economics and Politics of East-West Trade* (New York: Praeger, 1969); and Robert Starr, ed., *East-West Business Transactions* (New York: Praeger, 1974); Raymond Vernon, "The Fragile Foundations of East-West Trade," *Foreign Affairs* 57, 5 (Summer 1979), 1035–51; Samuel P. Huntington et al., "Trade Technology, and Leverage," *Foreign Policy* 32 (Fall 1978), 63–106.

[9]Information on the grain embargo is available in Michael R. Gordon, "The Grain Embargo," *National Journal* 12, 36 (September 6, 1980), 1480–84; Robert L. Paarlberg, "Lessons of the Grain Embargo," *Foreign Affairs* 59, 1 (Fall 1980), 144–62.

[10]Christopher Madison, "Anti-Soviet Ideology, Trade Goals at Odds on Russian Pipeline Deal," *National Journal* 13, 34 (August 22, 1981), 1498–1500.

[11]See "Sugar Imports to Be Limited, Reagan Decides," *Wall Street Journal,* May 5, 1982, p. 4.

[12]Poll results are summarized in Alvin Richman, "Public Perceptions of World Trade," a report prepared for the League of Women Voters Education Fund and reprinted in U.S., Congress, Senate Committee on Finance, *U.S. International Trade Strategy,* hearings (Washington, DC: Government Printing Office, 1980), pp. 456–91.

[13]Ibid.

CHAPTER 12

[1]Vernon Van Dyke, *Human Rights, the United States and World Community* (New York: Oxford University Press, 1970).

[2]Louis B. Sohn and Thomas Buergenthal, eds., *International Protection of Human Rights* (Indianapolis: Bobbs-Merrill, 1973).

[3]Van Dyke, *Human Rights,* p. 79.

[4]Charles Lewis Taylor and Michael C. Hudson, *World Handbook of Political and Social Indicators,* 2nd ed. (New Haven: Yale University Press, 1972), pp. 57–58, table 2.9.

[5]Taylor and Hudson, *World Handbook,* pp. 150–53, table 3.10.

[6]Ralph L. Lowenstein, Freedom of Information Center, School of Journalism, University of Missouri; data reported in Taylor and Hudson, *World Handbook,* pp. 51–53, table 2.7.

[7]U.S., House Committee on International Relations, and Senate Committee on Foreign Relations, *Country Reports on Human Rights Practices,* Joint Committee Print (Washington, DC: U.S. Government Printing Office, 1978); U.S., House Subcommittee on International Organizations of the Committee on International Relations, *The Status of Human Rights in Selected Countries and the U.S. Response* (Washington, DC: U.S. Government Printing Office, 1977); Rupert Emerson, "The Fate of Human Rights in the Third World," *World Politics* 27, 2 (January 1975), 201–26.

[8]U.S., House, *Status of Human Rights,* p. 19.

[9]Amnesty International, *Annual Report[s]* (London); *Report on Torture* (New York: Farrar, Straus, and Giroux, 1975).

[10]John R. Schmidhauser with Larry L. Berg, "The American Bar Association and the Human Rights Conventions," *Social Research* 38, 2 (Summer 1971), 362–410.

[11]Gernot Kohler and Norman Alcock, "An Empirical Table of Structural Violence," *Journal of Peace Research* 13, 4 (1976), 349.

[12]Paul R. Ehrlich and Ann E. Ehrlich, *Population, Resources, Environment* (San Francisco: W.H. Freeman, 1970), p. 72.

[13]Donella H. Meadows, Dennis L. Meadows, Jorgen Randers, William W. Behrens III, *The Limits to Growth,* 2nd ed. (New York: Potomac Associates; Signet-New American Library ed., 1972), pp. 56, 57, 114; Jan Tinbergen and others, *RIO: Reshaping the International Order* (New York: Dutton; Signet-New American Library edition, 1977), p. 280.

[14]David H. Blake and Robert S. Walters, *The Politics of Global Economic Relations* (Englewood Cliffs, NJ: Prentice Hall, 1981), p. 132.

[15]Joan Edelman Spero, *The Politics of International Economic Relations* (New York: St. Martin's, 1977), p. 144.

[16]U.S., President, *Economic Report of the President* (Washington, DC: U.S. Government Printing Office, 1978), p. 360, table B-3; pp. 373–74, table B-101; U.S., *Budget of the United States Government, FY 1985* (Washington, DC: U.S. Government Printing Office, 1984), pp. 5–21.

[17]Harold D. Lasswell, *A Pre-View of Policy Sciences* (New York: American Elsevier, 1971), p. 41.

Suggestions for Further Reading and Research

These suggestions include four kinds of publications: books containing basic reference information, books providing general introductions, periodicals containing serious specialized analyses, and other materials providing information and opinion on current topics. In addition, the items in the chapter notes and the sources cited in the tables and figures can be consulted for more information on specific topics.

GENERAL REFERENCE

Guides

BURNS, RICHARD, *Guide to American Foreign Relations since 1700*. Santa Barbara, CA: ABC-Clio, 1983.
PLISCHKE, ELMER, *U.S. Foreign Relations: A Guide to Information Sources*. Detroit: Gale, 1980.

Indexes and Abstracts

American Statistics Index. Washington, DC: Congressional Information Service.
ISI: International Statistics Index. Washington, DC: Congressional Information Service.
Public Affairs Information Service Bulletin. New York: Public Affairs Information Service.
Social Sciences Index. New York: H. W. Wilson.
United States Political Science Documents.

Information about Particular Countries and International Organizations

BANKS, ARTHUR S., VIVIAN CARLIP, WILLIAM OVERSTREET, and DWIGHT LINDER, eds., *Economic Handbook of the World*. New York: McGraw-Hill, new edition every few years.
Countries of the World and Their Leaders. Detroit: Gale, periodic.
Defense and Foreign Affairs Handbook. Washington, DC: Defense and Foreign Affairs, annual.
The Economist Intelligence Unit, *Country Reports*.
The Economist. The World In Figures. London: The Economist, new edition published every few years.
The Europa Yearbook. London: Europa Publications, annual.
Political Handbook of the World. New York: McGraw-Hill, annual.
The Statesman's Yearbook. London: Macmillan, annual.
TAYLOR, CHARLES LEWIS, and MICHAEL C. HUDSON, *World Handbook of Political and Social Indicators* (2nd ed.). New Haven: Yale University Press, 1972.
UN DEPARTMENT OF ECONOMIC AND SOCIAL AFFAIRS, *Statistical Yearbook*. New York: United Nations, annual.
U.S., Bureau of the Census, *Statistical Abstract of the United States*. Washington, DC: U.S. Government Printing Office, annual.
World Bank, *World Atlas*. Washington, DC: World Bank, annual.
————, *World Development Report*. Washington, DC: World Bank, annual.

U.S. Policies, Programs, and Agencies

Congressional Quarterly Almanac. Washington, DC: Congressional Quarterly, annual.
Congressional Quarterly, *Congress and the Nation*. Washington, DC: Congressional Quarterly, quadrennial.
U.S., *Budget of the United States Government*. Washington, DC: U.S. Government Printing Office, annual.
U.S., Congress, House of Representatives Committee on Appropriations, annual hearings on agency appropriations before various subcommittees. Also see similar documents of Senate Committee on Appropriations.
U.S., Congress, House of Representatives, annual hearings on agency authorizations before various committees and subcommittees, especially Committee on Foreign Affairs and Committee on Armed Services. Also see similar documents of Senate Committee on Foreign Relations and Committee on Armed Services, and other committees in issue area of interest.

Documents

Treaties and Alliances of the World. New York: Scribner's, updated periodically.
U.S., *United States Statutes at Large*. Washington, DC: U.S. Government Printing Office, annual.
U.S., Department of State, *Treaties in Force*. Washington, DC: U.S. Government Printing Office, annual.
————, *United States Treaties and Other International Agreements*. Washington, DC: U.S. Government Printing Office, annual.
————, *American Foreign Policy: Basic Documents*.
————, *American Foreign Policy: Current Documents*.
————, *Legislation on Foreign Relations*.
U.S., Congress, House Committee on Foreign Affairs, and Senate Committee on Foreign Relations. *Legislation on Foreign Relations through 19xx*. Washington, DC: U.S. Government Printing Office, annual.
U.S., Congress, House, *United States Code*. Washington, DC: U.S. Government Printing Office, updated periodically.
U.S., Office of the Federal Register, *Code of Federal Regulations*. Washington, DC: U.S. Government Printing Office, annual.

276 *Suggestions for Further Reading and Research*

INFORMATION AND OPINION ABOUT CURRENT POLICY ISSUES

Issues Before the General Assembly of the United Nations. New York: United Nations Association of the
U.S., annual.
U.S., Department of State, *Current Policy.*
————, GIST.
Christian Science Monitor
Congressional Quarterly Weekly Report
Current History
Defense Monitor
The Economist
Facts on File
Foreign Affairs (especially annual survey of world)
Foreign Policy
International Security
Keesing's Contemporary Archives
National Journal
New York Times
Orbis
Wall Street Journal
Washington Post
Washington Quarterly
Worldview

HISTORIES

BEMIS, SAMUEL FLAG, *A Short History of American Foreign Policy and Diplomacy.* New York: Holt,
Rinehart and Winston, 1959.
HAMMOND, PAUL Y., *Cold War and Detente* (rev. ed.). San Diego, CA: Harcourt Brace Jovanovich, 1975.
NATHAN, JAMES A., and JAMES K. OLIVER, *United States Foreign Policy and World Order* (2nd ed.).
Boston: Little, Brown, 1981.
ROBERTSON, CHARLES L., *International Politics Since World War II* (2nd ed.). New York: Wiley, 1975.
SPANIER, JOHN, *American Foreign Policy Since World War II* (9th ed.). New York: CBS College
Publishing, Holt, Rinehart and Winston, 1983.

MODELS OF POLICY MAKING

ALLISON, GRAHAM T., *Essence of Decision.* Boston: Little, Brown, 1971.
DOUGHERTY, JAMES E., and ROBERT L. PFALTZGRAFF, JR., *Contending Theories of International Relations.*
Philadelphia: Lippincott, 1971.
DYE, THOMAS R., *Understanding Public Policy* (6th ed.). Englewood Cliffs, NJ: Prentice Hall, 1987.
JACOBSON, HAROLD K., and WILLIAM ZIMMERMAN, eds., *The Shaping of Foreign Policy.* New York:
Atherton, 1969.
JENSEN, LLOYD, *Explaining Foreign Policy.* Englewood Cliffs, NJ: Prentice Hall, 1982.
ROSENAU, JAMES N., ed., *International Politics and Foreign Policy* (2nd ed.). New York: Free Press,
1969.
International Studies Quarterly
Journal of Conflict Resolution
Policy Science
World Politics

THE PUBLIC

HUGHES, BARRY B., *The Domestic Context of American Foreign Policy*. San Francisco: Freeman, 1978.
MUELLER, JOHN E., *War, Presidents and Public Opinion*. New York: Wiley, 1973.
ROSENAU, JAMES N., *Citizenship Between Elections*. New York: Free Press, 1974.
Journal of Conflict Resolution, 32, 2 (June 1988), several articles.
Gallup Report
Public Opinion
Public Opinion Quarterly
World Opinion Update

INTEREST GROUPS

BAUER, RAYMOND A., ITHIEL DE SOLA POOLE, and LOUIS ANTHONY DEXTER, *American Business and Public Policy* (2nd ed.). Chicago: Aldine-Atherton, 1972.
BERGSTEN, C. FRED, THOMAS HORST, and THEODORE H. MORAN, *American Multinationals and American Interests*. Washington, DC: Brookings Institution, 1978.
Congressional Quarterly Almanac. Washington, DC: Congressional Quarterly, annual.
———, *Congress and the Nation*. Washington, DC: Congressional Quarterly, quadrennial.
———, *The Washington Lobby* (4th ed.) Washington, DC: Congressional Quarterly, 1982.
HUGHES, KENT H., *Trade, Taxes, and Transnationals: International Economic Decision Making in Congress*. New York: Praeger, 1979.
PURVIS, HOYT, and STEVEN J. BAKER, eds., *Legislating Foreign Policy*. Boulder, CO: Westview, 1984.
RUSSETT, BRUCE M., and ELIZABETH C. HANSON, *Interest and Ideology: The Foreign Policy Beliefs of American Businessmen*. San Francisco: Freeman, 1975.

CONGRESS

CONGRESSIONAL QUARTERLY, *Guide to Congress* (3rd ed.). Washington, DC: Congressional Quarterly, 1982.
———, *Congress and the Nation*, Washington, DC: Congressional Quarterly, quadrennial.
———, *Almanac*. Washington, DC: Congressional Quarterly, annual.
CRABB, CECIL V., and PAT M. HOLT, *Invitation to Struggle: Congress, the President and Foreign Policy*. Washington, DC: Congressional Quarterly, 1980.
FISHER, LOUIS, *President and Congress*. New York: Free Press, 1972.
FRANCK, THOMAS M., and EDWARD WEISBAND, *Foreign Policy by Congress*. New York: Oxford University Press, 1979.
FRYE, ALTON, *A Responsible Congress*. New York: McGraw-Hill, 1975.
SPANIER, JOHN, and JOSEPH R. NOGEE, eds., *Congress, the President and American Foreign Policy*. New York: Pergamon, 1981.

BUREAUCRATS

ALLISON, GRAHAM, and PETER SZANTON, *Remaking Foreign Policy*. New York: Basic Books, 1976.
BLOOMFIELD, LINCOLN P., *The Foreign Policy Process*. Englewood Cliffs, NJ: Prentice Hall, 1982.
HALPERIN, MORTON, *Bureaucratic Politics and Foreign Policy*. Washington, DC: Brookings Institution, 1974.
———, and ARNOLD KANTER, eds., *Readings in American Foreign Policy: A Bureaucratic Perspective*. Boston: Little, Brown, 1973.
Armed Forces and Society
U.S., *Organizational Manual*. Washington, DC: U.S. Government Printing Office, annual.
———, *Report of the Commission on the Organization of the Government for the Conduct of Foreign Policy*. Washington, DC: U.S. Government Printing Office, 1975.

THE PRESIDENT

BARBER, JAMES DAVID, *The Presidential Character* (2nd ed.). Englewood Cliffs, NJ: Prentice Hall, 1977.
GEORGE, ALEXANDER, *Presidential Decisionmaking in Foreign Policy*. Boulder, CO: Westview, 1980.
HUNTER, ROBERT E., *Presidential Control of Foreign Policy*. New York: Praeger, 1982.
NEUSTADT, RICHARD, *Presidential Power: The Politics of Leadership With Reflections from F.D.R. to Carter*. New York: Wiley, 1980.
ROSSITER, CLINTON, *The American Presidency* (rev. ed.). San Diego, CA: Harcourt Brace Jovanovich, 1960.
WILDAVSKY, AARON, ed., *Perspectives on the Presidency*. Boston: Little, Brown, 1975.
Presidential Studies Quarterly

DEFENSE SPENDING

Setting National Priorities. Washington, DC: Brookings Institution, annual.
U.S., *Budget of the United States Government*. Washington, DC: U.S. Government Printing Office, annual.
U.S., Congress, House Committee on Appropriations, *Department of Defense Appropriations*. Washington, DC: U.S. Government Printing Office, annual. Also see Senate Committee on Appropriations, *Department of Defense Appropriations*. Washington, DC: Government Printing Office, annual.
————, Committee on Armed Services, *Hearing on Military Posture*. Washington, DC: U.S. Government Printing Office, annual. See also Senate Committee on Armed Services, *FYxx Authorization for Military Procurement, Research and Development, and Active Duty, Selected Reserve, and Civilian Personnel Strengths*. Washington, DC: U.S. Government Printing Office, annual.

NUCLEAR WEAPONS

BARTON, JOHN H., and LAWRENCE D. WEILER, *International Arms Control*. Stanford, CA: Stanford University Press, 1977.
DOUGHERTY, JAMES E., *How to Think about Arms Control and Disarmament*. New York: Crane, Russak, 1973.
DUNN, LEWIS A., *Controlling the Bomb*. New Haven: Yale University Press, 1982.
KAHAN, JEROME H., *Security in the Nuclear Age*. Washington, DC: Brookings Institution, 1975.
LODAL, JAN M., "An Arms Control Agenda." *Foreign Policy* 72 (Fall 1988), 152–172.
Stockholm International Peace Research Institute, *World Armaments and Disarmament: SIPRI Yearbook*. Cambridge, MA: MIT Press, annual.
U.S., Arms Control and Disarmament Agency, *Arms Control and Disarmament Agreements: Texts and Histories of Negotiations*. Washington, DC: U.S. Government Printing Office, annual.
The Military Balance. London: International Institute for Strategic Studies, annual.

MILITARY ASSISTANCE AND INTERVENTION

BLECHMAN, BARRY M., and STEPHEN KAPLAN, *Force Without War*. Washington, DC: Brookings Institution, 1978.
BOROSAGE, ROBERT L., and JOHN MARKS, eds., *The CIA File*. New York: Grossman, 1976.
FEINBERG, RICHARD E., *The Intemperate Zone: The Third World Challenge to U.S. Foreign Policy*. New York: Norton, 1983.
GODSON, ROY, ed., *Intelligence Requirements for the 1980's* (4 vols.). Washington, DC: National Strategy Information Center, 1979–1981.

RANSOM, HARRY HOWE, "The Intelligence Function and the Constitution." *Armed Forces and Society* 14, 1 (Fall 1987), 43–63.
U.S., Arms Control and Disarmament Agency, *World Military Expenditures and Arms Transfers.* Washington, DC: U.S. Government Printing Office, annual.

TRADE

BLAKE, DAVID H., and ROBERT S. WALTERS, *The Politics of Global Economic Relations* (2nd ed.). Englewood Cliffs, NJ: Prentice Hall, 1981.
COHEN, STEPHEN D., *The Making of United States International Economic Policy* (2nd ed.). New York: Praeger, 1981.
COHEN, STEPHEN D., and RONALD I. MELTZER. *United States International Economic Policy in Action.* New York: Praeger, 1982.
General Agreement on Tariffs and Trade, *International Trade, 19xx/xx.* Geneva: GATT, annual.
INTERNATIONAL MONETARY FUND. *International Financial Statistics.* Washington, DC: IMF, Monthly and annual.
KRASNER, STEPHEN D., "The Tokyo Round," *International Studies Quarterly* 23, 4 (December 1979), 491–531.
————, "U.S. Commercial and Monetary Policy," *International Organization* 31, 4 (Autumn 1977), 635–71.
PASTOR, ROBERT A., *Congress and the Politics of U.S. Foreign Economic Policy, 1929–1976.* Berkeley: University of California Press, 1980.
SPERO, JOAN EDELMAN, *The Politics of Economic Relations* (3rd ed.). New York: St. Martin's, 1985.
United Nations Conference on Trade and Development, *Trade and Development Report.* Geneva: UNCTAD, annual.
YERGIN, DANIEL, ed., *Global Insecurity: A Strategy for Energy and Economic Survival.* Boston: Houghton Mifflin, 1981.
International Organization.
The World Economy.

HUMAN RIGHTS

BAUMANN, FRED E., *Human Rights and American Foreign Policy.* Gambier, OH: Keynon College, 1981.
DOMINGUEZ, JORGE I., NIGEL S. RODLEY, BRYCE WOOD, and RICHARD FALK, *Enhancing Global Human Rights.* New York: McGraw-Hill, 1979.
GASTILL, RAYMOND D., *Freedom in the World, 19xx.* Boston: G. K. Hall, annual.
GEYER, ANNE E., and ROBERT Y. SHAPIRO, "The Polls—A Report: Human Rights." *Public Opinion Quarterly* 52, 3 (Fall 1988), 386–398.
GLASER, KURT, and STEFAN T. POSSONY, *Victims of Politics: The State of Human Rights.* New York: Columbia University Press, 1979.
KOMMERS, DONALD P., and GILBERT D. LOESCHER, eds., *Human Rights and American Foreign Policy.* Notre Dame: University of Notre Dame Press, 1979.
MILLER, WILLIAM, *International Human Rights: A Bibliography, 1970–1976.* Notre Dame: University of Notre Dame Law School, Center for Civil Rights, 1976.
NANDA, VED P., JAMES P. SCARRITT, and GEORGE W. SHEPHARD, JR., eds., *Global Human Rights.* Boulder, CO: Westview, 1981.
SCHWELB, EGON, "International Protection of Human Rights: A Survey of Recent Literature," *International Organization* 24 (Winter 1970), 74–92.
SOHN, LOUIS B., and THOMAS BUERGENTHAL, eds., *International Protection of Human Rights.* Indianapolis: Bobbs-Merrill, 1973.
U.S., House Committee on Foreign Affairs and Senate Committee on Foreign Relations, *Country Reports on Human Rights Practices.* Washington, DC: U.S. Government Printing Office, annual.
U.N., *Yearbook on Human Rights.* New York: United Nations, biannual.
Human Rights Quarterly
Universal Human Rights

ECONOMIC DEVELOPMENT

OLSON, ROBERT K., *U.S. Foreign Policy and the New International Economic Order*. Boulder, CO: Westview, 1981.

Overseas Development Council, *U.S. Foreign Policy and the Third World, Agenda 19xx*. New York: Praeger, biannual.

ROTHSTEIN, ROBERT L., *The Third World and U.S. Foreign Policy*. Boulder, CO: Westview, 1981.

TINBERGEN, JAN, and others, *RIO: Reshaping the International Order*. New York: Dutton, 1976; New American Library, 1977.

World Bank, *World Development Report*. New York: Oxford University Press, annual.

Index

India, 61, 141–42, 252
Indonesia, 204, 215
  human rights violations, 246
Indo-Pakistani War, 61–62, 141–43
Information Agency, U.S., 135
Intelligence activities. *See also* Central Intelli-
    gence Agency (CIA); Covert paramili-
    tary action
  agencies, 117
  purpose, 223
  reorganization, 133
Inter-American Convention of the Granting of
    Civil Rights to Women, 245
Interdependence, international
  economic, 9–12
  energy, 10–12
  nuclear weapons, 9
Interest groups, 74–92. *See also* Lobbying
    organizations; Multinational corpora-
    tions (MNCs)
  congressional response, 96–98
  definition, 74
  executive agencies, 125–26
  iron triangles, 80
  military-industrial complex, 169–71, 199
  pluralistic and bureaucratic decision making,
    35–39
Intergovernmental Council of Copper Export-
    ing Countries, 235
Intermestic affairs, 12, 54
International Atomic Energy Agency, verifica-
    tion safeguards program, 195
International Bauxite Association, 235
International Emergency Economic Powers
    Act, 102
Internationalism, 54, 56–58, 59
International Monetary Fund (IMF), 3
International politics decision-making model,
    42–43
  balance of power, 42
  empirical limitations, 43
  normative value, 43
  protectionism, 42
  security and status, 42
Investments, foreign, 9–10, 84
Iran, 12, 64, 204, 247, 248
Iran-Contra scandal, 108, 210–11
Iraq. *See also* Persian Gulf War
  coup (1958), 207
  Kuwait, 3
  military forces, 8
  sanctions against, 3
  war with, 1, 6, 64, 175, 232
  television coverage, 64
Iron triangle, 80, 242
Irwin, John, 141
Isolationism, 54, 56–57, 59
Israel, 57, 76, 83, 231, 253

Jackson Amendment, 238
Jamaica, 235
Japan
  competition with, 9
  energy, 10
  GNP, 8–9
  interest groups, 76–77
  investment in U.S., 9–10
  trade with, 2, 76–77, 85, 228–30, 239
Johnson, Lyndon
  personality, 149–50
  public opinion ratings, 71, 72, 146
  reelection decision, 69, 72
Johnson administration
  leaks, 127
  military intervention policy, 129–30, 208,
    209
  nuclear weapons policy, 130–31
  trade policy, 229
Joint Chiefs of Staff (JCS)
  ABM deployment, 130–31
  National Security Council participation, 140
  structure, 133
Jordan, 207
Jordan, Hamilton, 140

Kennedy, John F., 41
  public opinion ratings, 71, 146
Kennedy, Robert, 156
Kennedy, Ted, 41
Kennedy administration
  Cuban missile crisis, 61, 71, 100, 155–57,
    183
  defense budget, 166
  military intervention policy, 100, 128, 209
  nuclear weapons policy, 197
  press relations, 62
  trade policy, 238
Krushchev, Nikita, 157
Kissinger, Henry, 140, 141–43, 148, 158–59,
    199
Korea, 206–7
Korean War, 99–100, 154–55
Kosygin, Alexei, 131, 159
Kuwait, 3, 12, 253. *See also* Persian Gulf War

Laissez-faire trade policy, 227
Lasswell, Harold, 161
Laos, 101, 204, 208–9
Latin America. *See also* Central America
  arms sales, 214
  covert activities, 204–6, 210–11
  economic assistance, 252, 253
  military interventions, 208, 210–11
  oil reserves, 234
  trade with, 239